Economic Liberties
and the Constitution

Bernard H. Siegan

Economic Liberties
and the
*C*onstitution

University of Chicago Press
Chicago & London

BERNARD H. SIEGAN is distinguished professor
of law and director of law and economic studies
at the University of San Diego School of Law. He
is the author or editor of six books, has written
numerous scholarly articles, and was a practicing
lawyer in Chicago for over twenty years.

The University of Chicago Press, Chicago 60637
The University of Chicago Press, Ltd., London

Library of Congress Cataloging in Publication Data

Siegan, Bernard H
    Economic liberties and the Constitution.

    Includes bibliographical references and indexes.
    1. Trade regulation—United States—Cases.
2. United States—Constitutional law—Cases. I. Title.
KF1600.A7S53   343.73′07   80-15756
ISBN 0-226-75663-7

To Sharon

Contents

I

Current and Past Status of Economic Liberties under the Constitution

1 Interpreting the Constitution

Current Judicial Policy in Reviewing Economic Legislation

Throughout its 190-year history, the United States Supreme Court has established and revised policy many times. However, probably no change has been so drastic as that which occurred in the early 1940s, when the Court abandoned judicial review of economic and social legislation, review which it had carried out during much of its existence. This change substantially affected the large number of individuals and corporations engaged in private economic activity and had a profound impact on our political and economic systems. Government institutions and agencies at all levels acquired greater power over the economic system. For those denied the judicial forum for redressing grievances, the American government thereafter consisted of only two branches, not three.

Under its former policy, the High Court examined federal and state laws dealing with social and economic matters, and (under either the Fifth or Fourteenth Amendment) declared many unconstitutional because they deprived a plaintiff of property or liberty without due process of law. By comparison, the contemporary Court will uphold such legislation unless it violates certain specially protected liberties or is devoid of all rationality. Laws fixing prices, entry, and output, or otherwise restricting production and distribution of goods and services, which could not have passed constitutional muster under the prior standard, have little difficulty surviving under the contemporary

Court's rulings. Legislation restraining the exercise of what the contemporary Court considers fundamental liberties, such as speech and press, receives much less deferential treatment, and ordinarily will be set aside as unconstitutional unless the government can justify it as serving a compelling state interest.

For a great many in our society, the opportunity to engage freely in a business, trade, occupation, or profession is the most important liberty society has to offer. Consider, for example, the harm sustained by one who, in reliance on existing law, invests in a business only to have it terminated within two years by edict of the local city council. That was the situation presented in the case of *New Orleans v. Dukes,* decided by the United States Supreme Court on 25 June 1976.[1]

In August 1972, Nancy Dukes was operating her pushcart business in the New Orleans French Quarter, as she had been for approximately two years, selling hot dogs, drinks, confections, and novelties. About that time, the New Orleans City Council adopted an ordinance prohibiting pushcart vendors from selling foodstuffs in the Quarter. However, the ordinance carried a grandfather clause allowing all licensed vendors who had continuously operated the same business for eight years prior to 1 January 1972 to continue selling. Thus, the ordinance terminated Dukes's business in the area, but did not affect two other vendors who qualified under the time exception. One of these, Lucky Dogs, Inc., sold hot dogs and thereby was left with a monopoly in this business.

Dukes's challenge to the law lost in the federal district court,[2] won in the circuit court of appeals,[3] and was unanimously rejected by the eight United States Supreme Court Justices who considered the case. The federal High Court was concerned only that some reason existed for the city council's passing of the ordinance—a standard that even the most derelict lawmakers invariably can meet. The Court's per curiam decision declared that "in the local economic sphere, it is only the invidious discrimination, the wholly arbitrary act, which cannot stand consistently with the Fourteenth Amendment."[4] The Justices reasoned that the city might have thought that tourism would be enhanced by allowing only the veteran vendors to remain because their operations had become part of the unique character and charm of the Quarter. However, as the circuit court suggested, that same purpose could have been achieved through the far less onerous alternative of regulating the location and appearance of pushcarts.

Nancy Dukes would have fared much better during other periods of our judicial history. In fact, originally a major purpose for federal judicial review of national and state legislation was to protect property rights, possibly of the kind involved in the *Dukes* case. In the first part of this book, I shall describe and analyze the judicial treatment accorded the material liberties during the years between 1789, when the Constitution was ratified, and 1941, when the United States High Court withdrew from review of this area.

For now, let me acquaint the reader with this portion of our judicial history by briefly enumerating the constitutional protections to which Dukes might have been entitled in those years. The next three chapters will discuss these guarantees in considerable detail.

1. Article I, section 10 of the United States Constitution prohibits a state from passing an ex post facto law. The evidence is exceedingly persuasive that the Framers intended this provision to prevent passage of all retrospective laws, such as the New Orleans ordinance that deprived Dukes of her existing property and economic interests to vend food in the French Quarter. However, in 1798, three of four Justices deciding a case relating to this issue concluded that the ex post facto clauses in the Constitution applied only to criminal and not to civil matters.[5] Despite considerable criticism of that position over the years, the High Court has never departed from it.

2. The same section of the Constitution also bars a state from impairing the obligation of contracts. Chief Justice John Marshall and Justice Joseph Story, among the most capable Justices to serve on the Supreme Court, believed that this provision prohibited the state from interfering with an individual's freedom of contract. The New Orleans ordinance had this effect by preventing Dukes from entering into contracts relating to the purchase and sale of her wares. In a 4–3 decision in 1827, the United States Supreme Court confined the prohibitions of the contracts clause to laws affecting existing contracts,[6] thereby removing it as a bar to the regulation of future agreements and consequently of economic activity. Marshall wrote a lengthy dissent in which Justices Story and Duval concurred. His failure to prevail is attributable not to his lack of wisdom in the matter, but rather to the fact that the validity of state bankruptcy laws was involved and that his opinion would have prevented the states from enacting these statutes.

3. From the ratification of the Constitution through approximately the first quarter of the nineteenth century, Dukes might have had the benefit of natural rights–social compact doctrines employed by the United States Supreme Court to strike down state legislation that deprived individuals of property interests.

4. Several years following ratification of the Fourteenth Amendment in 1868, four of the nine Justices of the Supreme Court would have argued that the ordinance abridged Dukes's privileges and immunities

as a citizen of the United States to engage in a calling of her own choice.[7] Although this theory never prevailed, the same result would in time be achieved through the due process clause of the Fourteenth Amendment.

5. Possibly by 1876, a majority of the Court would have held that the ordinance violated Dukes's property rights under the due process clause of the Fourteenth Amendment. In a case decided during that year, the Court observed in dictum that for businesses not affected with a public interest, the Fourteenth Amendment "prevents the States from doing that which will operate" as a deprivation of the right to private property.[8] The likelihood of such a ruling increased in succeeding years,[9] and there is little doubt that by 1897, the New Orleans ordinance would have been considered a deprivation of property and liberty in violation of the due process clause.[10] This policy continued until 1937, when the Court adopted a far less exacting standard of review for economic legislation, but one that nonetheless allowed some judicial supervision.[11] In 1941, it abandoned even this modest control.[12]

From that time until now, a period when, with the blessing of the judiciary, liberty has flowered for many, individuals and corporations thrown out of business by government have, except for one case, obtained no relief from the federal courts unless the law also denied a political or some other specially protected right. The sole exception was the Court's 1957 ruling in *Morey v. Dowd*.[13] However, this decision was reversed by the *Dukes* case. Accordingly, almost regardless of how unfair, inequitable, unreasonable, arbitrary, or capricious legislators may be in depriving people of their business interests, the federal courts will not invoke their powers to safeguard the aggrieved party.

Yet the judiciary is the branch of government to which those who are adversely affected by legislation must look for relief. Justices are not intended to be government agents, furthering the interests of the executive and legislative branches in their disputes with citizens. Thousands of people and billions of dollars are already devoted to this cause. A judicial system more concerned to protect the power of government than the freedom of the individual has lost its mission under the Constitution. In a society that extols private property and private enterprise, those who engage in economic activities in reliance on existing laws are entitled to be secure against arbitrary and confiscatory government actions. If at all possible, society should not penalize or punish people who observe the rules and commit no wrongs.

This is one of the major reasons that we have a Supreme Court and that we grant it enormous power over lawmakers.

Nor is the problem confined to the individuals and corporations directly harmed by legislation. Society as a whole may suffer greatly when government intrudes into the operation of the marketplace. In the *Dukes* case the New Orleans City Council, by creating a monopoly, acted in a manner seemingly unpardonable in a competitive society. While the effect of this particular restriction may be minor in scope, it obviously can be reproduced on a broad scale with more serious societal consequences. For example, New Orleans subsequently extended the French Quarter ordinance to the downtown section.

The preceding discussion describes the general problem with which this book is concerned. In subsequent pages, I shall attempt to further persuade the reader that contemporary construction of the Federal Constitution that prevents its application to restrictions upon economic activity is erroneous and should be corrected. In the balance of the first chapter I shall present a brief background for this position by broadly surveying the operation of both the interpretive process and the interpretive body, the United States Supreme Court. This discussion introduces the reader to the judicial doctrine of economic due process, under which the High Court in the past safeguarded economic opportunities. The discussion also prepares for the historical and technical analysis of the doctrine contained in the balance of Part I and in Part II. In Part III, I shall describe the existing pattern of federal constitutional law affecting individual liberties, with special reference to economic liberties. Part IV explains the great need under our governmental system for judicial oversight of economic legislation.

The Quandary of Interpretation

Any endeavor to solve problems and ameliorate inequities in our judicial process must admit its inherent limitations. Under even optimum circumstances, legal interpretation is extremely arduous and complex. As a practicing attorney, I labored long hours drafting documents that I regarded as models of clarity and fairness, only to learn from counsel for the other parties that my efforts to exorcise ambiguities and maintain equities were not always successful. Fortunately my humiliation was usually short lived, lasting only until my role reversed from draftsman to critic. As Chief Justice John Marshall conceded, "Undoubtedly there is an imperfection in human language, which often exposes the same sentence to different constructions."[14]

The problems of construing private agreements tend to be minor
compared with the difficulties of interpreting the meanings of terms,
phrases, and clauses in the laws of the land—each of which has numerous professional and amateur authors. And it is that most important
legal document, the United States Constitution, that presents the most
trying construction problems.

Constitutional adjudication "must surely be the largest and hardest
task of principled decision-making faced by any group of men in the
entire world."[15] The Constitution's most crucial terminology is elusive
and nebulous, allowing the interpreter wide discretion. The annota-
tions of constitutional cases readily reveal the imprecision of such
seemingly straightforward terms as *speech, press, contract, religion,
property,* and *commerce* and the indeterminate character of clauses
concerned with *due process* and *equal protection.* When language is
not clear and precise, venturing beyond the written text may be necessary in order to supply meaning. This process usually requires examining the intentions of those who formulated the words. In the case of
the United States Constitution, intent is frequently not plain enough to
obviate further inquiry. Perhaps no consensus existed about meaning,
or it is now not discernible. Even when we are confident of the intent,
the problem may remain of applying that intent to a particular situation
unknown in an earlier era. In these circumstances, the interpreters may
have to determine what the Framers would have done had they been
confronted with this issue.

In their attempts to accomplish these tasks, Justices have often been
excoriated by historians for poorly supported findings and explanations. The use of history to untangle meaning is fraught with difficulty.
Perhaps no decision illustrates the situation better than the
Slaughter-House Cases, decided just five years after the 1868 ratification of the Fourteenth Amendment.[16] In this decision the United States
High Court split 5–4 on its first interpretation of the amendment's
meaning. The majority held that its coverage was largely confined to
race relations, while the dissenters believed it spanned a much broader
spectrum, including economic activity.

Consensus does not exist even on the issue of whether the Framers'
intent should be binding. For example, the equal protection clause has
been applied to a variety of societal ills not related to race. Yet, the
majority in the *Slaughter-House Cases* doubted "very much" that
state action for any other purpose would ever be held to come within
the purview of this provision.[17] The law reports are replete with similar
illustrations. Confronted with historical evidence supporting the poll

tax, Justice Douglas responded that such evidence is not binding: "In determining what lines are unconstitutionally discriminatory, we have never been confined to historic notions of equality...."[18] Chief Justice Hughes was more ingenious in confronting the problem. Recognizing the historical deficiency of his opinion upholding Minnesota's mortgage moratorium, Hughes nevertheless maintained that the Court was following the course that the Framers would have chosen:

> [W]e find no warrant for the conclusion that...the founders of our Government would have interpreted the [contracts] clause differently had they had occasion to assume that responsibility in the conditions of the later day.[19]

The speech and press guarantees provide another example of a willingness to ignore history. In a leading work on the subject, Professor Leonard Levy concludes that the First Amendment may have been based on the highly restrictive Blackstonian position concerning the limits of protected expression.[20] Nevertheless, Levy does not believe that the amendment's history should be controlling because the case for civil liberties is so powerfully grounded in principles and experience "that it need not be anchored to the past."[21]

Interpretation of any document, from the ordinary real estate contract to the Constitution, is influenced by the circumstances, mores, conventions, and prevailing notions of the contemporary society; and clearly, the meanings given words may change over the years. That which was reasonable, proper, and logical in one century may be unacceptable in another. Many concerns of yesteryear that prompted certain interpretations have now faded and been replaced with new attitudes. Ideas and feelings about labor, property, producers' and consumers' interests, the environment, and human rights do not remain static. Inventions and discoveries have occurred that were beyond the contemplation of those who lived centuries ago. The certainties of one period may appear as mistakes in another.

Nonetheless, the nation retains its commitment to a supreme legal document establishing the terms of the relationship between the governor and the governees. The American Constitution is the world's oldest still in use, and regardless of how distraught some of us become about certain judicial decisions, the people continue to honor and respect it as the fundamental law of the land.

For example, during the recent debates over ratification of the Panama Canal treaties that so consumed the United States Senate, no one could have credibly suggested that the constitutional requirement of a two-thirds concurring vote by that body is obsolete. The Framers' intent in this matter is final because it cannot be avoided or distorted. Why should other provisions be subject to a less exacting standard of compliance? The interpreter's great task is fulfilling the will of the authors of the fundamental document and of its amendments without damaging the fabric of the society. Giving primacy to the Framers' wishes also alleviates at least some construction problems. If we ascertain the goals that the Framers sought, some ambiguity is removed and the meaning of the words becomes clearer.

The nation has had almost two centuries in which to contemplate and develop rules of constitutional interpretation, and this opportunity has not been disregarded. Although the number of theories available to aid Supreme Court Justices in interpreting the fundamental law seems unlimited, most revolve about the critical question of how much authority the judiciary has or should have in departing from the meanings and purposes of the Framers. They range from those advocating a considerable policy-making role for the Court to those attempting to restrict judicial discretion almost completely. Many observers believe that the Constitution is a flexible and evolving document, always adaptable to changes in our society's conditions and circumstances. Others insist that judges be strictly bound by its words and by the historical record of what the framers of both the original text and the amendments intended. One commentator concludes that our highest tribunal has become a "Legiscourt" and urges the Justices to decide issues on direct policy rather than on strained constitutional grounds.[22]

A Theory of Constitutional Construction

Although these views are divergent and even contradictory, their proponents have no trouble in finding support in either the decisions or the practices of the courts, for our Justices themselves have not settled on any single theory of constitutional construction. Expressly or through their decisions, judges have displayed great differences in their approaches to the problem. My view is that we must look to the history, background, and purpose of judicial review in order to understand its meaning and power in relation to the constitutional scheme. I shall pursue this subject more fully in chapters 2 and 4. For now, consider some brief conclusions about the constitutional mission of the judiciary.

Judicial review of legislative action is America's contribution to the science of government. When our Constitution was ratified, no nation had yet accepted this idea as a principle of government. In England legislative authority over the judiciary was then and continues to be absolute. Judicial review was inevitable, however, in our country, given the diffusion of power among the various federal branches and between the national and state governments. It was also necessitated by the desire to secure individual liberties from governmental infringement. My reading in the history of judicial review leads to the conclusion that its purpose is to guarantee two distinct parts of the American plan of government: first, the structure of government as set forth in the Constitution, and second, the liberties of the people. Structural matters include the organization, composition, powers, and limitations of the various branches of the federal government, and their relationships to state governments. Some of this structure is defined in numerical figures about which there can be no quarrel. Disputes over other structural matters should be resolved in accordance with the Framers' will, as I shall describe below.

The second responsibility of our High Court is conceptually different. The conflicts in this area are not among governmental institutions, but rather between the individual and the state. The Court's obligation is to safeguard the individual from government, and this task requires judicial discretion in the cause of freedom. Although the over-all purpose of the Constitution is to protect and preserve liberty, the original document and its amendments do not define the extent and nature of this commitment. Moreover, the people's liberties are involved here, and they are too numerous and varied for the Framers to have enumerated. Consequently, in this area, a different approach to interpretation is required, as I shall subsequently explain.

Structure of Government

Let us first deal with the judiciary's responsibility to preserve structure and organization—a responsibility that involves construction of constitutional language. The strict constructionists' solution to interpretation is precise, uncompromising, relatively simple in application, and best implements neutral principles. According to this view, those who demand change must observe the constitutional mandate for amendment. Once the difficult problems of intent and purpose have been resolved, this theory leaves little room for judicial discretion. It is most consistent with the notion that justice demands the rule of laws and not of individuals. By comparison, those who refuse to be bound "by the hand of the past" confront the very troublesome question of how much discretion courts should have in departing from the document's original meaning. Because no absolute answer to this question exists, omitting the restraint of strict construction accords immense discretion to five of the nine people who, at any one time, happen, for various reasons, to occupy the highest judicial seats of power.

But, it might be said, why not accord this power to these learned people rather than to a group of individuals who lived two centuries ago in a world that has little relevance to our own? One reply to this often repeated query is that its underlying assumption is inaccurate. Basically, the Constitution speaks to the general political condition of the human species—a condition that has changed little if at all since the eighteenth century. The Framers' major concerns about the distribution, excesses, and abuses of political power are as pressing today as they were two hundred years ago. Their desire to secure individual liberties remains as compelling a concern as ever.

As the Constitution attests, the Framers' basic perceptions and views relating to governmental roles and functions are shared to a remarkable extent in the twentieth century. Thus the Framers believed that liberty and personal security are the ultimate purposes of society; they favored limited government and dispersal of power, feared the tyranny of political majorities, and viewed lack of governmental control as a boon to the economy and social well-being. They subscribed to the belief that individuals have fundamental and inalienable rights with which government may not interfere.[23]

The *Federalist Papers,* which present the ideas of the more influential Framers, continue to be regarded as among the greatest works of political philosophy. Many decisions of our earliest judges are as representative of modern thought and aspirations as are those issued by contemporary judges. The concepts and analyses of Blackstone, the foremost legal authority of the Constitutional period, remain highly relevant to our generation.[24] And Chief Justice John Marshall and Associate Justice Joseph Story, the most prestigious jurists of early America, would have a large and dedicated following today. Thus although almost two centuries have elapsed since the framing of the Constitution, we may conclude that our generation shares many basic philosophical and political beliefs with that of the Framers. In fact, the antigovernment perspective of recent years makes the current generation closer in philosophy than some that were nearer in time. Economic studies of regulation in recent times (discussed in later chapters) also demonstrate that the philosophical ideals of the Framers are pragmatically sound and desirable in our day.

Some prominent historians contend that the Framers were motivated by personal and selfish reasons. Other commentators assert the good faith and wisdom of the Founders.[25] The original Constitution (prior to the appending of the Bill of Rights) speaks for itself in its protection of human rights. The limitation, enumeration, and separation of powers restrain and confine the authority of governmental branches, agencies, and officers. The document prohibits suspension in peacetime of the writ of habeas corpus, the passage of bills of attainder, ex post facto laws, and laws impairing the obligation of contracts (by the states); it requires trial of all crimes by jury, and creates safeguards for those accused of or tried for treason. Furthermore, ratification of the Constitution did not alter the safeguards accorded under the common law for many other individual rights, including most of those later embodied in the Bill of Rights.

That the Framers' perspectives were not unique among their countrymen is evident from the fact that the states were already operating under governmental structures similar to the national model. Four of the twelve states which framed new constitutions during the Revolutionary period did not include specific bills of rights. And, as I have indicated, most of the common law liberties which the Bill of Rights guaranteed were already safeguarded under the political system the Framers established.

That the written word be observed to the maximum degree possible is a basic precept of a society of laws. This statement is true for both public and private sectors. A meaningful legal system cannot exist if those who follow recognized procedures in putting their intentions in writing cannot expect that these intentions will be honored and observed. Contracts, wills, deeds, and other documents are drafted in the belief that the words they contain will be fully implemented. Presumably legislators vote for laws under the assumption that they will be carried out as intended. Not infrequently, circumstances change after a legal document has been made final; therefore, some parties may wish its rescission or modification. However, the purpose of written arrangements is precisely to prevent this result.

Although the binding effect of legal documents is of paramount importance in a free society, this doctrine is subordinate to the even higher principle that absolutes in law do not exist. There are exceptions to all rules, even in a system emphasizing the sanctity of rules. Thus special circumstances may require that a rule not be enforced. In the event of an extreme emergency—for instance, war, insurrection, or fire—a government may assume powers expressly denied it.[26]

Although ours has always been a commercial society, dependent on financial commitments, courts in exceptional cases have set aside private agreements for policy reasons.[27] The people's fundamental rights may be circumscribed if such action is justified by compelling state interests.[28]

It follows therefore that even the strictest rules of construction do not always demand faithful adherence to the intention or purpose of the Constitution's Framers. No strict constructionist demands the reversal of all judicial decisions contrary to original meaning and understanding.[29] However, under the theory suggested, the justification for departing from adherence must be compelling and exceptional.

To be sure, many changes uncontemplated by the Framers have occurred in this world since the ratification of the Constitution. Their lack of prescience is not unique to lawyers and others involved in drafting binding documents. The length of many legal papers reveals how hard lawyers strive to cover all eventualities, but experience reveals that even the most brilliant legal minds do not necessarily succeed. It is when the unforeseen occurs that ascertaining intent and purpose becomes important. Courts try to determine as accurately as possible the course that the original parties would have followed had they thought about the situation in question. The difficulty of this undertaking is hardly reason for rejecting the Framers' will. Contracts are, after all, not thrown out of court because of a failure to predict all future eventualities.

A court's linking its decision to intent and purpose limits judicial discretion. This limitation is also accomplished by imposing the special-situation standard to justify departures from the Framers' will. Here the Justices would have to scrupulously explain why they are following a different course. In contemporary times the United States Supreme Court has adopted a comparable policy in deciding cases involving fundamental interests and suspect classifications. The Justices apply a standard of strict review and compelling state interest to test the validity of laws affecting these areas, limiting judicial discretion to evaluating the allegedly compelling interest. A great burden rests on the state to justify its restraint. A similar approach to constitutional construction would place a comparable burden on those demanding departure from the Framers' intent and purpose.

Liberties of the People

The second form of judicial responsibility—the protection of liberty —is no less derived from the will of the Framers, but it is not limited by language of the fundamental law. In fact, the Constitution does not define the nature and scope of judicial power. However, we know that leading figures of the Constitutional period regarded the judiciary as the individual's guardian against arbitrary rule by government. Although the original document, mainly in Article I, sections 9 and 10, enumerates relatively few individual guarantees, the Framers did establish a limited government. As we shall see in chapter 2, James Madison and Alexander Hamilton, among others, believed that a bill of rights was unnecessary because the federal government was given no power to diminish fundamental liberties. When the Bill of Rights was adopted, the Ninth Amendment was included to provide that the enumeration of certain rights should not be construed to deny or disparage others retained by the people.

The Court's discretion in protecting liberties is qualified by its constitutional responsibility, which it may not limit or exceed. Like other grants of undefined power, the review power should be construed in accordance with "the reason and spirit of it; or the cause which moved the legislator to enact it."[30] The judiciary must not, of course, violate provisions of the Constitution, or decide questions that Chief Justice Marshall referred to as in their nature political. The original understanding about the judiciary binds its powers in enforcing rights in two other respects.

First, the Court should protect those liberties necessary to maintain the form of government that had been created. Thus, in the economic sphere, the Framers sought to perpetuate a system based on private property and private enterprise. Accordingly, the Court should safeguard liberties consistent with this objective. Second, the judiciary must function within the confines of a structure separating and limiting the powers of each branch of government. The Constitution does not delegate policy-making authority to the judiciary, except as may be implied by the nature of the judicial process. The judges were to be interpreters, exercising no more than a veto or negative power over legislation, even when this form of remedy did not provide a complete solution to the problem.

Implementing or Creating Constitutional Rights

The preceding constitutional theory would require the same judicial priority for economic as for other rights. Economic liberties once enjoyed this status, but the courts that extended it are now criticized for following such policy.

Thus, according to a constitutional law casebook, "[f]rom *Lochner* in 1905 to *Nebbia* in 1934...the [Supreme] Court frequently substituted its judgment for that of the Congress and state legislatures on the wisdom of economic regulation interfering with contract and property interests."[31] Other commentators have referred to the decisions of those years as being the product of a "discredited," "rejected and reviled"[32] judicial period whose notions "have been repudiated."[33] They believe that the Justices undertook the functions of "a superlegislature to determine the wisdom, need, and propriety of laws that touch economic problems, business affairs, or social conditions." This last quotation is from Justice Douglas, writing in the 1965 case *Griswold v. Connecticut*,[34] a major Warren Court decision which I shall discuss shortly.

All these references concern the period between the late 1890s and the late 1930s, when the High Court, relying on the doctrine of substantive due process, frequently overturned legislation on the ground that it violated economic liberties protected by the Constitution. *Substantive due process* usually refers to a judicial policy that substantively protects, under the due process clauses of the Fifth and Fourteenth Amendments, activities that are not elsewhere secured in the Constitution. A more precise term for the doctrine protecting economic endeavors is *economic due process*.

Parts I and II of this book are mostly about substantive due process, and in them I shall show that the prevailing image of this doctrine is incorrect. The inference that there is something unique and extraordinary about the Supreme Court's conduct during the substantive due process era is, I believe, erroneous in light of that body's historical record. Let me explain this point by returning to the much-discussed *Griswold* decision and by considering some of the positions presented in the six opinions delivered in that case—four in the majority and two in dissent. This 7–2 decision was favorably received by many commentators and is illustrative of a contemporary judicial approach to the protection of individual liberties.

The issue in *Griswold* was the constitutionality of a Connecticut statute making criminal the use of any drug, article, or instrument intended to prevent human conception. The Court confronted the problem of how to deal with state legislative restraints on liberties that many people regarded as extremely important but that are not even remotely referred to in any constitutional provision and that the Framers of the original Constitution or the Fourteenth Amendment never imagined. For some of the Justices, however, more was at issue than the constitutionality of a single statute. Douglas and Black, among others on the Court, were dedicated opponents of substantive due process, and a decision against the law would seem to support that doctrine. Since the 1937 demise of substantive due process, the Court had managed to avoid striking down any economic or social law on the ground it violated due process.

The two defendants in *Griswold* were active participants in a birth control center that supplied information and advice to married couples on how best to prevent conception and that prescribed contraceptive devices. Payment for these services followed a graduated scale of fees based on family income, with some families paying nothing. The state complained that these practices violated a law making it illegal to assist and abet the commission of an existing offense. The defendants were found guilty as accessories under the latter section and fined. The dominant purpose of the anticontraceptive law was said to be the prevention of promiscuous or illicit sexual relationships, whether premarital or extramarital.

After inveighing against the Old Court's practice of striking down economic and social legislation, Justice Douglas, delivering the majority opinion, said that the Connecticut statute raised an entirely different issue because it affected an intimate relationship between husband and wife. The Justice ruled that the enactment violated the right of marital privacy, which he found within the penumbras of specific guarantees of the Bill of Rights, "formed by emanations from those guarantees that help give them life and substance."[35] His opinion mentions six provisions in the Bill of Rights and asserts that the combination of these individual safeguards creates a separate right of marital privacy protected from state action under the Fourteenth Amendment's due process clause.

Douglas chose an uncharted and circuitous route to arrive at a destination that the use of the rejected substantive due process doctrine would have made readily accessible. Applying pre–1937 substantive due process, a court might have disposed of the case in the following manner. By selling a professional service to married couples, the defendants were exercising liberty of contract. Connecticut's ban was an arbitrary and unjustifiable infringement of this liberty. Furthermore, the statutory means was excessive to accomplishing the legislative end of discouraging premarital or extramarital sexual relations. As Justices Goldberg and White noted in their concurring opinions, a statute more discriminately tailored to people engaged only in the prohibited sexual activity would have served the same purpose, without invading the marital relationship. Douglas also employed a means-ends test in declaring that the statute had an overly destructive impact by prohibiting use, rather than regulating manufacture or sale.[36] But this holding is only one facet of his complex endeavors. In formulating its opinion, the Old Court might have determined that liberty within the meaning of the due process clauses encompasses the marriage relationship. That Court had entered such a ruling with respect to family life in two cases to be discussed in chapter 7.[37]

Justice Goldberg concurred with Douglas and in addition analyzed the issue within an even broader context, not tied to any enumerated guarantees.[38] Goldberg contended that not all the rights our constitutional system intended to preserve are mentioned in the fundamental document, and as evidence of this position, he cited the Ninth Amendment, which states that "[t]he enumeration in the Constitution, of certain rights, shall not be construed to deny or disparage others retained by the people." The right of marital privacy is so basic to and deep-rooted in our society, he argued, that it has to be a protected right, whether or not specified in the Constitution. Goldberg concluded that failure to protect it would be a transgression of the Ninth Amendment.

The drawback to this particular reasoning is that the Ninth Amendment is applicable only to the federal government and does not safeguard liberties against infringement by the Connecticut legislature. Goldberg worked around this obstacle by deciding that rights secured under the Ninth Amendment are also secured under the due process clause of the Fourteenth Amendment, and thus protected from state laws. Chief Justice Warren and Justice Brennan concurred with Goldberg. Whatever else these opinions signified, they reinstituted substantive due process analysis, which was supposed to have been banished forever from the Court's deliberations.

Justice Black was not impressed by the ingenuity of his two colleagues, and he filed a strong dissent.[39] Rejecting recognition of a privacy right in the marital relationship, he accused Douglas and Goldberg of using the condemned substantive due process formula in striking down the Connecticut statute. Black believed that constitutional construction should be predicated upon natural meaning in contrast to what he referred to as natural law. He felt that the latter concept was the guiding force both for the substantive due process Court and the opinions of his two colleagues. Although he abhorred the statute in question, Black could find nothing in the Bill of Rights that created a right of privacy. This and other of his vigorous dissents display Black's belief that the Constitution must be given a natural interpretation. For him, the words in the Bill of Rights are self-limiting and may not be used to fashion guarantees that are not explicitly set forth; penumbras are obviously illusory. Moreover, Goldberg's view of the Ninth Amendment, which Black thought was not supported by the provision's history, would have broadened the Court's powers immeasurably and unjustifiably.

Interestingly, Black's dissent was not viewed as an appropriate application of judicial restraint by Justice Harlan, himself a professed believer in restraint (and a critic of substantive due process). Harlan concurred in the result, but not in the other majority opinions. He stated that judicial restraint in due process as in other constitutional areas could be brought about "only by continual insistence upon respect for the teachings of history, solid recognition of the basic values that underlie our society, and wise appreciation of the great roles that the doctrines of federalism and separation of powers have played in establishing and preserving American freedoms."[40] He suggested that Black's acceptance of two recent reapportionment decisions, which Harlan believed had no basis in history,[41] was not appropriate for a strict constructionist.

Black completely rejected the subjective approach implicit in Harlan's criteria. In an important decision on the Constitution's contract clause, which mandates that no state shall pass any law impairing the obligation of contracts,[42] Black stood alone in insisting that its words should be construed literally.[43] He also dissented in another major Warren Court decision because he could find nothing in the Constitution that forbade the poll tax.[44]

Black was endowed with that unique form of objectivity in constitutional construction that frequently seems to accompany the high position he occupied. Although he usually emphasized that each word of the Constitution is entitled to a natural interpretation, he was willing to omit the critical term *liberty* from the due process clauses. In *Griswold,* he expressed concern that the word could be extended "limitlessly to require States to justify any law restricting 'liberty' as my Brethren define 'liberty.' This would mean at the very least, I suppose, that every state criminal statute—since it must inevitably curtail 'liberty' to some extent—would be suspect, and would have to be justified to this Court."[45]

This approach does not succeed in settling the issue it raises; the difficulty of construing language is not reason for omitting it. Justice Powell has observed that the history of the due process provision teaches caution and restraint, but not abandonment.[46] Interpreters do not enjoy the privilege of rejecting or ignoring words at their pleasure.

The course preferred by Black denies constitutional benefits to those who might claim certain protections. Chief Justice Marshall made the point when he said that his Court "never sought to enlarge the judicial power beyond its proper bounds, nor feared to carry it to the fullest extent that duty required."[47]

Although many jurists complain about substantive due process in the economic sphere, they have not been reluctant to accept the course pursued by Douglas in which he recognized—some would say created—a privacy right entitled to substantive protection. This suggests that such criticism relates to the ends and not to the means. In *Griswold,* Justice Douglas enumerated some protected rights that are not mentioned in either the Constitution or its amendments. These rights include freedom of association and freedom of the university community. His opinion was also predicated on rights of family life relating to parental control over children's education that had been established by the substantive due process Court.[48]

Throughout our constitutional history Justices have espoused the view that certain personal rights—once referred to by Justice Cardozo as those "implicit in the concept of ordered liberty"[49]—are so fundamental that they are protected whether or not they appear in the Constitution. Most members of the Warren and Burger Courts accept this position. As I have indicated, Justices in the early years of the nation applied natural law–social compact theories to uphold property rights. In the abortion cases, which struck down laws in all states, Justice Blackmun, for the majority, expressed the opinion that the right of privacy that ensures freedom of choice in terminating pregnancy emanates from the due process clause of the Fourteenth Amendment's concept of personal liberty.[50] More recently, Justice Powell, writing for himself and three other Justices, found the right of an extended family to live together to be a liberty protected by this due process clause.[51]

Consider also contemporary decisions on the right to travel. The Court has used this right as the basis for invalidating residency requirements for welfare assistance[52] and public nonemergency hospital or medical care.[53] However, the right to travel is nowhere mentioned in the Constitution; it is a product of judicial construction. In the residency-requirement opinions, the Court elevated travel to a fundamental right, thereby entering the area of local fiscal programming ordinarily considered as within the legislative province; it did so possibly, one suspects, in order to accomplish certain social and economic goals—the identical objective ascribed to the Court of the "discredited'' substantive due process period. Justice Harlan, dissenting in the welfare assistance case, stated that the Court's reasoning reflected

> the current notion that this Court possesses a peculiar wisdom all its own whose capacity to lead this Nation out of its present troubles is contained only by the limits of judicial ingenuity in contriving new constitutional principles to meet each problem as it arises.[54]

What to some is judicial diligence, creativity, and ingenuity, to others translates as legalized transgressions. Although much of this book is devoted to discussing the highly criticized substantive due process Court, this fact should not obscure the strong feelings that have been directed at Courts of other days; efforts to restrict Supreme Court powers are almost as old as the institution itself.[55]

Substantive Due Process and Economic Liberties

The number and extent of rights created by the Supreme Court since the presumed demise of substantive due process continues to grow. However, economic liberties, which significantly touch almost every person's life, have not been accorded appreciable protection. Freedom to contract for the production or distribution of goods and services has been relegated to a low priority since the late 1930s. Economic and social legislation that does not affect some explicit or specially protected constitutional right will be upheld as we saw in the *Dukes* case, unless it is wholly arbitrary and constitutes invidious discrimination. For all practical purposes this standard means that the Constitution does not insulate economic activities from the exercise of legislative or administrative fiat. Omission of protection is not less defective or arbitrary than is its exaggeration. Given the Constitution's extensive umbrella, it is difficult to understand why the document fails to provide safeguards for conduct important to large numbers of people in this nation.

However, conventional history does not accept economic due process as benefiting the common people. A great many judges and commentators apparently believe that application of the concept proved little or no aid to the bulk of the population; they assume that the liberties of wealthy commercial interests and not those of the ordinary citizen were protected. Constitutional freedom was seen as a cover under which the ambitions of big business could be nourished. The implication is that Justices of the period abused their official and professional responsibilities. These accusations deserve to be rejected as fallacious.

Economic due process usually favored economic competition—a state of affairs not always pleasing to big business. Nevertheless, when the Court invoked the doctrine to invalidate welfare measures, they were seen as encouraging big business to the detriment of workers. But the Justices most dedicated to the concept also rejected much special interest legislation, such as a New York minimum price law for milk that had been promoted by dairy interests[56] and a statute advocated by the Oklahoma ice manufacturing industry barring free entry into that business.[57] Such positions protect economic competition and are therefore highly advantageous to consumers. Further, the acts designated as welfare provisions are not necessarily regarded as ameliorative by all those they were designed to benefit; one who loses her job as a result of a minimum wage law for women will hardly regard the law positively.[58]

Frequently, legal decisions help certain individuals or groups in ways that the Justices did not directly intend. For instance, judicial policy supportive of free press has greatly benefited the publishing industry, which includes some of the richest and most powerful corporations in the country.[59] The establishment of stringent proof-of-libel standards[60] and the invalidation of judicial gag orders,[61] government secrecy restraints,[62] and right-to-access statutes[63] have been financially advantageous to newspaper owners. The equal access, or right-to-reply statutes, which have been declared unconstitutional,[64] would have reduced the power of newspapers to influence elections and public policies. If judicial decisions are to be graded by the extent to which they aid the rich and powerful, those protecting the right of free press will receive high marks.

In general, the Supreme Court's present policy of abdication with respect to socioeconomic legislation has been more beneficial to the rich than to the poor—a matter to be considered in Part IV. This policy has caused an increase in the number and personal power of government officials. Political power monopolies, prevalent at federal, state, and local levels, exist at the expense of individual liberties. Big and small businesses have sought and obtained regulation curbing competition that meaningful judicial review might not have permitted. Those who benefit from certain official policies maintain silence or express support verbally or with campaign contributions rather than risk confrontation with influential politicians or a government agency. This state of affairs is hardly one from which to hurl condemnation at the "unreconstructed" Court.

Whether we approve or not, the legal experience of this country shows that over-all the many substantive due process judges were motivated by basically the same kinds of interests and concerns that courts have responded to throughout our history. Judges do not now and never have issued opinions from hermetically sealed environments. Because judges can be expected to undertake and perform their duties in light of their own visions of justice, there was, in this sense, nothing special or peculiar about the Supreme Court's work during the substantive due process era. Experience shows that while elevation to high office does not eliminate the innate desire to prevail, it also does not obliterate the tempering qualities of duty and service.

The contention that the Old Court capriciously interfered with the legislative process loses credibility when advanced by those who applaud much greater interventions by the Warren and Burger Courts. Judicial process is not the issue for many of these critics; they are guided rather by results. Decisions and procedures of the last quarter century, with vague or remote bases in constitutional law, have not aroused the animosity and contempt that erupted against the far more legally justifiable opinions delivered prior to 1937. *Lochner v. New York*,[65] to be discussed subsequently, is one of the most condemned cases in United States history and has been used to symbolize judicial dereliction and abuse. Yet it has as solid a constitutional basis as numerous contemporary decisions that have elicited little criticism and, frequently, lavish praise. Recent commentaries comparing *Lochner* and the abortion cases are clarifying the record in this regard and exposing the widespread tendency to be swayed by ends and not means.[66]

At the time of this writing, the idea of restoring a high legal priority to economic liberties is not acceptable to most judges. Economic due process and the Justices who enforced it continue to receive adverse treatment in the opinions and commentaries. However, many states continue to adhere to the doctrine.[67] In addition, recently decided cases that expand protected speech to include commercial publication[68]—pharmaceutical and lawyers' advertising, and "For Sale" and "Sold" signs—and that apply the contracts clause (Art. I, Sec. 10) to protect economic interests,[69] as well as a variety of Supreme Court opinions[70] and journal comments over the years, suggest that the ideological gap may not be so immense as commonly supposed. The overreaction seems to be subsiding. Before this hypothesis is explored and comparisons are made, it is appropriate to probe in some depth the history, experience, and philosophy that created and supported economic due process.

2 The Origins and Growth of Substantive Due Process

The Original Meaning of Due Process

The admonition in the Fifth and Fourteenth Amendment that a person shall not be deprived of "life, liberty or property without due process of law" had its origin in chapter 39 of the Magna Carta accepted by King John in 1215. This chapter provides that no freeman "shall be arrested, or detained in prison, or deprived of his freehold, or outlawed, or banished, or in any way molested...unless by the lawful judgment of his peers and by the law of the land." State constitutions usually contain either law of the land or due process clauses. It is generally understood that both have the same meaning. There is little dispute that at the time of the framing of the American Bill of Rights in 1789, law of the land and due process of law clauses related to certain procedures and processes of the common law. The difficult question is whether they also were restraints on substantive matters.

Citing in support a section of Edward Coke's *Institutes*, both Chancellor James Kent (1826) and Justice Joseph Story (1833) wrote that due process of law (which they understood to be the same as law of the land) required certain processes and procedures in criminal prosecutions. Neither considered whether these concepts had meaning in relation to legislative deprivations of property interests. However, Coke, in an earlier section explaining disseisin of property, cited two civil cases in which denials of property interests without judicial process were adjudged "against the law of the land." In discussing protection for liberties (as provided for under a subsequent issue of the charter), he concluded that "[g]enerally all monopolies are against this great charter, because they are against the liberty and freedom of the subject, and against the law of the land."[1] Thus Coke identified law of the land with common law rights.

Blackstone can be similarly construed. He enumerates many laws, both legislative and judicial in origin, that have to be observed before a subject can be deprived of life, liberty, or property. Some limited substantially certain powers of goverment. For example, in his discussion of the protection afforded the right of property, he writes that the legislature can acquire property "[n]ot by absolutely stripping the subject of his property in an arbitrary manner; but by giving him a full indemnification and equivalent for the injury thereby sustained." Blackstone asserted that this is but one instance "in which the law of the land has postponed even public necessity to the sacred and inviolate rights of private property."[2]

The first time the U.S. Supreme Court considered the issue was in 1819 in the *Okely* case, when Justice Johnson interpreted the law of the land clause of the Maryland Constitution as "intended to secure the individual from the arbitrary exercise of the powers of government, unrestrained by the established principles of private rights and distributive justice."[3] In 1792, the South Carolina Supreme Court decided that an act of the colonial assembly taking away a freehold from one person and vesting it in another without any compensation or jury trial was invalid "as it was against common right, as well as against magna charta."[4] The North Carolina Supreme Court held in 1805 that the law of the land clause in the state constitution prohibited the legislature from repealing a prior grant of lands to a university.[5]

Consequently, considerable basis existed for the broad definition of law of the land that Daniel Webster presented in the *Dartmouth College* case (1819) which became widely quoted in the cases and commentaries.

> By the law of the land is most clearly intended the general law; a law, which hears before it condemns; which proceeds upon inquiry, and renders judgment only after trial. The meaning is, that every citizen shall hold his life, liberty, property and immunities, under the protection of the general rules which govern society. Everything which may pass under the form of an enactment, is not, therefore, to be considered the law of the land . . . .[6]

In the Constitutional period, there was no need to resort to due process or other constitutional guarantees to find restraints on legislative action. Thus, like many of his contemporaries, Alexander Hamilton believed that limitations upon government are found in a higher law. Property could be safeguarded without invoking due process, which Hamilton thought was limited to processes in criminal law. In a 1796 opinion that he wrote as a practicing attorney, he said, in regard to the validity of land titles, that considerations based on natural justice and social policy exist aside from constitutional provisions that would protect purchasers in good faith from the Georgia legislature's attempted revocation of their title.

> Without pretending to judge of the original merits or demerits of the purchasers, it may be safely said to be a contravention of the first principles of natural justice and social policy, without any judicial decision of facts, by a positive act of the legislature, to revoke a grant of property regularly made for valuable consideration, under legislative authority, to the prejudice even of third persons on every supposition innocent of the alleged fraud or corruption; and it may be added that the precedent is new of revoking a grant on the suggestion of corruption of a legislative body.[7]

Over time, the federal and state courts that initially accepted the narrow view broadened their interpretation of the due process clauses to give them substantive meaning similar to the limitations on government that Hamilton thought already existed. One reason for this evolution is that the phrase denotes fairness and equity in treatment—notions that cannot always be reduced to criminal law safeguards, particularly when serious personal loss is threatened. Many judges believed that legislative acts depriving people of property interests have the same impact as punitive impositions but without trial or other protections, and therefore should be subject to judicial standards. For example, Chancellor Kent was of the opinion

> that there is no distinction in principle, nor any recognized in practice, between a law punishing a person criminally, for a past innocent act, or punishing him civilly by devesting him of a lawfully acquired right. The distinction consists only in the degree of the oppression, and history teaches us that the government which can deliberately violate the one right, soon ceases to regard the other.[8]

The concept of substantive due process evolved not only from notions of reasonable governmental process but also from the natural law and social compact theories popularly accepted by eighteenth-century Americans and applied by their courts. Substantive due process par-

takes of the same broad natural law doctrine that forbids legislative
bodies from imposing arbitrary restrictions on a person's fundamental
and inalienable rights and that holds that duly enacted statutes violative
of the natural law are not binding. Commentators have observed that
cases decided on the basis of natural law and social compact would
later have received the same disposition under a substantive due process theory.[9] When they eventually became hesitant or distrustful
about using unwritten laws, the courts began turning to provisions of
federal or state constitutions. They found the most appropriate to be
the due process clauses (or law of the land).

Human Rights in the Revolutionary and Constitutional Periods

Corwin, among others, advises us that during the initial period of federal constitutional history, which closed about 1830, leading judges and
advocates accepted the ideas of natural rights and the social compact
as bases for constitutional decisions.[10] Our constitutional and bills-of-
rights models were constructed at a time when the natural law school of
judicial thought was highly influential, and the early evolution of
American law coincided with a high tide of individualistic ethics and
economics.[11] As Cox has observed, "[b]elief in natural rights and natural law were deeply ingrained in the eighteenth-century American mind
despite uncertainty whether their source was the King of Kings and
Lord of all the earth, the immutable maxims of reason and justice, or
the accumulated wisdom of English common law."[12]

Recent historical analysis of the Revolution is very persuasive that
the dominant political ideology among the Colonists was predicated on
fear and distrust of government.[13] In *Ideological Origins of the American Revolution,* historian Bernard Bailyn discusses the philosophy of
those who made the Revolution. He is convinced that fear of a comprehensive conspiracy against liberty lay at the heart of American
Revolutionary thought. For protection against this conspiracy, many
looked for guidance to the advocates of a new liberty that espoused
natural rights and sought elimination of old institutions and practices
that harbored despotism.

> The ideas and writings of the leading secular thinkers of the Euro-
> pean Enlightenment—reformers and social critics like Voltaire,
> Rousseau, and Beccaria as well as conservative analysts like
> Montesquieu—were quoted everywhere in the colonies, by everyone
> who claimed a broad awareness. In pamphlet after pamphlet the
> American writers cited Locke on natural rights and on the social and

governmental contract, Montesquieu and later Delolme on the character of British liberty and on the institutional requirements for its attainment, Voltaire on the evils of clerical oppression, Beccaria on the reform of criminal law, Grotius, Pufendorf, Burlamaqui, and Vattel on the laws of nature and of nations, and on the principles of civil government.[14]

Although these authors' works were often only superficially understood, they were astonishingly well known. The key concepts were natural rights, the contractual basis of government, the uniqueness of English liberty, and the preservation of constitutions founded on dispersed authority. Government was thought to be by its nature hostile to human liberty and happiness and especially susceptible to corruption and despotism. Therefore, it should exist only at the tolerance of the people whose needs it serves.

The means for restricting governmental powers was through a constitution, which would define authority and create a mixture of functions that would prevent any one group from gaining ascendency. Creating this balance of forces was essential to preserve the capacity to exercise natural rights—those God-given, inalienable, and indefeasible rights founded on immutable maxims of reason and justice and inherent in all people by virtue of their humanity. Those rights were expressed—not created—in the English common law, in the statutory enactments of Parliament, and in the charters and privileges promulgated by the Crown. However, because not even these sources could exhaust the great treasure of human rights, they delineated the minimum, not the maximum, boundary of liberty. Government had to be so constituted that it could not infringe these rights, for the legitimacy of positive law and legal rights rests on the degree to which they conform to abstract universals of human rights.

While the passions may have subsided and the explanations become more pragmatic, these libertarian ideas were prominent and influential during the time when the United States Constitution was drafted and ratified. It is evident from the ratification debates that the protection of the individual from government was then the predominant political concern. Opponents of the proposed Constitution displayed great apprehension, suspicion, and antagonism toward centralized government, while its supporters responded that the federal government would have no more power than necessary to secure the people from foreign and domestic perils.[15] It is doubtful the Constitution would have been ratified by the necessary number of states had the Federalists not agreed to add amendments protecting individual rights. Professor

Wood advises that the search for a way to control and restrict the powers of elected representatives dominated the politics and constitutionalism of the Confederation period.[16]

The absence of a bill of rights in the original Constitution does not suggest the Framers were otherwise motivated. A proposal made during the Constitutional Convention to establish a committee to draft a bill of rights was rejected by a vote of ten to zero.[17] While no one can be certain about why a bill of rights was not included in the original document, four related explanations present themselves: First a limited government was established with little authority to interfere with fundamental liberties. Second, the rights codified in the Constitution were those most important and vital to society. Third, the enumeration of many liberties in a bill of rights might reflect adversely on the many others that were not expressed. Fourth, the common law in this country as in England provided sufficient protection for the essential liberties not secured in the Constitution.

In the ratification debates the Federalists contended that a bill of rights was unnecessary and that an enumeration of specific rights would provide a basis for abuse of power. In Number 84 of the *Federalist Papers*, Hamilton argued against the need for including a bill of rights in the Constitution. He asserted that the proposed document was intended to regulate not personal and private concerns but rather the nation's general political interests. "[T]he people surrender nothing; and as they retain everything, they have no need of particular reservations."[18] Therefore, a bill of rights was superfluous. Such a declaration might even be dangerous, Hamilton thought, because it would contain various exceptions to powers that were not conferred and to this extent would furnish a "colorable pretext" for claiming more than was granted—possibly by those disposed to usurpation. "For why declare that things shall not be done which there is no power to do?"[19]

According to this view, establishing a constitutional government does not affect the rights of the governed unless such an outcome is expressly provided for. The Constitution did not create these rights and therefore was not the source to which courts could turn for guidance about their breadth and character except insofar as the document restrained and modified them.

The addition of the Bill of Rights to the Constitution did not alter this understanding, for the Ninth Amendment provides that "enumeration...of certain rights shall not be construed to deny or disparage others retained by the people." James Madison introduced this

amendment to meet Hamilton's concerns about enumeration. Justice
Story later explained that the Bill of Rights "presumes the existence of
a substantial body of rights not specifically enumerated but easily perceived in the broad concept of liberty and so numerous and so obvious
as to preclude listing them."[20] Although he had stated that "every
power not granted thereby remains with the people, and at their
will,"[21] Madison in time supported the addition of the Bill of Rights
despite his initial opposition.

The fact that the original Constitution did expressly secure certain
liberties indicates the Framers had certain priorities. This is evident
from the records of their proceedings. By a vote of 6–5, the convention
rejected a provision mandating "that the liberty of the press should be
inviolably observed."[22] In opposing this motion, Connecticut's Roger
Sherman said that the provision was unnecessary, for Congress had no
authority over the press.[23] During the debates on the ex post facto
clauses, prominent members of the Convention also argued that these
were superfluous. When the prohibitions on attainder and ex post facto
laws were introduced, Oliver Ellsworth, a Connecticut delegate who
later became Chief Justice of the United States Supreme Court, said
that "there was no lawyer, no civilian who would not say that ex post
facto laws were void of themselves."[24] James Wilson of Pennsylvania,
also subsequently appointed to the Supreme Court, opposed inserting
the ban, explaining that "[i]t will bring reflections on the
Constitution—and proclaim that we are ignorant of the first principles
of Legislation . . . ."[25] Gouverneur Morris of Pennsylvania and William
Samuel Johnson of Connecticut also thought the prohibition unnecessary.[26] Nevertheless, ex post facto prohibitions were included.

That the original Constitution contains no express prohibitions
against confiscation of property does not prove that the Framers were
unconcerned about this liberty. As the next chapter will explain, the
evidence is persuasive that the Framers considered the ex post facto
provisions as guarantees against such actions. Despite this probable
understanding, the Supreme Court in 1798 construed these provisions
as applying only to criminal matters, and removed the protection of
ownership from their reach.[27]

A principal right intended to be safeguarded by the appeal to natural
rights and the social compact was that of property. A common contemporary opinion was that a major function of government was protecting
and preserving property rights. The leading constitutional Framers,
believing that these rights have a tenuous position under representative
government, often asserted on the Convention floor the necessity of
protecting them. For instance, considerable sentiment existed to re-

strict to property owners the privileges of voting and office holding. Apparently this qualification was not adopted, on grounds that it was unfeasible and not necessarily protective of property interests. Opinion favoring a restrictive franchise was not unusual for those times, since most states mandated some landed property ownership for voters, and the vast majority of males qualified under this limitation.

For many Framers, a freeholder was the ideal voter. Frequently he was financially independent with a stake in the preservation of established society. For people to become freeholders required protection of liberty of contract, for that is the only way to acquire property by one's own efforts. For freeholders to benefit from their property and remain independent of government also required protection of liberty of contract to use and dispose of property.

The Framers probably subscribed to Blackstone's definition that the right of private property is "absolute ...[and] consists in the free use, enjoyment and disposal [by man] of all his acquisitions, without any control or diminution, save only by the laws of the land." This right was "probably founded in nature" but was subject to the state's powers of eminent domain (with full indemnification), of taxation (only by Act of Parliament), and of regulation (gentle and moderate).[28]

James Madison attributed the convening of the Constitutional Convention less to the necessity of remedying the deficiencies of the Articles of Confederation than to that of providing some effective security for private economic rights. In a letter to Jefferson, written in October 1787, he explained this position:

> The mutability of the laws of the States is found to be a serious evil. The injustice of them has been so frequent and so flagrant as to alarm the most steadfast friends of Republicanism. I am persuaded I do not err in saying that the evils issuing from these sources contributed more to that uneasiness which produced the Convention, and prepared the public mind for a general reform, than those which accrued to our national character and interest from the inadequacy of the Confederation to its immediate objects. A reform, therefore, which does not make provision for private rights, must be materially defective.[29]

Here Madison was referring to state laws that were passed on behalf of debtor interests and that devalued promissory and contractual obligations. He voiced similar sentiments during the convention and in the *Federalist Papers*.[30]

A primary consideration for the Framers, according to Madison, was to guard against the dangers that will arise when a majority of the people own no property.[31] Although Hamilton believed that the Senate would protect the interests of property owners, he looked also to the federal judiciary to perform this function.[32] Judicial review is in fact intimately associated with protecting property rights. Those who feared legislative or majoritarian tampering with property rights considered the judiciary to be the branch of government that would guard owners' interests. For many leaders of that day, protecting the property rights of the minority was a major justification for granting courts review powers over legislation.[33]

Early cases at both federal and state levels elicited strong statements to the effect that the legislature could not limit property rights except when public necessity clearly demanded such a course and then only when equitable compensation was paid. The Framers' perspective on property was brought into the purview of constitutional law by William Paterson, a member of the Constitutional Convention who later became a Supreme Court Justice. In 1795 Justice Paterson, in an opinion he delivered while on circuit in Pennsylvania, stated that:

> [T]he right of acquiring and possessing property, and having it protected, is one of the natural, inherent and inalienable rights of man.... No man could become a member of a community, in which he could not enjoy the fruits of his honest labour and industry.... Every person ought to contribute his proportion for public purposes and public exigencies; but no one can be called upon to surrender or sacrifice his whole property, real and personal, for the good of the community, without receiving a recompence in value. This would be laying a burden upon an individual, which ought to be sustained by the society at large. The English history does not furnish an instance of the kind; the parliament, with all their boasted omnipotence, never committed such an outrage on private property; and if they had, it would have served only to display the dangerous nature of unlimited authority; it would have been an exercise of power and not of right. Such an act would be a monster in legislation and shock all mankind. The legislature, therefore, had no authority to make an act divesting one citizen of his freehold, and vesting it in another, without a just compensation. It is inconsistent with the principles of reason, justice and moral rectitude; it is incompatible with the comfort, peace and happiness of mankind; it is contrary to the principles of social alliance in every free government; and lastly, it is contrary both to the letter and spirit of the [Pennsylvania] constitution.[34]

The early Supreme Court did not depart from the position advanced by Paterson. For instance, Justice Story, speaking for the Court in 1829, stated:

That government can scarcely be deemed to be free, where the rights of property are left solely dependent upon the will of a legislative body, without any restraint. The fundamental maxims of a free government seem to require, that the rights of personal liberty and private property should be held sacred.[35]

Legal and Philosophical Origins of Economic Due Process

Understanding the role that the due process concept has played in our constitutional history requires consideration of a long line of opinions beginning with early cases. *Calder v. Bull*[36] provides a starting point. At issue there was a Connecticut statute upsetting a probate court decree and granting a new hearing at which the formerly disapproved will was accepted. The Justices found that under Connecticut law the original decree had not vested property rights and that therefore no divestiture of property interests had occurred. In the course of his opinion, Justice Samuel Chase, who had signed the Declaration of Independence, stated that the people possess natural or immune rights and that the social compact limits the extent to which legislatures may abrogate these rights.

> I cannot subscribe to the omnipotence of a state legislature, or that it is absolute and without control; although its authority should not be expressly restrained by the constitution, or fundamental law of the state. The people of the United States erected their constitutions or forms of government, to establish justice, to promote the general welfare, to secure the blessings of liberty, and to protect their persons and property from violence. The purposes for which men enter into society will determine the nature and terms of the social compact; and as they are the foundation of the legislative power, they will decide what are the proper objects of it. The nature, and ends of legislative power will limit the exercise of it.... There are acts which the federal, or state legislature cannot do, without exceeding their authority. There are certain vital principles in our free republican governments, which will determine and overrule an apparent and flagrant abuse of legislative power.... An act of the legislature (for I cannot call it a law), contrary to the great first principles of the social compact, cannot be considered a righful [*sic*] exercise of legislative authority.
>
> ... A law that punished a citizen for an innocent action...; a law that destroys or impairs the lawful private contracts of citizens; a law that makes a man a judge in his own cause; or a law that takes property from A. and gives it to B.: it is against all reason and justice, for a people to intrust a legislature with such powers; and therefore, it cannot be presumed that they have done it. The genius, the nature

and the spirit of our state governments, amount to a prohibition of such acts of legislation; and the general principles of law and reason forbid them.[37]

Justice Iredell wrote a concurring opinion that rejected the idea of natural justice because such justice is regulated by no fixed standard: "[T]he ablest and purest men have differed upon the subject; and all that the court could properly say, in such an event, would be, that the legislature (possessed of an equal right of opinion) had passed an act which, in the opinion of the judges, was inconsistent with the abstract principles of natural justice."[38] The correct approach, according to Iredell, is

> to define with precision the objects of the legislative power, and to restrain its exercise within marked and settled boundaries. If any act of congress, or of the legislature of a state, violates those constitutional provisions, it is unquestionably void; though, I admit, that as the authority to declare it void is of a delicate and awful nature, the court will never resort to that authority, but in a clear and urgent case. If, on the other hand, the legislature of the Union, or the legislature of any member of the Union, shall pass a law, within the general scope of their constitutional power, the court cannot pronounce it to be void, merely because it is, in their judgment, contrary to the principles of natural justice.[39]

The debate between Chase and Iredell has continued in one context or another throughout our constitutional history, as Justices have disagreed about the extent to which they are bound by the terms and provisions of the fundamental document. History discloses that Chase's position was more consistent with the predominant opinion of his contemporaries—and probably with the High Court's record from that day to this.[40]

From the sixteenth through the eighteenth century, the natural law concept commanded a great deal of scholarly attention, and by the time of the Constitutional Convention, a considerable number of philosophers, ecclesiastical scholars, social commentators, and jurists had written on the subject. Although the precise extent of the consensus about its meaning and application is difficult to determine, the thinking of three highly respected commentators provides insight and perspective about how natural law and natural rights were viewed by the political and judicial leaders of those times. These commentators are Edward Coke (1552–1634), John Locke (1632–1704), and William Blackstone (1723–1780). The Revolutionary generations accepted much of Locke's political philosophy and were committed to many legal doctrines espoused by Coke and Blackstone.

Locke wrote that people sought the sanctuary of political society because of the uncertain conditions existing in the state of nature, in which everyone who lacked the personal power to defend himself might be victimized by the unscrupulous and evil. In forming society, men and women entered into a social compact, defining the authority and purposes of government and relinquishing most of their individual powers to the state, which then became responsible for protecting life, personal liberties, and possessions, all of which were included in the term "property." "The great and chief end, therefore, of men's uniting into commonwealths, and putting themselves under government, is the preservation of their property; to which in the state of nature there are many things wanting."[41]

In the state of nature, some individuals might not possess sufficient physical power to protect their lives and valuables; those involved in a dispute over them might not be sufficiently knowledgeable to apply equal justice in all cases. The legislature, as the supreme body of the organized state, must have the power to rectify these defects; but that power must necessarily be limited, at least to the extent that lawmakers could not impose conditions worse than those existing in the state of nature. Therefore, organized society is based on a social compact defining the powers and purposes accorded government and limiting its sovereignty over the individual. The legislature may not deprive the individual of fundamental rights—first, because the social compact does not provide government with this power, and second, because government's purpose is to play a fiduciary role in safeguarding and enhancing these rights. Limitations on governmental power are central to Locke's theory.

> It cannot be supposed that they [individuals] should intend, had they a power so to do, to give to any one, or more, an absolute arbitrary power over their persons and estates, and put a force into the magistrate's hand to execute his unlimited will arbitrarily upon them. This were to put themselves into a worse condition than the state of nature, wherein they had a liberty to defend their right against the injuries of others, and were upon equal terms of force to maintain it, whether invaded by a single man or many in combination.[42]

The supreme power cannot take from any man any part of his property without his own consent. For the preservation of property being the end of government, and that for which men enter into society, it necessarily supposes and requires that the people should

have property, without which they must be supposed to lose that by
entering into society, which was the end for which they entered into
it, too gross an absurdity for any man to own.[43]

Lord Coke, the eminent attorney general, jurist, legislator, and
legal commentator, had provided an institutional framework for
Locke's theories. Judicial review can be traced to his famous dictum
in *Dr. Bonham's Case*,[44] decided by the court of common pleas in
1610. There Coke ruled that the London College of Physicians was
not entitled, under an Act of Parliament, to punish Bonham for
practicing medicine without its licence. Coke declared:

And it appears in our books, that in many cases, the common law
will controul Acts of Parliament, and sometimes adjudge them to be
utterly void; for when an Act of Parliament is against common right
and reason, or repugnant, or impossible to be performed, the common law will controul it, and adjudge such Act to be void . . . .[45]

Although precedent for this conclusion is doubtful, the dictum was
used in the colonies to justify resistance to the British Parliament and
by jurists after the Revolution as a basis for judicial review. Supported
by Locke's premises, Coke's views that positive laws are subject to the
higher laws of "common right and reason" provided a foundation for
the creation of a system of limited government under which the courts,
through judicial review, would be able to preserve the social compact's
essential character.

Although he is regarded as a leading exponent of legislative supremacy, Blackstone's perceptions are not at variance with these natural
law concepts, when viewed within the context of the American system.
He believed in the ultimate authority of the British Parliament to "do
everything that is not naturally impossible . . . . True it is, that what
they do, no authority upon earth can undo."[46] However, Blackstone's
position on this issue has limited application to the American constitutional system, under which legislative powers are limited. More
relevant is Blackstone's chapter, "Of the Absolute Rights of Individuals," for in this country the legislature is not the final authority as it is
in England. Blackstone identified these absolute rights as life, liberty,
and property.

I.   The right of personal security consists in a person's legal and
uninterrupted enjoyment of his life, his limbs, his body, his health
and his reputation. . . . II. [T]he personal liberty of individuals
. . . consists in the power of loco-motion, of changing situation or removing one's person to whatsoever place one's own inclination may
direct, without imprisonment or restraint, unless by due course of

law.... III. The third absolute right, inherent in every En-
glishman...of property: which consists in the free use, enjoyment,
and disposal of all his acquisitions, without any control or diminution, save only by the laws of the land.[47]

Blackstone believed that the principal end of society is to protect
the enjoyment of these absolute rights, which were subject only to
"[r]estraints in themselves so gentle and moderate, as will appear
upon further inquiry, that no man of sense or probity would wish to
see them slackened." To vindicate these rights when violated, the
people were entitled first, to seek judicial relief; second, to petition the
king and parliament; and lastly, to use armed force.

Thus Locke, Coke, and Blackstone, among others, provided the
foundation for the approach to constitutional interpretation, set forth
by Justice Chase, under which the judiciary is obligated to respect and
honor certain rights that the people have never relinquished.

Other early constitutional decisions expounded on natural law and
natural rights. For example, in *Fletcher v. Peck* (1810)[48] the Supreme
Court applied both the Constitution's contracts clause (no state shall
pass any law impairing the obligation of contracts)[49] and natural law
precepts to overturn a Georgia law canceling purchasers' title to millions of acres of land in what is now most of Alabama and Mississippi.
This land had been bought in good faith from grantors who had acquired it through legislative corruption. In his opinion Chief Justice
Marshall appealed to the nature of society and government as setting
limits on the legislative power, for "where are they to be found, if the
property of an individual, fairly and honestly acquired, may be seized
without compensation."[50] Marshall stated that the opinion was based
on constitutional provisions as well as on "general principles which are
common to our free institutions."[51]

Justice Johnson (a Jeffersonian and therefore presumably not disposed to accept Marshall's Federalist outlook) concurred on this issue
despite his inability to find a provision in the Constitution denying a
state power to revoke its own land grants. "But I do it, on a general
principle, on the reason and nature of things; a principle which will
impose laws even on the Deity."[52] As previously reported, in *Bank of
Columbia v. Okely*,[53] Johnson interpreted the phrase *law of the land* in
the Maryland Constitution to have substantive meaning:

> As to the words from Magna Charta, incorporated into the constitu-
> tion of Maryland, after volumes spoken and written with a view to
> their exposition, the good sense of mankind has at length settled
> down to this: that they were intended to secure the individual from

the arbitrary exercise of the powers of government, unrestrained by the established principles of private rights and distributive justice.[54]

In *Terrett v. Taylor* (1815),[55] Justice Joseph Story invoked the spirit and letter of the Constitution, principles of natural justice, and the fundamental laws of all free governments to strike down a Virginia statute that would have deprived the Episcopal Church of its property. Infringing the church's rights would be "utterly inconsistent with a great and fundamental principle of a republican government."[56]

Chief Justice Marshall, who had joined in Story's opinion, spelled out his views on natural law many years later. In dissenting in *Ogden v. Saunders* (1827) (discussed in chapter 3),[57] which involved the validity of state bankruptcy laws, he asserted that the contracts clause limits a state from restricting freedom of contract. Marshall strongly asserted his belief that the right of contract is both original and natural.

[I]ndividuals do not derive from government their right to contract, but bring that right with them into society; that obligation is not conferred on contracts by positive law, but is intrinsic, and is conferred by the act of the parties. This results from the right which every man retains to acquire property, to dispose of that property, according to his own judgment, and to pledge himself for a future act. These rights are not given by society but are brought into it. The right of coercion is necessarily surrendered to government, and this surrender imposes on government the correlative duty of furnishing a remedy....

This reasoning is, undoubtedly, much strengthened by the authority of those writers on natural and national law, whose opinions have been viewed with profound respect by the wisest men of the present, and of past ages.[58]

Moreover, according to Marshall, the Framers of the Constitution were intimately acquainted with writings on natural law that declare that contracts possess an original, intrinsic obligation not given by government. Because of this knowledge, Marshall opined that "[w]e must suppose, that the framers of our constitution took the same view of the subject, and the language they have used confirms this opinion."[59] Thus natural law was also a guide, if not necessarily the paramount consideration, in constitutional interpretation.

Subsequently, in *Wilkinson v. Leland* (1829),[60] the Supreme Court, per Justice Story, explained its role in implementing natural rights concepts.

The fundamental maxims of a free government seem to require, that

the rights of personal liberty and private property should be held
sacred. At least no court of justice in this country would be warranted in assuming, that the power to violate and disregard them; a
power so repugnant to the common principles of justice and civil
liberty; lurked under any general grant of legislative authority, or
ought to be implied from any general expressions of the will of the
people. The people ought not to be presumed to part with rights so
vital to their security and well being....[61]

Justice Bushrod Washington, while on circuit in 1823, attempted to
import the natural rights doctrine into the Constitution by way of the
privileges and immunities clause of Article IV. In *Corfield v. Coryell*,[62]
the first federal interpretation of the clause, Washington held it
protects those privileges "which are, in their nature, fundamental;
which belong, of right, to the citizens of all free governments...."[63]
He declared that the Federal Constitution guarantees nonresidents'
fundamental rights against encroachment by a state.[64]

Support for the prerogatives of ownership declined in the Supreme
Court presided over by Marshall's successor, Roger Taney, who held
the office from 1836 to 1864. One of Marshall's last major decisions was
Barron v. Mayor of Baltimore,[65] decided in 1833, which held that the
states were not affected by the Bill of Rights. This left the Court with
only two means to protect property owners from arbitrary state
laws—the principles of the higher law, and a broad interpretation of the
contracts clause, both of which Marshall utilized in *Fletcher v. Peck*.
The Taney Court was not disposed to employ either one for this purpose. Unlike his predecessor, Taney inclined to identify the public
interest with authority. He developed the police power concept which
justified government control over property in situations that would not
have been acceptable to the Marshall Court.[66]

Gelpcke v. City of Dubuque,[67] decided in 1864, illustrates, however,
that the natural rights approach remained viable. This action concerned
bonds issued in 1857 by the city of Dubuque, which had complied with
all requirements mandated by the Iowa Supreme Court for this type of
financing. However, in 1862, the Iowa court had reversed itself on
some of the questions involved in issuing bonds and thus rendered
Dubuque's action violative of the state constitution. The applicability
of the Federal Constitution's contract clause was in doubt because it
provides that "no state...shall...pass any" such law, and no state
legislation was in issue. Nevertheless, Justice Swayne, writing for the
majority, declared that "the plainest principles of justice" forbid a
state from abrogating an interest acquired under a bond that was valid

when issued. Refusing to follow the most recent holding of the Iowa Supreme Court, he stated that "[w]e shall never immolate truth, justice, and the law, because a State tribunal has erected the altar and decreed the sacrifice."[68]

Ten years later, Justice Miller, who had vigorously dissented in *Gelpcke,* invoked the higher law against an Iowa city's ordinance levying a tax whose purpose was to make possible the issuing of municipal bonds that would have assisted private industry.[69] The Justice believed that this plan enacted an illegal redistribution of resources from one citizen to another. Included in his supporting citations were state decisions in which Chase's dictum in *Calder* on natural law had been applied. The sole dissenter in the case based his reasoning in part on Iredell's *Calder* concurrence.[70]

Federal Substantive Due Process Prior to the Civil War

From its earliest days, then, the High Court substantively protected property rights even without explicit constitutional authority to do so. De Tocqueville would have us believe that in following this course the judiciary was responding to the wishes of the people: "In no country in the world is the love of property more active and more anxious than in the United States; nowhere does the majority display less inclination for those principles which threaten to alter, in whatever manner, the laws of property."[71] Eventually the due process clauses provided the positive foundation previously absent. The first Supreme Court applications of substantive due process notions can be traced to Justice Johnson's dictum in the *Okely* case and to the 1855 *Hoboken Land* decision,[72] in which the Court determined that due process relates to civil processes at common law. The latter opinion asserted that the Court would make the final determination about whether due process had been achieved. To this extent it made it possible to impose on the legislature substantive restraints.

In 1857 Chief Justice Taney invoked substantive due process as one basis for his decision in the *Dred Scott* case.[73] The major ruling is that a Negro could not be a citizen of a state (for federal purposes) or of the United States. Taney also held that Congress had no power to prohibit slavery in specified areas because the "powers over person and property . . . are not granted to Congress, but are in express terms denied, and they are forbidden to exercise them."[74] Taney explained this "express" limitation as follows:

And an act of Congress which deprives a citizen of the United States of his liberty or property, merely because he came himself or brought his property into a particular Territory of the United States, and who had committed no offence against the laws, could hardly be dignified with the name of due process of law . . . .

. . .[I]f the Constitution recognises the right of property of the master in a slave, and makes no distinction between that description of property and other property owned by a citizen, no tribunal, acting under the authority of the United States, whether it be legislative, executive, or judicial, has a right to draw such a distinction, or deny to it the benefit of the provisions and guarantees which have been provided for the protection of private property against the encroachments of the Government.[75]

Each of the Justices delivered an opinion in this case, and it is difficult to find a concurring majority on any one issue except that the lower court did not have the jurisdiction to entertain the suit brought by the Negro because of the federal courts' diversity of citizenship requirement.[76] On the due process point the Chief Justice was supported by only two of the eight other Justices (Grier and Wayne), both of whom concurred in his opinion. This was not the first time that Taney had thought in these terms. In speaking for the Court in *Bloomer v. McQuewan* (1852),[77] he had observed that a special act depriving licensees of their right to use property protected by patent "certainly could not be regarded as due process of law";[78] however, the case was resolved on other grounds.

A new era in this country's due process experience began with the ratification of the Fourteenth Amendment. The first clause of the first section of that amendment was framed to overcome the part of *Dred Scott* relating to citizenship. The due process definition in Taney's opinion was not affected, but carried little weight as part of a discredited opinion.[79] Taney's use of the term reveals that the meaning of due process was not then confined to criminal and procedural matters. Before exploring the impact of the amendment, I shall consider the chronology of due process at the state level.

Substantive Due Process at the State Level
Prior to the Fourteenth Amendment

The states had their own constitutions under which aggrieved individuals could seek relief. In interpreting their constitutions, the state courts at times applied natural rights and social compact doctrines to void legislation that eliminated vested property rights.[80] The early state constitutions did not offer much protection for the right of ownership.

As of 1800, only Vermont, Massachusetts, and Pennsylvania constitutionally provided compensation for the taking of property under
the eminent domain power,[81] which was regarded as an inherent attri-
bute of sovereignty. Although, as of 1820, a majority of states had not
enacted constitutional provisions ensuring compensation for land takings, by that time statutes accomplishing this purpose had been enacted
in every state except South Carolina.[82] Nor was a constitutional provision regarded as essential to such relief. Thus Stoebuck asserts that
compensation was the regular practice in England and America during
the entire colonial period.[83]

Confronted with a lack of explicit constitutional or statutory authority, state courts nonetheless began to protect existing property interests on the bases of both the natural law and the constitutional due
process and law of the land clauses, to which they accorded substantive meaning. According to Corwin, one-half of the original fourteen
states first recognized judicial review in cases involving acceptance of
what he refers to as the doctrine of vested rights.[84] Pursuant to this
doctrine, the courts protected the right of a person who had, under the
law, acquired title to tangible property to continue exercising control
over such property. Although police power regulation was permissible,
destruction of the interest without compensation would not be allowed.

Using natural law principles, the courts of Massachusetts, New
York, and New Hampshire early advanced the doctrine of vested
rights.[85] In 1829, Justice Story said he knew of no case in any state "in
which a legislative act to transfer the property from A. to B. without his
consent, has ever been held [constitutional]."[86] Professor Grant reports that between 1816 and 1860, high or federal courts in New York,
New Jersey, New Hampshire, Georgia, Maryland, Arkansas, and Iowa
held or expressed the belief that natural justice required that compensation must be paid when private property is taken for public use.[87]
The only decisions he found that did not adhere to this principle were
from the Carolinas. The South Carolina cases were less a rejection of
this higher law than an acceptance of the reasonableness of established
conduct. The North Carolina high court required compensation by
its interpretation of the law of the land clause of the state constitution.
During the period Grant writes about, actual court practices varied
considerably among the states in the extent to which the rights of
property owners were protected.[88] In 1907, Justice Moody asserted
that state courts had applied either positive or natural law to hold that a
public use was required for an eminent domain acquisition.[89]

In the 1805 *University of North Carolina* decision previously mentioned, the North Carolina Supreme Court held invalid an act repealing a prior land grant to the university. The court relied in part upon a law of the land clause, which it ruled was a limitation on legislative power and which it interpreted as meaning that no one could be deprived of liberty or property without proper judicial proceedings. On the basis of this clause, North Carolina's high court, in 1816, held invalid an act emancipating two slaves whose owner had, before he died, expressed the wish that they be freed.[90] Also pursuant to this clause, that same court, in *Hoke v. Henderson* (1833), overturned an election law that operated in some instances to deny appointed incumbents their governmental positions.[91] In the latter case, the court in effect granted to vested property rights constitutional immunity against legislative abridgements. The court asserted

> that there are limitations upon legislative power, . . . and that the clause itself means that such legislative acts, as profess in themselves directly to punish persons or to deprive the citizen of his property, without trial before the judicial tribunals, and a decision upon the matter of right, as determined by the laws under which it vested, according to the course, mode and usages of the common law as derived from our forefathers, are not effectually "laws of the land," for those purposes.[92]

Five years later, the Alabama Supreme Court expanded the term *property* to include the right to practice law by overturning restrictive legislation as being contrary to the due-course-of-law provision of the state's constitution.[93]

These cases portended subsequent developments.[94] Corwin opines that the destiny of the due process of law doctrine was not that it should enter the general constitutional jurisprudence of the United States Supreme Court through the decisions of the Alabama or Carolina tribunals.[95] An opinion of a court more eminent in the world of citation and precedent was necessary, and the jurisdiction that best fitted this description was New York, domicile of the celebrated Chancellor James Kent. Corwin credits Kent with giving the doctrine of vested rights its finally perfected form in his commentaries on American law, which he began publishing shortly after his 1823 retirement as chancellor of New York State.[96]

Consistent with prevailing common-law concepts, Kent maintained that the right of property could be limited only through taxation, eminent domain, and regulation under the police power. Although strongly committed to the inviolability of ownership, he wrote that in exceptional circumstances the government could interdict without compensation property uses creating nuisances or actual perils to the populace's health, safety, peace, and comfort.

One of Kent's best-known decisions is *Gardner v. Trustees of the Village of Newburg* (1816),[97] which involved a statute authorizing the village to install conduits to supply its inhabitants with water from a stream that flowed through Gardner's farm. Compensation was provided for the owner over whose land the conduits were laid, but not for Gardner, who would suffer loss because, as a result of the improvements, the water level on his property would be substantially reduced. Although the New York Constitution did not mention the eminent domain power, Kent granted an injunction to restrain operation of the statute because it made no provision for compensating Gardner for the loss to his land. For his ruling Kent relied on the principles of natural equity as expounded by European thinkers—namely, Grotius, Pufendorf, Bynkershoek, and Blackstone—and commented that the state has the inherent power of eminent domain when public necessity or utility requires, but that it could be employed only with adequate regard for the rights of property ownership. Several opinions in New York and New Jersey followed this line of reasoning.[98] However, Kent's approach to consequential damages did not receive general recognition for a lengthy period after this decision.[99]

Kent regarded the 1833 North Carolina decision in *Hoke v. Henderson* as replete with sound constitutional doctrine.[100] Relying in part on that decision, the New York high court in *Taylor v. Porter* (1843)[101] brought the vested rights concept within the ambit of the state constitution's due process of law clause. At issue in this case was a statute authorizing a private road to be laid over the plaintiff's land without his consent. Holding that the law violated both the law of the land and the due process clauses, the court reasoned that impairment of existing property rights has a punitive result and was therefore inherently beyond legislative power. Another important decision relying on due process was entered by the New York court in 1854, when it held unconstitutional a portion of a married woman's act depriving a husband of rights in a legacy to his wife that had vested prior to the law's enactment. The court stated:

> Due process of law undoubtedly means, in the due course of legal proceedings, according to those rules and forms which have been established for the protection of private rights. Such an act as the legislature may, in the uncontrolled exercise of its power, think fit to pass, is, in no sense, the process of law designated by the constitution.[102]

The leading pre–Civil War decision on due process at the state level is *Wynehamer v. People*,[103] an 1856 New York case, in which a state penal statute forbidding the sale of intoxicating liquors owned at the time of enactment (except for medicinal and religious purposes) and requiring the destruction of such as were intended for sale was declared unconstitutional. The majority held that the clause provides substantive protection for rights acquired under existing law. By this time case precedent in New York had reached the stage at which invoking natural law was unnecessary, and the court specifically rejected use of any such theory as the basis of its decision. *Wynehamer* enlarged the scope of judicial protection to include not only the possession of particular property but also the right to use that property in a manner permissible at the time it had been acquired. While allowing for some regulation, the opinion emphasized that a retroactive ban on use of property was forbidden.

> The true interpretation of these constitutional phrases is, that where rights are acquired by the citizen under the existing law, there is no power in any branch of the government to take them away.... Where rights of property are admitted to exist, the legislature cannot say they shall exist no longer....[104]

Insofar as it applied to legislative power to restrict liquor traffic, the *Wynehamer* precedent was generally not followed. With the exception of Indiana, in all other states where the issue was raised, the courts ruled that the police power enables the legislature to adopt laws for this purpose.[105] In 1855 the Indiana Supreme Court held that the state prohibition law was void because prohibiting the manufacture, sale, and consumption of spiritous liquors unlawfully interfered with individual liberty and the pursuit of happiness.[106] However, this decision was overturned seven years later.[107] Despite the criticism it received from contemporary courts, Corwin believes that *Wynehamer* was enormously influential. "In less than twenty years from the time of its rendition the crucial ruling in Wynehamer v. the People was far on the way to being assimilated into the accepted constitutional law of the country."[108]

That the *Wynehamer* perspective was not extraordinary is suggested in the writings of Thomas M. Cooley, a justice of the Supreme Court of Michigan, dean and professor of law at the University of Michigan, and probably the leading legal commentator in the last third of the nineteenth century. His treatise on constitutional limitations was first published in 1868, the same year in which the Fourteenth Amendment was ratified.[109] In his discussion of law of the land and due process

clauses, he asserts that both meant the same and provided substantive
protection for property interests. The definitions of these terms contained in the reported cases vary so greatly that some difficulty arises in
fixing upon one that is generally applicable. However, he concludes
that the principles upon which governmental processes are based determine whether due process has been achieved,

> and not any considerations of mere form. . . . When the government,
> through its established agencies, interferes with the title to one's
> property, or with his independent enjoyment of it, and its act is
> called in question as not in accordance with the law of the land, we
> are to test its validity by those principles of civil liberty and con-
> stitutional defence which have become established in our system of
> law, and not by any rules that pertain to forms of procedure
> merely. . . . Due process of law in each particular case means, such
> an exertion of the powers of government as the settled maxims of law
> sanction, and under such safeguards for the protection of individual
> rights as those maxims prescribe for the class of cases to which the
> one in question belongs.[110]

Cooley concedes that private rights to property may be interfered with
by any branch of government.

> The chief restriction is that vested rights must not be disturbed; but
> in its application as a shield of protection, the term "vested rights" is
> not used in any narrow or technical sense, as importing a power of
> legal control merely, but rather as implying a vested interest which it
> is equitable the government should recognize, and of which the indi-
> vidual cannot be deprived without injustice.[111]

The justice goes on to discuss those property interests protected by
due process or law of the land clauses.[112] Thus, according to this
authoritative commentator, due process at the time the Fourteenth
Amendment came into being provided substantive safeguards for property interests; he rejected the view that it had no more than procedural
significance in civil matters.

The Impact of the Fourteenth Amendment

The next significant phase in the history of due process commenced
with the adoption of the Fourteenth Amendment. By then *Okely, Dred
Scott, Bloomer,* and decisions in New York and other states had given
some substantive civil law connotation to due process of law. Due
process of law in 1868 could not therefore have been considered as

restricted solely to criminal and procedural matters. Cooley's commentaries confirm an expanded definition of the term.

Eventually, both federal and state tribunals further enlarged the amendment's substantive content, bringing intangible economic interests within the protected area, and later political and civil rights as well. The scope of the protections for the criminally accused grew larger. Thus over the decades the phrase's definition and application slowly and significantly changed. This evolutionary process is not unusual in American and English jurisprudence. It is similar to that carried on under the common law, which is characterized by great flexibility and capacity for growth and adaptation. In no event can substantive due process be regarded as an invention of a particular group of federal justices.

The first test of section 1 of the Fourteenth Amendment occurred in the famous *Slaughter-House Cases,* decided in 1872.[113] This section reads as follows:

> All persons born or naturalized in the United States, and subject to the jurisdiction thereof, are citizens of the United States and of the State wherein they reside. No State shall make or enforce any law which shall abridge the privileges or immunities of citizens of the United States, nor shall any State deprive any person of life, liberty, or property, without due process of law, nor deny to any person within its jurisdiction the equal protection of the laws.

Section 5 authorizes Congress to enforce the amendment. Also at issue in the *Cases* was the Thirteenth Amendment, ratified in 1865, which prohibits slavery and involuntary servitude.

The problem presented did not directly involve the Fourteenth Amendment's central concern, which was securing for the recently emancipated blacks the civil rights that the rest of the population enjoyed and providing them federal protection against infringement of such rights by the states. In 1869 Louisiana's legislature granted a twenty-five year exclusive privilege to a private corporation it had created to operate a regulated livestock and slaughterhouse business within a specified area of about 1150 square miles, comprising New Orleans and two other parishes. The privilege required that all cattle brought into this area for commercial purposes be slaughtered by the corporation or in its facilities. An association of butchers adversely affected brought suit on the basis that the monopoly grant violated the Thirteenth and Fourteenth Amendments—the former by creating an involuntary servitude and the latter by depriving plaintiffs

of their privileges and immunities as United States citizens, of liberty
and property without due process of law, and of equal protection under
the laws. However, the argument revolved principally about the
privileges and immunities clause. The Supreme Court upheld the
monopoly grant by a 5–4 vote, with the dissenters contending that
despite the facts' seeming remoteness to the Fourteenth Amendment's
purposes, the Louisiana statute violated one or more of the last three
clauses of section 1.

As their counsel, the butchers hired John Campbell, a former
member of the Supreme Court, who had resigned when his home state
of Alabama seceded from the Union. He argued that the privileges and
immunities clause extended to all citizens federal safeguards for a variety of civil rights, including the protection of the plaintiffs' interests in
pursuing their businesses. According to Campbell, the amendment's
framers intended to convert the privileges and immunities of state
citizenship into privileges and immunities of national citizenship. "The
States...have been placed under the oversight and restraining and
enforcing hand of Congress."[114] Supporting Campbell's position was
the definition Justice Washington gave, in *Corfield v. Coryell*,[115] to
the privileges and immunities phrase contained in Article IV, section 2.
Washington's decision contains this oft-quoted passage, which was
cited, but not considered as applicable, by the *Slaughter-House* majority.

We feel no hesitation in confining [the constitutional provisions] to
those privileges and immunities which are, in their nature, fundamental.... They may, however, be all comprehended under the
following general heads: Protection by the government; the enjoyment of life and liberty, with the right to acquire and possess property of every kind, and to pursue and obtain happiness and
safety.... The right of a citizen of one state to pass through, or to
reside in any other state, for purposes of trade, agriculture, professional pursuits, or otherwise; to claim the benefit of the writ of
habeas corpus; to institute and maintain actions of any kind in the
courts of the state; to take, hold and dispose of property, either real
or personal; and an exemption from higher taxes or impositions than
are paid by the other citizens of the state; may be mentioned as some
of the particular privileges and immunities of citizens, which are
clearly embraced by the general description of privileges deemed to
be fundamental: to which may be added, the elective franchise, as
regulated and established by the laws or constitution of the state in
which it is to be exercised. These, and many others which might be
mentioned, are, strictly speaking, privileges and immunities, and the

enjoyment of them by the citizens of each state, in every other state, was manifestly calculated (to use the expressions of the preamble of the corresponding provision in the old articles of confederation) "the better to secure and perpetuate mutual friendship and intercourse among the people of the different states of the Union." But we cannot accede to the proposition . . . that, under this provision of the constitution, the citizens of the several states are permitted to participate in all the rights which belong exclusively to the citizens of any other particular state . . . . [116]

Justice Samuel F. Miller, writing for the majority, rejected Campbell's argument that the Fourteenth Amendment provides federal protection for the rights specified by Justice Washington. In the process the Court virtually removed the privileges and immunities clause from the Fourteenth Amendment. Miller said that this clause was not intended as protection for the citizens of a state against the legislative power of their own state. Instead it places the privileges and immunities of United States citizens under federal protection. These privileges and immunities include the right to come to the seat of government, to assert claims against it, to seek its protection from foreign governments, to transact business with it, to have free access to the nation's seaports and courts, to assemble and petition for redress of grievances, and to be protected by the writ of habeas corpus. Preservation of these rights hardly required an extensive constitutional amendment. However, Miller contended that the construction that was sought by the butchers would

constitute this court a perpetual censor upon all legislation of the States, on the civil rights of their own citizens, with authority to nullify such as it did not approve as consistent with those rights, as they existed at the time of the adoption of this amendment. . . . [W]hen . . . these consequences are . . . so great a departure from the structure and spirit of our institutions; when the effect is to fetter and degrade the State governments by subjecting them to the control of Congress, in the exercise of powers heretofore universally conceded to them of the most ordinary and fundamental character; when in fact it radically changes the whole theory of the relations of the State and Federal governments to each other and of both these governments to the people; the argument has a force that is irresistible, in the absence of language which expresses such a purpose too clearly to admit of doubt. [117]

Miller was even less impressed with the plaintiffs' arguments on due process and equal protection. He did not address at all their contention concerning deprivation of liberty and he demolished their property arguments almost in passing. He stated that inquiring into the meaning of the due process clause was unnecessary, for

> it is sufficient to say that under no construction of that provision that we have ever seen, or any that we deem admissible, can the restraint imposed by the State of Louisiana upon the exercise of their trade by the butchers of New Orleans be held to be a deprivation of property within the meaning of that provision.[118]

Miller claimed that the equal protection clause was intended to remove discrimination against Negroes and doubted very much whether any state action not directed to such discrimination would ever be held to come within the purview of this provision.[119]

Some commentators find that Miller's answer to Campbell's conception of national citizenship is both liberal and progressive, emphasizing the right and ability of the majoritarian political power to enact social and economic regulation.[120] However, if economic liberties were not included in the Fourteenth Amendment's protection, neither was free expression. The debates in Congress and the ratifying conventions reveal an emphasis on securing property and commerce and relatively little reference to safeguarding expression. Justice Washington's definition of privileges and immunities covers a wide spectrum but is devoid of any specific reference to freedom of expression. Few in that period would have associated expression with due process or equal protection. While opinion is divergent as to the full meaning of the first section of the amendment, commentators generally agree that it was intended to guarantee and constitutionalize the Civil Rights Act of 1866.[121] The act enumerates economic and not political concerns. A chief objective was to strengthen the economic position of the freed slaves; their rights to expression were not an important consideration. Berger concludes that the act was intended to guarantee to blacks personal security, freedom of movement, and property rights, and that political and social rights were "unmistakably excluded" from it.[122] The Act declares that all persons born in the United States are citizens and that such citizens (with a few designated exceptions) shall

> have the same right to make and enforce contracts, to sue, be parties, and give evidence, to inherit, purchase, lease, sell, hold, and convey real and personal property, and to full and equal benefit of all laws and proceedings for the security of person and property, as is enjoyed by white citizens, and shall be subject to like punishment, pains, and penalties, and to none other.

Notwithstanding what may be implied by the quoted portion of his opinion, there is reason to conclude that Justice Miller did believe that due process encompasses certain substantive protection. A literal reading of Miller's language suggests no more than that the activities in question were not covered by due process. This conclusion, however, does not mean that vested property rights were outside the clause's scope. That Miller was inclined to include such rights is revealed by his decision in a case that was submitted in briefs at the time that *Slaughter-House* was argued but that was not decided until the following year.[123] In this case Iowa's statewide prohibition law, which had been enacted in 1851, came under attack as a violation of due process. Miller wrote that a statute prohibiting the sale of property would raise "very grave questions" under the Fourteenth Amendment's due process clause and cited *Wynehamer* as supporting such a proposition. However, according to Miller, the Iowa case did not present this issue, for it was "absurd to suppose that the plaintiff, an ordinary retailer of drinks, could have proved [in 1870]...that he had owned that particular glass of whisky prior to the prohibitory liquor law of 1851."[124] Miller again acknowledged the substantive aspects of the clause in an 1877 decision in which he asserted:

> It seems to us that a statute which declares in terms, and without more, that the full and exclusive title of a described piece of land, which is now in A., shall be and is hereby vested in B., would, if effectual, deprive A. of his property without due process of law, within the meaning of the constitutional provision.[125]

In 1869 a 6–3 majority of the Supreme Court had held that the Legal Tender Act of 1862[126] violated, among other provisions, the Fifth Amendment's due process clause by impairing the value of property held by creditors.[127] This act had compelled creditors to accept legal tender worth far less than any amount originally contracted for. Although two years later the Court reversed its holding, it did not reconsider that portion of the decision relating to due process.[128]

Therefore, had vested property rights been at issue in the *Slaughter-House Cases,* the due process clause might possibly have demanded a different outcome. However, at that time the majority was not prepared to regard a person's calling, trade, occupation, or labor as property, or the right to engage in it as liberty (or as property).

Each dissenting *Slaughter-House* opinion viewed property and liberty in the more expansive terms that would in time become judicially acceptable. Justices Field, Bradley, and Swayne filed separate dissents, with Chief Justice Chase and the two other dissenters joining with Field. Justice Swayne concurred in Bradley's opinion. The dissenters acknowledged that the well-being of Negroes may have been the amendment's primary concern, but they nevertheless maintained that its language was purposefully made general in order to embrace all citizens. They accepted Campbell's argument that the amendment provided federal safeguards for all people in the United States against deprivation of their fundamental rights by state legislatures.

The written dissents contain many memorable passages on the relationship between the government and the governed. For the most part Field limited his remarks to privileges and immunities, but in later opinions he applied this same reasoning to due process. Bradley and Swayne argued that all three clauses had been violated. Field castigated legislative monopoly as encroaching "upon the liberty of citizens to acquire property and pursue happiness"[129] contrary to the privileges and immunities clause; and Bradley declared that "a law which prohibits a large class of citizens from adopting a lawful employment, or from following a lawful employment previously adopted, does deprive them of liberty as well as property, without due process of law."[130] For Justice Swayne the language of all three clauses is unqualified in its economic scope: "There is no exception in its terms, and there can be properly none in their application."[131] Field, who also asserted that the Fourteenth Amendment was intended to give practical effect to the Declaration of Independence, interpreted the privileges and immunities clause to mean that all pursuits were open to citizens, subject to some regulations imposed equally upon everyone similarly situated.

> What the clause [in Art. IV] did for the protection of the citizens of one State against hostile and discriminating legislation of other States, the fourteenth amendment does for the protection of every citizen of the United States against hostile and discriminating legislation against him in the favor of others, whether they reside in the same or in different States. If under the fourth article of the Constitution equality of privileges and immunities is secured between citizens of different States, under the fourteenth amendment the same equality is secured between citizens of the United States.[132]

The minority Justices saw no problem in considering the butchers' loss to be one of both liberty and property. Thus as Bradley stated, "[t]his right to choose one's calling is an essential part of that liberty which it is the object of government to protect; and a calling, when chosen, is a man's property and right .... Their [citizens'] right of choice is a portion of their liberty; their occupation is their property."[133]

Swayne gave the following meaning to property:

Property is everything which has an exchangeable value, and the right of property includes the power to dispose of it according to the will of the owner. Labor is property, and as such merits protection. The right to make it available is next in importance to the rights of life and liberty. It lies to a large extent at the foundation of most other forms of property, and of all solid individual and national prosperity.[134]

Thus four Supreme Court Justices believed that the Fourteenth Amendment safeguarded from state limitations the production and distribution of goods and services. For them the amendment meant that the federal judiciary would have the power to perpetuate individual liberties by the exercise of a veto over state economic regulation. They saw the amendment as achieving a free society's goals of maintaining liberty at a maximum and removing restraints that impede individuals from fulfilling their rightful ambitions. Under this view the amendment would have codified the libertarian foundations of American constitutional government.

Bradley and Field were strong opponents of slavery (Field was appointed by Lincoln and Bradley by Grant), and the opinions they expressed in this case reflect the convictions of the antislavery movement and the principles of what has been referred to as the "jurisprudence of antislavery."[135] Among the rights to which the abolitionists gave prime attention were those of property and contract. They urged that these liberties be extended to all people, including (of course) Negroes, for these natural rights could enable the dependent poor to become financially secure and thus independent.[136] The abolitionists wanted section 1 of the Fourteenth Amendment to be the federal government's broad and sweeping guarantee of political, material, and intellectual rights.[137] The *Slaughter-House Cases'* ruling that, with relatively few exceptions, fundamental rights are not attributes of United States citizenship and therefore not constitutionally protected against state action was a severe blow to the contemporary civil rights movement.[138]

In 1879 Louisiana adopted a new constitution, abolishing monopoly grants, and in 1884 the United States Supreme Court, confronted with the issue of whether Louisiana could limit the slaughterhouse monopoly under the terms of the Federal Constitution's contracts clause, unanimously upheld this power.[139] Justices Field and Bradley, along with two Justices who had been appointed after the *Slaughter-House* decision, concurred in the result, contending that the grant had never been valid. Both of the former reiterated the positions they had taken eleven years earlier. Bradley's remarks provided one of the foundations for the 1897 decision in *Allgeyer v. Louisiana*,[140] in which the federal High Court constitutionalized liberty of contract and thereby formally commenced the economic due process period. Although Bradley's interpretation of the due process clause had not been accepted by the majority, his opinion was an affirming one, and courts were therefore able to accord it greater significance than they could have given a dissent. Field's opinion also embraced due process and had far-reaching influence among the state courts in fostering acceptance of the liberty of contract doctrine.[141]

Field subsequently wrote a number of opinions emphasizing the inclusiveness of due process. In his *Munn v. Illinois*[142] dissent, he maintained that the Fourteenth Amendment's due process clause prohibits regulation of prices charged by public warehouses. He interpreted the provision as safeguarding from government regulation a wide variety of economic activities. "There is, indeed, no protection of any value under the constitutional provision, which does not extend to the use and income of the property, as well as to its title and possession."[143] He denied the power of any legislature to fix the price that a person should receive for his property, regardless of what that property might be.

Justice Field also wrote the unanimous opinion in the leading case of *Barbier v. Connolly*,[144] upholding under the police power a San Francisco ordinance prohibiting washing and ironing of clothes in public laundries and washhouses within prescribed areas from ten o'clock at night until six o'clock the next morning. After reiterating his position that the due process and equal protection clauses protect freedom of contract and prevent arbitrary deprivation of economic liberties, he distinguished the ordinance as not imposing unequal or unnecessary restrictions but rather as promoting the general good with as little individual inconvenience as possible. He explained that laws do not furnish valid grounds for complaint if they operate alike upon all people and property similarly situated. Under the San Francisco regulation no person or class of people was treated invidiously.

Powell v. Pennsylvania,[145] decided in 1888, upheld a statute outlawing the manufacture and sale of oleomargarine but assumed that ordinary economic pursuits were protected by the due process clause. Justice Field again dissented on the same grounds as in the past, stating that the makers of oleomargarine should be rewarded instead of punished for contributing to social progress.

The famous 1886 case of *Yick Wo v. Hopkins*[146] applied due process as well as the equal protection doctrine for which it is usually cited. In that case San Francisco had adopted an ordinance making it unlawful for any person to operate a laundry business in a wooden building without permission from the city's board of supervisors. Though disguised in public welfare rhetoric, the ordinance's true purpose became clear in the manner of its administration: permits were granted to Caucasian applicants, but denied to Orientals. The unanimous opinion considered the ordinance unconstitutional because it "intended to confer . . . not a discretion to be exercised upon a consideration of the circumstances of each case, but a naked and arbitrary power to give or withhold consent, not only as to places, but as to persons."[147] To the Supreme Court of that day, such power was repugnant in a society governed by the force of laws rather than by the will of selected individuals.

> [T]he very idea that one man may be compelled to hold his life, or the means of living, or any material right essential to the enjoyment of life, at the mere will of another, seems to be intolerable in any country where freedom prevails, as being the essence of slavery itself.[148]

That same year the Supreme Court expressed its disapproval of state regulation of railroads that would reduce charges to levels that could be deemed confiscatory under the due process clause of the Fourteenth Amendment.[149] Justice Waite wrote for the majority that "[t]his power to regulate is not a power to destroy, and limitation is not the equivalent of confiscation."[150] As the Court stated in a subsequent case, the reasonableness of rates was therefore "eminently a question for judicial investigation, requiring due process of law for its determination."[151]

The Justices who in 1890 were concerned with fair rate-setting procedures[152] moved in 1898 to substantive adjudication and examined the reasonableness of the rates.[153] Their conclusion was that an owner could not constitutionally be denied a fair return, because such a return was deemed to be the essence of ownership. Thus the Supreme Court had recognized that *market earning power* is property; depriving owners of the exchange value of their property is equivalent to depriving them of their property.

Substantive Due Process at the State Level after the Civil War

For almost thirty years following the ratification of the Fourteenth Amendment, the United States Supreme Court remained unsettled in its view of economic due process. However, state courts took much less time in adopting the doctrine. The New York high court continued the lead by holding, in 1865, that a statute fixing the amount that a person who had been drafted during the Civil War might pay for a substitute was invalid as a deprivation of property without due process of law.[154] In 1885 that same court ruled that a statute forbidding the manufacture and sale of oleomargarine violated the constitutional provision protecting life, liberty, and property.[155] In that year the court also held that prohibiting the manufacture of cigars or preparation of tobacco in tenements in large cities infringed rights of liberty and property.[156] The following excerpt from the opinion in the cigar tenement case (*In re Jacobs*) is revealing of the New York court's perspective:

[I]t is plain that this is not a health law, and that it has no relation whatever to the public health. Under the guise of promoting the public health the legislature might as well have banished cigarmaking from all the cities of the State, or confined it to a single city or town, or have placed under a similar ban the trade of a baker, of a tailor, of a shoemaker, of a woodcarver, or of any other of the innocuous trades carried on by artisans in their homes. The power would have been the same, and its exercise, so far as it concerns fundamental, constitutional rights, could have been justified by the same arguments. Such legislation may invade one class of rights to-day and another to-morrow, and if it can be sanctioned under the Constitution, while far removed in time we will not be far away in practical statesmanship from those ages when governmental prefects supervised the building of houses, the rearing of cattle, the sowing of seed and the reaping of grain, and governmental ordinances regulated the movements and labor of artisans, the rate of wages, the price of food, the diet and clothing of the people, and a large range of other affairs long since in all civilized lands regarded as outside of governmental functions. Such governmental interferences disturb the normal adjustments of the social fabric, and usually derange the delicate and complicated machinery of industry and cause a score of ills while attempting the removal of one.[157]

Between 1885 and 1894 high courts in Pennsylvania, West Virginia, Massachusetts, Missouri, Illinois, Ohio, Nebraska, Colorado, California, and Arkansas followed the same general approach. One line of cases denied the legislature the power to regulate the terms of employment between employer and employee, except when health and life were clearly affected and when one of the parties was either a minor, a sailor, or a woman who had not been granted the privileges of the married woman's acts. The basis for these decisions was that such regulation constituted unreasonable denial to the employer and employee of liberty or property without due process of law, and/or was class legislation, for the legislature had attempted to interfere with the private rights of certain individuals. Thus the Pennsylvania court, in striking down legislation regulating wage rates, asserted that such an act was

> an insulting attempt to put the laborer under a legislative tutelage, which is not only degrading to his manhood, but subversive of his rights as a citizen of the United States.
>
> . . . He may sell his labor for what he thinks best, whether money or goods, just as his employer may sell his iron or coal, and any and every law that proposes to prevent him from so doing is an infringement of his constitutional privileges, and consequently vicious and void.[158]

Under this view liberty means being allowed to choose any lawful occupation for the exercise of one's abilities and faculties so long as no harm to others results. In a lengthy review of this issue, the Arkansas Supreme Court explained:

> The right to acquire and possess property necessarily includes the right to contract; for it is the principal mode of acquisition, and is the only way by which a person can rightly acquire property by his own exertion. Of all the "rights of persons" it is the most essential to human happiness . . . . A person living under the protection of this government has the right to adopt and follow any lawful industrial pursuit, not injurious to the community, which he may see fit; and, as incident to this, is the right to labor or employ labor, make contracts in respect thereto upon such terms as may be agreed upon by the parties, to enforce all lawful contracts, to sue and give evidence, and to inherit, purchase, lease, sell or convey property of any kind. The enjoyment or deprivation of these rights and privileges constitutes the essential distinction between freedom and slavery; between liberty and oppression.[159]

Using a comparable approach, other state courts struck down an array of laws that had attempted to accomplish the following:

1. forbidding barbers from keeping their shops open or working at their trade on Sunday;[160]
2. forbidding women from working in any factory or workshop in excess of eight hours during any one day or forty-eight hours during any one week;[161]
3. forbidding mine and factory owners from selling merchandise to employees at prices above those charged to others;[162]
4. forbidding employers from firing workers who joined or remained in unions;[163]
5. paying wages in anything other than money;[164]

6. restricting entry into the horseshoeing business;[165]

7. instituting an eight-hour-per-day maximum (except in emergencies) for workers in underground mines and smelters in one state[166] and in another for all classes of mechanics, servants, and laborers, except those engaged in farm and domestic labor (and requiring extra compensation in geometrical progression for overtime);[167]

8. regulating laborers' hours under public or municipal contract.[168]

Federal Acceptance of Substantive Due Process

Justice Field traced the origins of his interpretation of property to Adam Smith, who had said: "The property which every man has in his own labor, as it is the original foundation of all other property, so it is the most sacred and inviolable."[169] Two other distinguished men influential in our history also devised broad definitions of property. For John Locke all tangible property originally derives from labor. In ancient times perishable products resulted from labor and were exchanged for other objects and/or for a coinage equivalent that had a fixed value. Thus material possessions were the equivalent of reward for labor. Locke also wrote that every man has a property in his person.[170] James Madison offered this explanation of the meaning of property:

> This term [property], in its particular application, means "that dominion which one man claims and exercises over the external things of the world, in exclusion of every other individual." In its larger and juster meaning, it embraces everything to which a man may attach a value and have a right; and *which leaves to every one else the like advantage*. In the former sense, a man's land, or merchandise, or money, is called his property. In the latter sense, a man has a property in his opinions and the free communication of them. He has a property of peculiar value in his religious opinions, and in the profession and practice dictated by them. He has property very dear to him in the safety and liberty of his person. He has an equal property in the free use of his faculties, and free choice of the objects on which to employ them. In a word, as a man is said to have a right to his property, he may be equally said to have a property in his rights.[171]

In the 1890s the members of the United States Supreme Court were in accord with respect to the material aspects of property. The progression to this awareness had been deliberate and slow. Because the federal judiciary was in fact following trends already established in many states, the *Allgeyer* decision, which marks the formal beginning of the economic due process period, was not unexpected.

Protection of property and economic rights has been a dominant theme since the creation of the federal government. Some contend, as we shall see in the next chapter, that had the ex post facto clauses been correctly interpreted, the federal and state governments would have been, from the first, severely limited in regulating economic activity. A change of one vote on the Supreme Court in *Ogden v. Saunders* would have, in 1827, brought economic due process into being through the contracts clause. One vote likewise separated the majority and minority positions on the constitutional status of economic rights in the 1872 *Slaughter-House Cases*. As subsequent chapters explain, economic due process was unanimously accepted in 1897 and fell by one vote in 1937. These events suggest that under our system economic liberties, if not deserving the highest priority, are surely not to be relegated to lower levels of importance—a position that they have continuously occupied for about forty years.

3

Economic Due Process and the Ex Post Facto and Obligation of Contracts Provisions

In his opinion in the *Slaughter-House Cases,* Justice Samuel Miller contended that if the Supreme Court found that the butchers had a constitutionally protected right to engage in their business, the Union's federal character would be radically altered. Moreover, he believed that finding such a right would make "this court a perpetual censor"[1] of all state legislation affecting civil rights. Countless other commentators have echoed this perspective whenever economic liberties are at issue. These commentators have accepted the position that the United States Constitution does not give the national judiciary any, or at most very limited, power to outlaw federal or state regulations relating to economic activity. Economic due process and liberty of contract are looked on as judicial aberrations or abuses.

However, very persuasive evidence exists that the Constitution's Framers sought to safeguard property and economic interests from infringement by both federal and state governments. In the preceding chapter I described the thinking, prevalent during the eighteenth century, that supported substantial limitations on the government's authority to abridge individual autonomy. Under initial interpretations of the Constitution, the various organs of the federal government were thought to have only those powers that were expressly delegated to them, that were necessary and proper to carrying out such powers, or that they might be entitled to assume under the common law.[2] Opinions in *Vanhorne's Lessee v. Dorrance,*[3] *Calder v. Bull,*[4] *Fletcher v. Peck,*[5] and *Terrett v. Taylor*[6] considered state laws violating principles of natural justice as invalid under the federal or state constitutions.

60

Two sections of the Federal Constitution were also available to the judiciary for protecting property and economic interests. Article I, section 9, clause 3 mandates that "No Bill of Attainder or ex post facto Law shall be passed" by the federal government. Section 10 of the same article provides that "No State shall ... pass any Bill of Attainder, or ex post facto Law, or Law impairing the Obligation of Contracts...." Early in its history the attainder provision was given criminal and limited civil application as a result of Chief Justice Marshall's statement in *Fletcher* that "[a] bill of attainder may affect the life of an individual, or may confiscate his property, or may do both."[7] The High Court has maintained and broadened this definition over the years to provide protection against legislative actions intended to deprive specified or easily ascertainable individuals or groups of economic interests previously enjoyed.[8] The attainder provision would not have affected general economic interests such as those involved in the *Slaughter-House Cases*. However, the other two provisions of section 10 are relevant to that controversy.

As we have seen, Chief Justice Marshall and two Associate Justices believed that the obligation of contracts provision severely limited the states' power to restrict economic activity. In *Fletcher* the Chief Justice suggested that the ex post facto provision was not strictly confined to criminal matters, as *Calder v. Bull* had earlier held.[9] Justice William Johnson and some commentators have asserted that the ex post facto ban was intended to cover both civil and criminal retroactive laws.[10] Under such broad construction, either of these constitutional provisions would protect rights recognized under existing law—including the butchers' interests in the *Slaughter-House Cases*.

Had Marshall's interpretation of the contract clause prevailed, and/or had *Calder* given a civil law content to the ex post facto requirement, these provisions would have guaranteed somewhat the same haven for economic rights that substantive due process subsequently did. Marshall's interpretation would have allowed only regulation of the contractual remedy and would have generally forbidden a state from limiting an individual's right to enter into voluntary agreements. The application of ex post facto to civil matters would have forbidden the national and state governments from removing previously established legal rights.

Thus application of a broad interpretation of the contract and ex post facto clauses in the *Slaughter-House Cases* likely would have achieved the results sought by the minority Justices. Louisiana's monopoly grant limited the butchers' right to pursue their occupations and to contract for the purchase and sale of goods and services. It also limited the use of their property. The restraints on an existing occupation and on property might have been considered illegal if the ex post facto provision had been deemed applicable to retroactive civil statutes, and that portion of the law infringing the making of contracts might have been invalid under Marshall's dissent in *Ogden v. Saunders.*[11] Because two highly controversial decisions (*Calder* and *Ogden*) had profound economic and social consequences for the nation, questions naturally arise about the correctness of these decisions and about the true meaning of the clauses that they interpreted. The remainder of this chapter considers these issues.

No State Shall Pass Any Law Impairing the Obligation of Contracts

The principal support for a broad and inclusive interpretation of the contracts clause comes from the dissenting argument presented by Chief Justice Marshall for himself and two other Justices in *Ogden v. Saunders.* This action arose on a contractual debt between the parties. The defendant pleaded that he had been discharged as an insolvent debtor under New York laws and that he therefore no longer owed the debt. The issue was whether the New York bankruptcy law, which had been in effect prior to the time that the note became legally binding between the parties, was an impairment of a contractual obligation. By a 4–3 vote, the Supreme Court held that the constitutional provision was not violated by the bankruptcy statute. The first great restriction upon the scope of the contract clause was thus applied by a bare majority of the Supreme Court.

This decision was contrary to Marshall's dictum in an 1819 decision that the contract clause was violated even when the law at issue had been passed before a debt was contracted.[12] In *Ogden,* Marshall wrote for the three dissenters, one of whom was Joseph Story, the distinguished legal scholar and writer of the well-known *Commentaries on the Constitution of the United States.* No dispute existed on the Supreme Court concerning the question of whether the clause forbids retroactive laws diminishing the obligation of existing contracts.

Each of the four Justices constituting the majority (Washington, Johnson, Thompson, and Trimble) authored an extensive opinion. Justice Washington was quite equivocal about his decision, acknowledging that the issue was far from certain. Both he and Justice Thompson expressed a reluctance to overrule a state enactment in the absence of a clear constitutional mandate, and neither was able to construe the contract provision as affording them absolute authority to do so. Washington made plain his reservations about the question.

I am far from asserting that my labours have resulted in entire success. They have led me to the only conclusion by which I can stand
with any degree of confidence; and yet, I should be disingenuous
were I to declare, from this place, that I embrace it without hesitation, and without a doubt of its correctness. The most that candour
will permit me to say upon the subject is, that I see, or think I see,
my way more clear on the side which my judgment leads me to
adopt, than on the other, and it must remain for others to decide
whether the guide I have chosen has been a safe one or not.[13]

Clouding the determination of whether the clause relates to prospective laws was the involvement of the bankruptcy issue. The Constitution's only reference to bankruptcy occurs in Article I, section 8,
clause 4, which authorizes Congress to enact "uniform Laws on the
subject of Bankruptcies throughout the United States." The Supreme
Court had previously ruled that until Congress enacted statutes of an
exclusive nature, this provision did not preclude states from adopting
bankruptcy laws, provided that such laws did not impair the obligation
of contracts or any other prohibition on state action contained in Article I, section 10.[14] Marshall's opinion would have effectively deprived
the states of this power.

The majority Justices argued that had the Framers intended to prohibit the states from exercising bankruptcy authority, they would have
expressly so provided. This concern does not appear in any convention
records and was largely ignored at state ratification conventions. Justice Johnson was confident that the Constitution never would have
been adopted had the delegates imagined that the states would not be
able to exercise this authority.[15]

Commentators postulate that the *Ogden* decision was largely
brought about by a quarter century of failure to obtain a national
bankruptcy law, following the repeal in 1803 of such a law enacted
three years previously.[16] Just thirteen days before *Ogden* was decided,
a national bankruptcy law had again failed passage in Congress.[17] In
addition, "[t]he continued failure to obtain a national bankruptcy law
was a phase of a constantly waged battle, particularly by the Southern
states, for what was termed 'States' Rights.' To the success of that
battle, the destruction of the Contracts Clause was highly essential...."[18] Thus, had the Constitution expressly recognized state
bankruptcy powers, the outcome in *Ogden* might well have been different.

The majority opinions likewise evidence fear that a broad interpretation of the clause would severely limit the states' power over commerce. Justice Trimble wrote that Marshall's construction would

"transform a special limitation upon the general powers of the States, into a general restriction."[19] The opinions noted that this issue also had not been raised during the state ratifying conventions—again, the Justices assumed, because most delegates had not comprehended that the clause could have so broad an impact.

In denying that the clause applies to all contracts, the majority contended that impairing the obligation of any contract before it was formed was impossible, for prior to creating a contract, there is no contractual obligation to impair. Thus an ordinary reading of the clause did not lead to the broad interpretation suggested by the dissent. In any event, when parties enter into a contract, they do so subject to the laws then in existence, which thereupon control or become part of the agreement. In this respect bankruptcy laws were not extraordinary.

Chief Justice Marshall's dissent was also extensive and, according to some commentators "bitter," "emphatic," and "one of the most powerful opinions he ever wrote."[20] In thirty-four years as Chief Justice, this was the only published constitutional decision in which Marshall was part of the minority; *Ogden* also marked the first time in twenty-seven years that a majority opposed him on a constitutional law issue. Essentially Marshall argued that the contracts clause secured freedom of contract from molestation by the states. Under this view, the states would have very limited power to regulate commerce. His opinion can be summarized as follows:

1. The nature of the Union makes us "one people, as to commercial objects."[21] The prohibition in the clause is broad and inclusive, complete and total: "There is no exception from it."[22] The Constitution protects all contracts, past or future, from state enactments limiting the commitments sought by the parties. Had the intention of the convention been to confine the prohibition to retroactive laws, it would have been so expressed; "it is scarcely conceivable that some word would not have been used indicating this idea."[23] The word *impairing* applies to agreements executed subsequent to the adoption of a law. If a law limits the understanding that the parties desire to create, it impairs a contractual obligation regardless of when it is enacted.

2. If one law, such as the bankruptcy statute under consideration, becomes part of all subsequent contracts, so does every other law affecting contracts. Thus a legislative act declaring that all contracts should be subject to its control and should be discharged as the legislature might decide could become a part of every contract and be one of its conditions.[24] Therefore the majority interpretation would effectively negate the constitutional provision. (Marshall's fears were re-

alized in 1934, when the Supreme Court declared that the reservation
of essential attributes of sovereign power is read into contracts.)[25]

3. "[I]ndividuals do not derive from government their right to contract, but bring that right with them into society . . . ."[26] The obligation
is not conferred by positive law, but rather is intrinsic and conferred by
act of the parties. The obligation of contract is confined to that which is
actually written into the instrument.[27]

4. Marshall construed the prohibition literally. It barred regulation of
the obligation but not of its formation and enforcement. The Constitution did not require a state to enforce contracts (but every state surely
would). A state could make certain contracts illegal (such as usurious
and mischievous ones), since if there were no contract, nothing existed
that could be impaired. He apparently did not view these qualifications
as significantly limiting freedom of contract.

5. To be meaningful, the prohibition has to apply prospectively.

> [I]f the inhibition be of retrospective laws only, a very short lapse of
> time will remove every subject on which the act is forbidden to
> operate, and make this provision of the constitution so far useless.
> Instead of introducing a great principle, prohibiting all laws of this
> obnoxious character, the constitution will only suspend their opera-
> tion for a moment, or except from it preexisting cases. The object
> would scarcely seem to be of sufficient importance to have found a
> place in that instrument.[28]

Marshall was a delegate to the Virginia ratifying convention, the
author of a five-volume biography of George Washington, and the
holder of important federal posts before his appointment to the Supreme Court. He was also probably the Justice most knowledgeable
about the original definition and significance of the contract clause.[29]
Beard wrote that Marshall, more than anyone else on the Court, should
have known the Framers' intent.[30] Miller observes that "the text of the
Constitution was the distillation of a history that Marshall knew
well."[31] For Marshall the contract clause was a vital part of the American scheme of government.

> We cannot look back to the history of the times when the august
> spectacle was exhibited of the assemblage of a whole people by their
> representatives in Convention, in order to unite thirteen independent
> sovereignties under one government, so far as might be necessary for
> the purposes of union, without being sensible of the great importance
> which was at that time attached to the tenth section of the first
> article. The power of changing the relative situation of debtor and

creditor, of interfering with contracts, a power which comes home to every man, touches the interest of all, and controls the conduct of every individual in those things which he supposes to be proper for his own exclusive management, had been used to such an excess by the State legislatures, as to break in upon the ordinary intercourse of society, and destroy all confidence between man and man. The mischief had become so great, so alarming, as not only to impair commercial intercourse, and threaten the existence of credit, but to sap the morals of the people, and destroy the sanctity of private faith. To guard against the continuance of the evil was an object of deep interest with all the truly wise, as well as the virtuous, of this great community, and was one of the important benefits expected from a reform of the government.[32]

Marshall's explanation is generally accepted.[33] However, the proposed contract clause apparently occasioned no debate during the Philadelphia convention and very little during the state ratifying conventions; early drafts of the proposed constitution did not include the clause, although they did incorporate other prohibitions contained in the paragraph in which it appears. The matter was first raised in a motion made on 28 August, to prohibit the states from interfering with private contracts. This motion was replaced with one to insert attainder and ex post facto bans, which passed.[34]

Wright, the author of a leading work on the clause, believed that Marshall desired a general limitation on state powers over contracts.[35] Crosskey postulates that state power over the subject would have been brought largely to an end as of 1789, if the clause had been observed as the Framers had intended.[36] *Ogden* did not, of course, destroy the clause as a barrier to certain state regulation, as recent opinions have revealed.[37]

Although Marshall did not present historical evidence for his position, some subsequently became available. The contracts clause came into the Constitution as part of the report presented on 12 September 1787 by the Committee on Style. The clause, as the committee reported it, read: "No State shall...pass any...laws altering or impairing the obligation of contracts...."[38] George Mason of Virginia seems to have proposed the insertion of the word *previous* after the words *obligation of*—a change that would have limited the provision to contracts previously formed. In his records of the various proposals that he presented, Mason reported that this change was refused.[39] One may surmise, therefore, that the generality of the clause was considered and purposeful; it was to apply to both prospective and retrospective laws.[40] (On 14 September the words *altering or* were removed.)[41]

Neither the Federal Government nor the States
Shall Pass an Ex Post Facto Law

Both clauses in the Constitution (Art. I, secs. 9 and 10) are unequivocal
and would invalidate any law designed to operate ex post facto. The
problem is one of defining that term. From the time that the Constitutional Convention adopted these clauses, there has been doubt
whether the term applies to all retroactive legislation or only to retroactive penal statutes. While no body of law has developed on the
subject, it is accepted that a law removing legally acquired valuable
interests is retroactive. According to Justice Story, "every statute,
which takes away or impairs vested rights acquired under existing
laws, or creates a new obligation, imposes a new duty, or attaches a
new disability, in respect to transactions or considerations already
past, must be deemed retrospective...."[42] A broad judicial interpretation of what constitutes an ex post facto law can operate as a
severe restraint on the legislature, because statutes frequently adversely affect existing interests.

The Supreme Court's first pronouncement on the clauses came in
Calder v. Bull, and three (Chase, Paterson, and Iredell) of the four
Justices wrote opinions limiting them solely to criminal law. The fourth
Justice (Cushing) did not comment on the issue. Although some might
consider these observations as dicta and not essential to resolving the
controversy, the *Calder* case has, for the most part, settled the law on
the subject. It did not, however, put to rest the controversy about the
"true" meaning of the clauses.

Justice Chase predicated his opinion on history, previous definitions,
and policy.

> The expressions "*ex post facto* laws," are technical, they had been
> in use long before the revolution, and had acquired an appropriate
> meaning, by legislators, lawyers and authors. The celebrated and
> judicious Sir William Blackstone, in his commentaries, considers an
> *ex post facto* law precisely in the same light as I have done. His
> opinion is confirmed by his successor, Mr. Wooddeson; and by the
> author of the *Federalist,* who I esteem superior to both, for his
> extensive and accurate knowledge of the true principles of govern-
> ment.
>   I also rely greatly on the definition or explanation of *ex post facto*
> laws, as given by the conventions of Massachusetts, Maryland and
> North Carolina, in their several constitutions or forms of govern-
> ment....
>   ...If the term *ex post facto* law is to be construed to include and
> to prohibit the enacting any law, after a fact, it will greatly restrict

the power of the federal and state legislatures; and the consequences
of such a construction may not be foreseen . . . .

It is not to be presumed, that the federal or state legislatures will
pass laws to deprive citizens of rights vested in them by existing
laws; unless for the benefit of the whole community; and on making
full satisfaction. The restraint against making any *ex post facto* laws
was not considered by the framers of the constitution, as extending
to prohibit the depriving a citizen even of a vested right to property;
or the provision "that private property should not be taken for public
use, without just compensation," was unnecessary.[43]

Justice Paterson (a delegate to the Constitutional Convention who
left Philadelphia before the ex post facto clauses were discussed)[44]
considered the attainder, ex post facto, and contract bans together and
asserted that the latter covers civil acts and that therefore a similar
application of ex post facto would be redundant. The Framers "understood and used the words in their known and appropriate signification,
as referring to crimes, pains and penalties, and no further."[45]

Justice Iredell, reasoning more on policy grounds, stated that:

[T]he act or resolution of the legislature of Connecticut, cannot be
regarded as an *ex post facto* law; for the true construction of the
prohibition extends to criminal, not to civil cases. It is only in criminal cases, indeed, in which the danger to be guarded against, is
greatly to be apprehended. The history of every country in Europe
will furnish flagrant instances of tyranny exercised under the pretext
of penal dispensations.
    . . . The policy, the reason and humanity of the prohibition, do not,
I repeat, extend to civil cases, to cases that merely affect the private
property of citizens. Some of the most necessary and important acts
of legislation are, on the contrary, founded upon the principle, that
private rights must yield to public exigencies.[46]

Twelve years later Chief Justice Marshall, writing in *Fletcher v.
Peck,* saw the clause in a somewhat different light. The issue in that
case, the reader may recall, related to a Georgia statute that sought to
divest title from a purchaser in good faith of land acquired from a seller
who obtained the property under a legislative grant that was influenced
by corrupt politics. Marshall did not bring ex post facto fully into the
civil law, although he did suggest that it was not strictly confined to the
criminal.

An *ex post facto* law is one which renders an act punishable in a
manner in which it was not punishable when it was committed. Such
a law may inflict penalties on the person, or may inflict pecuniary

penalties which swell the public treasury. The legislature is then prohibited from passing a law by which a man's estate, or any part of it, shall be seized for a crime which was not declared, by some previous law, to render him liable to that punishment . . . . [The law in litigation] would have the effect of an *ex post facto* law. It forfeits the estate of Fletcher for a crime not committed by himself, but by those from whom he purchased. This cannot be effected in the form of an *ex post facto* law, or bill of attainder; why, then, is it allowable in the form of a law annulling the original grant?[47]

Marshall's *Fletcher* opinion did not modify the *Calder* decision, for in subsequent years the Supreme Court retained the interpretation of the latter case on ex post facto laws. Justice Johnson, who served on the Marshall Court, observed in some opinions that the ex post facto provisions had been wrongly interpreted and urged the Court to alter its position to include all retroactive laws. In *Ogden* he proposed such a change.

[Ex post facto] applies to civil as well as to criminal acts . . ., and with this enlarged signification attached to that phrase, the purport of the clause would be, *"that the States shall pass no law, attaching to the acts of individuals other effects or consequences than those attached to them by the laws existing at their date; and all contracts thus construed, shall be enforced according to their just and reasonable purport."*[48]

In a memorandum attached to an 1829 decision, Johnson analyzed in detail the grounds presented by Chase to support his *Calder* opinion and found them in the main to be erroneous.[49] Johnson cited a 1724 English decision by Lord Raymond concerning an Act of Parliament adopted in 1720 requiring the registration of certain existing contracts to prevent their being declared void.[50] Raymond had referred to the act as being ex post facto. The case served as Johnson's authority for concluding that as of the time of Raymond's decision, the phrase was not confined to criminal statutes, and the Justice could not understand how it had acquired a different meaning in 1798 when *Calder* was decided. He then proceeded to give examples of legal commentators (such as Sheppard, Godolphin, and Bulstrode) who also had applied the phrase to civil matters. Johnson disagreed with Chase's interpretation of Wooddeson and Blackstone, stating that neither should be considered as having restricted ex post facto to criminal matters. Chase had referred to the constitutions of Maryland, Delaware, Massachusetts, and North Carolina as illustrating the restrictive meaning. Johnson countered by noting that the Massachusetts and Delaware

constitutions did not contain the phrase and that the other two did not
provide authority for Chase's holding—or if they did, that the rest of
the country should not suffer from these states' errors. "Maryland first
used it in this restricted sense, and North Carolina copied from Maryland; and if the evidence of contemporaries may be relied on, Mr.
Chase was one of the committee who reported the constitution of
Maryland; and thus stands the authority for the restricted use."[51]
Johnson also rejected the policy basis of the *Calder* opinion.

[T]he learned judges could not then have foreseen the great variety
of forms in which the violations of private right have since been
presented to this Court. The case of a legislature declaring a void
deed to be a valid deed, is a striking one to show, both that the
prohibition to pass laws violating the obligation of contracts, is not a
sufficient protection to private rights; and that the policy and reason
of the prohibition to pass ex post facto laws, does extend to civil as
well as criminal cases. This Court has had more than once to toil up
hill in order to bring within the restriction on the states to pass laws
violating the obligation of contracts, the most obvious cases to which
the constitution was intended to extend its protection: a difficulty,
which it is obvious might often be avoided by giving to the phrase ex
post facto its original and natural application. It is then due to the
venerable men whose opinions I am combating, to believe that had
this and the many other similar cases which may occur and will
occur, been presented to their minds, they would have seen that in
civil cases, the restriction not to pass ex post facto laws could not be
limited to criminal statutes, without restricting the protection of the
constitution to bounds that would import a positive absurdity.[52]

Johnson closed his memorandum by warning that unless the clause
was restored to its intended meaning, the Justices might have to employ remedies that the Constitution might not fully sanction. Thus at
some time the Court might have to revert to such an alternative "in
order to maintain its own consistency, and yet give to the constitution
the scope which is necessary to attain its general purposes in this
section, and to rescue it from the imputation of absurdity."[53] As we are
now aware, in developing the doctrines of economic due process and
liberty of contract, succeeding Justices did follow the kind of course
that Johnson probably envisioned. At the time he wrote, the Court may
have already expanded the protection of the contract clause to offset
the ex post facto ban in its ruling in *Fletcher* and in the celebrated
Dartmouth College case,[54] which limited the states' powers to alter
corporate charters.
    The records of the Constitutional Convention are ambiguous about

the meaning of ex post facto laws and do not confirm the existing construction. Together with the ban on bills of attainder, the provision was first introduced while the first draft of the Constitution was already under consideration. James Madison made extensive notes concerning the debates and discussions carried on at the Constitutional Convention, and they are the principal and most complete source of information available on what transpired. In contrast, the convention's official journal is generally considered a source of only secondary reliability. However, despite their over-all length, Madison's notes are often cursory and provide only cryptic summaries of an unknown fraction of the speeches, comments, and questions. Moreover, before his death, Madison made changes in his original notes, compromising their reliability.

The excerpts that follow are the most significant references in Madison's notes to ex post facto laws and are quoted verbatim for the dates as specified.[55]

Wednesday, 22 August 1787

Mr. GERRY and Mr. McHENRY moved to insert, after the second Section, Article 7, the clause following, to wit:

"The Legislature shall pass no bill of attainder, nor any *ex post facto* law."

Mr. GERRY urged the necessity of this prohibition, which he said was greater in the National than the State Legislature; because the number of members in the former being fewer, they were on that account the more to be feared.

Mr. GOUVERNEUR MORRIS thought the precaution as to *ex post facto* laws unnecessary; but essential as to bills of attainder.

Mr. ELLSWORTH contended that there was no lawyer, no civilian, who would not say, that *ex post facto* laws were void of themselves. It cannot, then, be necessary to prohibit them.

Mr. WILSON was against inserting any thing in the Constitution, as to *ex post facto* laws. It will bring reflections on the Constitution, and proclaim that we are ignorant of the first principles of legislation, or are constituting a government that will be so.

The question being divided, the first part of the motion relating to bills of attainder was agreed to, *nem. con.*

On the second part relating to *ex post facto* laws,—

Mr. CARROLL remarked, that experience overruled all other calculations. It had proved that, in whatever light they might be viewed by civilians or others, the State Legislatures had passed them, and they had taken effect.

Mr. WILSON. If these prohibitions in the State Constitutions have no effect, it will be useless to insert them in this Constitution. Besides, both sides will agree to the principle, but will differ as to its application,

Mr. WILLIAMSON. Such a prohibitory clause is in the Constitution of North Carolina; and though it had been violated, it has done good there, and may do good here, because the Judges can take hold of it.

Doctor JOHNSON thought the clause unnecessary, and implying an improper suspicion of the National Legislature.

Mr. RUTLEDGE was in favor of the clause.

On the question for inserting the prohibition of *ex post facto* laws,—

New Hampshire, Massachusetts, Delaware, Maryland, Virginia, South Carolina, Georgia, aye—7; Connecticut, New Jersey, Pennsylvania, no—3; North Carolina, divided.[56]

Tuesday, 28 August 1787

Mr. KING moved to add, in the words used in the ordinance of Congress establishing new States, a prohibition on the States to interfere in private contracts.

Mr. GOUVERNEUR MORRIS. This would be going too far. There are a thousand laws relating to bringing actions, limitations of actions, &c., which affect contracts. The judicial power of the United States will be a protection in causes within their jurisdiction; and within the State itself a majority must rule, whatever may be the mischief done among themselves.

Mr. SHERMAN. Why then prohibit bills of credit?

Mr. WILSON was in favor of Mr. KING's motion.

Mr. MADISON admitted that inconveniences might arise from such a prohibition; but thought on the whole it would be overbalanced by the utility of it. He conceived, however, that a negative on the State laws could alone secure the effect. Evasions might and would be devised by the ingenuity of the Legislatures.

Col. MASON. This is carrying the restraint too far. Causes will happen that cannot be foreseen, where some kind of interference will be proper and essential. He mentioned the case of limiting the period for bringing actions on open account—that of bonds after a certain lapse of time—asking, whether it was proper to tie the hands of the States from making provisions in such cases.

Mr. WILSON. The answer to these objections is, that retrospective *interferences* only are to be prohibited.

Mr. MADISON. Is not that already done by the prohibition of *ex post facto* laws, which will oblige the Judges to declare interferences null and void.

Mr. RUTLEDGE moved, instead of Mr. KING's motion, to insert, "nor pass bills of attainder, nor retrospective laws."

On which motion,—New Hampshire, New Jersey, Pennsylvania, Delaware, North Carolina, South Carolina, Georgia, aye—7; Connecticut, Maryland, Virginia, no—3.[57]

Wednesday, 29 August 1787

Mr. DICKINSON mentioned to the House, that on examining Blackstone's Commentaries, he found that the term *"ex post facto"* related to criminal cases only; that they would not consequently restrain the States from retrospective laws in civil cases; and that some further provision for this purpose would be requisite.[58]

Friday, 14 September 1787

Colonel MASON moved to strike out from the clause (Article 1, Sect. 9,) "no bill of attainder, nor any *ex post facto* law, shall be passed," the words, "nor any *ex post facto* law." He thought it not sufficiently clear that the prohibition meant by this phrase was limited to cases of a criminal nature; and no Legislature ever did or can altogether avoid them in civil cases.

Mr. GERRY seconded the motion; but with a view to extend the prohibition to "civil cases," which he thought ought to be done.

On the question, all the States were no.[59]

Madison's entries do not prove that the ex post facto clauses apply to retroactive civil legislation, but clearly they do not foreclose that possibility. Thus, the discussion on 28 August when the ban on the states was adopted relates only to civil affairs. One can hardly avoid giving considerable significance to the fact that Madison quotes himself on that day as being under the impression that the ex post facto provision bars retrospective interferences in civil matters. Madison does not reveal whether his inquiry was answered or whether the assumption that he made regarding ex post facto laws was disputed. As Madison recorded, Rutledge's 28 August motion contains the word *retrospective;* however, the official journal uses the words *ex post facto*[60]—an occurrence suggesting that the two terms were used synonymously. Dickinson's comment on 29 August suggests he was calling the delegates' attention to something they might not have been aware of—that ex post facto might be interpreted to relate only to criminal matters.

As we shall see, the legal commentators are far from uniformly convinced that the three *Calder* opinions are correct expositions of the Constitution.[61] The research of Justice William Johnson, the most vigorous judicial opponent of the prevailing view, has been noted pre-

viously.[62] The most exhaustive examination of the issue by a commentator was conducted by Professor William Crosskey, who entertained little doubt that the term *ex post facto* was intended to cover
civil legislation. In two law review articles[63] and a two-volume work[64]
he set out an impressive array of evidence to support his thesis. The
following is a brief summary of his analysis.

1. Crosskey maintains that popular publications appearing in the
years immediately prior to, during, and after the drafting of the Constitution used the term as descriptive of all forms of retrospective laws.
To illustrate both this point and the nature of the abuses intended to be
cured by the ban on ex post facto laws, he reproduced an item that
appeared in Philadelphia and Charleston newspapers in 1785 entitled
"On Ex Post Facto Laws," and was afterwards reprinted in a monthly
that circulated throughout the states. The writer referred only to contracts and promissory obligations, and criticized legislatures for setting
aside or otherwise interfering with these commitments to the disadvantage of creditors.[65]

2. Crosskey writes that if, in 1787, interested Americans had referred
to contemporary law books, they would have found that the general
usage of the words *ex post facto* accorded with the broad view taken by
the popular publications. Although Chase and later judges cite Blackstone in support of the limited meaning, Crosskey explains that Blackstone (and his successor Wooddeson) did not himself actually confine
the definition. Some commentators thought Blackstone had done so,
merely because he illustrated his definition with an example from the
criminal law. Justice Johnson took a view similar to Crosskey's, and
William G. Hammond's edition of Blackstone, published in 1890, states
that "The original meaning of ex post facto applies to civil and criminal
law alike."[66]

3. Justices Paterson and Iredell had on previous occasions considered ex post facto as applicable to civil litigation. Ten years before
Calder, Iredell had expressed this view during the North Carolina convention that considered ratification; and three years prior to *Calder,*
Paterson had ruled to this effect in his 1795 decision in *Vanhorne's
Lessee v. Dorrance.*[67]

4. Virginia and New Jersey decisions in the 1790s and early 1800s
supported an extensive definition of the term pursuant to which it
would govern civil laws.[68] A 1792 Virginia opinion stated:

> [The legislature] may amend [the law] as to future cases, but they
> cannot prescribe a rule of construction, as to the past. For a legisla-

tive interpretation, changing titles founded upon existing statutes,
would be subject to every objection which lies to ex post facto laws,
as it would destroy rights already acquired under the former statute,
by one made subsequent to the time when they became vested. A
power to be deprecated, as oppressive and contrary to the principles
of the constitution.[69]

5. Crosskey presents portions of the debates that took place during
the Virginia and North Carolina ratifying conventions and that relate to
the ex post facto clauses. The extensive definition was accepted in
North Carolina without demur, but the Virginia convention split on the
issue, with both James Madison and Edmund Randolph contending that the clauses were limited to criminal matters and with
George Mason insisting that they also covered civil affairs. (Note that
in the Federal Convention proceedings of 14 September 1787, Mason
had unsuccessfully sought to eliminate the clauses, because he thought
it not sufficiently clear that they were limited to criminal cases.)[70] At
the Virginia convention, Patrick Henry, who had been appointed to but
declined to attend the Federal Convention, strongly supported Mason
in this interpretation. Crosskey asserts that Madison and Randolph
adopted their positions in order to facilitate ratification of the Constitution. Madison subsequently reiterated this position in congressional
debate in early 1790, but was challenged by five other congressmen
who argued that the clauses applied to civil matters. Madison's view
appears to be contrary to the one he entertained on 28 August 1787,
when the Convention was in session.
6. Crosskey disputes in detail Justice Chase's assertions in *Calder*
that the experience of the states with constitutional provisions against
ex post facto or retrospective laws confirmed the limited view. Justice
Johnson had similarly contended that Chase's analysis in this respect
suffered from inaccuracies. That Chase's citation of state constitutional provisions, writes Crosskey, "did not have the character he
gave them or support the conclusions he drew from them is evident."
Another detailed analysis of the issue is contained in a *University of
Michigan Law Review* article by Oliver Field, who generally supports
the position of Justice Johnson and the one that Crosskey would later
offer.[71] Field also sought to determine the Framers' intention and considered common and technical usage of the term *ex post facto* in his
inquiry. Summarizing all references to the term in Madison's notes,
Field finds that the Framers did not use it in a technical sense but rather
with a common, nontechnical understanding that seemed to include

retrospective laws affecting both civil and criminal matters. He adds
that his study of the debates of the states of Virginia and North
Carolina strengthens this conclusion. The article closes by quoting
from a letter written by two Connecticut delegates to the Constitutional
Convention, Sherman and Ellsworth (later to be Chief Justice of the
United States Supreme Court), to their governor, and accompanied by
a copy of the proposed Constitution.

> The restraint on the legislatures of the several states respecting
> emitting bills of credit, making anything but money a tender in pay-
> ment of debts, or impairing the obligation of contracts by *ex post
> facto* laws, was thought necessary as a security to commerce, in
> which the interest of foreigners, as well as of the citizens of different
> states, may be affected.[72]

The position of Justice Johnson and Mssrs. Field and Crosskey is
supported in other writings. Corwin asserts that many of the Framers
expected that the ex post facto clause applying to the states would
remedy those serious evils Madison referred to as "interferences with
the steady dispensation of justice." These evils included enactments
for revising or setting aside court decisions, suspending the general law
for named individuals, interpreting the law in particular cases, and
even deciding cases.[73] Justice Story believed in a broad exposition of
the term.[74] Cooley thought that *Calder* is "in opposition to what might
seem the more natural and obvious meaning of the term *ex post
facto*."[75] Professor Haines doubted that Chase's limitation is in accord
with the intention of the Framers.[76] Chancellor Kent believed "laws
impairing previously acquired civil rights are equally within the reason
of that prohibition, and equally to be condemned."[77]

In the congressional debates in 1805 (after the *Calder* decision) over
proposals that the federal government compensate innocent purchasers
in the Georgia land sale litigated in *Fletcher,* some congressmen still
assumed that the ex post facto ban applied to civil laws. Thus Findley
contended that

> as long as we pay respect to Constitutional obligations and the dis-
> tribution of the powers of Government, and as long as we respect the
> Federal Constitution, which expressly asserts that no *ex post facto*
> law, or law impairing the obligation of contracts, shall be made, we
> must agree that one session of a Legislature cannot annul the con-
> tracts made by the preceding session.[78]

Root described the Georgia Legislature of 1796 as "[d]isregarding the
sacred nature of contracts, setting at defiance the Constitution of the

United States, which declares that 'no State shall pass any *ex post
facto* law, or law impairing the obligation of contracts'. . . and sporting
with the rights of innocent individuals. . . ."[79] Horwitz relates that
during a 1736 action in debt on a Virginia statute barring usurious
interest, the defendant, who had contracted with the plaintiff before the
act was passed, maintained that it was "against natural justice to
punish any man for an action, innocent in itself with respect to human
laws, by a law made *ex post facto*."[80] Here again the implication is that
ex post facto covers civil statutes.

Because of contemporary circumstances and attitudes, I submit it is
likely that the Framers sought to ban retroactive civil legislation to
protect property interests. No provision other than ex post facto
clauses fully achieves this purpose. Complaints about retrospective
civil statutes were common in the Confederate and Revolutionary
periods. The Framers, as we saw in chapter 2, had great concern about
the preservation of ownership rights. That this was one of the liberties
most important to them can hardly be doubted. Madison voiced this
concern during the convention.

> An increase of population will of necessity increase the proportion of
> those who will labour under all the hardships of life & secretly sigh
> for a more equal distribution of its blessings. These may in time
> outnumber those who are placed above the feelings of indigence.
> According to the equal laws of suffrage, the power will slide into the
> hands of the former. No agrarian attempts have yet been made in this
> Country, but symptoms of a leveling spirit. . . have sufficiently ap-
> peared in a certain quarters to give notice of the future danger.[81]

On another occasion, Madison said that in civilized communities, preservation of property as well as of personal rights was an essential
object of the law.[82] Later he wrote that the protection of the "faculties
of men, from which the rights of property originate" is the first object
of government.[83]

At the convention, other delegates emphasized the property right.
Gouverneur Morris of Pennsylvania observed: "Life and liberty were
generally said to be of more value than property. An accurate view of
the matter would nevertheless prove that property was the main object
of Society." Rufus King of Massachusetts and John Rutledge of South
Carolina also asserted that property was the primary or principal object
of society. Pierce Butler of South Carolina contended that "property
was the only just measure of representation. This was the great object
of Government: the great cause of war, the great means of carrying it
on."[84] William R. Davie of North Carolina, Abraham Baldwin of

Georgia, and Charles Pinckney of South Carolina thought the Senate should represent property or wealth. George Mason of Virginia stated that an important objective in constituting a Senate was to secure the right of property. John Dickinson of Delaware considered freeholders to be the best guarantors of liberty.[85]

Although not all Framers shared them, these views on property were not challenged at the time they were expressed, and in all probability, the vast majority agreed on the primacy of the property right. As Professor Katz has observed, the right to property was an unquestioned assumption of that period.[86] This perspective was not confined to England and America. Thus, leaders of the French Revolution favored perpetuating the existing property system.[87] In the Declaration of the Rights of Man of 1789, the French asserted the right of property. In the constitutions that followed, the guarantee became stronger. The Constitution of 1793 read: "No one shall be deprived of the least portion of his property without his consent, except when public necessity, legally proven, evidently demands it, and then only on condition of just compensation previously made." This guarantee was preserved in later constitutions and is no less compelling than that provided in the taking clause (i.e., eminent domain clause)[88] of the Fifth Amendment.[89]

Leaders of that era were not too far removed from the times when monarchs and lords could control or seriously affect individuals' lives through their power to confiscate wealth. Personal experience may also have augmented some delegates' concern for property rights. Thirty-one delegates were lawyers, presumably with an education that emphasized the importance of property. The delegates included members of financial, mercantile, and large planter classes. These men, even if not concerned about their personal finances, should have fully understood the perils of uncurbed governmental power over private investment and holdings. As previously indicated, the Confederation had experienced a number of state laws prejudicial to the owners of credit and contract paper. Legislatures so oriented might limit the use and alienability of property or even divest an owner of title.

Nevertheless, in spite of such obvious perils to ownership, a study of the original Constitution (without the Bill of Rights) reveals that no provision other than the ex post facto clauses would protect owners from state or federal laws confiscating their property. If *Calder* is correct, we must conclude that the Framers refused to bar the states from confiscating property interests, yet prohibited them (in Art. I, sec. 10) from impairing the obligation of contracts, inflating the currency, imposing imposts and duties, and granting letters of marque and reprisal and titles of nobility. Such an outcome would be possible only if the Framers were not concerned about securing property interests—which we know they were—or if they were grossly negligent about a subject that occupied a considerable portion of their deliberations. Nor did they expect, as Hamilton put it in referring to laws violating private contracts, that "a more liberal or more equitable spirit would preside over the legislations of the individual States hereafter, if unrestrained by any additional checks, than we have heretofore seen in too many instances disgracing their several codes."[90] Some might speculate that the Framers were content to rely upon natural law doctrines to protect property interests. However, as previously reported, in matters they deemed most important, the delegates specified restraints that the natural or common law also imposed.[91] As we shall see in the next chapter, the Framers also sought to restrain economic powers of the federal government. The most probable conclusion is that *Calder* was wrong on the meaning and intent of the ex post facto provisions.

The Opinions in Calder

Chase indicated that the Framers did not consider that the ex post facto restraint extended to vested rights. If they had, the Fifth Amendment's taking provision would have been unnecessary.[92] However, the record of a debate relating to this issue held in the First Congress, which framed the Bill of Rights in September 1789, does not support Chase's thinking. It reveals that a number of Congressmen in February 1790 believed the ex post facto clauses applied to civil matters. Arguing against a proposed law that certain debts of the United States should not be paid, five Congressmen from four states expressed views that such a law would violate the ex post facto clause affecting the federal government.[93] As previously indicated, similar opinions were voiced in Congress even after the *Calder* decision. In any case, it should not be assumed that the Bill of Rights was a well reasoned, coherent document. Professor Levy suggests it was more a chance product of political expediency than a principled commitment to personal liberties.[94]

Scholars have been unable to discover the reasons for including an eminent domain clause in the Bill of Rights except for the obvious one of providing owners with protection. It is probable that the Amendment's framers understood that the ex post facto clauses did not affect government's inherent power of eminent domain (as I shall explain shortly) and inserted the clause to clarify this power. The Fifth Amendment codified the common-law restraints on eminent domain (the requirements of a public use and just compensation), neither of which are of course referred to in the ex post facto provisions. In this respect, the taking clause served to assuage fears, such as those of Justice Iredell, that the ex post facto clauses eliminated the government's eminent domain powers.

Iredell argued that giving ex post facto a civil application would deny eminent domain powers to government.

> The policy, the reason and humanity of the prohibition, do not, I repeat, extend to civil cases, to cases that merely affect the private property of citizens. Some of the most necessary and important acts of legislation are, on the contrary, founded upon the principle, that private rights must yield to public exigencies. Highways are run through private grounds; fortifications, light-houses, and other public edifices, are necessarily sometimes built upon the soil owned by individuals. In such, and similar cases, if the owners should refuse voluntarily to accommodate the public, they must be constrained, so far as the public necessities require; and justice is done, by allowing them a reasonable equivalent. Without the possession of this power, the operations of government would often be obstructed, and society itself would be endangered.[95]

The answer to this contention is that the condemnation power of government is not barred by a comprehensive ex post facto clause. Iredell's thesis is wrong. The eminent domain power is regarded as an inherent and necessary power of government, essential to its independent existence.[96] Neither the United States Constitution nor to my knowledge any state constitution contains an express grant of this power, and eminent domain provisions in these documents do no more than qualify its application by requiring just compensation and a public purpose. All land is subject to the sovereign's power of condemnation and therefore an eminent domain proceeding is not ex post facto. Iredell's colleague, Justice Paterson, had stated in *Vanhorne's Lessee v. Dorrance* just three years earlier, that "[t]he despotic power, as it is aptly called by some writers, of taking private property, when state necessity requires, exists in every government . . . government could not subsist without it . . . ."[97] This inherent-power concept traces back to the early writers on eminent domain, the civil law jurisprudents who wrote in the late seventeenth to mid-eighteenth century. Thus, Bynkershoek, in a work published in 1737, commented:

> Now this eminent authority extends to the person and the goods of the subject, and all would readily acknowledge that if it were destroyed, no state could survive . . . . That the sovereign has this authority, no man of sense questions . . . .[98]

That a court would have interpreted the ex post facto clause as eliminating government's authority to condemn property is highly remote.

Justice Paterson concluded that the obligation-of-contracts clause would have been unnecessary had the Framers regarded the ex post facto clause as unlimited. His observation of course does not relate to the federal government, which is not affected by the contracts clause. Using Paterson's reasoning, one would have to conclude that on the federal level no protection against retroactive civil laws was intended. Nor was the contracts clause intended to protect vested property rights. Further, as Chief Justice Marshall believed, the contracts clause may have been inserted in part to prevent passage of state laws impacting future contractual arrangements—a situation not necessarily affected by ex post facto bans. Justice Johnson presented a tenable position when he concluded that the ex post facto clause was placed as a bridge between the attainder and contract provisions because unlike either of them, it possessed both civil and criminal aspects and covered areas to which the others were not applicable.

The case against the correctness of the *Calder* holding is extremely strong. Clearly, each of the three opinions considering ex post facto laws was deficient in factual presentation and reasoning. To suggest its reversal now is not outside the realm of reason, inasmuch as Justice Brennan was not deterred from declaring the Sedition Act of 1798 invalid "in the court of history" 166 years after it was passed.[99] Most important, however, is the lesson to be derived from this analysis of *Calder*. The Framers intended strong safeguards against the destruction or modification of the property right. This is a perspective acceptable to a great many Americans who today are no less devoted to the sanctity of private property. As I shall argue in subsequent pages, these beliefs of the Framers are as compelling and as relevant now as they were then.

Concluding Comments

During the substantive due process period the United States Supreme Court in essence implemented a broad interpretation of the ex post facto and the obligation-of-contracts provisions in the Federal Constitution. In so doing that Court *sub silentio* reversed *Calder* and *Ogden*. No one can state with any degree of certainty that these clauses were not thereby given their true meaning and that the intention of the Framers was not thereby fully recognized. Similar doubts will always exist about the highly restrictive interpretation of the Fourteenth

Amendment annunciated in the *Slaughter-House Cases*. The argument
in behalf of economic due process becomes even stronger when one
considers the basic character of the American social compact, under
which legislative authority over individual liberties is limited. Given
this background, one should not be surprised that the Supreme Court
eliminated unrealistic distinctions between procedural and substantive
due process. If transgression occurred under economic due process, it
related mostly to form; perhaps other provisions of the Constitution
were more appropriate to the issue. The error of succeeding Courts is
greater. By totally ignoring or rejecting relevant constitutional meanings and background, the contemporary Supreme Court has committed
substantive mistake—a higher degree of fault.

4
The Judicial Obligation to Protect Economic Liberties

As indicated in chapter 2, judicial review of federal or state legislation was intimately associated in the early years of this nation with the protection of property interests. In this capacity, review served to implement what Framers James Madison, Gouverneur Morris, Rufus King, John Rutledge, and Pierce Butler declared was a prime object of government: the preservation of the property right.[1] Given the Framers' desire to safeguard and enhance ownership, judicial review became an essential pillar in the governmental structure they had created.

The question arises whether judicial protection of the property right is similarly important and appropriate for contemporary society, which does not seem to have the same dedication to ownership that prior generations did. My answer is that the underlying basis for securing property interests has not changed. A free society cannot exist unless government is prohibited from confiscating private property. If government can seize something owned by a private citizen, it can exert enormous power over people. One would be reluctant to speak, write, pray, or petition in a manner displeasing to the authorities lest he lose what he has already earned and possesses. As Hamilton stated, a power over a man's subsistence amounts to a power over his will.[2] Justice Story explained that the Constitution's just compensation requirement "is laid down by jurists as a principle of universal law [because] in a free government, almost all other rights would become utterly worthless, if the government possessed an uncontrollable power over the private fortune of every citizen."[3]

Likewise, individual investment and saving would be insecure. In fact, the system of private ownership and enterprise that the Framers sought to preserve could not exist in the absence of substantial protection for property rights. Individual and collective welfare in both periods is accordingly bound to the integrity of the property right. This chapter will examine the judicial role in this relationship.

Origin and Scope of Judicial Review

Almost 200 years following ratification of the Federal Constitution, judicial review, which is not specifically mentioned in that document, remains an incompletely defined power. Interpreters have generally assumed that the supremacy clause of Article VI, which makes the national Constitution "the supreme law of the land," thus binding on state judges, and Article III, which establishes the federal judiciary and its authority in constitutional matters, provide the bases for the United States Supreme Court's authority over state action involving federal questions. However, dispute continues concerning the origin of judicial power over congressional action. The records of the Constitutional Convention do not reveal whether the Framers intended to give the judiciary power to annul federal laws. No resolution was submitted to the convention granting this power, and despite exhaustive research, scholars have not been able to determine how a majority of the delegates felt about the issue.[4] Most of the reported discussions on the relationship between the judiciary and other branches center on a proposal, made initially by Virginia's Edmund Randolph, that the "Executive and a convenient number of the National Judiciary" compose a council of revision with authority to examine and if necessary to veto laws before they became operative. Congress, by specified majorities, could have overridden any veto.[5] At that time a comparable body, consisting of the governor, chancellor, and judges of its highest court, existed in New York, having been created by that state's 1777 constitution.

Proponents of the council thought that it would be a restraint on the legislature and at the same time would encourage wise and reasonable legislation. However, the plan would have made Congress and not the judiciary the final interpreter of the Constitution. The matter was twice brought to a vote and defeated each time, 8 states to 3, and 4 to 3. James Madison and James Wilson thereafter proposed a veto that could be exercised over federal legislation by either the president or the Supreme Court and that could be overturned by a greater-than-majority vote of Congress. This proposal was rejected 8 to 3.[6]

The *Federalist Papers* (per Hamilton) and *Marbury v. Madison*[7] (per Chief Justice Marshall) are the most important written sources for the concept of judicial review of federal legislation, and both strongly support it. At the time *Marbury* was decided, the Union consisted of seventeen states, in eight of which the judicial power to determine the validity of statutes had been asserted or expressed.[8] Marshall was not a delegate to the Philadelphia convention but did participate in the Virginia ratification convention in 1788, during which he asserted the same theory of judicial review that he would announce from the bench fifteen years later.[9] Hamilton, of course, spoke with the authority of a Framer.

Marshall's and Hamilton's views are supported by the background and history of the Constitutional period. It was inevitable that, given the historical and philosophical antecedents of the American constitutional system, legislative power would be prescribed and the judiciary accorded the responsibility of interpreting and protecting the nation's fundamental law. Judicial review was a "natural outgrowth of ideas that were common property in the period when the Constitution was established."[10] Wright observes that some delegates to the Constitutional Convention assumed that the power of review would be exercised by both federal and state courts, and over both congressional and state legislation.

> The number is not large and many of the statements relied upon as evidence of belief in judicial review are of an equivocal nature. But the very fact that such views were expressed and seldom questioned is indicative of the existence of a belief that no express constitutional sanction would be needed for the exercise of that power.[11]

Given the sentiments and circumstances of their day, the Framers must have understood that unless they restrained it, the Supreme Court would exercise, to some degree, the power of judicial review over both federal and state legislation. During the sessions, delegates Dickinson, Gerry, King, Madison, Martin, Mason, Mercer, Gouverneur Morris, Williamson, and Wilson made various statements referring to this power, suggesting that it would be applied by the national judiciary in the future, or alluding to previous instances of its exercise by state courts.[12] While the convention was in session, the Philadelphia press carried stories about judicial decisions in New Hampshire and North Carolina declaring statutes unconstitutional.[13] The delegates must have comprehended the nature of the review power, since it is generally agreed they accepted its application by the Supreme Court to state acts that affected the Federal Constitution.

Professor Haines reports six other cases in five states, decided between 1778 and 1786, in which a court exercised or expressed a right of review over a legislative act.[14] Professor Crosskey dismisses these instances as being totally imaginary, or imaginary in their supposed reference to judicial review. He writes that the right of review was disputed vigorously whenever it was asserted.[15] Nevertheless, some of these cases were publicly reported and discussed as involving judicial review, and one case was referred to by Madison on the convention floor in a manner suggesting it related to review.[16]

The Framers, as reasonably informed men of their time, would have been aware of contemporary views concerning judicial review. Coke's opinion in *Dr. Bonham's Case* in 1610, asserting the power of judicial review, was familiar to American lawyers of the late colonial period through digests as well as lawbooks which reasserted it as sound authority.[17] As we have seen, leading thinkers of the late eighteenth century generally accepted the fundamental idea that underlies judicial review—the idea of a higher law or constitution limiting legislative authority.

The strongest argument against review was provided by Blackstone's opinion that the legislature is sovereign. The difficulty with this position is that Blackstone's views can be regarded as relevant to the English governmental structure and experience, and not applicable to the American situation and a written constitution which limited legislative power. Further, Blackstone's emphasis on natural and absolute rights encourages restraint on legislative power.

Crosskey contended that the controversial nature of judicial review would have motivated a convention that favored it to protect the Supreme Court in the exercise of that right.[18] (He acknowledged that the Court was so empowered with respect to state infringements of the Federal Constitution, and to preserve its judicial prerogatives from molestation by the other federal branches.) The converse of this position is more persuasive. Article III, section 2 states that the "judicial power shall extend to all cases, in law and equity, arising under this Constitution." While not conferring it, this language tends to imply judicial review power.

Could it be the intention of those who gave this power, to say, that in using it, the constitution should not be looked into? That a case arising under the constitution should be decided, without examining the instrument under which it arises? This is too extravagant to be maintained. In some cases, then, the constitution must be looked into by the judges. And if they can open it at all, what part of it are they forbidden to read or to obey?[19]

Persons concerned with the abuse of power, as the Framers were, would not have been satisfied with language that implied power if they intended to deny it. Moreover, given existing theory and practice, a convention opposed to judicial review would have restricted the Supreme Court in this respect. Its failure to do so indicates to me a willingness to accept a judicial function as then understood, and that would have to include the strong likelihood that the judges would pass on the constitutionality of legislation. As Charles Beard has put it, "it cannot be assumed that the convention was unaware that the judicial power might be held to embrace a very considerable control over legislation and that there was a high degree of probability (to say the least) that such control would be exercised in the ordinary course of events."[20]

Haines, in his authoritative work on judicial review,[21] sets forth at length the legal theories and principles involved in establishing the American doctrine of judicial review of legislative acts. These theories and principles may be summarized as follows:

1. *Doctrines of natural law and natural rights.* Judicial review originated at a time when the idea was rather generally accepted that natural and inalienable rights exist with which government may not justly interfere. The courts were seen as barriers protecting the individual from the coercive and arbitrary designs of the legislative and executive branches.

2. *Distrust of legislative power.* By 1787, a commonly held belief was that the greatest peril to liberty comes from the expanding power of legislative bodies.

[T]here was more concern as to the restrictions under which governments should operate than as to the functions to be performed. Governments were to be prohibited from interfering with freedom of person, security of property, freedom of speech and of religion. The guaranty of liberty was, therefore, to give the rulers as little power as possible and then to surround them with numerous restrictions—to balance power against power.[22]

3. *Theory of separation of powers.* The judiciary was considered the branch able to maintain lawful prohibitions and restrictions upon exercise of unauthorized powers by other governmental bodies as well as by individual officeholders.

4. *Theory of checks and balances.* While the trend in other countries had been to centralize authority and place supreme power in one branch, usually the legislative, the American system separated governmental powers and divided authority. Again, the judiciary was considered the most appropriate branch to implement this separation, for the nation had less to fear from possible usurpation by it than by the executive and legislative departments.

5. *Need to protect minorities.* A generally supported opinion during the Constitutional period was that government should safeguard minorities against oppression by majority rule.

> The conviction of leaders among both conservatives and radicals that the judiciary would become the greatest bulwark for the protection of individual interests because it secured the rights of the minority, was undoubtedly one of the chief reasons for the adoption by the courts of the right to declare laws invalid.[23]

6. *Protection of property rights.* Eighteenth-century political leaders were greatly concerned with safeguarding private property rights, and for this protection they looked to the judiciary, the governmental entity that was esteemed above all others as a counterweight to popular rule. Some of the earliest and most emphatic statements favorable to judicial review were directed toward legislative attempts to interfere with property rights.

7. *Written constitutions as fundamental law.* The written constitution was considered a supreme law, superior to any legislative enactment. The belief was prevalent that as authorized interpreters of this law, the courts, when conflicts arose, had to define and apply the Constitution as fundamental law.

8. *Judges as guardians of written constitutions.* Had they been so inclined, the Framers could have designated the legislature as chief guardian of the document's terms and provisions as well as arbiter of the scope of its own power. Therefore, the conclusion that a fundamental law demands final interpretation by the judiciary does not follow. According to Haines, Lord Coke's concept favoring the supremacy of the common law became the prime authority for judicial review.

Haines's conclusions accord with those of McLaughlin, another constitutional scholar, who in an earlier work had described the thinking of those who helped to establish judicial review. McLaughlin summarized the "series of fundamental principles" that influenced Revolutionary ideas in these words:

> The chiefest among the principles I have given are these: first and foremost, the separation of powers of government and the indepen-

dence of the judiciary, which led courts to believe that they were not bound in their interpretation of the constitution by the decisions of a collateral branch of the government; second, the prevalent and deeply cherished conviction that governments must be checked and limited in order that individual liberty might be protected and property preserved; third, that there was fundamental law in all free states and that freedom and God-given right depended on the maintenance and preservation of that law, an idea of the supremest significance to the men of those days; fourth, the firm belief in the existence of natural rights superior to all governmental authority, and in the principles of natural justice constituting legal limitations upon governmental activity, a notion that was widely spread and devoutly believed in by the young lawyers and statesmen of the Revolutionary days who were to become the judges of the courts and the lawyers that made the arguments; fifth, the belief that, as a principle of English law, the courts would consider that an act of Parliament contrary to natural justice or reason was void and pass it into disuse, a belief which was especially confirmed by the reference to Coke. Back of all of these ideas was a long course of English constitutional development in which judges had played a significant part in constitutional controversy. In English history courts had held an influential if not an absolutely independent position; Parliament itself had long played the rôle of a tribunal declaring existing law rather than that of a legislative body making new law. The principle of legislative sovereignty as a possession of Parliament was, on the other hand, a comparatively modern thing.[24]

Corwin, who generally concurs with Haines and McLaughlin, noted:

The idea of judicial review is today regarded as an outgrowth of that of a written constitution, but historically both are offshoots from a common stock, namely the idea of certain fundamental principles underlying and controlling government. In Anglo-American constitutional history this idea is to be traced to feudal concepts and found its most notable expression in Magna Carta.[25]

Thus prevailing opinion did not dispose the Framers to reject judicial review or discourage judges from exercising it. This power implements the Framers' goal of constructing a government strong enough to carry out certain important national functions and firm enough to secure the rights of persons and property against popular majorities, no matter how large.[26]

For Hamilton, the review power did not establish the judiciary's supremacy over any other branch. The judiciary was the interpretative body implementing the will of the people, as originally expressed in a fundamental law. All the reservations of particular rights or privileges

would amount to nothing if the Supreme Court could not declare voi
those acts contrary to the Constitution. For, said Hamilton, no princ
ple is clearer than that which states that an act of a delegated authorit
is invalid if contrary to the tenor of the commission under which it i
exercised.[27]

In *Marbury,* Chief Justice Marshall generally followed Hamilton'
reasoning, and he also emphasized in several passages the Court's rol
in protecting the individual from government.

> The very essence of civil liberty certainly consists in the right c
> every individual to claim the protection of the laws, whenever h
> receives an injury. One of the first duties of government is to affor
> that protection . . . .
> . . .The government of the United States has been emphaticall
> termed a government of laws, and not of men. It will certainly ceas
> to deserve this high appellation, if the laws furnish no remedy for th
> violation of a vested legal right.[28]

If we equate democracy with representative government, judicia
review is clearly undemocratic, for its purpose is to undo that whic
the majority has decreed. As we have seen, the judiciary was intende
as a means to limit the power of popular majorities. The Framers feare
the effect of majority rule on the liberties they prized. They recognize
that the difference between democracy and liberty can be immense. I
allowed free reign, majorities can extinguish the liberty of expressio
upon which a democratic system relies for dissemination of politica
information. They can confiscate property, eliminate economic op
portunity, and incarcerate the unpopular. Of course, the majority ma
in time learn from its errors and restore liberty. Moreover, liberties d
exist and flourish in countries that have not granted the judiciary th
power of review and where legislative enactments are absolutely bind
ing on the judiciary (as in England). In fact many might argue tha
liberty would have benefited more under the protection of the legis
lators than of the judges; but this alternative was not suited to ou
constitutional system. Instead the historical and philosophical back
ground of our governmental structure mandated an independent con
trol over popular and legislative majorities.

McIlwain reminds us that the legislature is not the people. "Popula
sovereignty is, in fact, possible only in a pure democracy without rep
resentative institutions . . . . In choosing a legislature, whether we like i
or not, we are choosing a master, and because we choose it, it is legall
no less a master than a monarch with a hereditary title."[29]

The underlying assumption of many who condemn judicial review a
undemocratic is that the legislature's actions tend to represent th

majority's wishes. These people assume that laws brought before the courts are the results of democratic processes. I will show in chapters 2 and 13 that these assumptions are highly questionable. Many measures adopted by legislatures are less representative of the people's will than are judicial decisions striking them down. The actual operation of the election system and the legislative process makes effectuating the popular will difficult. Therefore concluding that any particular measure is prima facie a product of public demand is a mistake. Critical provisions in bills may be inserted for a variety of reasons that have little relation to the public's wishes. The legislative function is quite susceptible to capture by small, special-interest groups. Because so many laws have only a tenuous connection to the popular will, it is reasonable to subject them to additional scrutiny before they are applied to a public that might not have approved their enactment. Both judicial review and executive veto provide such oversight. Hamilton's support of the executive veto is pertinent also to judicial review.

> The oftener the measure is brought under examination, the greater the diversity in the situations of those who are to examine it, the less must be the danger of those errors which flow from want of due deliberation, or of those missteps which proceed from the contagion of some common passion or interest. It is far less probable that culpable views of any kind should infect all the parts of the government at the same moment and in relation to the same object than that they should by turns govern and mislead every one of them.[30]

The Natural Rights Perspective of Early Justices

The preceding history and background reveal an original understanding about the function of judicial review that consists of two parts. First, the Federal Supreme Court would preserve the structure and organization of the government that had been created. Second, it would protect the people's liberties from infringement by the other branches and organs of government. Early judicial decisions used different approaches to accomplish these purposes. Preserving structure required construing the Constitution's text to maintain the organization of government and of its branches and to define the powers of the various governmental institutions in relation to each other. This endeavor involved ascertaining meaning, intention, and purpose within textual confines. In theory the judiciary merely applied the Framers' will as evidenced in the fundamental document.

Justices did not always fulfill their second responsibility in the same manner. When rights were set forth in the document, as in the case of

the ex post facto and contracts clauses, the Court used similar tech
niques to interpret constitutional design. However, as we have seen
they did on occasion go outside the text and in the name of natural o
fundamental principles secure rights that were nowhere enumerated ir
the Constitution. This practice was engaged in by, among others, the
three leading jurists of the time—Marshall, Story, and Kent—each o
whom may be regarded as staunchly dedicated to the integrity of a
fundamental law. As previously indicated, this policy was quite ac
ceptable in the judicial climate of that era. This resort to doctrine
external to the Constitution's text seems inconsistent with a strict con
structionist perspective. However, in the instance of individual liber
ties, these and other contemporary justices believed that the Con
stitution did not peclude consideration of rights not alluded to in the
document.

Dicta in *Vanhorne's Lessee v. Dorrance,*[31] *Calder v. Bull,*[32] anc
Wilkinson v. Leland[33] maintained that principles of natural law anc
social compact limited the power of state legislatures to abrogate indi
vidual rights. In *Fletcher v. Peck,*[34] per Chief Justice Marshall, anc
Terrett v. Taylor,[35] per Justice Story, the United States Supreme Cour
struck down legislation in part or in whole on the basis that the nature
of society restrained the legislative power even where the federa
or state constitutions are silent on the matter. In these cases the state
legislatures had enacted retrospective legislation divesting owners o
property that they had acquired in good faith. Had the ex post factc
clause applied to civil legislation, or the taking provision of the Fiftl
Amendment to state actions, either would have been relevant to sucl
facts. In lieu of these provisions, Marshall fell back on the contract:
clause and Story on the "spirit and letter" of the Constitution. How
ever, both also reached for the principle of a higher unwritten law tha
forbade the legislature from appropriating the title of a property owner
As we shall learn, the Justices had common-law authority for thei
position.

Were it not for technical, procedural reasons, more instances of thi:
form of natural law–social compact jurisprudence would obtain in the
early law reports. For example, Beveridge indicates that Justice Story
thought that the famous *Dartmouth College* decision,[36] actually basec
on the contracts clause, would have been more correctly founded on a
violation of the fundamental principles of government. Story believec
that the case should have been instituted in a federal court in order tc
enable this position to be propounded. Suit had originally been brough
in a state court, and the U.S. Supreme Court jurisdiction was predi

cated solely on the alleged violation of a federal constitutional right (the contracts clause). Its holding could not be based on any federal doctrine relating to natural principles. Beveridge suggests that Marshall agreed with Story's analysis. Chancellor Kent also believed that the legislative action in *Dartmouth College* violated natural justice.[37]

These natural rights judges believed that the American legislatures were inherently limited bodies, without power to deprive individuals of fundamental and inalienable rights. Only express constitutional authority could overcome this limitation. The English Parliament served as a model to support this proposition. Although it possessed absolute and final authority to enact and repeal legislation, English custom and tradition required that it honor and observe the unwritten constitution of the country that protected individual rights. Thus, as a practical matter, the English Parliament was limited in its authority to infringe on liberties. Justice Bradley once explained that "England has no written Constitution, it is true; but it has an unwritten one, resting in the acknowledged, and frequently declared, privileges of Parliament and the people, to violate which in any material respect would produce a revolution in an hour."[38] In this opinion, Bradley espoused the natural rights position that the American legislatures possessed no greater power over individual rights than Parliament in actuality did, or as he put it, the "people of this country brought with them to its shores the rights of Englishmen."[39]

The views expressed by Bradley were quite acceptable during his and other periods in the nation's history. Hamilton voiced a similar, and similarly common, opinion when he said: "Our ancestors, when they emigrated to this country, brought with them the common law, as their inheritance and birthright . . . ."[40] Justice Cooley wrote in 1868:

> The maxims of Magna Charta and the common law are the interpreters of constitutional grants of power, and those acts which by those maxims the several departments of government are forbidden to do cannot be considered within any grant or apportionment of power which the people in general terms have made to those departments. The Parliament of Great Britain, indeed, as possessing the sovereignty of the country, has the power to disregard fundamental principles, and pass arbitrary and unjust enactments; but it cannot do this rightfully, and it has the power to do so simply because there is no written constitution from which its authority springs or on which it depends, and by which the courts can test the validity of its declared will. The rules which confine the discretion of Parliament within the ancient landmarks are rules for the construction of the powers of the American legislatures;

and however proper and prudent it may be expressly to prohibit those things which are not understood to be within the proper attributes of legislative power, such prohibition can never be regarded as essential, when the extent of the power apportioned to the legislative department is considered, and appears not to be broad enough to cover the obnoxious authority. The absence of such prohibition cannot, by implication, confer power.[41]

Leading constitutional Framers accepted the idea that legislatures are inherently limited in power. The reader may recall that Wilson and Ellsworth and some other Framers believed that ex post facto laws are invalid and that no specific prohibition on them was needed.[42] James Madison wrote in *Federalist* Number 44 that bills of attainder, ex post facto laws, and laws impairing the obligation of contract are "contrary to the first principles of the social compact and to every principle of sound legislation. The two former are expressly prohibited by the declarations prefixed to some of the State constitutions, and all of them are prohibited by the spirit and scope of these fundamental charters."[43] Mention has already been made of Hamilton's acceptance of this perspective.

In *Calder v. Bull*,[44] Justice Chase presented an explanation for the position espoused by these Framers. He asserted that the federal and state legislatures were without power to overrule certain vital principles of free republican government. It was against reason and justice for the people to entrust a legislature with such powers, and therefore they will not be presumed to have done it. To maintain that the federal or state legislatures possess such powers unless they are expressly restrained would be a political heresy, altogether indefensible in free republican government. Consequently, Justice Story later concluded, no court of justice in the country would be warranted in assuming that the power to violate and disregard the rights of personal liberties and private property lurked under any general grant of legislative authority, or ought to be implied from any general expression of the will of the people.[45] Chancellor Kent emphasized that the judges were not to be confined by rights enumerated in the Constitution. "Our Constitutions do not admit the power assumed by the Roman Prince and the principle we are considering [no retroactive laws] is now to be regarded as sacred. It is not pretended that we have any express constitutional provisions on the subject; nor have we any for numerous other rights dear alike to freedom and to justice."[46]

The reader may recall Justice Iredell's complaint that Chase's natural rights theory gave unlimited discretion to judges. This charge does not lack basis, but experience has shown that the problem is not much different from that confronted by courts when they interpret the array of imprecise terms and provisions that permeate the Constitution. Courts are similarly endowed with great discretion in construing the common law which governs relations between people. According to Alexander Hamilton, the common law was principally the application of natural law to the state and condition of society.[47] In the late eighteenth century, the common law provided numerous protections for individual liberties. Essentially the natural law jurists were applying common-law concepts to protect interests not expressly safeguarded by the Constitution.

It is not unusual that the Constitution makes no provision for this procedure; the document is devoid of reference to other specific governmental functions and relationships. For instance, although the Constitution does not authorize the federal government to institute eminent domain proceedings or to invoke police powers, both powers are considered integral to the existence and sovereignty of government. The Constitution extends judicial authority to all cases of admiralty and maritime jurisdiction, but does not define the meaning of such jurisdiction. These gaps or silences are filled by common-law jurisprudence. Similarly, words used in the Constitution—for example, *jury, writ of habeas corpus, crime,* and *felony*—could be expounded only by the rules of common law.

Interpreters must bear in mind that the Constitution was framed against the background of the common law. At the time of the Constitutional Convention, the common-law system and tradition were generally accepted in the states. Although it vigorously condemned the English abuse of power, in 1774 the First Continental Congress declared that the English colonies in North America were entitled to the common law of England.[48] American law has never departed from this position.[49] Chancellor Kent explained:

> It was not to be doubted that the constitution and laws of the United States were made in reference to the existence of the common law .... In many cases, the language of the constitution and laws would be inexplicable without reference to the common law; and the existence of the common law is not only supposed by the constitution, but it is appealed to for the construction and interpretation of its powers.[50]

The common law was dedicated to the rule of right and reason. English judges and Parliament steadily expanded common-law protections; at one time only the meagre rudiments of criminal procedure were required, while by Blackstone's day "absolute rights" to life, liberty, and property were acknowledged. During the late eighteenth century, the system was highly regarded as a guardian of individual rights.[51] Many Americans then equated the common law with the natural law. For them the English constitution which consisted of common-law rights provided the greatest measure of human freedom. As Professor Wood has put it, "what made their Revolution so unusual [was that] they revolted not against the English constitution but on behalf of it."[52]

Most personal guarantees contained in the Bill of Rights were already accepted and applied under the common law at the time that document was ratified. Referring to advances in the criminal law, Prof. Grant concludes that common-law processes, with occasional help from statutes, remade, in a little over two centuries, a cruel, one-sided system into the one inserted into the Constitution, which provided numerous guarantees for an accused. He notes that the same general pattern of growth continued after ratification in accordance with common-law procedures.[53]

The Common Law of Liberties

If we assume that the natural law judges were acting consistently with the law of their day, a further inquiry must be made into whether the rules then in effect are forever binding on the judiciary. Arguably, the Constitution was framed with reference to the rules of the extant common law, implementing that era's law relating to individual rights, and the delegates intended that document be interpreted on the basis of those rules and none other. For those seeking to fulfill the intent and purpose of the Framers, the question is whether the common-law definitions of the late eighteenth century should be valid for all time, except as they might be altered by constitutional amendment. (The "loose" constructionists of course are not disturbed by such problems.) Strict constructionists might find appealing the conclusion that the Constitution guarantees only those rights within the Framers' knowledge and understanding. Because people cannot fully comprehend something unknown, it might be expected that the Framers would have been exceedingly reluctant to endorse unfamiliar ideas.

Another approach to interpreting the Framers' intent and purpose with respect to individual liberties is to conclude that they accepted the common-law system that encompasses continually changing meanings adopted pursuant to new understandings and conditions. Common-law tradition at the time of the framing of the Constitution espoused the progressive enlargement of the people's liberties. Framers who were willing to accept common-law jurisprudence must have understood that it is constantly being altered and reformed. Certainly the many lawyers at the convention were fully aware of this process and some exerted considerable influence in the constitutional deliberations. Therefore if codification did occur, it was of a system and process, and not of a specific set of rules. The first section of the Fourteenth Amendment, with its generalized phraseology, did not alter this understanding.

I am persuaded that the Framers accepted, as part of the constitutional government that they created, the common-law system and tradition to preserve and protect the liberties of the people. Their acceptance would necessarily have to be qualified in several respects.

First, judicial discretion should always be subject to and not violative of constitutional provisions.

Second, the reason and spirit of the review power should be of paramount consideration in adjudicating rights. The law in this area should reflect and complement the ideals, principles, and orientation of government, which in the American situation included, among other things, strong dedication to the preservation and enhancement of property and economic interests. In view of their other commitments to these rights, the Framers must have assumed judicial law would secure and surely not destroy them. In this connection, it might well be argued that legislative bodies never acquired more power to restrain individual liberties than they possessed when the Constitution was ratified, and therefore that at least the same recognition should be given material rights now as was accorded then. Thus Cooley takes the position that freedom of expression "must mean a freedom as broad as existed when the constitution which guarantees it was adopted."[54] In criminal law, it is accepted that the Constitution sets only minimum standards below which we cannot sink.[55]

Third, in exercising its jurisdiction, the judiciary should not intrude on the powers of the other branches. As early judges and authorities asserted, in constitutional matters, the functions of judges were strictly and exclusively judicial. The judiciary was an interpretative body not possessed of executive and legislative authority. Our contemporary federal courts have not abided by this limitation and have engaged in executive and legislative actions. The pragmatic implications of this change in policy will be discussed in chapter 14, and the historical aspects covered later in this chapter after we focus again on the Framers' perspectives on the material rights.

Political Economy and Economic Liberties

For the Framers the most fundamental of all rights were those which protect individuals from death or incarceration at the will of the state, and an owner of real or personal property from confiscation. These are the liberties of person and property and the only ones regarded as sufficiently important by the Framers to protect specifically in the text of the original Constitution. These liberties constitute the three absolute rights of life, liberty, and property proclaimed by Blackstone.

The significance of the property right is not always apparent in the literature of our times. In contrast, people of the constitutional period had more reason to comprehend the great harm that results when monarchs, lords, and officials deprive individuals of their lawfully acquired possessions and interfere in the lawful pursuit of commerce. An individual's right to own and use property free of governmental restraint (except for taxation) meant emancipation, independence, and autonomy. People could produce, develop, create, and invent, secure in the knowledge that the government could not confiscate the products of their own labor and ingenuity. They could speak, write, and pray without suffering material loss. This right ensured equality of burden, with no person or group having to bear the cost of installations or improvements benefiting the entire community.

I have previously referred to the abuses inflicted by legislatures upon creditors during the Confederation. The American colonists also suffered considerable economic indignities. The British imposed taxes on many commodities, required soldiers to be quartered, and controlled customs, imports, exports, and currency. They prohibited purchase by the colonists of Indian lands beyond a certain western boundary line. They removed from local officials and granted to royal officers the power of licensing persons engaged in trade with the Indians, thereby obtaining control of the lucrative fur trade. During the Revolution, on the other hand, a large amount of property owned by Loyalists was confiscated by Congress and the states. This historical experience made it evident that legal protection for property and commerce is essential in a state dedicated to maximizing freedom.

Whatever the purposes of judicial review, it followed that high priority had to be accorded its power to annul legislative infringements of the rights of property. "The right of the judiciary to declare laws invalid, and thus to check the rapacity of legislative assemblies was in the opinion of many to be the chief cornerstone of a governmental structure planned with particular reference to preserving property rights inviolate and to assuring a special sanction for individual liberties."[56]

Chief Justice Marshall referred to courts as "tribunals which are established for the security of property, and to decide human rights." According to Kent and Story, "[p]ersonal security, and private property, rest entirely upon the wisdom, the stability, and the integrity of the courts of justice."[57] Within this context, the property right necessarily included contractual and other economic interests.

The Framers' perspectives on political economy reveal their intentions toward protecting material interests. As explained in chapters 2 and 3, there is little doubt they sought to limit the powers of states over both local and national commerce. One reason for the convening of the Constitutional Convention was to secure economic rights in the states. Article I, section 10 prohibits the states from engaging in numerous activities that would limit private commerce. The Framers were concerned not only with the protection of individual rights, but also about future growth and development. Thus, several commentators maintain that the diversity of jurisdiction clause in the Constitution permitting out-of-state residents to sue local residents in a federal court was intended to protect and encourage investment in the country.[58] According to these commentators, the Framers were most interested in assuaging the apprehensions of domestic and foreign investors that state-appointed or elected judges might favor local interests. Nationally appointed judges were thought to be less subject to local pressures.

The Framers' intentions regarding protection of property and economic liberties at the federal level are not as clear, although inclined in the same direction. The contracts clause does not affect the federal government, but as explained in chapter 3, the ex post facto clauses might have covered much of the same area. Complicating the analysis is that for some leaders, such as Madison, Hamilton, and Marshall, lodging larger powers in the national government was a means for preserving liberty. They feared that the same powers in the hands of state authorities would result in greater limitations on personal freedoms.

In the ratification debates, the Federalists insisted that the national government was one of enumerated and limited powers. Opponents of the Constitution replied that three clauses ceded broad and unrestricted powers. These were the necessary and proper (Art. I, sec. 8, cl. 18), supremacy (Art. VI, cl. 2), and the common defense and general welfare (Art. I, sec. 8, cl.1) clauses. In the *Federalist Papers,* Madison and Hamilton strongly denied such views with respect to the first two provisions.[59] Madison was similarly emphatic that the defense and welfare clause did not expand the powers granted Congress.[60]

However, Hamilton contended this clause allowed for taxation and appropriation to provide for the common defense, an explanation that can be considered as also applicable to the "general welfare."[61] (Hamilton later explained that the appropriations under the welfare clause were confined to purposes that were general and not local in nature.)[62] Chiefly to resolve ambiguities about the national powers, the Tenth Amendment, proposed as part of the Bill of Rights by the Federalist-controlled First Congress, was added, declaring that the "powers not delegated to the United States by the Constitution, nor prohibited by it to the States, are reserved to the States respectively, or to the people." The Constitution might never have been ratified had the Federalists' representations in this regard not been accepted by a portion of the public.

It is consequently important to understand that the Framers rejected granting significant economic powers to the federal government. The convention refused to empower the national government to grant charters of incorporation; to establish seminaries for the promotion of literature and the arts; to establish public institutions, rewards, and immunities for the promotion of agriculture, commerce, trades, and manufactures; to regulate stages on the post road; to establish a university; to encourage, by proper premiums and provisions, the advancement of useful knowledge and discoveries; to provide for opening and establishing canals; to emit bills on the credit of the United States (which would include notes for circulation as currency); and to make sumptuary laws. Each of the proposals was introduced and either voted down or not further considered outside of committee.[63] The delegates may have also rejected other efforts to empower Congress to grant monopolies except for patents and copyrights.[64]

It may be, as some believe, that almost all of the foregoing powers are implied in the commerce and other powers given Congress. As of 14 September, three working days before final adjournment, and after the commerce and other major national powers had been settled, some influential and prominent delegates apparently believed either that the convention did not confer extensive economic powers on the federal government or the constitutional language in this regard was not clear. On that day, Benjamin Franklin moved to add to Article I, section 8 "a power to provide for cutting canals where deemed necessary." Madison moved to enlarge the motion "to grant charters of incorporation when the interests of the U.S. might require and legislative provisions of individual states may be incompetent." James Wilson seconded the first motion, and Edmund Randolph the second. Under these proposals, the federal government would be able to encourage or subsidize public and private enterprises to engage in public works or other activities.[65]

Franklin's motion was rejected 8 to 3, and Madison noted, the "other part fell of course, as including the power rejected."[66] Madison and Charles Pinckney then moved to empower Congress to establish a university, and this motion was defeated six noes, four ayes, and one divided.[67]

We cannot, of course, be certain why these proposals were voted down. However, the episode does lend credence to the position that the Constitution did not grant Congress very extensive economic powers. In opposing, in 1791, legislation before the House of Representatives to authorize a national bank, Madison (a member of the House) argued the measure was unconstitutional citing (among other things) the convention's rejection of federal chartering of corporations.[68] Years later Madison explained that the proposal on canals had been rejected either as improper to be invested in Congress, or as a power not likely to be yielded by the states.[69]

In the *Federalist Papers*, Madison minimized the scope of the power to "regulate Commerce . . . among the several states." (Art. I, sec. 8, cl. 3.) The commerce clause, which also allows regulation of trade with foreign nations and Indian Tribes, is one, he asserted, "which few opposed and from which no apprehensions are entertained."[70] This clause was not an important issue in the ratification debates and met with only scattered opposition, the domestic portion apparently not being thought of as a grant of extensive power to the national government. Hamilton did not expound on the domestic power in the *Federalist Papers*. Madison explained that the domestic power was supplemental to the foreign one without which the latter would have been incomplete and ineffectual. A material object of the domestic provision, he wrote, was to relieve states which import and export through other states of improper contributions levied on them by the latter. Were the states at liberty to regulate trade between themselves, some would find ways and contrivances to impose duties even though the Constitution elsewhere barred them from doing so.[71] In 1829 he stated that the power over domestic commerce was not intended to be as extensive as that over foreign commerce; the former was negative and preventive against injustice among the states rather than for the positive purposes of the federal government.[72]

To be sure, many dispute Madison's assessment. But even if he were incorrect, and the Framers intended to grant a large commercial power to the national government, it is doubtful their purpose was to increase economic regulation in the country. Believing that economic liberties were more secure under federal than under state authorities, they sought to preempt state economic controls. They inserted the contracts clause and other restraints to prevent economic abuses by the states. The commerce clause was similarly inspired. Madison asserted in his famous *Federalist* Number 10 that a "rage for paper money, for an abolition of debts, for an equal division of property, or any other improper or wicked project, will be less apt to pervade the whole body of the Union than any particular member of it...."[73] He echoed the views of prominent nationalists such as Hamilton and Marshall who wanted to confine governmental authority over people. Thus, Professor Mann concludes that decisions of the Marshall Court supporting a broad interstate commerce power nationalized private rights and personal liberties to secure them against arbitrary state interference.[74] Framers may not have sought to impose an Adam Smith program, for, as we know, Hamilton (as the first Secretary of the Treasury) and the Federalist-dominated First Congress favored some mercantilist policies. However, they did believe individual liberties, private property, and private enterprise were safer under federal auspices. Under this interpretation, the domestic commerce clause, a major source for the growth of national controls over the years, was originally intended to accomplish just the reverse: to curb government regulation. This grant of power would in actuality limit power.

The Framers provided Congress with a limited number of economic powers in addition to the regulation of commerce (some of which would not be needed if the commerce power were very broad). These are the power to tax (but restricted on the basis of population with respect to direct taxes) and spend for constitutional purposes, borrow money, establish uniform bankruptcy laws, coin and regulate the value of money, fix standards of weights and measures, establish post offices and post roads, and grant copyrights and patents. Professor Grampp observes that the economic controls the Constitution expressly authorizes are quite modest when compared with those France and England exercised or tried to exercise during the period of mercantilism, from the sixteenth to the middle of the eighteenth century: the fixing of prices, wages, and interest rates, prohibition of forestalling and engrossing, regulating the quality of goods, licensing of labor, programs to increase the population, sumptuary control, monopoly grants and other exclusive rights, incorporation, state enterprise, and the control of foreign trade and finance, including the protection of domestic industries.[75]

Not even proposed [at the Philadelphia Convention] were the powers to control prices, wages, interest rates, the quality of goods, the conditions of their sale, and the allocation of labor. All of these powers were cherished by the *practitioners* (although not the theorists) of mercantilism, and could they have been asked for an opinion of the Constitution, they would have said it provided a feeble economic policy indeed. Those who today believe the Federal government has extensive economic authority to exercise, if it will, cannot support their belief by the records of the constitutional convention (nor the Constitution of course), because the delegates were not agreed upon the issue.[76]

The only authority allowing the establishment of a private monopoly is contained in the provision in Article I, section 8, cl. 8 that Congress may safeguard patents and copyrights for limited periods. Unlike other monopolies, patents and copyrights establish exclusive rights that enhance social and economic well-being. By enabling owners to receive increased compensation for their creativity, these rights offer individuals and corporations added incentive to spend resources and time toward making important contributions to society. Both monopolies were acceptable to Adam Smith, an archenemy of monopolies.[77] As Milton Friedman, another opponent of monopoly power, has observed, patents and copyrights advance property rights and therefore are in a different class from other government-supported monopolies. He concludes that a strong prima facie case clearly exists for our society's protecting them.[78]

Professor Martin Diamond notes that the functions of the new government most frequently discussed and "most vehemently emphasized" in the *Federalist Papers* are its abilities to strengthen the nation against the danger of "foreign war" and to secure it from the danger of "domestic convulsion."[79] These are, of course, the most justifiable reasons for restraining liberty and granting power to government. They correspond to the principle that limitations on freedom are acceptable only when they are necessary to safeguard a compelling interest of the state. Separation, enumeration, checks, balances, and protection of rights were all intended to limit the dominion of government.

Madison and Hamilton were apprehensive about perils all governments pose to freedom. Thus, in *Federalist* Number 10, Madison addressed what he and other Framers deemed a major problem of republican government: the threat which "factions" present to property, economic, and other public interests. *Faction* he defined as a "number of citizens, whether amounting to a majority or minority of the whole, who are united and actuated by some common impulse of passion, or of interest, adverse to the rights of other citizens, or to the permanent and aggregate interests of the community."[80] Madison and Hamilton each thought, for different reasons, that the new government would overcome this problem.

The Framers might well be described as commercial republicans. Professor Lerner writes that a group of influential eighteenth-century thinkers—Charles Montesquieu, Adam Smith, David Hume, Benjamin Franklin, John Adams, and Benjamin Rush—advocated development of a state dedicated to commerce, regarding it as "a more sensible and realizable alternative to earlier notions of civic virtue and a more just alternative to the theological-political regime that had so long ruled Europe and its colonial periphery."[81] While Lerner does not discuss the attitudes of the Framers (except for Franklin), he describes a philosophy of government they would have found acceptable. The men Lerner writes about harbored diverse views concerning the nature of society and man, but he believes they were brethren-in-arms in preferring the kind of commercial republic which can be defined best by what it rejects: constraints and preoccupations based on visions of perfection beyond the reach of all or most; disdain for the common, useful, and mundane; judgments founded on a man's inherited status rather than on his acts.

The commercial republic substituted the wants, preoccupations, and designs of "the great mob of mankind" (Adam Smith's words) in place of those that appealed to the ruling classes. The destiny of the state was to be tied to the predominant concerns of the people—economic and other liberties—which meant releasing them from an obligation to support the visions of the politically powerful. This system would provide goods and services more abundantly and with greater humanity. Commerce, states Lerner, commended itself to these thinkers because it promised a cure for destructive prejudices and irrational enthusiasms, many of them clerically inspired. Their apprehensions about the new state were less than their misgivings about the old.

Decisions reached at the Constitutional Convention indicate to me that it was similarly inspired. The Framers' plan of diffused power could not be achieved if the ultimate economic authority rested with monarchs or majorities. A nonauthoritarian republic had to rely on the individual liberties of the people, who must be allowed to pursue their personal interests and concerns. It could not endure if the state could select the goals of their lives. In the eternal contest between liberty and authority, the existence of a commerically oriented state demanded preference for the former.

Limitations on the Judicial Power

The function traditionally exercised by the judiciary in protecting personal interests has taken a significant turn in contemporary times. Federal judicial review is no longer confined to vetoing legislative encroachments on liberty, but now dispenses what I term "affirmative jurisprudence" that supervises public expenditure and influences taxation policy.[82] Instead of exercising a negative on the other branches and limiting the power and size of government—and therefore the impositions upon ownership and enterprise—the judiciary has become another producer of laws and expander of government. Professor Nagel describes the development as follows:

> In recent years, both popular and academic attention has begun to focus on the innovative and expansive remedies that federal courts have utilized with increasing frequency, especially against state governments. These forms of relief raise the question whether the judiciary has begun to tolerate in itself a blending of functions that would never be tolerated in another branch of government. Federal district courts largely have assumed the duties of administering a state mental health system and a state prison. Many federal courts are intimately involved with operating public school systems, and one court has placed a public high school directly under judicial control. For some years, of course, courts have mandated state apportionment schemes. One court has ordered the reorganization of an entire city government. In short, courts have exercised traditionally executive functions by appointing executive and quasi-executive officers responsible to the judiciary and by determining administrative processes in elaborately detailed decrees; they have exercised legislative functions by setting policy standards for the operation of state and federal programs, including the setting of budgetary requirements.[83]

This new role comes at the expense of our constitutional system. The structure of the federal government expressly contemplates a separation of legislative, executive, and judicial powers, except as otherwise provided. Thus the Constitution delegates a series of legislative or policy-making powers to Congress and authorizes it to make all laws necessary and proper for executing these powers. The organizational intention is that Congress should not exercise any powers beyond or not implicit in the delegation, thereby limiting its legislative authority.

No policy-making or executive authority is granted to the judiciary. Consequently, the courts are left to exercise only those policy-making powers that are inherently related to the judicial function. These implied powers are those that must necessarily refer to the judiciary in the nature of that institution.[84] The judicial power is distinguishable from one enabling the legislature or other governmental bodies to adopt various laws and regulations to deal with contemporary problems, and to enact taxation and spending measures. Nor does this power contemplate administering government agencies.

Under the American system of separation of powers, there are necessarily times when courts must be limited in the relief they can provide. "It is also essential to the successful working of this system that the persons intrusted with power in any one of these branches shall not be permitted to encroach upon the powers confided to the others, but that each shall by the law of its creation be limited to the exercise of the powers appropriate to its own department and no other."[85] The U.S. Supreme Court has in the past accepted this course, even when the equities dictated otherwise. Thus, in response to demands that a court assume local governmental functions through a judicial receivership to prevent Memphis from dishonoring its obligations to creditors, Justices Field, Bradley, and Miller, all strong believers in property rights, replied in a concurring opinion that the judiciary is limited in its powers:

> If the State will not levy a tax, or provide for one, the Federal judiciary cannot assume the legislative power of the State and proceed to levy the tax. If the State has provided incompetent officers of collection, the Federal judiciary cannot remove them and put others more competent in their place. If the State appoints no officers of collection, the Federal judiciary cannot assume to itself that duty. It cannot take upon itself to supply the defects and omissions of State legislation. It would ill perform the duties assigned to it by assuming power properly belonging to the legislative department of the State.[86]

Whatever else its role may be, the judiciary was not perceived in the eighteenth century as a policy-making body capable of substituting its will for that of the legislature. In reviewing legislation, its power was to be exercised entirely through negative action in the sense that it would do little more than annul laws that violated the Constitution. At the time of the Constitutional Convention, I am not aware that any court had ever assumed any other stance with respect to interpreting written constitutions. The few precedents for judicial review then existing involved negative actions.[87] Justice Cardozo advises that similar principles guided the interpretation of the common law. "The theory of the older writers was that judges did not legislate at all. A pre-existing rule was there, imbedded, if concealed, in the body of the customary law.

All that the judges did was throw off the wrappings, and expose the statue [*sic*] to our view."[88] John Marshall said that "Courts are the mere instruments of the law, and can will nothing."[89] Hamilton explained that the judiciary "has no influence over either the sword or the purse" and would have "neither FORCE nor WILL but merely judgment."[90] Blackstone theorized about rules of law that were found but not made by judges, whom he referred to as repositories of the law and living oracles.[91]

Judges theorized their role to be discovering and applying custom, tradition, and precedent, not creating new rules. While unreasonable or invalid existing rules could be rejected, judicial innovation was thought to be an impermissible exercise of will. Justice Iredell maintained "that the distinct boundaries of law and Legislation [not] be confounded," for "that would make Courts arbitrary, and in effect *makers of a new law,* instead of being (as certainly they alone ought to be) *expositors of an existing one.*"[92] According to Chief Justice Marshall: "The province of the court is, solely, to decide on the rights of individuals, not to inquire how the executive, or executive officers, perform duties in which they have a discretion. Questions in their nature political, or which are, by the constitution and laws, submitted to the executive, can never be made in this court."[93]

The Framers' generation viewed the judiciary as another means for achieving libertarian objectives of government. The Framers surely never would have accepted judicial review if they thought it would have been used in an antilibertarian fashion. The debates and votes on the proposed council of revision indicate that the majority rejected an affirmative constitutional role for the judiciary. Courts now exercise these affirmative powers under the assumption they are necessary to redress constitutional violations. However, need (a highly subjective determination) does not create authority. The limitations on power are themselves predicated on the highest moral principles. Madison and Hamilton believed that a judiciary "not separated from the legislative and executive powers" was a threat to "general liberties"[94] and its members potential "oppressors."[95]

Concluding Observations

The federal judiciary has wandered far from its mission. Persons who should have access to these courts are effectively denied it, and the courts engage in practices belonging to other governmental bodies. Such departures from original design should be of concern to more than strict constructionists. They represent fundamental change in the function of a most powerful institution brought about by that body itself—the very one which the Framers relied upon most to maintain constitutional integrity. To this extent, the trust originally reposed in the judiciary has been compromised.

However, in interpreting the Constitution, many do not regard the pursuit of neutral principle as the highest and ultimate objective. Eminent members of the legal community believe the United States Supreme Court is generally fulfilling its constitutional responsibility, consistent with contemporary wisdom, needs, and understandings. Theirs is a pragmatic outlook which accepts judicial accommodation to events.

Most of those who hold this position consider economic due process as no longer appropriate to our times. Part II of this book attempts to evaluate this thesis by describing and analyzing the High Court's record between 1897 and 1937, when this doctrine was in vogue. The balance of this book speaks further to this issue by exploring the role of courts in the pursuit of a free, humane, and plentiful society. In essence, this inquiry seeks to determine whether constitutional principle has been needlessly breached.

II *The Substantive Due Process Era*

5   The Allgeyer-Lochner-Adair-Coppage Constitutional Doctrine

This chapter is devoted to discussing what Justice Black contemptuously referred to as the *Allgeyer-Lochner-Adair-Coppage* constitutional doctrine.[1] In these four cases, the United States Supreme Court employed concepts that frequently guided its substantive due process decisions handed down between 1897 and 1937. The last three, which concern labor disputes, are probably the most controversial of the due process decisions and should not necessarily be considered representative of the period, in that in other cases the Old Court sustained most labor legislation. Nevertheless, they are important for the magnitude of their impact. In the next chapter I shall analyze other important economic due process decisions that are both more representative of the era and more palatable to today's tastes and that, perhaps to the surprise of some, express positions similar to those taken by many modern economists. In chapter 7 I shall conclude the analysis with a discussion of the substantive due process Court's major opinions dealing with intellectual and family liberties.

Liberty of Contract

The historical background presented in chapter 2 should help the reader understand the judicial perspectives of the era in which these cases were decided. The expansion of the due process concept during the late nineteenth century occurred in the fashion of the common law to progressively extend its coverage. In each of the four decisions, the Justices stated they were not intruding on the legislative function, but were enforcing constitutionally guaranteed rights. They asserted that the Constitution limited the power of government to diminish the right of contract. The decision that gave constitutional status to liberty of contract is *Allgeyer v. Louisiana,* an 1897 unanimous opinion,[2] which aroused few passions.

A Louisiana statute made it illegal and punishable for any person, firm, or corporation to obtain marine insurance on Louisiana property from an out-of-state company that had not been licensed to carry on such business in the state. The Allgeyer company was charged with violating the statute by entering into a contract for marine insurance with a New York insurance company that had not complied with Louisiana's law. The defendant objected that the law violated both the equal protection and due process clauses of the Fourteenth Amendment. The trial court entered judgment for the company, but the Louisiana Supreme Court reversed.

Justice Peckham, writing for the United States Supreme Court, overruled the Louisiana high court, declaring that the statute violated the Fourteenth Amendment by depriving the defendant of its liberty to contract for insurance:

> The liberty mentioned in that amendment means not only the right of the citizen to be free from the mere physical restraint of his person, as by incarceration, but the term is deemed to embrace the right of the citizen to be free in the enjoyment of all his faculties; to be free to use them in all lawful ways; to live and work where he will; to earn his livelihood by any lawful calling; to pursue any livelihood or avocation, and for that purpose to enter into all contracts which may be proper, necessary and essential to his carrying out to a successful conclusion the purposes above mentioned.[3]

Peckham cited two sources to support this holding, Justice Bradley's concurring opinion in the second New Orleans slaughter-house case and Justice Harlan's majority decision in the oleomargarine case. Justice Bradley had asserted:

> The right to follow any of the common occupations of life is an inalienable right. It was formulated as such under the phrase "pursuit of happiness" in the Declaration of Independence, which commenced with the fundamental proposition that "all men are created equal, that they are endowed by their Creator with certain inalienable rights; that among these are life, liberty and the pursuit of happiness." This right is a large ingredient in the civil liberty of the citizen.... I hold that the liberty of pursuit—the right to follow any

of the ordinary callings of life—is one of the privileges of a citizen in the United States.[4]

Justice Harlan amplified these observations:

> The main proposition advanced by the defendant is that his enjoyment upon terms of equality with all others in similar circumstances of the privilege of pursuing an ordinary calling or trade, and of acquiring, holding and selling property, is an essential part of his rights of liberty and property, as guaranteed by the Fourteenth Amendment. The court assents to this general proposition as embodying a sound principle of constitutional law.[5]

Thus the right to make all proper and necessary contracts must be included in the right to pursue an ordinary calling or trade and to acquire, hold, and sell property. Every individual and corporate entrepreneur could now claim the protection of the Federal Constitution against local and state restrictions that limited economic opportunity. Thus did economic due process arrive officially for a long stay at the nation's highest judicial level. Pursuant to the police power, government could seek to impose regulation, but its authority had to be justified in each situation. For the challenged legislation to survive, the state had to persuade the Court that the legislation did not diminish arbitrarily the aggrieved party's protected rights.

The technique by which liberty of contract was established was neither unique nor extraordinary in American jurisprudence. The Court's conception of due process had evolved to a new level. The declarations of Justices Peckham, Bradley, and Harlan have been reiterated in substance, in one form or another, throughout the history of the Supreme Court. Rights do not have to be named in the Constitution to be accorded the full authority of that document. Justices have, as shown previously, found limitations on state authority, not necessarily because of a specific constitutional command, but because in their ultimate but finite wisdom, they believed such limitations promoted justice.

The reversal in the Court's position from the *Slaughter-House Cases* to *Allgeyer* has been detailed and explained in chapter 2. To that discussion may be added several pragmatic factors. The Court's composition had changed almost completely. The origins and primary intent of the Civil War amendments became blurred as the concerns of the Reconstruction period subsided. Society was also changing; the shift from agriculture to industry became more pronounced. And, as I shall explain later in this chapter, laissez-faire was serving well, and allowing the nation to attain a dominant position in world affairs. The system offered an abundance that mankind had never before experienced.

Lochner

The second and undoubtedly most famous of the "discredited" cases is *Lochner v. New York*.[6] In 1895, New York had enacted, as part of a measure establishing sanitary and other working conditions for bakeries and confectioneries, a provision limiting to sixty the number of hours an employee in such establishments could "be required or permitted" to work each week, with a maximum of ten hours a day. The defendant employer had been indicted for a violation of this provision and found guilty by the trial court. His conviction was upheld by both the appellate division of the New York Supreme Court (3–2)[7] and the state's court of appeals (4–3).[8] The defendant had demurred to the indictment, partly on the ground that the law violated his liberty under the due process clause. Again, Justice Peckham delivered the opinion of the United States Supreme Court, but this time he spoke for only a bare majority.

The state argued that the law was a legitimate exercise of police power, intended to preserve the health of workers by limiting work hours in a potentially unhealthful occupation. In support of this argument, the state presented evidence of hazards to bakers' health from long working hours.

As in all cases involving regulatory legislation, the Court could pursue one of three alternative inquiries. First, it could select the approach, set forth in Justice Holmes's dissent, that would usually allow the legislative judgment to prevail in socioeconomic matters. Legislation would be upheld "unless it can be said that a rational and fair man necessarily would admit that the statute proposed would infringe fundamental principles as they have been understood by the traditions of our people and our law."[9] Second, it could accept the thesis of another dissenter, Justice Harlan (grandfather of the Warren Court's Justice Harlan), that the law's benefit to the workers' health was debatable and that, therefore, allowing for an honest difference of opinion, the Court should not interfere with the legislative determination. The third alternative, the one used by the majority, required the state to show beyond question the wisdom of and need for the law:

> The act must have a . . . direct relation, as a means to an end, and the end itself must be appropriate and legitimate, before an act can be

held to be valid which interferes with the general right of an individual to be free in his person and in his power to contract in relation to his own labor.[10]

Justice Peckham's opinion builds on the base established in *Allgeyer*. The right to contract for the purchase and sale of labor is protected by the due process clauses unless special circumstances overcome that strong presumption. The state must demonstrate to the Court's satisfaction the existence of such circumstances. "There must be more than the mere fact of the possible existence of some small amount of unhealthiness to warrant legislative interference with liberty."[11] Laws tending to make people healthier were not necessarily valid as health laws enacted under the police power. The proclaimed purpose of the law was not controlling, and more than speculative conclusions and paternalism had to be shown. New York had not proven that a material danger to the employees' or the public's health would exist if working hours were not curtailed pursuant to the legislation. Unless the courts restrained the legislatures, all individual actions would in time be at the mercy of majorities, and none could escape this all-pervading power.

Peckham observed that the Court previously had upheld a Utah law limiting employment in underground mines and in smelters to eight hours a day except in cases of emergency.[12] However, because the New York law covered a situation considered by the majority far less perilous, and because it allowed no exceptions, it was distinguishable from the Utah statute. As Justice Harlan noted, the Court would have come to an opposite conclusion had the law limited employment to eighteen hours a day, for working a longer period would indeed be detrimental to health. Peckham implied that the other parts of the New York law relating to sanitation and working conditions were valid exercises of the police power.

As indicated in chapter 2, considerable precedent existed at the state level for the majority decision, and Peckham cited five state cases invalidating legislative "interferences" with ordinary trades and occupations. Three struck down on due process or equal protection grounds the regulation and licensing of the horseshoeing trade.[13] These laws required that the person practicing the trade be examined and certified for competency by an administrative board. In one of the cases, New York sought unsuccessfully to justify such a law as a health regulation.[14] Peckham also included the Nebraska holding invalidating a maximum hours law that required substantial pay increases for work in excess of eight hours a day and the Pennsylvania decision outlawing a statute fixing the rate of wages for puddlers.[15] In these cases, Peckham stated, the courts had upheld the rights of free contract, including the purchase and sale of labor upon mutually acceptable terms.

That the substantive due process Court was not totally averse to welfare measures is demonstrated by the fact that it sustained many challenged labor laws. Its upholding of the Utah law limiting hours of work has already been noted. In 1908, the Court accepted a statute imposing a ten-hour workday on women employed in a factory or laundry,[16] and in 1917, it found valid a regulation that limited to ten hours the working day of any person employed in any mill, factory, or manufacturing establishment but that allowed some exceptions, including a three-hour overtime period with time-and-a-half pay.[17] Other instances are set forth in the next chapter.

Under substantive due process, a legislature could circumscribe liberty of contract to purchase or sell labor if the measure clearly secured worker health and well-being. In *Lochner,* Harlan cited considerable professional support for the legislative determination that the hours limitation accomplished this result. However, even if correct in this respect, such evidence does not resolve the issue. Means-ends analysis requires consideration of the benefits as well as detriments of legislation. Harlan's opinion fails to consider that the mandated reduction in working hours might also create appreciable problems for workers. First, their pay might be decreased, possibly near the same proportion as the reduction in hours. Peckham noted that limitations upon hours "might seriously cripple the ability of the laborer to support himself and his family."[18]

Second, if wages were not reduced proportionately to hours and there was no compensating improvement in worker productivity, the price of labor would rise and less of it would be utilized (because the higher the wage, the less amount of labor demanded). Shortening long working hours generally tends to increase labor productivity and thereby operates to raise hourly wages. The extent to which this will occur in any specific situation is, however, speculative. The *Lochner* statute would have reduced average working hours roughly by about 15–20 percent.[19] Labor experience suggests that a like increase in the productivity of the bakery workers would be extraordinary.[20]

Third, only part of the industry maintained long working hours, as I shall shortly explain, and this portion (obviously) would be most adversely affected. Many of the employers included in this group would not be able to recoup sufficiently their added labor costs through higher prices, and consequently would be forced out of business. The employees would lose their jobs.

Professor William Panschar has described the nation's turn-of-the-century baking industry as a study in contrasts. The largest segment of the industry was the small-scale bakeries, which differed little from their colonial counterparts. The other portion consisted of industrial bakers using the more mechanized baking techniques and distribution methods familiar to contemporary society. The trend was clearly toward greater industrialization.[21] New York's law, aimed at regulating structural, sanitary, mechanical, and working conditions, would have only hastened the process by adding to the small owners' costs, but would not have significantly altered this movement over the long run.

Kyrk and Davis supply national statistics showing the industry's changing structure. In 1899, only 2 percent of the baking establishments were owned by corporations, as compared with 7 percent in 1919. During this period the corporate portion of the industry's output rose from 28.7 to 51.8 percent. Between 1909 and 1919, the average number of wage-earners in corporate-controlled bakeries was about forty-four, as contrasted with an average work force of fewer than three people in the bakeries under other forms of ownership.[22]

In New York, as elsewhere, the baking industry was split between sizable bakeries whose plants had been specifically built or fully converted for such purposes, and small bakeries, operating out of limited, often subterranean quarters not originally intended for such use. The Bureau of the Census reports that in 1905, there were 3,164 bakeries in New York State, of which 2,870 were owned by individuals, 228 by firms, and 64 by corporations. In that year, the individuals employed 10,804 workers, the firms 1,672, and the corporations 5,232—averaging 3.76, 7.33, and 81.75 workers per enterprise, respectively. Percentage of total bakery output maintained by each group was 62.5, 9.7, and 27.8. The New York trend was also toward bigger operations: in 1900, individuals had owned 2,767, firms 188, and corporations 44 bakery establishments.[23]

Contemporary articles in the *New York Times* reported that sanitary, health, and working conditions in the small bakeries were far below those in the large ones. Referring to the statute in question, Frederick Endres, secretary of a journeyman bakers' and confectioners' union, explained: "Of course the bill was not aimed at the big bakeries, for they invariably comply with sanitary regulations, but it was directed against the small bakeries, where every sanitary consideration is disregarded.''[24] The same sentiment was echoed by Edward Thimme, editor of the *Bakers' Journal,* who argued ''The cause of this trouble is that the small bakeries are owned by ignorant persons. The large bakeries are conducted in an exemplary manner.''[25] Conrad Moll, president of a small bakery owners' association, complained: ''It is impossible for the small bakeries to comply with all the laws. The laws are all in favor of the large bakeries and the aim seems to be to drive the small bakeries out of business.''[26]

Working hours were much longer in the small bakeries than in the large ones, and the maximum hours provision hit employers and employees of the former much more. In a report dated 27 January 1896, almost seven months after the effective date of the law, state factory inspectors reported that workers in some small bakeries (''found in noisesome cellars and unfit surroundings'') remained on the business premises (if not actually on the job) from twelve to as many as twenty-two hours a working day. The workday in the larger firms (''those conducted on a modern plan with improved appliances and proper workrooms'') met or was close to the statutory maximum of ten hours.[27]

A survey by the State Labor Bureau in 1896 of eight New York cities disclosed that the bakers' average working time per week was 72⅔ hours.[28] Many workers in the small bakeries of New York City, and probably elsewhere in the state, were recent immigrants unable to speak English, who were attracted to owners speaking their language. The small owners frequently provided their laborers with sleeping quarters, enabling them to spend long hours on the job. The time limitation on working hours would have forced the small owners to hire additional help. Because the reduction in hours might be less than a day's work, it might be difficult to hire someone at the existing rate of pay. As for current employees, it is unlikely that weekly wages, which already were very low, could be cut proportionately to approximate the decrease in working hours, or that worker productivity would increase sufficiently to compensate for this difference. Consequently the restrictions on working hours meant higher labor costs for the small bakers, who, due to competition from the corporate bakers, were limited in the amount they could pass on in the form of higher prices. A number of the small bakers would have to terminate their businesses.

The effect on the larger bakeries would be far less adverse. They were much closer to the hour standard, and unlike the small bakeries, they might sustain a modest increase in costs if they had to hire more workers. However, extra production costs would be offset by the lessened competition from the small bakeries, which would lead to higher prices. I have been unable to learn the large bakeries' position on New York's statute, but their support for all of its provisions would certainly not be surprising.[29]

Presumably, the bulk of the workers in the small bakeries were engaged in the most remunerative employment they could find. This was particularly true for the new immigrants, whose knowledge of English and their new country was limited. The question arises of how the health and welfare of the people who worked long, arduous hours for relatively small wages would be helped by substantially lowering their working time and wages, leaving them with more leisure but much less to spend on the necessities of life. Perhaps worst of all, those employed by bakeries driven out of business by the added costs would lose their jobs. Nor could a law under these circumstances be very effective: violations (prior to the law being declared unconstitutional) probably were extensive.[30] The law could not alleviate the needs of an ever-increasing flood of immigrants, eager to satisfy their wants and ambitions.

The reaction to *Lochner* might have been less harsh had the critics recognized that the law probably would have reduced considerably the wages of many low-paid workers, and caused others to lose their jobs. Commentators may still insist that from the perspective of the workers' health less pay is preferable to long hours in an unpleasant environment. This is far more true for workers in underground mines and smelting than, say, clerks in commercial offices. Bakery workers are somewhere in between, and for the *Lochner* majority the evidence in this regard, given prevailing labor conditions, was not sufficiently clear to allow for legislative interference.

In any case, the average length of the working day for bakery employees nationally declined from about ten hours in 1909, to nine hours in 1914, to eight hours in 1919, lengthening slightly in 1921.[31] A survey of working hours for union workers in various industries shows that on the average, union bakers worked 64.5 hours per week in 1890, 59.3 in 1905, 52.5 in 1915, and 47.8 in 1926.[32]

Over the years, this nation has learned that a considerable amount of social and economic legislation has not served its intended purpose and has been frequently counterproductive. From the foregoing data, one can conclude that New York's restriction on working hours would have had a relatively short-term impact. Moreover, if effective, it might have been a highly destructive influence on the lives of the workers it sought to help.

Some critics of the *Lochner* decision assume that the hours limitation reflected the will of the workers. They note that unions strongly supported the law, and contend that the elimination of "such drudgery" could only be a "blessing" for the workers affected. As previously suggested, this conclusion is questionable. Contemporary experience discloses that people at various stations in life willingly accept what to others might be unpleasant, difficult, dangerous, or unhealthful work, because it provides more pay and/or other personal satisfactions than less arduous or hazardous employment. Consider in this regard an article by Deborah Sue Yaeger in the 31 May 1979 Wall Street Journal, describing a contemporary situation reminiscent of the *Lochner* facts.[33] A summary of portions of the article follows.

In 1978 a fifty-hour work week, without overtime pay, would seem anachronistic in the continental United States. Federal and state laws mandate a shorter week, and unions compel employers to observe the legal maximum or even less. However, it is estimated that in 1978, 8,000 Chinese were working in 400 garment factories in New York City's Chinatown for longer hours at lower wages than are allowed under federal or union standards. Almost all of these workers are women—largely immigrants from Hong Kong, Taiwan, and mainland China. They work more than the union's hourly rate maximum of thirty-five hours a week and usually receive no overtime pay. They are paid on a piecework basis and may earn below the union's hourly minimum. Some workers receive limited additional benefits and gifts, but generally not enough to offset the union scale. Employers may sponsor immigrants, lend them money, and generally foster an air of paternalism that tends to minimize protests.

The lofts in which they work, often four stories above the streets, are walk-ups. Whirring and vibrating sewing machines create a constant din; finished clothing is hung on pipe racks, and in older factories peeling plaster is an added hazard. Because of the lint-filled air, workers have to wear surgical masks.

But this is America, and the International Ladies Garment Workers Union (ILGWU) claims it represents 90 percent of Chinatown workers—so how is such "exploitation" possible? The workers do not complain; some fear being fired, but all look upon these jobs as the best available to them. Attorney Norman Lou Kee, a member of the city's Human Rights Commission, explains that the "Chinatown garment industry is an employment resource for a large segment of our people. Without it, we would have suffered greatly in terms of immigrant families having a viable way of earning a decent living and becoming entrepreneurs themselves." Although they are aware of the situation,

union and government officials have not substantially increased polic-
ing of the factories. Apparently these officials accept conditions largely
as they are. Enforcement of the rules would destroy these companies
and greatly limit the workers' employment opportunities.

A Teaching of Lochner

An important teaching of *Lochner* lies in its analysis of legislative
tendencies to control people's livelihoods. Absent judicial review, the
legislatures and regulatory agencies will determine with finality when
and under what conditions individuals will be allowed to pursue a
business, trade, occupation, or profession. The *Lochner* Court explained the problem in this manner:

> It might be safely affirmed that almost all occupations more or less
> affect the health. There must be more than the mere fact of the
> possible existence of some small amount of unhealthiness to warrant
> legislative interference with liberty. It is unfortunately true that
> labor, even in any department, may possibly carry with it the seeds
> of unhealthiness. But are we all, on that account, at the mercy of
> legislative majorities? A printer, a tinsmith, a locksmith, a carpenter,
> a cabinetmaker, a dry goods clerk, a bank's, a lawyer's, or a physi-
> cian's clerk, or a clerk in almost any kind of business, would all come
> under the power of the legislature, on this assumption. No trade, no
> occupation, no mode of earning one's living, could escape this all-
> pervading power, and the acts of the legislature in limiting the hours
> of labor in all employments would be valid, although such limitation
> might seriously cripple the ability of the laborer to support himself
> and his family . . . .
>   It is also urged, pursuing the same line of argument, that it is to the
> interest of the State that its population should be strong and robust,
> and therefore any legislation which may be said to tend to make
> people healthy must be valid as health laws, enacted under the police
> power. If this be a valid argument and a justification for this kind of
> legislation, it follows that the protection of the Federal Constitution
> from undue interference with liberty of person and freedom of con-
> tract is visionary, wherever the law is sought to be justified as a valid
> exercise of the police power. Scarcely any law but might find shelter
> under such assumptions, and conduct, properly so called, as well as
> contract, would come under the restrictive sway of the legislature.[34]

The prophetic nature of these words was realized a half century later
in *Williamson v. Lee Optical Co.*,[35] which sustained a law requiring
(among other things) a prescription from an optometrist or ophthal-

nologist before an optician could fit old lenses into a new frame. The
act was challenged as violating both due process and equal protection.
Justice Douglas wrote that although the law may exact a "needless,
wasteful requirement in many cases,"[36] the legislature might have
concluded that the waste was justified in order to achieve the objective
of protecting health. Douglas did not rely on legislative history or declarations stating the purpose of the regulation. Instead, *Lee Optical* is
one of a number of cases in which the Supreme Court reasoned that the
legislature "might have" reached certain conclusions. In 1976, the
Court in *Dukes* essentially maintained this standard and held that in the
local economic sphere only "the inviduous discrimination, the wholly
arbitrary act" violated the Fourteenth Amendment.[37] It has been observed that under this rule any law that legislators pass will be
sustained unless they were in a complete state of lunacy at the time they
acted.[38]

   Under *Allgeyer* and *Lochner,* the legislatures had to show real and
substantial reasons for regulating people's lives; in contrast, under *Lee
Optical* and its succcessors, the courts will discover a plausible explanation even if the lawmakers have none. This approach necessitates a
complete judicial withdrawal from an area of vital importance to a great
many individuals in various stations of life and to the efficient operation
of our society. Thus, as Posner observes, a "state statute that, on
grounds of public health, forbids opticians to replace eyeglass frames
without a prescription signed by an optometrist or ophthalmologist can
have no real purpose other than to increase the income of optometrists
and ophthalmologists at the expense of opticians—and consumers."[39]
Individual freedom is left entirely to whatever compassion lawmakers
are prepared, or are in a position, to grant. The *Lochner* principle is
suited to a society of limited government. By creating an additional
hurdle that must be surmounted, its application screens the legislative
processes and requires due consideration for the plight of the losers in
political struggles. Unlike the contemporary Supreme Court, the
Lochner majority found it impossible "to shut our eyes to the fact that
many of the laws of this character, while passed under what is claimed
to be the police power for the purpose of protecting the public health or
welfare, are, in reality, passed from other motives."[40]

The Union Cases

Although demanding more than sixty hours of labor a week seems
exploitative to modern sensibilities, even more anguish surrounds the

thought of an employer firing an employee for engaging in union activ
ity. Today, a great many people would favor a law forbidding em
ployers from requiring a person, as a condition of employment, to
agree not to become or remain a member of a labor union. Proponents
of such a law probably would include most of the Supreme Cour
Justices appointed by President Franklin Roosevelt and his successors
It is doubtful that these jurists could ever be persuaded that such legis
lation is unconstitutional. In this regard, adverse reaction to the *Adai*
and *Coppage* decisions is understandable. But this attitude fails to
perceive the wisdom of an earlier day concerning the sanctity of con
tractual arrangements.

Both of these cases involved antiunion promises that the union
called "yellow dog" contracts. The constitutionality of a federal stat
ute outlawing such contracts in the railroad industry was at issue in the
1907 case of *Adair v. United States.*[41] There a railroad agent had been
convicted of violating the statute by firing an employee for belonging to
a union. The United States Supreme Court reversed on the con
stitutional ground that Congress could not make criminal the discharge
of an employee because of his membership in a labor organization. A
6–2 majority found that the law in question invaded both the persona
liberty and right of property protected by the Fifth Amendment. Jus
tices Holmes and McKenna dissented.

Seven years later, a majority of six Justices took a similar position in
Coppage v. Kansas,[42] setting aside, pursuant to the Fourteenth
Amendment, the conviction under a Kansas statute of a railroad agen
for discharging an employee who would neither sign an agreement to
withdraw from a union nor resign from it. Again Holmes was one o
three dissenters.

These cases presented essentially the same issue as *Lochner:* I
there sufficient reason for the legislation to qualify as an exception to
the prevailing doctrine of liberty of contract? The laws in these case
were advanced as promoting the growth of unionism, which, it was
argued, was essential for the public welfare. The court viewed the
controversy in much narrower terms, as Justice Harlan in *Adair* ex
plained:

> The right of a person to sell his labor upon such terms as he deem
> proper is, in its essence, the same as the right of the purchaser o
> labor to prescribe the conditions upon which he will accept such
> labor from the person offering to sell it. So the right of the employé to
> quit the service of the employer, for whatever reason, is the same a
> the right of the employer, for whatever reason, to dispense with the
> service of such employé.[43]

In *Coppage,* Justice Pitney asserted that the antiunion requirement was no more onerous than the condition that an employee work full time exclusively for a single employer. He wrote that whenever the right of private property exists, "there must and will be inequalities of fortune; and thus it naturally happens that parties negotiating about a contract are not equally unhampered by circumstances."[44] Accordingly, to deprive a negotiating party of the advantage of a superior situation, brought about by such circumstances, is to deprive that party of a property right. The quest for economic equality is constitutionally limited. The Justice continued:

> This applies to all contracts, and not merely to that between em-
> ployer and employé. Indeed a little reflection will show that wher-
> ever the right of private property and the right of free contract
> coexist, each party when contracting is inevitably more or less in-
> fluenced by the question whether he has much property, or little, or
> none; for the contract is made to the very end that each may gain
> something that he needs or desires more urgently than that which he
> proposes to give in exchange. And, since it is self-evident that, un-
> less all things are held in common, some persons must have more
> property than others, it is from the nature of things impossible to
> uphold freedom of contract and the right of private property without
> at the same time recognizing as legitimate those inequalities of for-
> tune that are the necessary result of the exercise of those rights.[45]

Such passages do not endear the Court to reformers determined to use the judiciary and legislatures to reduce social and economic inequalities. These people see *Adair* and *Coppage* as maintaining, if not augmenting, the superior powers of employers. However, serious questions exist about the effectiveness and desirability of laws intended to offset or ameliorate inequalities, about which I shall have more to say in Part IV. For now, the reader should remember that both decisions came at a time when unions were still highly controversial institutions in this country. It is estimated that in 1910, 8.6 percent of the employee class belonged to a union.[46]

Moreover, unions raised philosophical problems for judges. In his analysis of the antislavery movement's impact upon judicial reasoning, Nelson explains that judges who had received their education or commenced their professional careers during the Civil War era viewed labor and unions much differently than does our society. Freedom of contract for both employer and employee was strongly espoused by the antislavery movement. It was accepted that the right of the individual to bestow his labor as he pleased was among the rights for which the

Civil War had been fought. Many judges of the period feared that unions would obliterate these and other legal and natural rights. Given the values that emerged triumphantly from the war, some judges found it simply "preposterous" that unions replace slaveholders and "attempt to issue orders that free men are bound to obey . . . ."[47]

Labor union practices greatly disturbed adherents of the widely followed individualist philosophy. Those joining unions had to subordinate themselves to the will of the organization. Workers who went on strike insisted that they had not given up their jobs and claimed a right to those positions over other workers eager to work. Enforcing this "right" required picket lines, threats, and at times violence directed not only at employers but also at other workers. Moreover, union policies encouraged inefficiency. In 1869, John Stuart Mill wrote: "Some of the Unionist regulations go even further than to prohibit improvements; they are contrived for the express purpose of making work inefficient; they positively prohibit the workman from working hard and well, in order that it may be necessary to employ a greater number."[48]

Accordingly, Pitney's contention in *Coppage* that government has no legitimate interest in encouraging unions was far less controversial than contemporary generations might suppose. The Court believed that the labor market itself would operate to support the welfare of both workers and employers. The fact that today a large majority of workers do not belong to unions may suggest that they do not contest this conclusion.

Despite *Adair* and *Coppage,* unions did organize thousands of workers, and their existence aided numerous others. Many workers must have received compensation for pledging not to join unions, the amounts depending on the fluctuations of the labor market.[49] These promises would have been costlier to obtain when unemployment was relatively low, as it frequently was during the first quarter of the century. That *Adair-Coppage* kept workers from flocking to unions is most doubtful. As of 1976, about forty years after legislation turned favorable to their growth, labor organization members constituted 23.2 percent of the entire labor force and 28.3 percent of nonagricultural employees.[50] The percentages of union membership peaked in the middle 1950s, reaching about 25 and 35 percent for the respective groups. These figures suggest that the laws struck down in *Adair* and *Coppage* would have denied many employees an opportunity to receive compensation for entering into antiunion agreements. Workers who rejected joining unions and/or worked for employers who overestimated the union threat received more than they relinquished when they bargained away their right to join a union. Nor would union membership necessarily be more materially rewarding. The *Coppage* Court believed that workers benefited from having the right to enter into such agreements.

In the era of *Lochner, Adair,* and *Coppage,* real wages were rising, working hours decreasing, and the country's wealth growing. By 1914, the national income exceeded that of the United Kingdom, Germany, France, Austria-Hungary, and Italy combined, and per capita income was well above that of any other great nation.[51] Between the end of the Civil War and beginning of World War I, real gross national product grew at a historically very high rate.[52] It is estimated that the purchasing power of wages (exclusive of agriculture), measured by the relationship of wages either to wholesale or to retail prices, trebled between 1840 and 1914–15.[53] Working hours declined substantially. Average daily scheduled work hours in manufacturing and mechanical establishments was 11.5 in 1850, 9.8 in 1900, and 8.5 in 1920,[54] a reduction of about 25 percent for the entire period. The average work hours per week in all manufacturing industries declined from 60 in 1890 to 50.3 in 1926.[55]

Because relatively few welfare laws and unions existed in those decades, the betterment of life must be attributed to the success of the economic system. It was not difficult to conclude that this success could be undermined by limiting entrepreneurial freedom: that which harms business also injures the livelihoods of the people. The Supreme Court's concept of liberty enabled the economy to continue providing a great measure of material benefits.

6

The Role of the Old Court in Preserving Economic Liberties

This chapter will examine substantive due process decisions of the 1920s and 1930s dealing with economic issues. As previously discussed,[1] the substantive due process Justices believed that the United States Constitution limited the powers of the federal and state governments over private economic affairs. Regulation under the police power in these areas was permissible only if mandated by special situations or circumstances.

In applying substantive due process, Justices did what can hardly be considered novel or radical under our constitutional system. They usually balanced the restraint imposed on the individual against the public benefits achieved under the statute. This procedure required evaluating the legitimacy of the act's objectives and the means used to accomplish them. It entailed applying a means-end test to determine if the statute would generally achieve its purpose and not unnecessarily affect other matters, for otherwise the restraint would be in vain or excessive. As the Court explained in 1894, "the means [must be] reasonably necessary for the accomplishment of the purpose, and not unduly oppressive upon individuals."[2] If the same purpose could be achieved through less restrictive means, the law needlessly restrained freedom. For impositions to survive the Court's scrutiny, the weight of competing interests had to come down heavily on the side of government.

Because of the subjectivity of this analysis—the elements to be considered and the weight to be given each—critics contend that the Court was involved in policy-making, similar to that which takes place when legislatures evaluate the favorable and unfavorable aspects of the measures they consider. Obviously there is truth in this allegation. Frequently the Justices did evaluate factors in the same manner as did the legislators. However, judicial review is not possible unless courts can probe and appraise legislation, and this process requires the application of subjective considerations. Substantive due process accorded significant recognition to individual rights and in theory created a protective barrier surrounding the person that Congress and the state legislatures could not penetrate without showing what a majority of the Court believed to be exceedingly good cause. The doctrine operated as another check on a system not intended to be overwhelmed by the force and coercion of the state.

This kind of balancing continued for many years after the demise of the old substantive due process, but it was not applied to the same liberties. The protective barrier remained for conceptual freedoms and was largely removed for economic freedoms. Not long after the advent of the New Deal, the Supreme Court began creating a dichotomy between intellectual and economic rights by lowering the priority of the latter. Over a period of time, a spirited controversy ensued on the Court and among the commentators about the application of a balancing approach to freedom of expression. The most vigorous opponents of balancing did not argue that it intruded into the legislative function; on the contrary, they said that the standard was too lenient, for it allowed the legislators excessive powers. Their goal was to shield certain rights almost completely from legislative or majoritarian influences. In responding to this argument, the Court eventually created the concept of fundamental personal rights and thus made sustaining legislation in this area far more difficult than it had been under the balancing formula.

To further safeguard rights from the executive and legislature, the Supreme Court during contemporary times has also created the concept of suspect classifications, intended primarily to benefit members of racial minorities. Accordingly, the Court has held that legislative classifications based on race or national origins are suspect and thus require as stringent (or possibly even more stringent) legislative justifications than those needed to sustain restrictions upon fundamental rights. When considering the cases in this and the preceding chapter, the reader should be aware that the restraints imposed on the legislatures were not extraordinary in relation to the practices of the Court during other eras.

The old substantive due process period covered about one-third of a century. Many different Justices served on the Court during this time, and they confronted a large variety of controversies. Therefore, finding inconsistencies in reasoning and results is not difficult. For example, a recent article maintains that during its tenure the Court frequently was not true to its laissez-faire reputation.[3] Justice Roberts in 1934 and Chief Justice Hughes in 1937 wrote opinions citing large numbers of prior decisions upholding regulatory laws.[4]

In *Bunting v. Oregon,*[5] the Court upheld a regulation of work hours without even referring to *Lochner*. The latter case seems to have minimized the principle that legislation is presumed to be constitutional, while the former emphasized it. In fact, in *Adkins v. Children's Hospital,*[6] a dissenting Chief Justice Taft stated that he believed that *Bunting* had overruled *Lochner*.[7] However, Justice Sutherland did not accept this perception, for in the majority decision he relied heavily on *Lochner*. Professor Corwin believed that in 1934 enough precedents were available "to approach the question of factual justification from either one of two opposed angles, to sustain a statute or to overturn it."[8] To me, the most incomprehensible decision of this period is *Village of Euclid v. Ambler Realty Co.,*[9] which validated zoning. In that decision Justice Sutherland, one of the mainstays of economic due process, ignored concepts of liberty that he had often invoked in others.

Estimates have been made about the amount of legislation that the Court invalidated. One writer determined that from 1868 to 1912, the Supreme Court struck down legislation in somewhat more than 6 percent of the cases it heard. During the period between 1913 and 1920, the percentage rose to approximately 7, and from 1920 to 1928, to 28.[10] Professor Mendelson presents this comparison of judicial vetos for four different periods:[11]

Era	Acts Invalidated		Average Invalidation Per Year
	State	Federal	
Waite restraint (1874–89)	61	8	4.3
Laissez-faire activism (1890–1936)	359	45	8.6
Frankfurter restraint (1937–60)	120	9	5.4
Mature Warren Court activism (1961–69)	132	14	16.2

Supporters of economic due process assigned high constitutional priority to safeguarding individual liberties against regulations fixing prices, barring entry into commercial activity, and prohibiting the operation of a particular business. The major exemption from this protection was businesses "affected with a public interest," the definition of which was a continual problem.

The five principal cases to be considered in this chapter cover the era between 1922 and 1934. William Howard Taft was Chief Justice from 1921 to 1930 and was succeeded by Charles Evans Hughes, who retained the office until 1941. In addition to these illustrious personalities, the Court is noted for its two ideological extremes. At one end were Justices Van Devanter (1910–37), McReynolds (1914–41), Butler (1922–39), and Sutherland (1922–38), while at the opposite were Holmes (1902–32), Brandeis (1916–39), and Stone (1925–46). Justice Cardozo (1932–38) is often identified with the second group and McKenna (1898–1925), Pitney (1912–22), Taft, and Sanford (1923–30) with the first. At the beginning of their tenures, Hughes and Roberts (1930–45) occupied middle ground, but in time their changing perceptions provided crucial victories for the second group. As we shall see in this and the subsequent chapters, the two main camps were not always united, and at times divided on important issues.

Property

The two most important property-related decisions that the Court handed down during this period did not concern liberty of contract, and they remain the law of the land. The first is *Pennsylvania Coal Co. v. Mahon*,[12] decided under that portion of the due process clause of the Fourteenth Amendment that (by judicial decision) absorbs the Fifth Amendment's prohibition against the taking of private property for public use without just compensation. *Euclid v. Ambler Realty Co.* also rested on this provision. The earlier case established a balancing test for determining constitutionality, resembling the test then frequently in vogue for economic matters. However, in *Euclid*, Justice Sutherland invoked a test corresponding to that which Justice Harlan had sought to impose in *Lochner*: if the issue was fairly debatable, the legislation would be upheld.

When the Pennsylvania Coal Company sold the property at 7 Prospect Place in Pittston, Pennsylvania, in 1878, the deed of conveyance reserved to the grantor the right to mine all the coal beneath the surface without any liability for damages occasioned in so doing. Such reservations were common in the area at that time. In 1917, the Mahons purchased the house at that address subject to such a provision. Four

years later, the state passed the Kohler Act, which prevented the coal
company from any mining on the property that would cause surface
subsidence, thus virtually eliminating the company's property and
contract interests therein. The question before the Supreme Court was
whether the state could demonstate sufficient reason to uphold the law.

The famed dissenters of the Court split on the issue. From Justice
Holmes's perspective, the case involved a specific provision of the
Constitution (taking of property) and was not an instance of according
meaning to a nebulous term (liberty). He wrote the now famous opinion
striking down the statute. Justice Brandeis's dissent did not differ from
his regular position with respect to economic interests.[13] The Justices
also disagreed on the question of whether a nuisance was involved,
Holmes denying Brandeis's contention that the legislation served to
abate a noxious use that would occur when the coal company commenced mining operations on improved property.

The arduous circumstances confronting the Mahons did not deter
Justice Holmes from applying strict views about the taking of property.

> The protection of private property in the Fifth Amendment pre-
> supposes that it is wanted for public use, but provides that it shall not
> be taken for such use without compensation. A similar assumption is
> made in the decisions upon the Fourteenth Amendment.... When
> this seemingly absolute protection is found to be qualified by the
> police power, the natural tendency of human nature is to extend the
> qualification more and more until at last private property disappears.
> But that cannot be accomplished in this way under the Constitu-
> tion....
> ... In general it is not plain that a man's misfortunes or necessities
> will justify his shifting the damages to his neighbor's shoulders....
> We are in danger of forgetting that a strong public desire to improve
> the public condition is not enough to warrant achieving the desire by
> a shorter cut than the constitutional way of paying for the change.[14]

Holmes proceeded to establish the test that balanced the value to the
public of the regulation against the loss in value to the property owner.

> If we were called upon to deal with the plaintiffs' [homeowners']
> position alone, we should think it clear that the statute does not
> disclose a public interest sufficient to warrant so extensive a de-
> struction of the defendant's [company's] constitutionally protected
> rights.
> ... The general rule at least is, that while property may be reg-
> ulated to a certain extent, if regulation goes too far it will be rec-
> ognized as a taking. It may be doubted how far exceptional cases,
> like the blowing up of a house to stop a conflagration, go—and if they

go beyond the general rule, whether they do not stand as much upon tradition as upon principle.... As we already have said, this is a question of degree—and therefore cannot be disposed of by general propositions.[15]

This reasoning is analogous to the analysis often conducted by the Court when legislation impacted liberty of contract.

Brandeis argued that so long as title remained in the owner or the property had not been seized by government, reduction in value is irrelevant: "Restriction upon use does not become inappropriate as a means, merely because it deprives the owner of the only use to which the property can then be profitably put."[16] He would invalidate regulations either that did not protect the public or that were clearly beyond redemption as an appropriate means to a valid public purpose. Brandeis's position would have effectively destroyed the taking clause, for he did not believe that judicial intervention is appropriate to relieve loss in value. The clause would provide protection only in the event title is transferred or the owner removed from possession. Inasmuch as under this view regulation could destroy virtually all value, the protection of the title interest would represent mere vindication of form over substance.

Justice Sutherland's *Euclid* opinion reversed a lower court decision that zoning is a taking of property in violation of the Fourteenth Amendment. The lower court had proceeded on the theory that property ownership is a substantive right under the due process clause that may be limited only under few and special circumstances. Sutherland did not respond to this reasoning, suggesting rather that zoning was a reasonable and possibly essential restraint that would increase over-all property values although certain parcels would be diminished in value. The opinion discusses examples of damaging consequences of land use in the absence of government direction. Sutherland's opinion upheld zoning in principle and placed the burden on the landowner to show that a particular ordinance was unreasonable and arbitrary. "[B]efore the [zoning] ordinance can be declared unconstitutional, [it must be shown to be] clearly arbitrary and unreasonable, having no substantial relation to the public health, safety, morals, or general welfare."[17] This deference to the legislature is inconsistent with the typical approach employed by the same Court for legislation affecting liberty of contract, and understandably, the three remaining stalwarts of that theory (Butler, Van Devanter, and McReynolds) dissented.

The *Euclid* principle, while initially demanding a greater judicial scrutiny than *New Orleans v. Dukes* (discussed in chapter 1 *supra*) requires, has so eroded over time that by now it would probably not differ from it, were it not for the *Pennsylvania Coal* precedent. *Dukes* permits the adoption of laws eliminating existing economic interests. However, *Pennsylvania Coal* bars legislation that substantially removes real property values. Holmes favored both the kind of judicial submission provided for in *Dukes* and the judicial intervention required under *Pennsylvania Coal*. He once stated: "The truth seems to me to be that, subject to compensation when compensation is due, the legislature may forbid or restrict any business when it has sufficient force of public opinion behind it."[18] However, in *Lochner* and *Adkins*, Holmes did concede that economic and social legislation is subject to some judicial scrutiny.

In his long series of dissents, Holmes rejected the idea that the term *liberty* in the context of contractual understandings has a justiciable meaning. As he observed in one dissent,

> Contract is not specially mentioned in the text that we have to construe. It is merely an example of doing what you want to do, embodied in the word liberty. But pretty much all law consists in forbidding men to do some things that they want to do, and contract is no more exempt from law than other acts.[19]

This objection was not applicable to the word *property*, which appears in the Constitution and has a relatively clear meaning.

The distinction Holmes drew between the words *liberty* and *property* may operate quite arbitrarily. For example, the approach taken in *Dukes* enables states to bar the pursuit of a business, trade, or profession, frequently at substantial economic cost to the individuals concerned. In *Dukes* as well as the *Skrupa* case,[20] to be discussed subsequently in chapters 8 and 9, the Court upheld laws making a business worthless. The state in a very realistic, if not technical, sense is "taking" someone's valuable assets. Nevertheless, there is no judicial recourse such as exists when tangible property ownership is involved. In economic terms, it is a distinction without a difference.

Entry into Business

New State Ice Co. v. Liebmann[21] concerned a 1925 Oklahoma statute that declared that the manufacture of ice for sale and distribution is a "public business" and conferred upon the corporation commission powers of regulation customarily exercised in connection with public utilities. The act made it a misdemeanor to engage in this business without obtaining a certificate of public convenience and necessity from the commission. This agency was given wide discretion in issuing the certificate, the law authorizing a denial whenever the existing facilities "are sufficient to meet the public needs therein."[22] The ice industry strongly backed passage of the legislation. New State had for some time been engaged in the manufacture, sale, and distribution of ice in Oklahoma City and had invested $500,000 in the business. Liebmann purchased land in the city and commenced construction of an ice plant that would compete with New State. He never applied for a certificate from the commission, and New State sued to enjoin his operation.

In response to Liebmann's constitutional challenge, two philosophical opponents squared off: Sutherland for the majority of six, and Brandeis for the minority of two (one Justice not participating). The majority said that Oklahoma had not presented justification to warrant infringing Liebmann's liberty to enter the market. The facts did not disclose a natural monopoly, damages to public health and safety, or other characteristics of a business clothed with a public interest, a designation which would allow upholding the act. Brandeis's opinion, which outweighed (31–10 pages) and outpointed (55–0 footnotes) his opponent's, also dealt much more with economic theory than did Sutherland's. But it reflected a perspective that would find limited favor among economists today. He wrote that the statute was not unreasonable or arbitrary and that it therefore should prevail. According to him, Oklahoma should at least be allowed to experiment with this effort to provide a solution to a pressing problem.[23]

The main points of Sutherland's analysis are as follows:

1. The business is essentially as private in nature

> as the business of the grocer, the dairyman, the butcher, the baker, the shoemaker, or the tailor, each of whom performs a service which, to a greater or lesser extent, the community is dependent upon and is interested in having maintained . . . . It may be quite true that in Oklahoma ice is not only an article of prime necessity, but indispensable; but certainly not more so than food or clothing or the shelter of a home.[24]

2. Entry into the ice business was costly, but this fact applies to numerous other businesses in which competition exists. Moreover, appliances to make ice could be purchased "for a comparatively moderate outlay," providing a competitive restraint on price.

3. The practical tendency of the restrictions was to shut out new

enterprises and thus to create and foster monopoly in the existing establishments.

> The control here asserted does not protect against monopoly, but tends to foster it. The aim is not to encourage competition, but to prevent it; not to regulate business, but to preclude persons from engaging in it. There is no difference in principle between this case and the attempt of the dairyman under state authority to prevent another from keeping cows and selling milk on the ground that there are enough dairymen in the business; or to prevent a shoemaker from making or selling shoes because shoemakers already in that occupation can make and sell all the shoes that are needed. We are not able to see anything peculiar in the business here in question which distinguishes it from ordinary manufacture and production . . . . There is nothing in the product that we can perceive on which to rest a distinction, in respect of this attempted control, from other products in common use which enter into free competition, subject, of course, to reasonable regulations prescribed for the protection of the public and applied with appropriate impartiality.[25]

4. Brandeis's contention that Oklahoma should be allowed to engage in this experiment to ascertain the desirability and feasibility of the law would deny constitutional protection to would-be entrepreneurs. "[T]here are certain essentials of liberty with which the state is not entitled to dispense in the interest of experiments . . . . The opportunity to apply one's labor and skill in an ordinary occupation with proper regard for all reasonable regulations is no less entitled to protection [than freedom of the press]."[26]

Brandeis's lengthy dissent constitutes an engaging explanation of the regulatory process. Those who want to learn about the theory of airline or trucking regulation will find few better sources. The Justice sought to explain how regulation could prevent the needless "waste" and "destructiveness" of competition, provide for an equitable return to producers, and allow for a wider and less costly distribution of goods to the consumer. He cited the ice industry's aversion to competition and its approval of the law to support his argument. Brandeis was not concerned that competition would be eliminated.

> It is no objection to the validity of the statute here assailed that it fosters monopoly. That, indeed, is its design. The certificate of public convenience and necessity is a device—a recent social-economic invention—through which the monopoly is kept under effective control by vesting in a commission the power to terminate it whenever that course is required in the public interest. To grant any

monopoly to any person as a favor is forbidden even if terminable. But where, as here, there is reasonable ground for the legislative conclusion that in order to secure a necessary service at reasonable rates, it may be necessary to curtail the right to enter the calling, it is, in my opinion, consistent with the due process clause to do so, whatever the nature of the business. The existence of such power in the legislature seems indispensable in our ever-changing society.[27]

Despite the extensiveness of his inquiry, Brandeis did not probe the legislative conclusion that regulation would provide greater service at more reasonable rates than does the market. He willingly accepted the legislature's contentions in this regard. Yet, possibly even under Brandeis's standards for review, the law would have to fail if such an outcome were remote or unlikely.[28] At the time he wrote, the country had little experience with economic regulation, and theory thus had to substitute for practice.

When *New State Ice* arose, competition between ice producers was very keen in some areas of the state, quite limited in others. Apparently, large areas of the state were not then served by the ice manufacturers. Economic regulation comparable to that imposed by the Oklahoma statute is usually justified as serving two main purposes: first, to stabilize the industry by limiting competition, and second, to provide services that the market does not offer. Generally, only the first objective can be realized. Cost considerations tend to inhibit achievement of the second. Thus while Oklahoma could reduce competition in the industry, the expense involved would be too great for the state to demand that the icemakers serve the entire population. They would be required to sell only within designated areas, probably not much larger than the areas served by the unregulated market.

Accomplishing the regulatory goals necessitates that consumers in areas already served or capable of being served in time by the market pay increased prices. They would have to pay a greater than competitive price because competition is restricted, and they would also be charged for the cost of expanding services, involving the cross-subsidization of one group by another. Cost-benefit analysis of such programs usually reveals a net loss to society. A number of such studies are discussed in chapter 13.

Brandeis contended that conditions of natural monopoly prevailed in the ice-making business, that it was therefore not subject to economic competition, and that monopoly was inevitable. However, the fact that the case arose indicates that this belief was not universally shared among Oklahoma business people. It is not likely that Liebmann (and many others) sought entry simply in the hope that, despite the existence of others in the industry, he was destined to be the sole survivor. Natural monopolies do not occur frequently; some economists believe that almost no industry is immune to competition.

Nor does Brandeis's presentation support the view that ice-making was a natural monopoly. He wrote: ''[T]he relative ease and cheapness with which an ice plant may be constructed exposes the industry to destructive and frequently ruinous competition.''[29] He noted testimony that about 11 percent of the state's population was served by a ''semblance of competition'' and that eight plants located in Oklahoma City and Tulsa were capable of producing daily more than 200 tons of ice for sale. These statements refute the view that the business was then a natural monopoly, inasmuch as a variety of producers were able to exist in the market. The contention that competitive warfare between these producers would result in a single monopoly firm had no basis in fact. Brandeis's description is applicable to many markets, at particular stages of development, that then or in time serve the consumer adequately. Competitive industry is often highly fluid. Companies are constantly entering and leaving, a situation that necessitates maximum efforts by existing firms to remain profitable. Bars on entry protect companies from competitive forces that operate to restrain price increases and to reduce inefficiency. Without such bars, the most efficient survive, and often with the passage of time relative stability results.

Interestingly, Brandeis was not describing an industry subject solely to marketplace dynamics. His dissent reveals that for seventeen years prior to the passage of the 1925 statute, the corporation commission had exercised jurisdiction over rates, practices, and services of ice plants. Regulatory practices frequently inhibit investment and expansion; the limited growth of this business may well be attributable to existing regulation.

Although Brandeis's footnotes cite dozens of articles and texts, one authority, whose teaching might have tempered the Justice's emphasis upon the industry's advocacy of regulation, is strikingly absent. I refer to Adam Smith, who long before Brandeis wrote, warned about support for regulation from this sector:

> The interest of the dealers...in any particular branch of trade or manufacturers, is always in some respects different from, and even opposite to, that of the public. To widen the market and to narrow the competition, is always the interest of the dealers. To widen the market may frequently be agreeable enough to the interest of the

public, but to narrow the competition must always be against it. . . .
The proposal of any new law or regulation of commerce which
comes from this order, ought always to be listened to with great
precaution, and ought never to be adopted till after having been long
and carefully examined, not only with the most scrupulous, but with
the most suspicious attention.[30]

With the possible exception of some members of the industry involved, legislation of the kind struck down in *New State Ice* would
today face strong opposition. Professor Richard Posner believes that
this legislation was economically unsound. He writes that rather than
being intended to prevent wasteful duplication under conditions of natural monopoly, the statute was probably designed to foster cartelization of the Oklahoma ice industry to the benefit of established ice
companies and their shareholders and to the detriment, primarily, of
the poor. Posner suggests that Brandeis was not convinced that the ice
business was a natural monopoly, but that he possibly was favorable to
the proposed regulation as a remedy of general application to the economic dislocations created by the Depression.[31]
The Oklahoma regulations were similar to those that have been imposed in many other fields. Consider, for example, airline regulation,
discussed further in chapter 13. The bill establishing the Civil
Aeronautics Board was originally drafted by the Air Transport Association of America, which is the trade association of scheduled airlines in
the United States. It was patterned after the act that had instituted
trucking regulations (Motor Carrier Act of 1935) and was designed in
part to ensure the elimination of what was then considered excessive
competition among the carriers. The CAB was given the power to
control entry, fares, routes, and profits. A major reason for the recent
legislation deregulating the industry was the huge cost that regulation
imposed on the public. In 1976, Professor Levine cited conservative
estimates that put public cost of airline regulation at about half a billion
dollars each year; less conservative estimates range from $1.5 billion to
$3 billion annually in extra consumer cost.[32]
Individuals of such widely divergent persuasions as Milton Friedman[33] and Ralph Nader[34] have urged deregulation of the entire transportation industry, which is presently subject to the kind of regulatory
framework that the Oklahoma law established for the ice industry.
The *New State Ice* decision applied to limitations on entry into
common business ventures. Justice Sutherland expressed views accepting regulation when industry was affected with a public purpose
and when public health and safety are concerned.

It must be conceded that all businesses are subject to some measure of public regulation. And that the business of manufacturing, selling or distributing ice, like that of the grocer, the dairyman, the butcher or the baker may be subjected to appropriate regulations in the interest of the public health cannot be doubted; but the question here is whether the business is so charged with a public use as to justify the particular restriction here stated.[35]

Today, a court considering the justifications for curtailing Liebmann's freedom of entry would have to conclude that most of the beneficiaries of that legislation would be wealthy companies and individuals. Consumers and prospective entrants would be disadvantaged. "The people actually wronged by the statute were the poor, who were compelled to pay higher prices for ice than if free entry had been permitted; the well-to-do, as Brandeis pointed out, were more likely to have refrigerators."[36] Neither public health nor safety would be augmented. Given the narrow rewards of the statute, the state had little reason to deny Liebmann a liberty basic to a private enterprise society.

Brandeis wrote his *New State Ice* dissent during the Depression, and his comments reflect a disillusionment with economic competition characteristic of the time. To him, the law seemed neither arbitrary nor unreasonable, and therefore it was not unconstitutional. However, that he did not always follow the rule of complete abstention in economic regulatory matters is evidenced by two majority opinions that he authored overturning regulations imposed by Tennessee and Texas.[37] He conceded in *New State Ice* that "the reasonableness of every regulation is dependent upon the relevant facts."[38] Perhaps had Brandeis better comprehended the consequences of the Oklahoma statute, he might have voted with the majority.

Regulation of Prices

During 1931, milk prices in New York State declined drastically, and during 1932 prices farmers received for milk were below the cost of production. A joint committee of the state senate and assembly was created to investigate this situation and to recommend solutions. The committee was organized in May 1932, and its activities lasted almost a year. Responding to the committee's request for imposing regulation, the state legislature, in April 1933, adopted a statute, to expire in March 1934, effectively making the milk industry a public utility and establishing a three-member milk control board, with vast powers to regulate the industry, including setting prices at the retail level. In fixing prices, the board had to consider the amount necessary to yield a "reasonable return" to the milk producers and dealers. The primary object of the legislation was to improve the farmers' economic position.

The board made it a crime to sell milk below nine cents a quart in a retail store. Nebbia, who owned a small store in Rochester, sold two bottles of milk and a loaf of bread for eighteen cents and was subsequently convicted of committing a misdemeanor for violating the milk control law. Prices at which producers could sell were not then prescribed, nor was production in any way limited. In *Nebbia v. New York*, the United States Supreme Court, in a 5–4 decision, upheld the conviction against a challenge that it violated the seller's rights under the Fourteenth Amendment's due process and equal protection clauses.[39]

The opinion was historically significant in that it signaled the approaching end of economic due process, which actually terminated three years later.[40] Rejecting the standard that had previously applied, the majority held that the due process guarantee demands only that the law be not unreasonable or arbitrary and that it have a substantial relation to the objective sought to be achieved. The Justices repudiated the exception that the Court had reserved, in determining the validity of economic regulations, for businesses affected with a public interest. Under substantive due process, price restraint had been sanctioned only in unique circumstances. The majority, however, set forth a new rule embodying much more limited scrutiny of legislative action. Through Justice Roberts, it ruled that under existing circumstances, it was not unreasonable for New York to enact legislation that deprived Nebbia of the liberty to sell milk at a price of his own choosing. Roberts opined that price controls were subject to the same review test as any other form of economic regulation.

The dissenters totally rejected this standard of review. Justice McReynolds wrote the minority opinion, in which he was joined by Justices Van Devanter, Sutherland, and Butler. He pursued a reverse line of inquiry and contended that the only question presented by the case was whether justification existed for depriving Nebbia of his rights under the Fourteenth Amendment. McReynolds sought to determine whether the legislation could be upheld because it was a temporary response to an emergency, or because the milk business bears such a special relationship to the public that the price of milk may be prescribed irrespective of emergency conditions—that is, that it is a business affected with a public interest.

The minority opinion denied that either condition existed or that the statute could meet a means-ends test of validity. McReynolds wrote that the state had not met the burden of establishing the presence of an emergency whose magnitude justified the law. Nor was requiring the grocer to disprove its existence fair or appropriate: "If necessary for appellant to show absence of the asserted conditions, the little grocer was helpless from the beginning—the practical difficulties were too great for the average man."[41] Moreover, the legislative findings and report should not be deemed conclusive:

> May one be convicted of a crime upon such findings? Are federal rights subject to extinction by reports of committees? Heretofore they have not been. . . .
> The exigency is of the kind which inevitably arises when one set of men continue to produce more than all others can buy. The distressing result to the producer followed his ill-advised but voluntary efforts. Similar situations occur in almost every business. If here we have an emergency sufficient to empower the Legislature to fix sales prices, then whenever there is too much or too little of an essential thing—whether of milk or grain or pork or coal or shoes or clothes—constitutional provisions may be declared inoperative. . . .[42]

McReynolds found that the industry was a private calling not affected with a public interest. He questioned the wisdom of the regulation and denied that the means proposed would achieve the legislative purpose. How could the imposition of higher prices at the retail level—an imposition that would reduce consumption—raise prices at the production level? Because the legislation would compound rather than relieve the problem of excessive production, the Justice contended that it would not accomplish the proposed aim of increasing farmers' incomes. Nevertheless, the public was being forced to assume a heavy burden:

> Not only does the statute interfere arbitrarily with the rights of the little grocer to conduct his business according to standards long accepted—complete destruction may follow; but it takes away the liberty of twelve million consumers to buy a necessity of life in an open market. It imposes direct and arbitrary burdens upon those already seriously impoverished with the alleged immediate design of affording special benefits to others. To him with less than nine cents it says—You cannot procure a quart of milk from the grocer although he is anxious to accept what you can pay and the demands of your household are urgent! A superabundance; but no child can purchase

from a willing storekeeper below the figure appointed by three men at headquarters! And this is true although the storekeeper himself may have bought from a willing producer at half that rate and must sell quickly or lose his stock through deterioration. The fanciful scheme is to protect the farmer against undue exactions by prescribing the price at which milk disposed of by him at will may be resold![43]

McReynolds concluded:

The Legislature cannot lawfully destroy guaranteed rights of one man with the prime purpose of enriching another, even if for the moment, this may seem advantageous to the public. . . . Grave concern for embarrassed farmers is everywhere; but this should neither obscure the rights of others nor obstruct judicial appraisement of measures proposed for relief. The ultimate welfare of the producer, like that of every other class, requires dominance of the Constitution. And zealously to uphold this in all its parts is the highest duty intrusted to the courts.[44]

Roberts chose to ignore this argument, citing the numerous instances when regulation has been upheld under what he asserted amounted to a reasonableness standard. Nor did the majority seriously probe the effectiveness of the law. Yet, everyone on that Court would have agreed that any senseless and needless restraint is an unreasonable, arbitrary invasion of individual freedom that a court is obligated to overturn. McReynolds put it this way: "If a statute to prevent conflagration should require householders to pour oil on their roofs as a means of curbing the spread of fire when discovered in the neighborhood, we could hardly uphold it."[45]

That the means (setting minimum retail prices) was unlikely to accomplish the objective (increasing the farmers' income) is evident from an analysis of the background and economics of the legislation.

1. The New York Assembly adopted the statute in question in a crisis atmosphere. Farmers were striking and news reports told of violence. Legislators from farm areas called for passage as a means of terminating the strike and the bloodshed, and of restoring calm. They pleaded with their colleagues to do something, even if the results were far from perfect. The original draft of the bill allowed the board to fix minimum prices for producers and maximum prices for consumers. Changes were subsequently made to satisfy both the large milk dealers and farm representatives. Noticeably absent from the discussions and negotiations were representatives of the small retail stores. Although

the Nebbias were vitally affected, they appear to have had virtually no input into the legislative deliberations.[46]

2. Establishing a retail minimum price would not lead to the increased consumption upon which the farmers had to depend for improved revenues. Minimum price requirements impede market-clearing processes. While the precise impact of fixing minimum prices depends on the severity of the controls and the elasticity of demand, it is likely to cause a reduction in consumption, thereby exacerbating, not alleviating, the milk producers' woes. Per capita consumption in New York City had already dropped, because of the Depression, from four-fifths of a pint each day in 1930 to three-quarters in 1933.[47] These data suggest a significant causal relationship between consumption of milk and its price.

3. The large retailers argued otherwise. They asserted that their existence was threatened by price-cutting and that if they were forced out of business, milk distribution would be disastrously impaired, to the serious detriment of the producers. The lower and upper court opinions are devoid of any evidence substantiating these assertions, both of which are difficult to accept, especially because of the relatively short period the law was to be in effect. The large retailers could hardly be ruined within one year. Changes in economic conditions may affect entrepreneurs differently, and usually this does not justify preserving the existence or profits of those adversely affected. Any other policy would support inefficient enterprise. The large retailers' legislative success explains more about politics than economics. The price-cutters seem to have been sacrificed for political rather than economic reasons.

The legislation aroused much opposition in New York City. Within a month after passage of the statute, the milk board raised prices by one cent a quart. Mayor La Guardia, officials of the largest milk distributors in the city, and the health commission, among others, condemned the increase. The mayor sought federal help to protect consumers: if the city could obtain milk from the Department of Agriculture, this supply would not be subject to the price-fixing powers of the milk board.[48] The small dealers also protested the increase and other board policies. Approximately fifty members of an organization representing retail grocers accompanied their spokesman to city hall to complain that the board was "in league with the large distributors to discriminate against the small retailer," and that "gorilla tactics" were employed by the authorities against small retailers accused of violating the law.[49] The milk board subsequently issued a directive to dealers to pass along to the producers any profits accruing from the fixed minimum prices.

The milk price control law was inspired by unusual public passions and pressures, and its final form was dictated by lobbyists for farmers and large milk dealers. Only by accident can measures conceived under these circumstances justify the restraints they impose on people. The situation is precisely the type that warrants the kind of judicial oversight that the Supreme Court repudiated in this case.

The minority views in *Nebbia* did not mollify the critics of economic due process. By then the die had already been cast and the commentators were not prone to empathize with shopkeepers who labor for the sake of profits. Yet small entrepreneurs work long hours, and their returns resemble wages more than profits. At the time of *Nebbia*, "Ma and Pa" stores required very lengthy hours of labor weekly by at least one family member.[50]

Indeed, *Nebbia* had all the trappings of radical drama: powerful interests, depression, exploitation, excessive milk prices, and criminal sanctions. McReynolds's opinion eloquently speaks to these issues: "A superabundance; but no child can purchase from a willing storekeeper below the figure appointed by three men at headquarters!"[51] Still it has received no recognition from those who condemn the wickedness of substantive due process. Surely McReynolds's dissent would have been described as powerful, eloquent, and moving in a setting more to the liking of the critics. His prose is scarcely in keeping with the image of old-guard reactionaries and those who tread on the rights of the masses. And for lawyers, it should be very provocative. Why have so many legal commentators missed the point of economic due process? Were Holmes and Brandeis really the heroes of that Court?

Wage Rates

In 1918, Congress enacted a statute for the District of Columbia, establishing a board to fix minimum wages for women and minors in various industries.[52] Two suits filed to restrain the board from prescribing wages were consolidated for the decision of the United States Supreme Court. One was brought by the corporate owner of a children's hospital that employed a large number of women in different capacities and paid some less than the minimum wage specified by the board. Lyons, a twenty-one-year-old woman employed as an elevator operator in a hotel, brought the other action. She alleged that she would be fired because her employer would not pay the designated minimum wage. She stated that her pay was the highest that she was able to obtain for any work she was capable of performing. In 1923, in *Adkins v. Children's Hospital*,[53] the Supreme Court, per Justice Sutherland, held the law unconstitutional on a vote of 5–3, with Justice Brandeis not participating. Sutherland concluded that no exceptional circumstances existed to warrant this abridgment of freedom of contract.

He saw the D.C. statute as mandating employers to pay wages for which they received nothing in return. To the extent that the wage exceeds the fair value of the services rendered, it amounts to a compulsory exaction from the employer for the support of a partially indigent person, for whose situation the employer was not responsible. Therefore the law arbitrarily shifts to the employer a burden that, if it belongs to anybody, belongs to society as a whole. A comparable purpose could be applied to govern other transactions, for example, the purchase of goods likewise burdening entrepreneurs and the economy. In fact, if such legislation were to be held legally justified, the operation of the police power would have been substantially increased so that it would admit even the imposition of maximum wage controls. Thus, the arguments urged in this case to the disadvantage of the employer could later be invoked to the detriment of the employee.

Sutherland rejected the position that women require restrictions that could not lawfully be imposed on men under similar circumstances.

> [W]hile the physical differences must be recognized in appropriate cases, and legislation fixing hours or conditions of work may properly take them into account, we cannot accept the doctrine that women of mature age, *sui juris,* require or may be subjected to restrictions upon their liberty of contract which could not lawfully be imposed in the case of men under similar circumstances. To do so would be to ignore all the implications to be drawn from the present day trend of legislation, as well as that of common thought and usage, by which woman is accorded emancipation from the old doctrine that she must be given special protection or be subjected to special restraint in her contractual and civil relationships.[54]

The majority believed that the wage restriction would subject business to a substantial burden, especially because it applied both to big business and to small, weak employers without taking into account periods of economic difficulties or crippling losses, each of which could leave the employer without adequate means of livelihood. To the contention that the law would serve the public interest, Sutherland replied:

It has been said that legislation of the kind now under review is required in the interest of social justice, for whose ends freedom of contract may lawfully be subjected to restraint. The liberty of the individual to do as he pleases, even in innocent matters, is not absolute. It must frequently yield to the common good, and the line beyond which the power of interference may not be pressed is neither definite nor unalterable but may be made to move, within limits not well defined, with changing need and circumstance. Any attempt to fix a rigid boundary would be unwise as well as futile. But, nevertheless, there are limits to the power, and when these have been passed, it becomes the plain duty of the courts in the proper exercise of their authority to so declare. To sustain the individual freedom of action contemplated by the Constitution, is not to strike down the common good but to exalt it; for surely the good of society as a whole cannot be better served than by the preservation against arbitrary restraint of the liberties of its constituent members.[55]

Chief Justice Taft and Justice Holmes wrote dissents. Both accepted the differentiation of the sexes. The former argued that the law could be upheld on the basis of prior decisions and because sufficient reason existed for the congressional action. He believed that although some hardships would result, "the restriction will enure to the benefit of the general class of employees in whose interest the law is passed and so to that of the community at large."[56] Holmes denied that the Court had any power in this area, for the Constitution leaves such matters entirely to the wisdom of the legislators. He wrote that the statute did not compel anybody to pay anything and that women would not be employed at even the lowest wages allowed unless they earned them or unless the employer's business could sustain the burden. The legislature could differentiate between men and women and "I should not hesitate to take [differences] into account if I thought it necessary to sustain this act."[57]

In 1937, the United States Supreme Court, by a 5–4 majority, explicitly overruled *Adkins* by sustaining a Washington State statute that established minimum wages for women and minors. Employing the *Nebbia* standard, the majority determined that the law was a reasonable exercise of legislative discretion. Chief Justice Hughes authored the opinion in the case, *West Coast Hotel v. Parrish,*[58] which involved an adult hotel worker. This case marks the formal termination of economic due process. The same Justices who had dissented in *Nebbia* also dissented in *Parrish.* The Chief Justice explained the decision in part on the difficult economic conditions of the time and "the un-

paralleled demand for relief." Sutherland replied that the meaning of
the Constitution does not change with the ebb and flow of economic
events, a statement somewhat difficult to reconcile with the balancing
technique his group employed.

Hughes's decision contains a perspective about the role of government that had not often appeared in majority opinions. Rejecting
Sutherland's belief that the common good is predicated on individual
freedom, Hughes equated liberty with the application of the police
power.

> [T]he liberty safeguarded is liberty in a social organization which
> requires the protection of law against the evils which menace the
> health, safety, morals and welfare of the people. Liberty under the
> Constitution is thus necessarily subject to the restraints of due pro-
> cess, and regulation which is reasonable in relation to its subject and
> is adopted in the interests of the community is due process.[59]

With respect to both *Adkins* and *Parrish,* these observations are
submitted:

1. Were an appropriate challenge to be instituted at this time against
a law establishing a minimum wage for women, the primary legal issue
would be whether the statutory classification satisfies the equal protection requirements of the Fifth Amendment's due process clause or the
equal protection clause of the Fourteenth Amendment. To withstand
constitutional attack, classification by sex must serve "important governmental objectives and must be substantially related to the achievement of those objectives."[60] This recent terminology, coupled with
adjudications to that effect, indicate that the standard in sex classification is somewhere between the minimal *Dukes* test and the strict
scrutiny test applied to racial classifications,[61] probably closer to the
latter than the former. This test resembles the one used by Justice
Sutherland (but triggered in that case by liberty of contract) and subjects legislation to greater scrutiny than the one employed by
Hughes.[62]

The purpose of the *Adkins* statute was to enhance the living conditions of poor women and minors. While under current standards this
legislative objective is permissible and important, it is doubtful that
minimum wage legislation can accomplish this goal—as we shall see
below. In light of existing law on sex classifications and contemporary
economic understanding, the present Court, were it ruling on the matter for the first time, probably would agree with the result in *Adkins* and
not with that in *Parrish.*

2. The economic analyses of Sutherland, Taft, Holmes, and Hughes have one common element: they are all only partially correct. Laws that elevate the minimum wage above market will cause employers to pay some workers more and to fire (or not to hire) others. By raising the required pay of workers whose productivity does not justify the increase, the laws create and maintain unemployment. If the law mandates a $2.50 hourly wage, employers will be reluctant to hire or retain any employee whose productivity is valued below that figure. Thus Puerto Ricans strongly objected to the 25-cent minimum wage once passed by Congress because enforcement would wipe out a 40,000-worker needlework industry overnight.[63] In addition, the employers who do pay more have an incentive to minimize the added labor costs by installing work-saving machines and maintaining much closer supervision of their workers to obtain maximum productivity. Some workers will not accept such conditions and therefore will quit. These methods probably will not eliminate all the additional labor expense, and employers in time will be confronted with these alternatives: *(a)* reducing profits, *(b)* raising prices, *(c)* terminating their businesses. Obviously the last two options are disadvantageous to both wage earners and consumers (particularly the poorer ones). Nor is the first much better, for it will in time curtail plant maintenance and improvements and deter expansion and investment.

3. Limiting the law to women is an unsatisfactory means to the end of improving their condition. Such a measure will cause employers to fire women who had been hired because of their willingness to work at a lower wage than do men. Because of the law, the elevator operator in *Adkins* lost her job, and she was undoubtedly handicapped in obtaining other work. The workers who bear the primary burden of a general legislative minimum are the marginally employable ones—that is, the least productive, those who are hired last and fired first. Currently teenagers, minorities, women, the uneducated, and the physically handicapped are represented among the marginal segment in disproportionate numbers. In 1973, 66 percent of those persons with usual hourly earnings below $2.00 were women.[64] Eight studies published in the 1970s conclude on the basis of available information that wage minimums have reduced employment for those who would otherwise earn lower wages.[65] Workers with lowest skills suffered the most from such legislation. A law increasing the minimum wages of only one of the groups aggravates the employment problem of that group. The most frequently recommended remedy to relieve a particular group's unemployment situation operates on the reverse premise.

Thus, in recognition of the adverse effects of these laws on youth employment, some states and some European countries have established a differential lower minimum wage for youth.[66] For comparable reasons, minimum wage laws frequently have exempted the occupations in which the adverse impact would be most serious.[67]

Consequently, if a general minimum wage law would cause loss of employment for women, such a law limited to that group would have a much more devastating impact. As Justice Butler observed in a 1936 opinion upholding *Adkins*, "prescribing of minimum wages for women alone would unreasonably restrain them in competition with men and tend arbitrarily to deprive them of employment and a fair chance to find work."[68]

4. The advocacy of special working conditions for women has not always been premised on cultural or paternalistic or humanitarian grounds. Two economic explanations can also be found for these concerns. First, in the early part of this century, the majority of unions affiliated with the American Federation of Labor were not eager to spend money organizing the low-paid, unskilled trades that were dominated by women workers.[69] Second, many union men feared that women, who were entering the labor force in constantly increasing numbers, posed competitive problems. They thought women were a reserve force of cheap labor, available to replace more expensive males when mechanization made jobs simpler, or to break nascent unions.[70]

In 1914, the AFL, which had previously supported protective laws for men, reversed its position, adopting a resolution that opposed maximum-hours legislation for men.[71] Florence Kelley, head of the National Consumers' League and an advocate of protective laws for all workers, explained this reversal:

> In many cases, men who saw their own occupations threatened by unwelcome competitors, demanded restrictions upon the hours of work of those competitors for the purpose of rendering women less desirable as employees. In other cases, men who wished reduced hours of work for themselves, which the courts denied them, obtained the desired statutory reduction by the indirect method of restrictions upon the hours of labor of the women and children whose work interlocked with their own.[72]

Many feminists of the period saw dangers inherent in protective legislation. Like feminists of today, they decried all attempts at encouraging the paternalism that for centuries had "protected" and harmed them. In fact, the Women's Party filed a brief in *Adkins* urging the Supreme Court to strike down the D.C. minimum wage law for women.[73] An odd coalition of radical feminists and libertarian/conservative Justices triumphed, for a short time and in a small area, over the combined forces of liberals and unions.

In *Muller v. Oregon*,[74] the Supreme Court, which three years earlier had rejected the *Lochner* work limitation, unanimously upheld an Oregon maximum-hour work law for women as essential to protect their well-being. Much credit for this decision is given to a brief submitted by Louis D. Brandeis, then a private attorney, containing more than one hundred pages of statistics and other socioeconomic data on the harm suffered by women working excessive hours. This document is said to be the original "Brandeis Brief," which supports a particular position with an array of facts. Although presumably the information that he compiled was accurate, the author failed to recognize that it did not establish the desirability of the legislation. Women who were willing to work longer hours than allowed might well lose their jobs.

Equal rights advocates now appear to agree that laws limiting a woman's hours and types of work constrict her employment opportunities. Thus, women employees challenged a California statute limiting the number of hours women could work in enumerated industries to an eight-hour day and a forty-eight-hour week. These women, employees of North American Aviation, Inc., complained that the law gave male employees an unfair advantage because it denied women *(a)* overtime employment and *(b)* certain positions with the company. They alleged that the act violated their rights under the due process and equal protection clauses and the Civil Rights Act of 1964. A lower court dismissed the case on the theory that *Muller* and its progeny had foreclosed examination of the issue. A circuit court sent the case back for consideration, observing that circumstances and understanding of the problem had changed over the years.[75]

In another recent case, the employer refused promotion to a woman employee solely because she would have to engage in duties prohibited under the California labor code limiting hours and work of women. A federal court found that the statute discriminated against women on the basis of their sex and therefore violated the provisions of the Federal Civil Rights Act of 1964.[76]

5. Hughes's comments in *Parrish* quoted above stand the concept of liberty on its head. They are at variance with a fundamental idea of our society that the state's power over people is limited, and are more nearly in keeping with those political philosophies that subordinate the individual to the designs of the community. Hughes was similarly wrong in his economics. Imposition of higher wages brings unemployment and reduces the economy's flexibility, thereby impeding economic recovery. The *Adkins* majority did not have the economic data

that were later to emerge, and it probably did not sympathize with feminist ideology. But at that stage in our history, the *Adkins* law appeared to be a serious imposition on the employment relationship. Employers and employees could claim disadvantages to offset contentions that workers would generally benefit. Thus, the government's argument was not persuasive for a court majority that believed "the good of society as a whole cannot be better served than by the preservation against arbitrary restraint of the liberties of its constituent members."[77]

Exceptional Circumstances Justify Restraint

In declaring freedom of contract, the *Allgeyer* Court said that this right was not absolute and was therefore subject to regulation. During the substantive due process era, courts routinely reiterated this statement, emphasizing that freedom was the general rule and restraint the exception. The legislative authority to abridge could be justified only by special or exceptional circumstances, and the Court was frequently hard pressed to determine the boundaries of what was legislatively permissible. But as statistics at the beginning of this chapter show, a considerable amount of legislation was sustained. The *Nebbia* and *Parrish* decisions cite dozens of such instances. Perhaps the most far-reaching from that period is Justice Sutherland's opinion in *Euclid,* which fastened zoning regulation on one of the country's major industries. All of this raises the question of when and how the Court actually did draw the line on regulation. Just how laissez-faire was that tribunal?

One of the major exceptions to freedom of contract was that it did not apply to businesses "affected with a public interest." This proposition was formulated in *Munn v. Illinois*[78] (decided in 1876), sustaining the state's regulation of grain warehouse rates because this was a business "affected with a public interest" or a "public calling." The Court explained that the grain warehouse industry was not an ordinary calling but one of critical importance to the commerce of the country, likening it to the many callings that could be regulated at common law, such as common carriers, ferries, warfingers, grist mills, and innkeeping. The Court also found that the grain warehouse business in Chicago was a "virtual" monopoly because no price competition existed among the nine firms controlling the fourteen grain elevators in that city. Accordingly, *Munn* decided that history and economics could determine whether a business was a public calling.

This distinction between public and private callings received more precise elaboration in another leading decision, *Wolff Packing Co. v. Court of Industrial Relations*,[79] a unanimous opinion written by Chief Justice Taft in 1922. This case involved the Kansas Court of Industrial Relations Act, which declared that a number of pursuits were affected with a public interest, including the manufacture of food and clothing and production of fuel, and created an industrial court with powers to impose wage settlements on those businesses. In holding the act unconstitutional because these are ordinary callings, Taft classified into four categories those businesses clothed with a public interest justifying some public regulation:

1. those that are carried on under authority of a public franchise imposing the affirmative duty of rendering public service demanded by the public—e.g., a common carrier or a public utility;

2. certain occupations, regarded as exceptional, that historically have been subject to regulation—e.g., inns, cabs, and grist mills;

3. businesses in which an economic monopoly exists or is likely to occur;

4. businesses that are so important in the nation's economy that disruption or stoppage would endanger the public welfare.

Taft could find no monopoly in the preparation of foods (the business involved in the litigation), and a work stoppage would not imperil the public. Prices were set by competition, and the sources for food supply in Kansas were countrywide. In analyzing prior cases not included in the first two categories, but in which the Court had decided that the business was affected with a public interest, Taft found this distinction: "[T]he thing which gave the public interest was the indispensable nature of the service and the exorbitant charges and arbitrary control to which the public might be subjected without regulation."[80] The Court subsequently explained that the following businesses were not included within the affected exceptions: *(a)* a public exhibition, game, contest, or performance to which an admission charge is made; *(b)* employment agencies; and *(c)* roadside gasoline stations.[81] The exception sometimes seemed conclusive only as applied and was the source of continuing controversy among the Justices.[82]

The dissenters in *Nebbia* and the majority in *New State Ice* believed that reasonably competitive markets existed in those situations, although obviously the competition was far from textbook perfect. *New State Ice* provides another example of the distinction between the permissible and the forbidden. Some years prior to that decision, a federal circuit court had sustained the constitutionality of an Oklahoma law imposing regulations similar to those for the ice industry on the business of operating cotton gins.[83] Accepting this decision, Sutherland, in *New State Ice*, explained that the cotton-gin business was not an ordinary calling (like manufacturing, selling, and distributing ice) because it was the principal industry in Oklahoma upon which the prosperity of the entire state in large measure depended. Sutherland also noted an analogy to the grist mills that had been subject to regulation under the common law, explaining that competition was also limited in cotton ginning:

> The cotton gin bears the same relation to the cotton grower that the old grist mill did to the grower of wheat. The individual grower of the raw product is generally financially unable to set up a plant for himself; but the service is a necessary one with which, ordinarily, he cannot afford to dispense. He is compelled, therefore, to resort for such service to the establishment which operates in his locality. So dependent, generally, is he upon the neighborhood cotton gin that he faces the practical danger of being placed at the mercy of the operator in respect of exorbitant charges and arbitrary control.[84]

For both historical and economic reasons, the Justice concluded that the business had been devoted to a public use which justified its regulation.

Justice Stone, in a 1927 dissent to an opinion invalidating price control on theater ticket resales, commented that a common element permitting price regulation is the existence of circumstances materially restricting the regulative force of competition,

> so that buyers or sellers are placed at such a disadvantage in the bargaining struggle that serious economic consequences result to a very large number of members of the community. Whether this situation arises from the monopoly conferred upon public service companies or from the circumstance that the strategical position of a group is such as to enable it to impose its will in matters of price upon those who sell, buy or consume . . . or from the predetermination of prices in the councils of those who sell, promulgated in schedules of practically controlling constancy . . . or from a housing shortage growing out of a public emergency . . . the result is the same.[85]

Other regulatory measures had been upheld by the Court because of the existence of special circumstances:

1. The courts had sustained a variety of social legislation prior to *Lochner*, including the limitations on miners' working hours in *Holden*.[86] Three years after *Lochner*, the Supreme Court unanimously sustained a regulation of working hours for women,[87] and in 1917, a divided Court

upheld a state law limiting to ten hours the working day for men in major industries and providing for overtime pay.[88] Following the *Coppage* decision, three varieties of worker's compensation were sustained, two unanimously and the other by a bare majority.[89] A 1915 case affirmed congressional power to temporarily adjust railroad wages to keep the railroads moving pending wage negotiations and consideration of the controversy by a commission established for this purpose; the Court emphasized that this was a temporary measure to avoid a general strike in an industry affected by the public interest.[90] The Court upheld rent control laws during and after World War I.[91] Legislatures could regulate size and weight of loaves of bread,[92] insurance rates,[93] the size and character of packages in which goods are sold,[94] the practice of medicine, and the training of practitioners.[95] They could also require smallpox vaccination and prohibit the sale of adulterated food and drugs.[96] In certain instances, the lawmakers could impose absolute liability without fault.[97]

2. Uses of property could be abated if they would create nuisances and become dangerous, unhealthful, or highly damaging. These uses included infected cedar trees, brickyards, livery stables, billiard halls, oleomargarine factories, and breweries.[98]

3. The list of permitted regulation covers zoning, collusive practices by competitors, gambling, extortion, and usury.

These "exceptional" cases reveal the Court did not always conform to its laissez-faire reputation. The Justices seemed to have their own ideas on what was economically desirable. In the *Euclid* case, the zoning ordinance reduced the value of plaintiff's land by hundreds of thousands of dollars, a result that should have gravely concerned believers in economic rights but that in fact led to dissents only from the three Justices most dedicated to this cause. The explanation frequently given for the Court's acceptance of zoning is twofold: first, the majority believed that zoning would on the whole enhance property values by eliminating or reducing undesirable, incompatible, and near-nuisance uses; and second, the Justices lived in exclusive residential areas and reflected the typical sentiments of their class toward apartments and other diverse uses.

Justice Sutherland's language in the opinion suggests another possibility: he did not believe economic freedom was desirable in the land-use market. For him, it was not a question of the virtues of freedom versus the evils of restraint, because in this market economic freedom did not serve society well. Freedom of contract was not in the interests of homeowners and many other property owners, and therefore was not worthy of judicial protection. This manner of reasoning may explain some of the fine-line–drawing that occurred in the days of substantive due process. Professor Strong maintains that the rulings of that period were motivated by the Justices' belief in a pattern of economic organization founded on competitive economic practices espoused by Adam Smith and Herbert Spencer.[99] Another analysis in light of the *Euclid* opinion suggests that in the balancing process that the Justices used, restraint was likely to be upheld when they were not personally satisfied that the private market was performing well. Pragmatism has always held a high judicial priority.

Some Concluding Remarks

Despite the Court's many detours and diversions, an underlying theme during the judicial periods I have discussed in this and the preceding chapters is classic liberalism's philosophy of individual liberty: the only purpose for which power can be rightfully exercised over any member of a civilized community against his will is to prevent harm to others. Professor Aaron Director offers this interesting explanation of the classical view that applies quite well to the old Court's orientation.

> Laissez faire has never been more than a slogan in defense of the proposition that every extension of state activity should be examined under a presumption of error. The main tradition of economic liberalism has always assumed a well-established system of law and order designed to harness self-interest to serve the welfare of all. The institution of private property—at least since Hume—has always been defended on this ground. And, wherever it seemed that this institution might be modified without subverting the general framework of a competitive society, the tradition has shown a readiness—perhaps exaggerated—to modify this basic institution. But the tradition goes much beyond this. It has always assumed that there were some economic results which cannot be attained at all or attained only in inappropriate amounts if left to the free market.[100]

The substantive due process Justices believed liberty of contract to be basic in a free society and among the freedoms protected by the due process clauses of the Fifth and Fourteenth Amendments. This liberty was not absolute, but to support restraint, the state had the obligation of providing clear and convincing reasons for its curtailment. When restraints are applied to legislation affecting political and intellectual activity, these classical principles are now routinely reiterated and approved by judges and legal commentators. The early twentieth-century Justices treated economic liberty at a level approaching, but not nearly as high as, that which the contemporary Supreme Court accords the freedoms of expression, religion, voting, and privacy.

Substantive due process obligated the judiciary to secure essential individual freedoms and not to abdicate this constitutional responsibility to the legislature. This concern is as appropriate and necessary today as it was then. In reality, the complaints against the earlier Court are about the ends, not the means: critics who are angered by some results have destroyed a sound principle. The overreaction to some substantive due process decisions has unfortunately eliminated an important check in the government of checks and balances.

7   The Old Court and Personal Rights

This chapter deals with cases that commentators usually regard as involving personal rights. My purpose in including it is to present a broader perspective on the jurisprudence practiced in the days of economic due process. Critics have charged that the Old Court had a sterile record in the field of civil liberties; that its declarations on behalf of liberty were prompted chiefly by a desire to encourage laissez-faire economics. It is widely held that supporters of economic due process were limited in their desire to redress grievances, whereas opponents had a greater and more flexible concern for the individual. To explore these contentions, this chapter examines leading decisions of the period relating to family, conceptual, and political rights.

Family Rights

Justice McReynolds, the eloquent dissenter in *Nebbia v. New York,* authored two well-known and often cited opinions that gave substantive protection under the due process clauses to liberties relating to family life: *Meyer v. Nebraska* (1923)[1] and *Pierce v. Society of Sisters* (1925).[2] Each safeguarded two personal interests: first, the liberty of contract of the complaining parties, and second, the liberty of parents to make vital decisions about their children's education. McReynolds could have premised both opinions entirely on liberty of contract, but chose in addition to recognize certain family or parental liberties.

These opinions and others to be discussed in this chapter are persuasive evidence that McReynolds and like-minded Justices believed that the Fourteenth Amendment safeguards the exercise of a wide variety of human endeavors—a position at odds with the current Supreme Court policy of according nearly unlimited protection to some liberties and minimal recognition to others. The opinions also serve as excellent illustrations of the close ties between economic rights and those frequently referred to as "personal" or "civil" rights.

Meyer, considered a landmark case on family rights, involved a Nebraska law that made it a crime to teach grade-school children any language other than English, with the exception of the ancient or "dead" languages such as Latin, Greek, and Hebrew. The objective was to compel immigrants to learn English. A private school teacher was convicted for teaching a student to read German. He defended on the grounds that the law unreasonably interfered with his right to make a living and with the rights of parents to hire him to instruct their children. The United States Supreme Court reversed the conviction and invalidated the law by a 7–2 vote. The dissenters were the ideological odd couple of Justices Holmes and Sutherland. McReynolds presented a concept of liberty under the Fourteenth Amendment's due process clause that continues to be frequently quoted in cases and texts.

> While this Court has not attempted to define with exactness the liberty thus guaranteed, the term has received much consideration and some of the included things have been definitely stated. Without doubt, it denotes not merely freedom from bodily restraint but also the right of the individual to contract, to engage in any of the common occupations of life, to acquire useful knowledge, to marry, establish a home and bring up children, to worship God according to the dictates of his own conscience, and generally to enjoy those privileges long recognized at common law as essential to the orderly pursuit of happiness by free men . . . . The established doctrine is that this liberty may not be interfered with, under the guise of protecting the public interest, by legislative action which is arbitrary or without reasonable relation to some purpose within the competency of the State to effect.[3]

For McReynolds, the statute was another instance of an illegal means to achieve a laudable purpose.

> That the State may do much, go very far, indeed, in order to improve the quality of its citizens, physically, mentally and morally, is clear; but the individual has certain fundamental rights which must be respected. The protection of the Constitution extends to all, to

those who speak other languages as well as to those born with English on the tongue. Perhaps it would be highly advantageous if all had ready understanding of our ordinary speech, but this cannot be coerced by methods which conflict with the Constitution—a desirable end cannot be promoted by prohibited means.[4]

In contrast, Holmes believed that under the then existing circumstances the statute might be regarded as a reasonable or even necessary method of reaching a desired goal, for he thought that the law would ensure that children from homes where foreign languages were spoken would have the opportunity of hearing and speaking English. He maintained that if the act was reasonable, it did not constitute a violation of the liberty of either teacher or scholar. "[T]he only criterion of [the teacher's] liberty under the Constitution that I can think of is 'whether, considering the end in view, the statute passes the bounds of reason and assumes the character of a merely arbitrary fiat.'"[5]

Moreover, he stated, the Constitution did not forbid this experiment in education. Here Justice Holmes parted with Brandeis. Although Brandeis was also a supporter of social experimentation, *Meyer* suggests that his willingness to allow legislative experiments turned on the importance of the rights affected; he was not willing to speculate with those individual liberties he prized most.[6]

In *Pierce* the issue concerned an Oregon compulsory education law, adopted by popular vote, requiring every person in the state who was responsible for a child between the ages of eight and sixteen to send him or her to a public school. Noncompliance with the law was a misdemeanor. Exceptions were made for children who were subnormal, had completed the eighth grade, or lived a certain distance from a public school.

The plaintiffs were a private Catholic school and a private nonsectarian school. Although the issue could have been resolved under the liberty of contract concept, McReynolds again invoked the rights of parents in striking down the statute. The Justice stated that the practical results in enforcing the act would be the destruction of the primary schools operated by the parties and perhaps all other such private primary schools in the state. He concluded that no special circumstances or emergencies existed to warrant legislation having such dire impact. Then, relying on *Meyer,* McReynolds went on to buttress his opinion with this well-quoted passage:

[W]e think it entirely plain that the Act of 1922 unreasonably interferes with the liberty of parents and guardians to direct the upbringing and education of children under their control. As often heretofore pointed out, rights guaranteed by the Constitution may not be abridged by legislation which has no reasonable relation to some purpose within the competency of the State. The fundamental theory of liberty upon which all governments in this Union repose excludes any general power of the State to standardize its children by forcing them to accept instruction from public teachers only. The child is not the mere creature of the State; those who nurture him and direct his destiny have the right, coupled with the high duty, to recognize and prepare him for additional obligations.[7]

In both *Meyer* and *Pierce,* the Court acknowledged that the state did have the power to compel school attendance and to make reasonable regulations relating to curriculum and personnel, but held that the statutes in question abused this power.

These decisions have been extremely influential. *Pierce* has been discussed or used as precedent in scores of Supreme Court decisions concerning the limits of public school education. Thus in the recently decided *Moore v. City of East Cleveland, Ohio,* Justice Powell, writing for himself and three other Justices, sought to elevate the right of an extended family to live together to the status of a fundamental right under the due process clause, and relied in part on these precedents.[8] These were the first cases cited by Justice Douglas in *Griswold* (on the theory that they rejected limitations on acquiring knowledge) to support his reasoning that the Constitution protects rights peripheral to those specified. He incorrectly stated they were First Amendment cases. Douglas (as previously recounted—see chapter 1) preceded these citations by attacking the Court that produced them for its other forays into substantive due process. In more recent times, the Court might have made the same decisions under the First Amendment— which perhaps explains Douglas's error.

McReynolds had another opportunity to expound on the *Pierce* ruling in *Farrington v. Tokushige,* decided in 1927,[9] which augmented the independence of private, nonreligious schools. The legislature of the Hawaii territory imposed rules of conduct for private, foreign-language schools, prescribing teacher qualifications and contents of textbooks and requiring that teachers pledge to "direct the mind and studies of pupils in such schools as will tend to make them good and loyal Americans." These schools catered mostly to Japanese-American children. In invalidating these regulations under the due process clause of the Fifth Amendment, McReynolds wrote that they far exceeded the exceptions allowed in *Pierce* and *Meyer.*

[T]he School Act and the measures adopted thereunder go far beyond mere regulation of privately-supported schools where children
obtain instruction deemed valuable by their parents and which is not
obviously in conflict with any public interest. They give affirmative
direction concerning the intimate and essential details of such
schools, intrust their control to public officers, and deny both owners
and patrons reasonable choice and discretion in respect of teachers,
curriculum and text-books. Enforcement of the Act probably would
destroy most, if not all, of them; and, certainly, it would deprive
parents of fair opportunity to procure for their children instruction
which they think important and we cannot say is harmful. The
Japanese parent has the right to direct the education of his own child
without unreasonable restrictions; the Constitution protects him as
well as those who speak another tongue.[10]

Other "Personal" Rights

Before discussing the record of the substantive due process court on
freedom of expression cases, it is worth noting some other leading
decisions relating to personal rights. In *Jacobson v. Massachusetts*,[11]
the *Lochner* Court, speaking through Justice Harlan, sustained a state
law requiring vaccination against smallpox. Harlan wrote that the restraint on liberty was justified because such a law was essential to
protect the health of the majority from a minority or even an individual
who might be infected and spread the disease. In *Buck v. Bell*, Justice
Holmes delivered the opinion which, with one dissent, sustained a
Virginia statute authorizing a sterilization operation on an institutionalized, feeble-minded woman, who was the daughter of a
feeble-minded mother, and the mother of a feeble-minded child;
Holmes wrote that society would be better off by preventing the problems, instead of waiting to suffer the consequences: "Three generations of imbeciles are enough."[12] In *Powell v. Alabama*,[13] the Court
(7–2), per Justice Sutherland, held that in a capital case, where the
accused is unable to employ counsel and is incapable of making an
adequate defense, the trial court has a duty to assign a lawyer to
sufficiently counsel and advise him as a necessary requisite of due
process of law. The Court reversed the conviction of the "Scottsboro"
defendants on the ground that although counsel was assigned them, the
attorneys did not provide effective representation and advice. Sutherland declared that the right to the aid of counsel is of fundamental
character and requires full and not nominal or cursory implementation.

Truax v. Raich[14] invalidated a statute that required employers of more than five persons to employ at least 80 percent qualified electors or native-born citizens. The Court stated that the right to work for a living is secured by the Fourteenth Amendment's equal protection clause, but acknowledged that some discrimination might be upheld if the state could show a special interest in affording protection to its own citizens. The court subsequently upheld a state requirement that public contractors employ only citizens, a statute forbidding aliens to own land for the purpose of farming, and an ordinance barring aliens from operating pool and billiard rooms.[15] Regulations requiring separate railroad accommodations for whites and blacks as well as legislation establishing separate schools for the races were sustained.[16] In 1917, the Court struck down a Louisville, Kentucky ordinance barring whites or blacks from occupying houses in a block where a majority of houses are occupied by persons of the other race.[17]

The 1934–35 term revealed a certain consensus on racial matters. The Justices held unanimously that the Fourteenth Amendment forbids systematic exclusion of blacks from grand or petit juries despite official assertions of good faith.[18] However, they refused with the same unanimity to invalidate the exclusion of blacks from voting in a primary election of the all-white Democratic party in Texas, on the ground that the action was private and not that of the state.[19]

In view of the First Amendment status given advertising by the Burger Court (discussed in chapter 10), two other cases of the earlier Court deserve mention. The Court upheld an Oregon law forbidding dentists from advertising and a Utah statute barring cigarette advertising on billboards, streetcar signs, and placards.[20]

Early Freedom of Expression Cases

The opinions of the substantive due process Court defining the free expression guaranteed by the Constitution can be divided into two periods that are separated by World War I. By today's standards the Court's initial record on expression is bleak. Although after the war, the Justices began making determinations more acceptable to current viewpoints, not until 1927 was a defendant able to obtain relief under the Court's interpretation of the expression guarantees.

In the 1897 case of *Robertson v. Baldwin,* the Court, with one Justice absent and only Justice Harlan dissenting (but not on this point), declared that "the freedom of speech and of press (art. 1) [*sic*] does not

permit the publication of libels, blasphemous or indecent articles, or
other publications injurious to public morals or private reputation."[21]
In effect, the Bill of Rights did not protect publication deemed injurious
to the state.

That same year, in *Davis v. Massachusetts,* the Court upheld the
conviction of a preacher for making a public speech in the Boston
Common without a permit from the mayor, as was required under a
Boston ordinance. The United States Supreme Court affirmed the
lower court opinion, which had been written by Holmes, then a justice
on the Supreme Judicial Court of Massachusetts, who had asserted:
"For the legislature absolutely or conditionally to forbid public speaking in a highway or public park is no more an infringement of the rights
of a member of the public than for the owner of a private house to
forbid it in his house."[22]

Ten years later Holmes, now a member of the United States Supreme Court, wrote for the majority in *Patterson v. Colorado* (with
Harlan dissenting, joined by Justice Brewer on different grounds),
which sustained a state contempt-of-court conviction for publication of
articles and a cartoon disparaging the motives and conduct of the Supreme Court of Colorado in pending matters. The opinion contained a
dictum highly restrictive of the constitutional guarantee of expression,
with Holmes relying in part on Blackstone: "[T]he main purpose of
such constitutional provisions is 'to prevent all such *previous restraints*
upon publications as had been practiced by other governments,' and
they do not prevent the subsequent punishment of such as may be
deemed contrary to the public welfare."[23] (A previous or prior restraint is a governmental restriction imposed in advance of publication,
in contrast to a penalty exacted subsequent to publication.) The opinion left undecided whether the Fourteenth Amendment protected expression. Harlan disagreed that the legislature could abridge expression whenever the public welfare required. He asserted that the rights
of speech and press were attributes of national citizenship protected in
this instance by the due process clause of the Fourteenth Amendment.
"It is ... impossible to conceive of liberty ... which does not embrace
the right to enjoy free speech and the right to have a free press."[24]

In 1915, Holmes wrote the unanimous decision in *Fox v. Washington,* upholding a conviction for publishing matter alleged to have encouraged violation of the state of Washington's indecent exposure law.
The defendant was found guilty under a statute making illegal any
publication that had "a tendency to encourage or incite the commission

of any crime." Holmes found that the article in question "by indirection but unmistakably...encourage[d] and incite[d]" people to unlawful conduct. "[T]he disrespect for the law that was encouraged was disregard of it—an overt breach and technically a criminal act."[25]

As these cases demonstrate, in the early days of expression litigation, Holmes was the Court's authority and spokesman on the subject. This situation was soon to change.

The Clear and Present Danger Test

The contemporary judicial perspective on freedom of expression began with a series of post–World War I decisions concerning prosecutions under the Federal Espionage Acts of 1917 and 1918 for interference with the war effort. The postwar years also brought into question the legality of written and oral expressions of dissatisfaction with the prevailing political and social order. Considerable public anxiety existed about subversive and revolutionary groups and their attempts to change or overthrow the government. Judges at both state and federal levels were reluctant to overrule legislative bodies seeking to eradicate threats to the nation's political system. On the High Court, the major opponents of speech and press restraints were Holmes and Brandeis, whose opinions were by nature dissents but nevertheless provided the rationale that continues to influence the law on the subject.

The initial decision in this series was *Schenck v. United States*,[26] a unanimous 1919 decision in which Holmes first enunciated the famous "clear and present danger" test. The case. challenged the constitutionality of an application of the Espionage Act of 1917, which prohibited conduct interfering with the prosecution of the war. Schenck, general secretary of the Socialist party, and other defendants printed and circulated to men accepted for military service leaflets condemning and urging resistance to the draft. The defendants were convicted of violating the law, and Holmes's opinion affirmed the convictions.

Holmes indicated he had modified the views he expressed in *Patterson*. He no longer thought that prohibitions on laws abridging free speech were confined to prior restraints, although he acknowledged that to prevent them might have been the main purpose of the First Amendment. Holmes then went on to set forth the clear and present danger standard: "The question in every case is whether the words used are used in such circumstances and are of such a nature as to

create a clear and present danger that they will bring about the substantive evils that Congress has a right to prevent."[27] Writing for a
unanimous Court in what is considered the first important free speech
case, Justice Holmes explained the test in terms of balancing interests.

> [T]he character of every act depends upon the circumstances in
> which it is done.... The most stringent protection of free speech
> would not protect a man in falsely shouting fire in a theater and
> causing a panic. It does not even protect a man from an injunction
> against uttering words that may have all the effect of force.... It is a
> question of proximity and degree. When a nation is at war many
> things that might be said in time of peace are such a hindrance to its
> effort that their utterance will not be endured so long as men fight,
> and that no Court could regard them as protected by any con-
> stitutional right.[28]

In two important cases decided the same day, Holmes and his colleagues refused to reverse convictions for expression intended to encourage opposition to the war and to obstruct recruiting. One, *Debs v.
United States*,[29] upheld the defendant's conviction for giving an anti-
war speech at a state convention of the Socialist party. In 1912, Eugene
Debs had run for president on the Socialist ticket for the fourth time,
and because he represented an established and widely recognized
political position, the ruling stirred considerable opposition. Holmes's
opinion was not well received by many contemporary commentators,
and their criticisms might have influenced his later opinions.

The other case, *Frohwerk v. United States,* was factually similar to
Schenck; in it Holmes curtly rejected broad immunity under the First
Amendment: "We venture to believe that neither Hamilton nor Madison, nor any other competent person then or later, ever supposed that
to make criminal the counselling of a murder within the jurisdiction of
Congress would be an unconstitutional interference with free
speech."[30] Consequently, certain acts were beyond the area of protection (and presumably not subject to a clear and present danger
analysis). Unlike the position he would later espouse, his opinion here
found harmful impact because the circulation of the paper in question
"was in quarters where a little breath would be enough to kindle a
flame."[31]

Holmes's clear and present danger test almost immediately encountered complications that would remain with it until its apparent demise
in 1969. In *Abrams v. United States*,[32] decided in 1919 soon after
Schenck, the Court did not apply the test, and Holmes was later to

complain (in *Gitlow*) that it had been abandoned. And in *Gitlow v. New York*,[33] decided in 1925, Justice Sanford, writing for the majority, denied that the test was of constitutional stature, asserting instead that it had been used in *Schenck* solely to interpret the applicability of the statute to utterances for which the defendants had been convicted. The Justice distinguished between the statute in *Schenck*, which designated certain conduct unlawful and had to be applied to the speech in question, and the statute in *Gitlow*, which made speech itself the crime. In these and several other cases, Holmes and Brandeis reiterated and refined the formula, expelling any doubt that they considered it determinative of relevant constitutional issues on speech and press.

Holmes's intent in creating the danger standard has been subject to dispute by other than his colleagues. Justice Frankfurter believed that the test was not used by Holmes to express a legal doctrine or convey a formula for adjudicating constitutional issues. It was, instead, Frankfurter said, a "literary phrase not to be distorted by being taken from its context."[34] An opinion subscribed to by four Justices in the *Dennis* case explained that Holmes used the test only for determining whether a clear and present danger existed that the defendant's conduct would cause a military insubordination, which was illegal under the law.[35] Professor Kalven thought that the danger dictum did not become in Holmes's mind a constitutional test until sometime after *Schenck*, and Professor Strong concludes that Holmes employed it originally as essentially a rule of evidence.[36]

Holmes applied a version of his *Schenck* reasoning three years later in *Pennsylvania Coal Co. v. Mahon*.[37] There too, as we saw in chapter 6, he insisted that the constitutional guarantee was a matter of degree and could not be disposed of by general propositions. Thus a consistency of thought appears in these cases; in the latter, Holmes argued that the taking clause did not prevent the government from blowing up buildings to halt a conflagration, and in the former, that the speech guarantee did not forbid jailing those who falsely shout "fire" in a crowded theater. This approach was not novel to the Court on which he served: very good reason had to exist for subordinating the individual to the state. It was, to paraphrase Holmes, all a matter of degree.[38]

The majority, however, was unwilling to submit the constitutionality of all peacetime expression to this balancing test. Certain speech was never constitutionally acceptable. For example, incitement to force and violence was not protected and thus was outside the confines of a subjective standard that at times might have validated it. Similarly, because not all economic restraints were eligible for the balancing of substantive due process, liberty of contract, as we have seen, did not apply to industries "affected with a public interest."

The clear and present danger test had much in common with substantive due process. Both required judicial evaluation of the legislative judgment. Both were compromises between liberty and authority. Both required much more than a debatable legislative justification for upholding the law. And both embodied the idea that people should not be purposelessly restrained.

Holmes's and Brandeis's discussions of the clear and present danger test are excellent expositions for the proposition that laws unnecessarily limiting individual freedom are constitutionally defective. They were willing to curb expression only when required to protect people or the state from serious injury. The principle involved is basic in Anglo-American law. William Blackstone condemned as arbitrary and undesirable restraints that little served their purpose. By the 1920s this principle would seem to have acquired constitutional status under the due process clauses having been invoked repeatedly to preserve freedom of contract. Yet neither side of the Court seemed to comprehend the full meaning of a principle which they each strongly advanced in different contexts. Holmes and Brandeis declined to apply it across the spectrum of human activity (except when the law was beyond redemption), and the majority declined to recognize it in the area of expression (which they did protect under other theories).

Consider an analogy presented by the *Lochner* decision. In that case, the Court would have upheld the statute had it been convinced that long working hours create a clear and present danger to the health and well-being of the bakery workers. It had previously sustained an eight hour day for workers in underground mines and smelters because longer working hours in that situation constituted a clear and present danger to health and well-being. The Court was willing to limit freedom of contract to avert serious harm. The famous dissenters accepted suppression of expression when dangerous consequences threatened.

The Triumphant Dissenters

In *Abrams v. United States*,[39] also decided in 1919, Holmes and Brandeis dissented from the decision that affirmed the convictions of the five defendants for conspiracy to violate the law by publishing pamphlets condemning and urging resistance to the dispatch of American troops to Russia. Each was sentenced to twenty years in prison. The problem presented by the case was the necessity of establishing that the defendants violated a law intended to protect the American war effort against Germany.

Holmes maintained that *Schenck, Frohwerk,* and *Debs* were correctly decided because they concerned speech that produces or was intended to produce a clear and imminent danger. However, he doubted that any immediate danger to the success of the war effort was presented by the publishing in the *Abrams* situation of what he considered silly leaflets by unknown people who did not engage in further action. Anything more than nominal punishment would make the accused suffer not for committing a crime but rather for espousing an ideology. He said that a state of war in itself did not change the right of free speech; nothing less than "the present danger of immediate evil or an intent to bring it about"[40] warranted congressional limitation on expressing opinions. Holmes's famous rhetoric displays his belief that an almost unfettered interchange of ideas is necessary to establish political truth. He wrote that

> the ultimate good desired is better reached by free trade in ideas—that the best test of truth is the power of the thought to get itself accepted in the competition of the market, and that truth is the only ground upon which their [the people's] wishes safely can be carried out. That at any rate is the theory of our Constitution. It is an experiment, as all life is an experiment. Every year if not every day we have to wager our salvation upon some prophecy based upon imperfect knowledge. While that experiment is part of our system I think that we should be eternally vigilant against attempts to check the expression of opinions that we loathe and believe to be fraught with death, unless they so imminently threaten immediate interference with the lawful and pressing purposes of the law that an immediate check is required to save the country.[41]

Justice Clarke, writing for the majority, disagreed that the defendants' conduct was of negligible consequence.

> It will not do to say, . . . that the only intent of these defendants was to prevent injury to the Russian cause. Men must be held to have intended, and to be accountable for, the effects which their acts were likely to produce. Even if their primary purpose and intent was to aid the cause of the Russian Revolution, the plan of action which they adopted necessarily involved, before it could be realized, defeat of the war program of the United States, for the obvious effect of this

appeal, if it should become effective, as they hoped it might, would be to persuade persons...not to aid government loans and not to work in ammunition factories....[42]

Serious wartime restraints upon both economic and political freedoms were accepted by the "laissez-faire" Court. *Schenck, Frohwerk, Debs,* and *Abrams* are examples in the speech area. The Court also upheld economic restraints it would never have countenanced during peacetime. Included were laws establishing an eight-hour day and a minimum-wage scale for employees of interstate carriers.[43] In addition, it allowed the imposition of rent controls, with Holmes in that situation applying a criterion resembling the danger formula: "The regulation is put and justified only as a temporary measure.... A limit in time, to tide over a passing trouble, may well justify a law that could not be upheld as a permanent change."[44]

Debate over interpretation of protected expression extended to two famous peacetime cases: *Gitlow v. New York* and *Whitney v. California.*[45] Perhaps the most significant aspect of the former is that it is the first opinion to acknowledge that the prohibitions in the First Amendment against the abridgement of speech and press by the federal government are applicable to the state governments by virtue of the Fourteenth Amendment's due process clause. The majority "assumed" that the rights of speech "are among the fundamental personal rights and 'liberties' protected by the due process clause of the Fourteenth Amendment from impairment by the States."[46] Despite his position in the economic cases that the term had no justiciable meaning, Holmes in his dissent agreed that the word liberty in the Fourteenth Amendment's due process clause embraced free expression.

Gitlow was convicted under New York's criminal anarchy statute forbidding the advocacy of overthrowing organized government by force or violence.[47] He had arranged for the printing and distributing of 16,000 copies of a "Manifesto" calling for violent action and revolution. The trial produced no evidence of any effect from the dissemination of the manifesto.

Whitney was convicted of violating California's 1919 Criminal Syndicalism Act, penalizing membership in any organization advocating "unlawful acts of force and violence or unlawful methods of terrorism as a means of accomplishing a change in industrial ownership or control, or effecting any political change."[48] Whitney's crime consisted of organizing and being a member of the Communist Labor party of California, which was formed to promote the syndicalism illegal under the act. Justice Sanford wrote the *Gitlow* and *Whitney* opinions, and

Holmes and Brandeis disagreed with the reasoning in both, although they concurred with the result in *Whitney* on technical grounds.

In *Gitlow* Sanford asserted that utterances inciting to the overthrow of government by unlawful means present a sufficient peril to bring their punishment within the range of legislative discretion. He did not regard the defendant's expression as within the ambit of protected political speech. He believed that although the effect of a given utterance cannot be accurately foreseen, the danger it poses can be real and substantial.

A single revolutionary spark may kindle a fire that, smouldering for a time, may burst into a sweeping and destructive conflagration. It cannot be said that the State is acting arbitrarily or unreasonably when in the exercise of its judgment as to the measures necessary to protect the public peace and safety, it seeks to extinguish the spark without waiting until it has enkindled the flame or blazed into the conflagration. It cannot reasonably be required to defer the adoption of measures for its own peace and safety until the revolutionary utterances lead to actual disturbances of the public peace or imminent and immediate danger of its own destruction; but it may, in the exercise of its judgment, suppress the threatened danger in its incipiency.[49]

In light of this explanation, the case against Whitney was stronger. There, Sanford said that united action constitutes greater danger to the public peace and security than do isolated utterances and acts of individuals. If it had exercised more imagination and foresight, the majority could have defined both Gitlow's and Whitney's actions as clear and present dangers and in so doing would have rendered decisions more acceptable to future commentators. (This is the course the Vinson Court followed in 1951 in the *Dennis* case, which is discussed subsequently.)

In *Gitlow* Holmes contended that his danger formula applied and that the defendants' printed efforts to overthrow the government did not present a clear and present danger. To the allegation that expression can be an incitement, Holmes replied with the now familiar language:

Every idea is an incitement. It offers itself for belief and if believed it is acted on unless some other belief outweighs it or some failure of energy stifles the movement at its birth. The only difference between the expression of an opinion and an incitement in the narrower sense is the speaker's enthusiasm for the result. Eloquence may set fire to reason. But whatever may be thought of the redundant discourse before us it had no chance of starting a present conflagration. If in the long run the beliefs expressed in proletarian dictatorship are destined to be accepted by the dominant forces of the community, the only meaning of free speech is that they should be given their chance and have their way.[50]

Brandeis, in *Whitney*, asserted that the danger test was determinative of the constitutional question. Unlike his action in cases concerning economic rights, in which he strongly supported the legislative judgment, in this case he was willing to limit the weight given the legislative action, saying that it "creates merely a rebuttable presumption that these conditions [the existence of a clear and present danger] have been satisfied."[51] He rejected the majority's ruling that joining a political party formed to advocate a future proletarian revolution by mass action is not a constitutionally protected right.

Brandeis used the occasion of *Whitney* to present his famous historical essay on the meaning of free speech.

Those who won our independence believed that the final end of the State was to make men free to develop their faculties; and that in its government the deliberative forces should prevail over the arbitrary. They valued liberty both as an end and as a means. They believed liberty to be the secret of happiness and courage to be the secret of liberty. They believed that freedom to think as you will and to speak as you think are means indispensable to the discovery and spread of political truth; that without free speech and assembly discussion would be futile; that with them, discussion affords ordinarily adequate protection against the dissemination of noxious doctrine; that the greatest menace to freedom is an inert people; that public discussion is a political duty; and that this should be a fundamental principle of the American government. They recognized the risks to which all human institutions are subject. But they knew that order cannot be secured merely through fear of punishment for its infraction; that it is hazardous to discourage thought, hope and imagination; that fear breeds repression; that repression breeds hate; that hate menaces stable government; that the path of safety lies in the opportunity to discuss freely supposed grievances and proposed remedies; and that the fitting remedy for evil counsels is good ones. Believing in the power of reason as applied through public discussion, they eschewed silence coerced by law—the argument of force in its worst form. Recognizing the occasional tyrannies of governing majorities, they amended the Constitution so that free speech and assembly should be guaranteed....

Those who won our independence by revolution were not cowards. They did not fear political change. They did not exalt order at the cost of liberty. To courageous, self-reliant man, with confidence in the power of free and fearless reasoning applied through the processes of popular government, no danger flowing from speech can be deemed clear and present, unless the incidence of the evil apprehended is so imminent that it may befall before there is opportunity for full discussion.[52]

This passage, which resembles in thought and language the funeral oration of the Athenian leader Pericles,[53] is an eloquent tribute to essential premises of American society. However, Brandeis was engaged in a role not entirely characteristic of his tenure on the Court. He was using his impressive intellectual and rhetorical talents to defend liberty against authority. On many other occasions, the Justice assumed a different position, as illustrated by his dissent in *New State Ice*, where he found many reasons for the state to impose its will on a person or a corporation. Brandeis reserved his eloquence in behalf of freedom to cases involving conceptual and political rights.

Brandeis's rhetoric in *Whitney* pays tribute to a group of individuals whose political and economic philosophies were much different from his own. Unlike the Framers, he tended to observe a standard that considered government nearly always right when it restricts economic and property interests and nearly always wrong when it imposes restrictions in intellectual matters. The Framers' priorities were far different in this regard. In his laudatory 1933 biography of the Justice, Professor Mason advises us how distant Brandeis's views were from those who framed the Constitution he was obliged to interpret:

Urging *laissez faire* in politics, Mr. Justice Brandeis is an ardent advocate of government regulation in industry. Indeed his principles exhibit an element of collectivism so strong as somewhat to embarrass those who endorse his libertarian doctrines.[54]

Prominent Framers believed the property right was preservative of many other personal liberties (about their attitudes toward free expression we shall see more in chapter 11). A government that can control an individual's property, wealth, and livelihood can also dominate his or her life and actions, including the exercise of speech and press. Brandeis apparently was willing to accept these risks in the belief that economic justice depended on government intervention into the economy. In these instances, he was reluctant to follow his famous warning about expanding governmental authority:

In every extension of governmental functions lurks a new danger to civil liberty.

Experience should teach us to be most on our guard to protect
liberty when the government's purposes are beneficent. Men born to
freedom are naturally alert to repel invasion of their liberty by evil-
minded rulers. The greatest dangers to liberty lurk in insidious
encroachment by men of zeal, well-meaning but without understanding.[55]

Holmes and Brandeis owe much of their fame as defenders of individual rights to their opinions in the expression decisions that followed
World War I. In these cases neither Justice was willing to accept
popular legislative judgments, even in matters posing threats to public
tranquility, and thus voted to overrule them. In so doing, they sought
to impose a standard of judicial review that much legislation on the
subject could not meet. However, instead of being criticized for substituting their judgment for that of the lawmaking bodies, or of deciding
cases upon what, to use Holmes's own words, was a "theory which a
large part of the country does not entertain,"[56] the Justices were be-
stowed with the appreciation and admiration of history. In contrast,
their colleagues on the Court suffered scorn, ridicule, and contempt for
engaging in a similar process when economic regulation was concerned. The reason for this double standard is outcome and not process. Professor Alexander Bickel's description of the art of evaluating
courts is relevant here.

Where does the truth lie? One begins reluctantly to feel the suspicion that perhaps what is really decisive is not any theory of a proper
relationship between the Court and Congress, not any theory on the
Court's part of its proper function in a democracy, but where the
result comes out.[57]

An analysis of the Holmes-Brandeis opinions on speech and press
does little to inspire confidence that they are products of extraordinary
judicial craftsmanship. Holmes's opinions in the pre–World War I
cases —stated "when times were more settled and Brandeis's influence
was not yet felt"[58]—accepted a Blackstonian version of the First
Amendment's provision on speech and press; they offer no clue to the
perspective he would later adopt. Holmes began to retreat from his
original position when he proposed the clear and present danger test in
Schenck. There, he was satisfied that the statute in question was valid
and that under it speaking or writing with intent to obstruct the war
effort was illegal, even though the challenged action did not accomplish
its purpose.

Although everyone is entitled to correct errors in light of new understanding, Justices especially should explain why their comprehension of the law has changed. Such explanation is one reason for written decisions. However, in the expression cases Holmes never satisfactorily met this responsibility. He neither provided supporting precedent for the danger rule nor presented any historical basis for its application. These omissions are all the more striking because of Holmes's attacks on substantive due process as being without basis in the Constitution.

As for Brandeis, concurring with Holmes in *Whitney*, he maintained that the danger rule was controlling.[59] As a result of the Court's holding and reasoning in *Gitlow*, however, the danger test no longer had the authority of precedent, and Brandeis's statement to the contrary was wrong. This was not the only occasion when Brandeis and Holmes rejected existing precedent: they continually refused to accept the prevailing formulation of liberty of contract. One gets the impression Holmes and Brandeis were operating their own store.

Brandeis's concurrence in *Whitney* seeks to accord constitutional roots to the danger test. However, his historical perspective is not well founded. The evidence strongly supports Holmes's views in *Patterson*, that the main purpose of the expression guarantee was to prevent previous restraints on expression and not to prevent "the subsequent punishment of such as may be deemed contrary to the public welfare." It is most unlikely that Whitney would have been exonerated in the early decades of the nation. First, the First Amendment applies only to Congress and not to the states. Second, the Amendment would not have helped her, even assuming Congress had passed the law. This amendment (as will be further explained in chapter 11) did not abolish the common law of seditious libel. In the late eighteenth century, a publication that brought government into contempt or disrepute or excited hatred against it was considered a seditious libel. To be found innocent of this charge, an accused had to prove that publication was made for justifiable purposes and with good motives, regardless of whether it was in fact true.[60]

Holmes and Brandeis may have been the giants of the American judiciary as so many commentators believe, but that portion of their records discussed in these pages does not bear this judgment out. In highlighting some of their shortcomings, I do not mean to minimize or impugn their ability and integrity. Doubtless, students of that period could find comparable deficiencies in the opinions of their ideological opposites. My conclusion is that history has admired one group and condemned another for reasons that have to do more with ends than means. Prevailing professional opinion accepts the superiority of the conceptual rights over the material rights. The Justices associated with each perspective have benefited and suffered accordingly.

Political Speech

That the Supreme Court was not hostile to "pure speech" is evidenced by its decision in *Fiske v. Kansas,*[61] handed down on the same day as *Whitney.* The defendant in the case was the first to succeed before the Court on the basis of a claim that he was deprived of the liberty of speech. Fiske was an organizer for the Industrial Workers of the World (IWW) and was convicted under a Kansas syndicalism act, which was similar to the California statute considered in *Whitney.* His offense was promoting criminal syndicalism by recruiting new members for the IWW. The only evidence of the IWW's unlawful purposes was the preamble to its constitution that urged a continuous struggle between workers and employers to the end that workers "organize as a class, take possession of the earth, and the machinery of production and abolish the wage system." The preamble neither urged nor mentioned violence.

Justice Sanford, for a unanimous Court, reversed the conviction on the ground that although the statute was valid, the defendant, unlike Whitney, urged change through peaceful means and therefore was protected under the Constitution. The preamble differed from the manifesto involved in *Gitlow* because it did not advocate unlawful conduct. This distinction dominated the thinking of the majority of the Court. For these Justices, freedom of speech did not protect utterances tending to incite crime, disturbances of the public peace, or violent overthrow of the government, but did safeguard the advocacy of change through nonviolent means.

De Jonge v. Oregon,[62] decided by a unanimous Court in 1937 (with Justice Stone not participating), concerned Oregon's criminal syndicalism law. De Jonge, a Communist party member, was convicted and sentenced to seven years in prison for participating in a public meeting, held under the auspices of the Communist party, in order to protest the shooting by police of some strikers and raids on workers' homes and halls.

In reversing the conviction, the Supreme Court, through Chief Justice Hughes, asserted that an individual could not be punished for speech that did not incite to illegal conduct, despite the fact that the forum is under the sponsorship of an organization advocating subversive doctrine.

The greater the importance of safeguarding the community from incitements to the overthrow of our institutions by force and violence, the more imperative is the need to preserve inviolate the constitutional rights of free speech, free press and free assembly in order to maintain the opportunity for free political discussion, to the end that government may be responsive to the will of the people and that changes, if desired, may be obtained by peaceful means. Therein lies the security of the Republic, the very foundation of constitutional government.[63]

Hughes said that peaceful assembly for lawful discussion cannot be made a crime.

If the persons assembling have committed crimes elsewhere, if they have formed or are engaged in a conspiracy against the public peace and order, they may be prosecuted for their conspiracy or other violation of valid laws. But it is a different matter when the State, instead of prosecuting them for such offenses, seizes upon mere participation in a peaceable assembly and a lawful public discussion as the basis for a criminal charge.[64]

In *Herndon v. Lowry*,[65] relating to the charge of "an attempt to incite insurrection" in violation of Georgia law, the Court split 5–4 on the fact of whether Herndon, a black Communist organizer, was attempting to induce and incite others (mostly Southern blacks) to join in forceful resistance to the authority of the state. The majority opinion of Justice Roberts said that no evidence had been found that the defendant advocated violence against the state and thus rejected the dissenting views of Justice Van Devanter (joined by McReynolds, Sutherland, and Butler) that the purpose and probable effect of the literature distributed by Herndon should be tested in light of the impact on those who were sought to be influenced. Van Devanter said that the literature was largely directed to blacks, whose past and present circumstances would lead them to give unusual credence to its inflaming and inciting features.

Hughes's opinion in *Stromberg v. California*[66] held unconstitutional a California law making it a felony to display a red flag or any other flag "as a sign, symbol or emblem of opposition to organized government." He found this language so vague and indefinite as to permit punishment of free political discussion. This was one of many state "red flag" laws that had been adopted during the height of the antiradical feeling in the country following World War I. Justices McReynolds and Butler each dissented separately on other grounds.

Prior Restraint on Publications

Six years earlier the four minority Justices in *Herndon* had also dissented in *Near v. Minnesota*,[67] the leading case on prior restraint of the press. The defendants were publishers of a Minneapolis weekly, *The Saturday Press*, which had accused, over a period of time, the mayor and other local officials of gross misconduct for having condoned the activities of gangsters said to be responsible for gambling, bootlegging, and racketeering in the city. Minnesota law provided for abatement as a public nuisance of a "malicious, scandalous and defamatory newspaper, magazine, or other periodical." The county attorney sought and obtained under this statute a permanent injunction restraining the defendants from future publication of any "malicious, scandalous or defamatory newspaper." The trial court found that the defendants were engaged in the business of publishing defamatory articles creating a nuisance and that future articles would be of the same character.

On appeal, the United States Supreme Court ruled 5–4 to vacate the injunction, with both opinions agreeing that the Constitution prohibits certain kinds of prior restraints but differing on the kind affected.

To the majority, per Chief Justice Hughes, the restraint imposed by the trial court was the "essence of censorship."[68] According to the Chief Justice, the First Amendment prohibited all previous restraints except for special cases, such as when disclosure of wartime military deployment was threatened, when the material was obscene, and when the speaker incited others to acts of violence or revolution. Justice Butler, writing for the minority, replied that the ban applied historically only to the controls administered by licensors and censors and therefore did not affect a judicial remedy to be enforced by a suit in equity. Furthermore he could not perceive any distinction between a publication devoted to scandal and defamation, such as the one in question, and a lewd one, which Hughes said was subject to prior restraint.

Apparently the dissenters had the better historical argument.[69] The majority was more concerned about the meaning and significance attached by the Framers' generation to prior restraint and the need for a vigilant press in contemporary times. Consequently, for them, the historical distinction was not decisive.[70]

Butler viewed the defendants as not engaged in the dissemination of information, but as conducting a business which constituted a nuisance. Rejecting this distinction, Hughes asserted it did not matter that a newspaper or periodical is largely devoted to the publication of defamatory material. The majority maintained the state's libel laws afforded both public and private redress for wrongs committed by publishers. The dissent did not regard libel laws as adequate to suppress defamation. An insolvent publisher, for example, would not be deterred by the threat of a damage action.

This writer does not know if those harmed could, in a suit for defamation, have recovered adequately to make them whole. A subsequent penalty will deter defamation but may not cause truth to cancel out all the injurious effects of that which has been said or written. Obviously, no such problem would exist if a court prevented publication. However, because prior restraint can be injurious to both producers and consumers of speech, no solution will fully satisfy the interests of all concerned. Prior restraint enables government to make the critical decisions in this regard. This power lends itself to being oppressively and incompetently exercised to the detriment of the free flow of ideas. In a society dependent upon private sources of political information, the censor is more to be feared than the press. The *Near* majority accepted this analysis, and in spite of the damaging and provocative character of the publication, refused advance restraint. These Justices indeed displayed great confidence in the workings of the marketplace of ideas.

But at this same time the Justices were much less certain about a free marketplace for property. Zoning, whose constitutionality the Supreme Court upheld in 1926,[71] is essentially prior restraint on a use of property that poses no threat of nuisance. The zoning authorities determine in advance the likely harm that will result from certain uses and regulate development to avoid or minimize these frequently speculative problems. Thus, they too are censors, with the power of government to force their ideas on the public. Nevertheless, the High Court of that period removed almost all prior restraint from one business (publishing) and effectively imposed it on another (real estate and building).

A strong argument can be made, based on reasons comparable to those advanced in *Near,* that prior restraints on economic activity are likewise detrimental to the public. (This subject will be discussed subsequently in chapters 11 and 13.) However, the analogy between speech and property rights has been noticeably absent in judicial reasoning. The support for a free-speech marketplace displayed in *Near* contrasts sharply with the record of the judiciary in cases in which the use of property threatened economic interests of some members of the public.

In *Hadacheck v. Sebastian*,[72] a unanimous Supreme Court, in 1915, upheld criminal proceedings that restrained the operation of a brick-making factory—an action that resulted in a more than 90 percent loss in value to the owner (from $800,000 to $60,000), and possibly appreciable monies to consumers of the product—despite the fact that the brickyard had been the first development to locate in the area. Originally a benign use of property, the brickyard became a "nuisance" only when people moved into the neighborhood. The rationale of such decisions that owners of certain potentially harmful businesses assume the risk that they will in time become "nuisances" even without committing any wrong contrasts markedly with the willingness of the Court to safeguard from censorship publishers who deliberately create defamatory "nuisances."

In 1936 in *Grosjean v. American Press Co.*,[73] the Supreme Court committed itself further to the principle established in *Near*. Louisiana had imposed a 2 percent gross receipts "license tax" on all publications that sold advertising and had a circulation in excess of 20,000 a week. The reason for the law apparently was that the papers subject to the tax opposed the Huey Long regime, while the smaller ones supported it. Writing for a unanimous Court, Justice Sutherland declared the law unconstitutional as a violation of the expression guarantee.

> The tax here involved is bad not because it takes money from the pockets of the appellees [newspapers]. If that were all, a wholly different question would be presented. It is bad because, in the light of its history and of its present setting, it is seen to be a deliberate and calculated device in the guise of a tax to limit the circulation of information ....[74]

Interestingly, Sutherland relied heavily on the history which antedated and attended the adoption of the expression guarantee with apparently little more accuracy than Brandeis had achieved in *Whitney*.[75]

In *Associated Press v. National Labor Relations Board*,[76] decided the following year, the Supreme Court upheld application of the National Labor Relations Act to the press. The AP had discharged an employee for what the NLRB had concluded were prounion activities, and the Court ordered reinstatement, limiting to this extent AP's power to terminate employment. Sutherland, with the concurrence of Van Devanter, McReynolds, and Butler, dissented on the ground that governmental control over the employment relationship of news collection corporations violated freedom of press. While acknowledging the right and interest of employees to form and join unions, Sutherland argued that the constitutional immunity of the press would be circumscribed if publishers did not have the power to dispense with the services of an employee engaged in editorial services: "[I]f petitioner [AP] concluded, as it well could have done, that its policy to preserve its news service free from color, bias or distortion was likely to be subverted [by an employee], what power has Congress to interfere in the face of the First Amendment?"[77] Sutherland advocated the strongest regard for free expression:

> Freedom is not a mere intellectual abstraction; and it is not merely a word to adorn an oration upon occasions of patriotic rejoicing. It is an intensely practical reality, capable of concrete enjoyment in a multitude of ways day by day. When applied to the press, the term freedom is not to be narrowly confined; and it obviously means more than publication and circulation. If freedom of the press does not include the right to adopt and pursue a policy without governmental restriction, it is a misnomer to call it freedom. And we may as well deny at once the right of the press freely to adopt a policy and pursue it, as to concede that right and deny the liberty to exercise an uncensored judgment in respect of the employment and discharge of the agents through whom the policy is to be effectuated.[78]

In both *Grosjean* and *Associated Press,* Sutherland accords freedom of the press highest constitutional authority and voices sentiments comparable to those in contemporary speech cases. His language is eloquent and dramatic, perhaps for some even stirring. But Sutherland confronted the difficult problem of having to compete for historical honors with Brandeis and Holmes, in this area at least "rhetoricians of extraordinary potency,"[79] and an exceptionally hard act to follow.

Similarity of Approach to Liberties

How does one explain why Justices supposedly committed to freedom would uphold the *Abrams, Gitlow,* and *Whitney* convictions and favor prior restraint in *Near?* One explanation is that the Justices did not regard liberties equally—that is, that they had preferences for speech and economic rights exactly the reverse of Brandeis's. However, a number of factors cast doubt on this reasoning. First, the Justices in *Gitlow* included speech as a right protected against infringement by a state under the due process clause of the Fourteenth Amendment. This ruling represents one of the greatest advances for free expression.

Second, their votes to reverse the conviction of Fiske, De Jonge, and Stromberg, each of which had been upheld by all the lower courts, displayed acceptance—in face of considerable public opposition to "subversive" groups—of "peaceful speech" that urges changes in government through the usual political processes. Judged historically, Sanford's holding that advocacy of violence and revolution is not constitutionally safeguarded was hardly arbitrary or capricious.[80] A quarter of a century after *Gitlow*, Justice Learned Hand, for the Second Circuit Court of Appeals,[81] and Chief Justice Vinson, for the United States Supreme Court, applied the clear and present danger rule in upholding the 1949 conviction, under the Smith Act, of Eugene Dennis, Secretary General of the United States Communist party.[82] Three Justices joined Vinson's opinion and two others concurred. This law was essentially similar to the act sustained in *Gitlow*, making it illegal to advocate the overthrow of the state by force and violence.

Distinctions, the tool of the legal trade, have been much in evidence in speech theory. The Court has always accepted a tier of expression that is not constitutionally secured. Most Justices have not been willing to protect libel, slander, obscenity, perjury, false advertising, and solicitation of crime. Even Justice Black, the most fervent speech advocate ever to sit on the Court, distinguished between pure expression and expression associated with conduct, believing that the one merited absolute protection and the other was subject to regulation. Given the Blackstonian background of the First Amendment and the limited evolution of judicial thought on free expression, Sanford's distinction between advocacy of forceful and of peaceful means of change is quite understandable (although, as I have previously suggested, it was analytically shallow).

Third, Justice Butler's distinction in the *Near* case was not out of character with the position his group took in economic regulation cases. He viewed the conduct as constituting a nuisance and not entitled to exception under the prior restraint rule formulated by Hughes. He would have been no less adverse to property nuisances. Moreover, Sutherland wrote the opinion in *Grosjean*, augmenting the prior restraint rule and removing a threat to free press, as well as the dissenting opinion for the *Near* minority in *Associated Press*, rejecting the impediments that labor regulations would impose on the freedom of the news-gathering business.

A persuasive explanation for their opinions on expression is that these Justices were quite even-handed in interpreting the Constitution. The approach of Justices Sanford, Butler, Sutherland, Van Devanter, and McReynolds is not satisfactory to the strong proponents of free expression. These jurists did not exhibit the same enthusiasm for unrestrained speech that Holmes and Brandeis did. Nevertheless, the postwar Court did seem to display about the same standard of concern for the conceptual as for the material liberties. Liberty of contract for these Justices was no more inclusive than was freedom of utterance. However, the laissez-faire Justices made their reputation, for better or worse, on their approach to freedom in the economic sphere. History accords them no laurels for their attitudes toward the exercise of speech and press rights.

It requires more than the ordinary perceptions of this writer to discern whether or to what extent the substantive due process Justices who served after the First World War gave preference to some endeavors over others. Moreover, there might be an insuperable obstacle to such an evaluation. Liberties are not always neatly separable but are often linked and intertwined. In *Meyer* and *Pierce,* the plaintiffs would have triumphed regardless of whether the theory employed was economic rights or family rights. Likewise, newspaper and magazine publishers may gain equally from freedom of expression or liberty of contract. The liberty to become better informed, to advance ideas, to travel, to vote, and possibly even to procreate, may have been at stake for Leibmann, Nebbia, Lyon (a plaintiff in *Adkins*), and their families, in the cases discussed in the last chapter. Laws that deprive people of the opportunity to gain materially also inhibit the exercise of other personal liberties, such as those mentioned. Perhaps, as has been noted, Louisiana's restrictive laws on the commissioning of riverboat pilots (discussed in the next chapter) may have foreclosed the literary career of another Mark Twain.[83]

Rights are not ends in themselves, but means to the enhancement of the human condition, through self-fulfillment, personal gratification, enlightenment, and happiness. The judicial policy that most advances these is to be preferred. If that is the test, the account on the preceding pages discloses that the substantive due process judges adequately performed their responsibilities.

III Fall of the Old and Rise of the New Substantive Due Process

8   Judicial Abdication

The Road to Abdication

           As we have seen above (in chapter 6), the special recognition given liberty of contract under substantive due process was rejected in the 1934 case of *Nebbia v. New York*. In that situation, there was enough leeway in the exception relating to businesses affected with a public interest for the Supreme Court to cope with "emergency" conditions in the New York dairy industry, one of the state's most important businesses. But the 5–4 majority chose not to follow that course. Justice Roberts said that the exception was not susceptible of definition. Prior to *Nebbia,* businesses not clothed with the public interest designation were considered as largely exempt from price regulation. In eliminating the distinction, Roberts declared that legislation curbing economic activity would be upheld if not unreasonable or arbitrary and if reasonably related to a public purpose. Contrary to previous declarations, restraint was no longer the exception.

        Nevertheless, two years later Roberts voted with the dissenters in *Nebbia* to nullify New York's minimum-wage law for adult women and minors.[1] The majority rejected the contention of the state that the New York law was distinguishable from the one invalidated in *Adkins.* But this grace period was short lived. In *West Coast Hotel Co. v. Parrish,* decided the following year, Roberts switched sides again, enabling the majority, per Chief Justice Hughes, to follow the line established in *Nebbia.* This time the Court reversed *Adkins.* Hughes also overturned the premise that had sustained substantive due process by asserting that legislative restraints were consistent with, and not antagonistic to, the liberty contemplated by the due process clause. Hughes's single concern was whether regulation of women's minimum wages was reasonable, not arbitrary: "[The legislative judgment] cannot be regarded as arbitrary or capricious, and that is all we have to decide. Even if the wisdom of the policy be regarded as debatable and its effect uncertain, still the legislature is entitled to its judgment."[2]

This rule remained intact in two cases decided during the same term, sustaining against due process attack the Railway Labor Act and the National Labor Relations Act,[3] both of which require employers to bargain exclusively with the union chosen by a majority of workers. These decisions effectively overturned *Adair* and *Coppage*.

Judicial review of economic legislation was further circumscribed the following year in the filled-milk case, *United States v. Carolene Products Co.*[4] In 1923 Congress had enacted legislation prohibiting the shipment in interstate commerce of any product resembling milk or cream that was in fact a blend of skimmed milk and a fat or oil other than milk fat. The statute declared that filled milk as so defined "is an adulterated article of food, injurious to the public health, and its sale constitutes a fraud upon the public."[5] The defendant indicted for violating the act used due process grounds as one basis of its challenge. A divided Supreme Court upheld the indictment with four making up the majority, two concurring in the result, two not participating, and one dissenting. Sutherland and Van Devanter had by then retired. For the majority, Justice Stone set forth the following rules as governing review of legislative enactments:

> [T]he existence of facts supporting the legislative judgment is to be presumed, for regulatory legislation affecting ordinary commercial transactions is not to be pronounced unconstitutional unless in the light of the facts made known or generally assumed it is of such a character as to preclude the assumption that it rests upon some rational basis within the knowledge and experience of the legislators....
> ...[B]y their very nature such inquiries, where the legislative judgment is drawn in question, must be restricted to the issue whether any state of facts either known or which could reasonably be assumed affords support for it.[6]

Stone still left some review power over commercial regulation, although very few such statutes could fail under his guidelines. In his famous footnote 4, he sought to confine the rule to economic legislation and not have it apply also to political and "personal" liberties.

There may be narrower scope for operation of the presumption of constitutionality when legislation appears on its face to be within a specific prohibition of the Constitution, such as those of the first ten amendments, which are deemed equally specific when held to be embraced within the Fourteenth.

It is unnecessary to consider now whether legislation which restricts those political processes which can ordinarily be expected to bring about repeal of undesirable legislation, is to be subjected to more exacting judicial scrutiny under the general prohibitions of the Fourteenth Amendment than are most other types of legislation...

Nor need we enquire whether similar considerations enter into the review of statutes directed at particular religious... or national... or racial minorities... whether prejudice against discrete and insular minorities may be a special condition, which tends seriously to curtail the operation of those political processes ordinarily to be relied upon to protect minorities, and which may call for a correspondingly more searching judicial inquiry.[7]

In 1941, *Olsen v. Nebraska*[8] unanimously upheld a state statute limiting the fee that private employment agencies could charge. By then the only remaining members of the earlier Court were Stone and Roberts, neither a champion of economic due process. The *Olsen* case specifically overruled the 1928 decision, *Ribnik v. McBride*,[9] which had invalidated a similar statute and upon which the Nebraska Supreme Court had relied. Justice Douglas's opinion reasoned that the determinative standard used in *Ribnik* had been whether the business was affected with a public interest, and because that test had been discarded in *Nebbia*, the *Ribnik* precedent could not survive. However the complainants also alleged that the legislation would promote more harm than good and would not reasonably further a legitimate public purpose. To this contention Douglas responded:

We are not concerned, however, with the wisdom, need, or appropriateness of the legislation. Differences of opinion on that score suggest a choice which "should be left where...it was left by the Constitution—to the States and to Congress."... There is no necessity for the state to demonstrate before us that evils persist despite the competition which attends the bargaining in this field. In final analysis, the only constitutional prohibitions or restraints which respondents have suggested for the invalidation of this legislation are those notions of public policy embedded in earlier decisions of this Court but which, as Mr. Justice Holmes long admonished, should

not be read into the Constitution.... Since they do not find expression in the Constitution, we cannot give them continuing vitality as
standards by which the constitutionality of the economic and social
programs of the states is to be determined.[10]

Justice Black did not concur in that portion of *Carolene Products* in
which Justice Stone had retained a minimal due process review for
legislation, and one commentator has surmised that Black rejected any
jurisdiction over economic matters.[11] As a senator pressing for welfare
legislation at a time when the judiciary was predisposed to use its veto,
Black may have become sensitive about this power. In 1949, he authored the opinion in *Lincoln Federal Labor Union v. Northwestern
Iron & Metal Co.*,[12] sustaining state right-to-work laws that make illegal union shop arrangements. Black's opinion reinforced Douglas's
decision in *Olsen* and extinguished economic due process review.

This Court beginning at least as early as 1934, when the *Nebbia*
case was decided, has steadily rejected the due process philosophy
enunciated in the *Adair-Coppage* line of cases. In doing so, it has
consciously returned closer and closer to the earlier constitutional
principle that states have power to legislate against what are found to
be injurious practices in their internal commercial and business affairs, so long as their laws do not run afoul of some specific federal
constitutional prohibition, or of some valid federal law.... Under
this constitutional doctrine the due process clause is no longer to be
so broadly construed that the Congress and state legislatures are put
in a strait jacket when they attempt to suppress business and industrial conditions which they regard as offensive to the public welfare.[13]

The reversal was complete; liberty of contract survived only by
grace of constitutional provisions foreign to its origin. Constitutional
doctrines have come and gone, but as Professor Robert McCloskey has
stated, the abrupt demise of substantive due process was un-
precedented.

The judicial reaction against economic due process after 1937 is
unique in the history of the Supreme Court.... [I]t is hard to think of
another instance when the Court so thoroughly and quickly demolished a constitutional doctrine of such far-reaching
significance.... [T]he judicial power to strike down an economic
statute on the ground that it was "arbitrary, capricious, or unreasonable" had been frequently exercised and seemed to stand on a solid
base. Most of the Court's critics and some of its friends might have
hoped in the early 1930's that the "rational basis" standard would be

applied more leniently. But only a singularly prescient observer could have dreamed that the Court would soon abandon the concept altogether.[14]

Carolene Products' footnote 4 provided a widely heralded rationale for the two-level approach to individual liberties. It suggests the hazards of using footnotes to create constitutional doctrine. The footnote is supposed to limit judicial discretion by giving preference to specific prohibitions of the Bill of Rights. Presumably due process is not within this category. Yet, it accepts application of specific prohibitions to the states by way of the Fourteenth Amendment's due process and other section 1 clauses, all of which are nonspecific. The concern seems to be not with specification, but with substance, and this involves considerable judicial discretion.[15]

This footnote implies that a guiding principle for the extent to which legislation should be subject to judicial scrutiny depends on the availability of legislative relief for those who are denied meaningful access to the political process and who have little realistic chance of influencing the law makers. The thought is that if a group has a reasonable opportunity to avail itself of the electoral and legislative processes to accomplish change in its behalf, it does not require judicial aid.

Justice Stone considered racial, religious, and ethnic minorities to be discrete and insular groups. Clearly, he did not regard producers and sellers as falling within that category. However, in a representative government premised on majority rule, many economic minorities have little recourse at the ballot box or in the legislative halls. They too can be the victims of perverse, arbitrary, and capricious measures.

The filled-milk case concerned such a minority. The defendant was the producer of a new product, cheaper than, and a substitute for, milk, and therefore a serious competitive threat to the farm bloc and milk industry, together constituting a very powerful economic group. In time the filled-milk producers might have prevailed in the legislature, but the process would have been long and arduous, and the liberties of producers and consumers would have suffered.

Congressional committees found that the use of filled milk as a substitute for whole milk deprived users of the food value of milk fat. This was the extent of its hazard to health. Supposedly the legislators were concerned that consumers were using the product without knowledge that it was not pure milk. In actual fact, the legislators were probably more concerned about the power of the milk bloc.[16] Stone contended that the legislature, not the courts, should decide whether the public would be adequately protected by the prohibition on false labels and false branding imposed by the Pure Food and Drug Act or whether the product should be banned entirely. This perspective ignores the judicial responsibility in behalf of all minorities. Legislators respond to political pressures, campaign contributions, lobbying, and expert testimony. As a result producers of new products frequently are at great disadvantage in a legislative contest with a large industry or business association that feels economically imperiled. Under the logic of footnote 4, many would-be producers are insular minorities greatly in need of judicial oversight to protect their interests. The footnote incorrectly assumes that the infirmities of legislatures are confined to certain subject matter. Experience discloses that the problems are endemic to all law-making (see discussion later in this and in chapters 2 and 12).

Footnote 4 was a statement of philosophy about the role of the Court that had no basis in the original intention of the Framers. When made, the perspective it contained was the subject of dispute between the two major political parties. The Democrats emphasized the importance of political freedoms while the Republicans stressed economic liberties. The famous footnote provided constitutional sanction for the Democrats' position. Professor Martin Shapiro equates the footnote with New Deal politics. He writes that it forbids the Court to aid the business community, regarded by New Dealers as their enemy. Instead, the Justices would protect the political processes, which New Dealers believed favored them over the "monied interests." The footnote also advanced the interests of the New Deal's allies: the intellectuals, for whom free speech was very dear, and the ethnic, religious, and racial minorities.[17]

The judicial abdication advanced in footnote 4 impedes democratic processes. In the absence of judicial review, legislators have great power over the commercial community, effectively reducing freedom of political choice and expression for its members. In the two metropolitan areas in which I have lived, property owners and developers have contributed to incumbents and candidates expected to win local council seats, regardless of political persuasion or personal preferences. These persons feared that failure to make these contributions would jeopardize their zoning and development proposals. Such practices represent a failure of the political processes with which the footnote is concerned. Voters should not feel compelled to make political contributions. Legislators should not be put or kept in office by voters whose persuasion differs from their own. To be sure, even in the days of economic due process, legislators had enough power to affect the well-being of entrepreneurs. However, a judicial policy which substantially augments that power is not furthering the aspirations of representative government.

Less-Restrictive-Alternative Principle

The minimal review rule eliminates the various tests that the Old Court used to scrutinize economic and social legislation, one of which was the "less restrictive alternative" principle, intended like the others to forbid unnecessary restraints. A 1926 case, *Weaver v. Palmer Bros.*,[18] illustrates employment of this principle in the context of regulatory legislation designed to safeguard the consumer, the same concern involved in *Carolene Products*. To protect health and prevent fraud, a statute prohibited the use of secondhand shoddy in mattresses and similar articles. The Supreme Court found that used shoddy could be sterilized and that old material could not easily be passed off as new if identifying tags were required to be attached to articles containing it. On the premise that "it is a matter of public concern that the production and sale of things necessary or convenient for use should not be forbidden," the Court concluded that the legislative ban was not needed to protect the public. The measure needlessly restrained liberty of the manufacturer.

Under the less-restrictive-alternative principle, neither a business nor a product may be banned altogether if the evils associated with it can be eliminated by regulation. Although the use of this principle in economic matters was essentially rejected in *Olsen*, many state courts continue to apply it.[19] Contrary to the thrust of the filled-milk case, some state courts have presumed that labeling or warning requirements will suffice to protect the consumer. Interestingly, the West German and Swiss courts have recognized an economic less-restrictive-alternative of constitutional dimensions.[20]

As the reader may recall, Justice Douglas imposed the principle in *Griswold v. Connecticut* to strike down a statute banning the use of contraceptives, concluding that the legislative purpose could have been accomplished by a law regulating their manufacture or sale. Douglas said that a total prohibition could not be sustained under the familiar rule "so often applied by this Court, that a 'governmental purpose to control or prevent activities constitutionally subject to state regulation may not be achieved by means which sweep unnecessarily broadly and thereby invade the area of protected freedoms.'"[21] In *Olsen*, however, Douglas was not disposed to think in these terms because economic legislation was involved. In the *Ribnik* case, which *Olsen* overruled, Justice Sutherland had asserted that if the employment agency business peculiarly lent itself to fraud, extortion, and discriminatory practices, regulation related to these matters was the appropriate remedy and not the more onerous price-fixing that the *Ribnik* statute had imposed. Sutherland, in declaring that restrictive legislation must be narrowly drawn to avoid undue restraint, was applying the same rule that Douglas was to invoke in *Griswold*.

Results of Abdication

By 1939 it was clear that a party aggrieved by economic legislation had to find constitutional relief outside any notion of a substantive liberty of contract. As previously stated, the last case overruling state legislation on substantive due process grounds was the 1936 opinion nullifying New York's minimum wage law for women and minors. Thereafter, the Supreme Court became a very restrained reviewer of socioeconomic legislation. Some of the better known cases in which legislation has been upheld follow. Complainants in these cases advanced a due process or an equal protection theory or both without success.

Riverboat Pilots

Louisiana's pilotage law required that ocean-going vessels under that state's jurisdiction be piloted through the Mississippi River approaches to the Port of New Orleans and in the port itself only by pilots appointed by the governor. To be eligible for appointment, a candidate had to have been selected by a board, composed of state pilots, to serve a six-month apprenticeship. The complainants in the case were experienced in piloting coastal vessels on the river and in the port and possessed all the statutory qualifications except the six-month apprenticeship. They alleged that the incumbent pilots generally choose as apprentices their relatives and occasionally friends and therefore "membership...had been closed...to all except those having the favor of the pilots." In rejecting an attack based on a denial of equal protection, the Supreme Court, per Justice Black, said that the method adopted by Louisiana for the selection of pilots was not without relation to the objective of securing the safest and most efficiently operated pilotage system practicable.[22] In dissent, Justice Rutledge said: "The door is thereby closed to all not having blood relationship to presently licensed pilots. Whether the occupation is considered as having the status of 'public officer' or of highly regulated private employment, it is beyond the legislative power to make entrance to it turn upon such a criterion.''[23]

Barmaids

A Michigan statute banned women from working as barmaids in bars of cities with a population exceeding 50,000 unless they were wives or daughters of the male owners of licensed liquor establishments. The Supreme Court upheld the law as not violating the equal protection clause.[24] It refused to consider evidence that no morality problem existed and that the statute adversely affected large numbers of women. Three dissenting Justices believed the classification to be invidious, rejecting the assumption that the statute was motivated by legislative solicitude for women's moral and physical well-being. If such a statute were challenged today, it probably would be struck down under the standard of review that the Supreme Court now uses in gender classification cases, as explained in chapter 6. It is presented here as indicative of legislative propensities to disadvantage certain groups for whom no relief exists at the judicial level.

Morticians Barred from Selling Life Insurance

A South Carolina statute provided that undertakers may not serve as agents for life insurance companies and that life insurance companies and their agents may not operate undertaking businesses. A life insurance company sought to enjoin the law, which contained criminal sanctions, on the grounds that it contravened the due process and equal protection clauses. The evidence revealed that such insurance was sold by morticians in more than thirty states and that both morticians who did not sell insurance and insurance agents who were not morticians had lobbied for passage of the bill to protect them from competition. The record contained a speech by a member of the Life Underwriters of South Carolina in which he declared that "insurance writing by undertakers would endanger the livelihood of 4200 men in this state now engaged in the insurance profession."

The plaintiff insurance company submitted evidence that its rates were lower than those of any other insurance company doing business in the state and that it offered the only insurance available in the state to people over sixty-five. Under the rational relation test, this information was obviously not relevant, and the United States Supreme Court rejected it in upholding the statute:

[A] judiciary must judge by results, not by the varied factors which may have determined legislators' votes. We cannot undertake a search for motive in testing constitutionality....
...We cannot say that South Carolina is not entitled to call...funeral insurance...an evil. Nor can we say that the statute has no relation to the elimination of those evils. There our inquiry must stop.[25]

Opticians

The *Lee Optical* case, discussed before in chapter 5, dealt with Oklahoma's extensive law regulating visual care and prohibiting the following activities: fitting lenses and duplicating or replacing frame lenses without a written prescription from a licensed ophthalmologist or optometrist; soliciting or advertising the sale of eyeglasses, frames, lenses, mountings, or prisms; and renting space or subleasing departments by a retail merchandiser or otherwise permitting any person purporting to do eye examination or visual care to occupy space in a retail store. Sellers of ready-to-wear glasses were exempted.

The Supreme Court, reversing a three-judge district court, unanimously upheld the statute in its entirety.[26] Justice Douglas advised those aggrieved by such legislation to resort to the polls, not to the courts.[27] For the Justice, it was enough that there was a possible evil at hand awaiting correction and that the particular legislative measure *might* correct it. Although the evidence *might* have shown the law to be both "needless" and "wasteful," the legislature "might have concluded" otherwise.

The *Board of Pharmacy* advertising case discussed in chapter 10 effectively overrules the advertising portion of *Lee Optical;* however, the more recent *Friedman v. Rogers,*[28] upholding a Texas statute preventing optometrists from using trade names, provides support for the balance of it.

Voting Time Off

In *Day-Brite Lighting, Inc. v. Missouri,*[29] the High Court upheld a statute requiring employers to allow employees time off with full pay on election days in order to encourage voting. The law not only regulated commercial endeavor, but it also operated as a tax on employers without any relationship to business interest or activity. In dissent, Justice Jackson objected that "there must be some limit to the power to

shift the whole voting burden from the voter to someone else who
happens to stand in some economic relationship to him.''[30]

Debt-Adjusting Business

The Kansas statute litigated in *Ferguson v. Skrupa*[31] made it a misdemeanor for any person to engage in the business of debt adjustment
except as incident to the legal practice of law. Debt adjusting was
defined as making a contract under which the debtor undertook to pay
periodically a certain sum of money to the debt adjuster, who for a
consideration, distributed it among specified creditors according to an
agreed-upon plan. The state produced evidence that the debt-adjusting
business lends itself to abuses against distressed debtors, particularly
in the lower income groups. A number of other states strictly regulate
or prohibit this business. Skrupa, the complainant, maintained that his
business was useful and desirable, neither inherently immoral or
dangerous, nor in any way contrary to the public welfare. The law
would make his and other such businesses worthless.[32] The district
court invalidated the statute as an unreasonable regulation of a lawful
business, relying in part on *Adams v. Tanner,*[33] which had struck down
a state statute prohibiting employment agencies from collecting fees
from workers. In *Adams,* Justice McReynolds had asserted that the
evils associated with that business could be eliminated through the less
onerous alternative of regulation.

> Because abuses may, and probably do, grow up in connection with
> this business, is adequate reason for hedging it about by proper
> regulations. But this is not enough to justify destruction of one's
> right to follow a distinctly useful calling in an upright way. Certainly
> there is no profession, possibly no business, which does not offer
> peculiar opportunities for reprehensible practices; and as to every
> one of them, no doubt, some can be found quite ready earnestly to
> maintain that its suppression would be in the public interest. Skill-
> fully directed agitation might also bring about apparent condemna-
> tion of any one of them by the public. Happily for all, the fundamen-
> tal guaranties of the Constitution cannot be freely submerged if and
> whenever some ostensible justification is advanced and the police
> power invoked.[34]

In *Skrupa,* Justice Black, writing for the Court (with one Justice
concurring), vigorously rejected this philosophy:

> Unquestionably, there are arguments showing that the business of
> debt adjusting has social utility, but such arguments are properly
> addressed to the legislature, not to us. We refuse to sit as a ''super-

legislature to weigh the wisdom of legislation,'' and we emphatically refuse to go back to the time when courts used the Due Process Clause "to strike down state laws, regulatory of business and industrial conditions, because they may be unwise, improvident, or out of harmony with a particular school of thought."... Whether the legislature takes for its textbook Adam Smith, Herbert Spencer, Lord Keynes, or some other is no concern of ours.[35]

However, it should be of concern that Black was rejecting a fundamental basis of his power: the obligation to protect the liberties of people from violation by a legislature. The Court was countenancing the destruction of the livelihood of people whose principal offense may have been that they were not very persuasive in legislative halls. Unless the evils are overwhelming, a legislature is not likely to ruin the occupations of those who can assert political pressures effectively. Perhaps compelling reasons existed for abrogating what must have been to Skrupa a basic liberty, but refusal even to review these reasons is a dereliction of judicial responsibility. Many experienced debt adjusters surely have as much competence to engage in the business as does the average lawyer.

The persons deprived of their livelihood by this decision would have had to commit serious crimes to be fined an amount equivalent to the losses sustained—a point emphasized in some of the contemporary cases concerning fundamental rights. Beneficiaries of this decision are lawyers, who usually constitute a significant portion of a legislative body and who cannot be expected to be oblivious to the interests of their colleagues or possibly of their profession. Skrupa may well qualify as a member of an insular minority.

Practice of Law

Professional competition may also succumb to existing law. Under a rule promulgated by the Supreme Court of Kansas, a resident of the state who was licensed to practice law in Kansas and Missouri and who maintained law offices in both states and regularly practiced in Missouri was denied the right to appear in a Kansas court without local associate counsel. The High Court dismissed the appeal for want of a substantial federal question, holding that the rule was within the allowable range of state action under the Fourteenth Amendment.[36]

Mention should be made of rules in some states that deny appellants admission to practice law solely because they refuse to answer questions regarding their personal beliefs or affiliations with organizations that advocate certain political doctrines. These situations have created sharp conflict and close divisions on the Court, with some fervent supporters of judicial abdication in the economic area (i.e., Black and Douglas) supporting more extensive review.[37]

Chain Drugstores

In 1973, the High Court unanimously sustained a North Dakota statute requiring that a corporation operating a pharmacy have a majority of its stock owned by registered pharmacists, actively engaged in its management and operation.[38] This law effectively barred chain drugstores from the state. The case overruled *Louis K. Liggett Co. v. Baldridge*,[39] which had held invalid a comparable Pennsylvania law prohibiting entrance into the pharmacy business by nonpharmacists. Justice Sutherland, in delivering the *Liggett* opinion, rejected the claim that mere ownership of a drugstore by one not a pharmacist bore a reasonable relation to the public health, seeing it as based entirely on conjecture, unsupported by anything of substance. He observed that a state could protect the public by regulating the prescription, sale, and purchase of medicines. Under Pennsylvania law of the time a drugstore owner, whether a registered pharmacist or not, could not purchase or dispense what the state designated as impure or inferior medicines; he could not, unless he was a licensed physician, prescribe for the sick; he could not, unless he was a registered pharmacist, have charge of a drugstore or compound a prescription. "Thus, it would seem, every point at which the public health is likely to be injuriously affected by the act of the owner in buying, compounding, or selling drugs and medicines is amply safeguarded."[40]

> It is a matter of public notoriety that chain drug stores in great numbers, owned and operated by corporations, are to be found throughout the United States. They have been in operation for many years. We take judicial notice of the fact that the stock in these corporations is bought and sold upon the various stock exchanges of the country and, in the nature of things, must be held and owned to a large extent by persons who are not registered pharmacists. If detriment to the public health thereby has resulted or is threatened, some evidence of it ought to be forthcoming. None has been produced, and, so far as we are informed, either by the record or outside of it, none exists.[41]

Gasoline Stations

In *Exxon Corporation v. Governor of Maryland*,[42] the United States Supreme Court (with one dissent on grounds other than due process), upheld a Maryland statute that prohibited those oil companies that produce or refine petroleum products from operating retail service stations in that state. The companies could not continue operation of the stations they already owned, nor could they open new ones. The measure required companies to divest properties valued at more than $10 million. About 200 of the state's 3800 gasoline service stations were affected.

The major articulated purpose of the Maryland law was to promote competition. However, the trial court hearing the case concluded that "the statute is inversely related to the public welfare." It found that requiring the companies to divest themselves of the stations would be harmful to competition in the industry and would primarily serve to protect the independent dealers rather than the public at large. The court concluded that there was no proven detrimental effect on the retail market caused by company-owned-and-operated stations which could not be curbed by federal and state antitrust laws.[43] On appeal, the Federal Supreme Court refused to probe the legislation futher than determining it satisfied the minimal review test.[44]

The two opinions filed in the case disclose that the company-operated stations performed well for the consumer. They concentrated largely on high volume sales with consistently lower prices than those charged by independent dealer–major brand stations. The oil companies also used these stations to introduce new marketing ideas.

Auto Dealerships

The California Automobile Franchise Act provides that before an auto manufacturer or dealer may establish a new dealership or relocate an existing one, notice of such intention must be given to the state's new motor vehicle board and to all dealers handling the "same line make" of car in the relevant market area, which is about a 300-mile territory surrounding the proposed new location. Any dealer so notified may file a protest within fifteen days and the board is thereupon required to order a postponement pending decision on the merits of the protest. Similar statutes have been adopted in seventeen other states. The stated concerns that prompted enactment of the statute were "to avoid undue control of the independent...dealer by the vehicle manufacturer or distributor and to insure that dealers fulfill their obligations under their franchises and provide adequate and sufficient service to consumers generally."[45]

In a suit brought by General Motors and two Southern California retail automobile dealers, a three-judge district court enjoined enforcement of these provisions and expressed the view that "the right to grant or undertake a Chevrolet dealership and the right to move one's business facilities from one location to another" fell within the ambit of liberty interests protected by the Fourteenth Amendment and could be curtailed only after a hearing. The court reasoned that due process was violated because the plaintiffs were deprived of their "liberty" to move or establish a dealership for many months pending the board's decision.[46] By a margin of 8 to 1, the United States Supreme Court upheld the statute.[47] Justice Stevens in dissent concluded that the law denied procedural due process because it granted "private parties an exclusive right to cause harm to other private parties without even alleging that any general rule has been violated or is about to be violated."[48]

The law provides existing dealers with two opportunities: first, to block the entry of a competitor, and second, to hold back competition for a period of time. The experience of the two complainants in the case, a Buick dealer and a Chevrolet dealer, indicate the harm that the law can cause for those who desire to invest in new dealerships. The Buick dealer entered into a franchise agreement in May 1975, and because of various legal maneuvering, the board's hearing date was postponed until September 1976. In April 1976, General Motors and the Buick dealer filed suit in federal court to have the law declared unconstitutional, and the case was not decided until December 1978. The Chevrolet dealer was prepared to locate his new operation in December 1975, and the hearings were set by the board for June 1976. In August a hearing officer approved of the proposed location and the board had until the middle of September to concur. Before the waiting period ended, the dealer was advised that the property in which he proposed to locate was no longer available because of his long failure to take possession and otherwise assume the obligations of a lease.

Retroactive Burdens

Black lung disease, a malady that affects coal miners, was not recognized in the United States until the 1950s, and in 1969 the first laws were passed to provide benefits to its victims. In that year, Congress enacted legislation to compensate victims by creating liability on the part of the individual employers, both for miners suffering from the condition and employed at the time of or after the date of its passage and for miners suffering from the condition but no longer employed in the industry on that date. Thus a miner would be able to receive benefits from a particular employer even if he were no longer working in the industry at the time of the 1969 enactment.

In a suit to invalidate part of the statute, the mine operators challenged the provision for retroactive liability on the ground that it was arbitrary and irrational, in violation of the due process clause of the Fifth Amendment. Justice Marshall, for a 7–2 majority, upheld the act,[49] asserting:

> We find . . . that the imposition of liability for the effects of disabilities bred in the past is justified as a rational measure to spread the costs of the employees' disabilities to those who have profited from the fruits of their labor—the operators and the coal consumers. . . .
>
> . . . We are unwilling to assess the wisdom of Congress' chosen scheme by examining the degree to which the "cost-savings" enjoyed by operators in the pre-enactment period produced "excess" profits, or the degree to which the retrospective liability imposed on the early operators can now be passed on to the consumer. It is enough to say that the Act approaches the problem of cost spreading rationally . . . .[50]

Justice Powell, in concurring, argued that the facts suggested that Congress had acted irrationally in pursuing a legitimate end, but he said that the operators had not made a strong enough showing to override the presumption of constitutionality accorded such legislation. He denied that excess profits were feasible in the coal industry, which is highly competitive and whose returns are based on costs. Had the operators in the past been required to set aside funds for compensation, these monies would have been part of their costs and therefore passed on to the consumer. Some firms would now have difficulty passing on the retroactive costs because they were not uniformly spread among the operators: the newer companies would be obligated for a much smaller amount than would those long in service. Liabilities would also depend on a past, not a current, scale of operation. Powell pointed out that the extent of retroactive liability might be substantial for certain firms, inasmuch as the industry, during the middle 1970s, employed 150,000 people, a number substantially lower than the 450,000 employed in 1939.

It is possible that some of the older companies, particularly those whose operations have decreased over the years, will sustain serious financial problems. Congress has in effect seized one group's property and given it to another.

Property Use Regulation

The standard of review established in *Euclid* for zoning cases is more rigorous than minimal scrutiny. Recent cases suggest, however, that

the difference has virtually disappeared. In three major property use
regulation cases, the Court gave a high degree of deference to local
legislation, notwithstanding the presence of serious First Amendment
issues. In *Belle Terre*,[51] the Justices upheld (7–2) a zoning ordinance
restricting occupancy of single-family dwellings to traditional families
or to groups of not more than two unrelated persons. Justice Marshall,
in dissent, objected that the law violated the freedoms of association
and privacy and the stated purposes of the regulation could have been
achieved through less drastic means.

In *American Mini Theatres*,[52] a 5–4 majority upheld a provision of
Detroit's "Anti-Skid Row Ordinance" prohibiting the location of any
adult movie theatre exhibiting sexually explicit motion pictures within
1000 feet of two other similarly regulated "adult" businesses. Two
adult-motion-picture operators filed the action. Justices Stewart and
Blackmun entered strong dissents that the ordinance violated the complainants' rights of expression and was defectively vague.

In *Penn Central*,[53] the Court (5–3) upheld property use regulation
that censored artistic expression. The case concerned Grand Central
Terminal, which the city's landmarks commission designated a landmark, and therefore subject to its architectural control. Penn Central
sought permission from the commission to erect a 55-story office tower
that would be cantilevered over the terminal, leaving its existing Beaux
Arts facade intact. The proposed tower satisfied zoning requirements.
Although the commission had no rule against adding to protected
buildings, and had allowed such construction, it concluded that constructing the tower "above a flamboyant Beaux Arts facade seems
nothing more than an aesthetic joke." Any proposed addition would
have to "harmonize in scale, material and character"—a standard
allowing maximum discretion.

Occupational Licensing

Professor Walter Gellhorn, long a commentator in the field, recently
described the extent of occupational licensing requirements in the nation. He wrote that the Founding Fathers would be aghast to learn that
in many states aspiring beekeepers, embalmers, lightning rod sales-
people, septic tank cleaners, and taxidermists must obtain official approval before seeking the public's patronage. Gellhorn said that in at
least one state, about the only people who remain unlicensed are the
clergy and university professors, presumably because they are
nowhere taken seriously. As of 1969, the most restrictive state was

California, with 178 licensed occupations. Pennsylvania came next, with 165. With only 63, West Virginia was the least restrictive.[54]

Occupational licensing is invariably justified as a means of protecting the public against unscrupulous and incompetent practitioners. However, Gellhorn suggests that a much greater number of honest and able individuals are being excluded from their preferred work. He states that restricting entry is the real purpose and not merely a side effect of many if not most successful campaigns to institute licensing schemes.

> Licensing, imposed ostensibly to protect the public, almost always impedes only those who desire to enter the occupation or "profession;" those already in practice remain entrenched without a demonstration of fitness or probity. The self-interested proponents of a new licensing law generally constitute a more effective political force than the citizens who, if aware of the matter at all, have no special interest which moves them to organize in opposition.
>
> The restrictive consequence of licensure is achieved in large part by making entry into the regulated occupation expensive in time or money or both.[55]

Gellhorn summed up the objections to these practices as follows:

> [O]ccupational licensing has typically brought higher status for the producer of services at the price of higher costs to the consumer; it has reduced competition; it has narrowed opportunity for aspiring youth by increasing the costs of entry into a desired occupational career; it has artificially segmented skills so that needed services, like health care, are increasingly difficult to supply economically; it has fostered the cynical view that unethical practices will prevail unless those entrenched in a profession are assured of high incomes; and it has caused a proliferation of official administrative bodies, most of them staffed by persons drawn from and devoted to furthering the interest of the licensed occupations themselves.[56]

Some of the questionable occupational licensing requirements cited by Professor Gellhorn include the following:

1. In California a license to cut hair may be obtained after completion of a long apprenticeship, graduation from a barber college, and success in an examination that in past years has demanded knowledge of such esoteric things as the chemical composition of the bones and the name of the muscle in the hyoid bone. Most states insist that new recruits to the haircutting profession receive institutionalized instruction in bacteriology, histology of the hair, skin, nails, muscles, and nerves, and on diseases of the skin, hair, glands, and nails.

2. In some states virtually the only "profession" open to once
convicted felons is that of burglary; they are barred from other ac
tivities because they are presumed to possess a bad moral character
regardless of the nature of their felony or its relevance to their intended
occupation.

3. Georgia insists that those who seek to be commercial photog
raphers pass a Wasserman test for syphillis.

4. Some states mandate that regardless of national citizenship, a
potential licensee must have been a resident of the license-issuing state
for a certain period even though no relationship exists between prior
residence and occupational qualifications—for example, those of op
tometrist, accountant, masseur, and dentist.

5. Some state laws authorize towns and cities to make residence the
sine qua non, notwithstanding prior experience and proficiency, for an
auctioneer, plumber, fortune-teller, lawn-sprinkler installer, and sta
tionary engineer, among other professions.

Gellhorn has pointed out that in the 1950s, 75 percent of the occupa
tional licensing boards at work in the country were composed exclu
sively of licensed practitioners of their respective occupations
Although this requirement is understandable, it has the serious dis
advantage of giving authority to people who may be primarily con
cerned about the welfare of existing practitioners at the expense of
competition and entry. This process, which is reminiscent of the
medieval guilds that controlled their membership, may, warned Gell
horn, make us a "society of status."

The problem of licensing is mainly one for the legislature. But when
with little or no justification, lawmakers or regulators deny to some
people the opportunity to work, important personal freedoms are
abridged, which can only be redressed through judicial review.

Some relief in the federal courts presently exists against gross un
fairness in licensing procedure, but it does not approach meaningful
judicial oversight. On the basis of charges filed by the Alabama Op
tometric Association, the Alabama Board of Optometry instituted pro
ceedings against optometrists employed by Lee Optical Company on
the theory that they were practicing optometry illegally. All members
of the board were either members of the association or independent
optometrists who presumably would benefit financially from the exclu
sion of the "employed" competitors from the market. The United
States High Court disqualified the board from ruling on the charges
instituted against Lee Optical optometrists.[57] However, the decision
does not offer a significant victory for competition, for the legislature

could without judicial objection adopt statutes that accomplish substantially the same end.

Lochner in Retrospect

Holmes's dissent in *Lochner v. New York* contains some of the most lauded language in legal history. His position is now and has been for almost forty years largely consistent with federal law. However, the preceding cases show that his perspective has not influenced the human condition favorably; it has fallen far short of the expectations and excitement induced by the rhetoric. The economic marketplace on which so many in this country rely for their welfare has frequently and frivolously been disturbed as regulation and regulators wield enormous power. This power and authority spill over into the marketplace of ideas that Holmes in his later years was so concerned to maintain almost inviolate. Producers, sellers, and sometimes even consumers who require the approval or dispensation of the regulators surrender willingly their right to criticize rather than imperil their standing with the authorities. They are aware that political contributions, speeches, or articles unwisely directed may lead to unpleasant consequences, equal in result to sustaining a substantial fine or penalty. People whose only claim to expertise is their support of a winning candidate or their position as locally elected officials (sometimes representing a relatively minute constituency) have critical power over the well-being of a great many producers and consumers. It is difficult to believe that *Lochner* would have harmed so many so often.

9 Fundamental Rights and Interests

In the cases discussed in the last chapter, various Justices disparaged the Old Court because it had invaded the authority of the legislature. One must not conclude from their remarks, however, that they believed the judiciary should be highly deferential to the other branches of government. The cases cited involved economic issues. When it came to statutes concerning the other areas, these Justices were not nearly as hesitant in overruling legislators. As the statistics reported in chapter 6 show, the Warren Court, whose members frequently criticized the pre–New Deal tribunal for its supposed legislative propensities, was less submissive to legislatures than the Old Court. Our contemporary Court has targeted large areas of human affairs where the legislature may tread lightly, if at all. The Justices insist they are doing only what the Constitution mandates, but few are persuaded by that explanation. It is commonly accepted that they are making decisions largely consistent with their own ideas about the Constitution, life, and justice. In contrast with the information provided in the last chapter, we shall now examine judicial expansion in contemporary years. This chapter, together with the other two in Part III of this book, should inform the reader how the contemporary Court has responded to its constitutional mission to safeguard liberty.

Securing Certain Liberties

If the Constitution were rewritten for contemporary America, its drafters might resolve the conflict between authority and freedom in this manner:

1. Certain liberties are largely immune from executive, legislative, and administrative authority.

2. Government may restrict these liberties only when necessary to further a compelling state purpose.

3. Every restriction must be as precise and narrow as possible, to avoid imposing any unnecessary restraints on people.

4. The responsibility for safeguarding these liberties rests with the judiciary.

5. In cases challenging any diminution of these liberties, the state, not the aggrieved party, is obligated to prove that the statute is in accord with each of the foregoing rules.

Of course, no need exists for either a new constitution or a constitutional amendment because these provisions describe the present Supreme Court's approach to liberties it deems fundamental. What is required, as these pages will demonstrate, is a better allocation of judicial concern. The system outlined above may not designate rights as absolute, but it comes as close to guaranteeing them from molestation by the state as is possible in an organized society. The structure constitutes a contemporary acknowledgement that in certain significant areas government is limited, and has relatively little power over its constituents. In principle, therefore, it is consistent with the aspirations of the Framers; such a system might have alleviated some of their fears concerning the exercise of judicial power. If certain activities are placed beyond the reach of legislation, attempts to pass enactments affecting these areas occur infrequently; therefore less litigation is engendered and consequently fewer opportunities arise for the exercise of judicial discretion and for the possibility of its abuse.

The reasoning that supports this system appears also in contemporary interpretations of the equal protection clause of the Fourteenth Amendment and the judicially created equal protection component of the due process clause in the Fifth Amendment. Statutory classifications, which either imply suspect purposes or affect fundamental rights, will be held to deny equal protection unless necessary to further a compelling government interest. As applied to the equal protection clause, the compelling interest standard is almost the opposite of the more commonly employed standard (as in *New Orleans v. Dukes*)[1] that a statute does not violate the clause if some rational explanation might be found for the classification it creates.

These tests make up a two-tiered standard of construction for the equal protection clause. On the one tier, the state (as in the case of fundamental rights) has the onerous burden of establishing the existence of a compelling interest, while on the other tier, the private party has the even more difficult task of showing irrationality.[2] The contemporary court has not always confined itself to the two-tiered system, but has allowed for intermediate alternatives, particularly in more recent years.[3] It also employs the irrebuttable presumption doctrine (to be explained later in this chapter) to effect an intermediate standard of review.

We have previously discussed the adjudication of liberties during the substantive due process era, long before the High Court created this more elaborate system. This new structure and its specifications, which were created by the Supreme Court in recent years beginning in the middle 1960s, provide a much more systematized and programmed analysis than existed in the days of the Old Court. Thus, in theory at least, it removes such problems as where the burden of persuasion rests and the extent of the government obligation under that burden.

However, it has not solved the problem of which freedoms should be entitled to special status. Justices have reiterated that certain liberties stand out—that they are "fundamental," "transcendent," "preferred," and "special." The standard for ascertaining these rights has been variously expressed as whether the right is "implicit in the concept of ordered liberty,"[4] whether it "lie[s] at the base of all our civil and political institutions,"[5] whether it is "so rooted in the traditions and conscience of our people as to be ranked as fundamental,"[6] and whether it embodies "that fundamental fairness essential to the very concept of justice."[7] A collection of catchwords and catch phrases would fill pages, but would not be very helpful in establishing guidelines. As we have seen, the Court has accorded special preferences to liberties on the basis of the collective wisdom of the majority at a particular time. Judge Learned Hand provides insight:

> [J]udges are seldom content merely to annul the particular solution before them; they do not, indeed they may not, say that taking all things in consideration, the legislators' solution is too strong for the judicial stomach.[8]

Although some opinions refer to certain liberties as fundamental, these liberties do not achieve special status unless the Court also subjects infringements on them to the rigid scrutiny previously described. Thus the right of property protected under the taking clause of the Fifth Amendment is sometimes said to be fundamental. Nevertheless, unlike in litigation affecting other rights deemed fundamental, the burden of persuasion in property regulation cases does not shift to the government. Rather, it remains with the plaintiff who, to succeed, must show that the restraint is not substantially related to the public welfare. As a result, property rights, although based on an explicit provision in the Bill of Rights, have a relatively low priority in the hierarchy of constitutionally guaranteed liberties.

We saw in *Griswold* (discussed in chapter 1) that a right need not be mentioned specifically in the Constitution in order to be designated fundamental. The Court has held that the rights to certain personal privacies, to travel, to equal access to the criminal appellate process, and to voting are fundamental, and therefore it subjects restraints upon them to strict scrutiny. Thus the anomalous situation exists which accords higher priority to rights nowhere mentioned in the Constitution than is allocated to the right of property which is specifically recognized in the Fifth Amendment.

The fundamental rights concept has been used both as a means to remove the restraints imposed by the legislature and as a means to impose affirmative restraints upon the legislature and the executive. The judicial process is employed in the first instance negatively and in the second positively. As previously indicated, the former approach is consistent with the role of the judiciary, while the latter challenges the provinces of the legislature and the executive. For example, in the speech cases, the Supreme Court has not done more than eliminate impediments to the functioning of the marketplace of ideas, while in both the travel and abortion cases, the High Court sometimes has adjudicated by striking down laws and at other times by imposing affirmative obligations on government (as discussed later in this chapter and in 14).

Rights of Expression

At the time the Constitution was written, a fairly well-established natural-rights, social-compact tradition existed in this country (as described in chapter 2). Its adherents believed that the document was only an incomplete codification of a higher law whose principles were preexisting. Fundamental rights, it was believed, are so transcendent that they may not be abridged, even if they remain unwritten. However, because subsequent Courts have had their own conceptions of fundamental rights, some prior interpretations have been abandoned. In this sense, the immutable rules of the higher law have been muted.

The contemporary judiciary has replaced material rights with nonmate
rial rights as the major concern of a free society.

After the arrival of the "Reconstructed Court," two theories domi
nated the Supreme Court's decisions in expression cases: clear and
present danger, and balancing. Because the former is itself based on a
balancing of interests, the line of demarcation between the theories is
far from precise (except of course to proponents of either view). Jus
tices Black and Douglas rejected both positions. They insisted that the
First Amendment requires complete freedom of expression for all ideas
and repeatedly denounced the application of any balancing test in de
ciding cases on expression. "[T]he men who drafted our Bill of Rights
did all the 'balancing' that was to be done in this field," said Justice
Black.[9] The marketplace of ideas is self-regulatory and thus rejects
speech inimical to the public welfare. (However Black, unlike Douglas
did exempt speech intertwined with conduct from the expression
guarantee.)

The majority of the Court never accepted the absolutist position
adhering rather to Chief Justice Hughes's declaration in *Near v. Minnesota* that "[l]iberty of speech, and of the press, is . . . not an absolute
right, and the State may punish its abuse."[10] In this area Black's and
Douglas's chief protagonists on the Court were Justices Frankfurter
and Harlan. In his concurrence in *Dennis v. United States*,[11] Frankfurter argued that balancing in expression cases is essential to accommodate the will of the majority and the needs and security of the state
He rejected the interpretation of the clear and present danger test that
limited the scope of judicial review to determining the imminence and
gravity of the evil threatened, because "the interest in speech, pro-
foundly important as it is, is no more conclusive in judicial review than
other attributes of democracy."[12] Justice Harlan was willing to employ
balancing in those cases in which speech was indirectly affected by
some measure that presumably was enacted to further a different state
interest.

The Warren Court resolved the controversy by adopting rules that
followed Black and Douglas more than Frankfurter and Harlan
Brandenburg v. Ohio,[13] decided in 1969, appears to have rejected both
the balancing and the danger tests. *Brandenburg* involved a Ku Klux
Klan leader who was convicted of violating the Ohio syndicalism
statute, the text of which was quite similar to that of the statute upheld
in *Whitney*. The defendant made a speech before television cameras
threatening the president and other high government officials and an-
nouncing marches on Congress and throughout the South. In unani-

mously reversing the conviction, the Court overruled *Whitney* and set forth a new test defining punishable speech.

> [T]he constitutional guarantees of free speech and free press do not permit a State to forbid or proscribe advocacy of the use of force or of law violation except where such advocacy is directed to inciting or producing imminent lawless action and is likely to incite or produce such action.[14]

The wording differs from the danger test in that the advocacy that is punishable must not only be directed to inciting imminent, lawless action, but must also be likely to produce such action. This standard protects a greater variety of utterances than any previous test relating to this subject matter.

The thinking that in time produced the contemporary Court's position on fundamental rights is evident in the 1958 decision, *Speiser v. Randall*.[15] Under a constitutional amendment adopted by initiative, the state of California required as a condition for obtaining a war veteran's property tax exemption, that an applicant file an oath stating that he or she would not advocate either the violent overthrow of government or the support of a foreign power in the event of hostilities against the United States. Some veterans refused to file such an oath, contending that the requirement violated the speech guarantees of the Constitution.

The California Supreme Court held that "by no standard can the infringement upon freedom of speech imposed . . . be deemed a substantial one."[16] In a 7–1 opinion,[17] written by Justice Brennan, then the Court's chief spokesman on speech and press, the High Court reversed, holding that to deny tax exemptions because people have exercised First Amendment rights is in effect to penalize those people through fines. Under the statute those seeking the exemptions would have the burden of proving their right to receive them in the event that their oaths were challenged.

Using an analogy to the protections accorded the accused in criminal proceedings, Brennan held that the state should instead bear this burden. The right of speech had a "transcendent value" that is nearly, but not quite, absolute. "[T]he line between speech unconditionally guaranteed and speech which may legitimately be regulated, suppressed, or punished is finely drawn."[18] To reduce the margin of error in separating the lawful from the unlawful, Brennan required "that the State bear the burden of persuasion to show that the appellants engaged in criminal speech."[19] He stated that "[i]n all kinds of litigation it is plain that where the burden of proof lies may be decisive of the outcome,"[20] and he further explained:

The vice of the present procedure is that, where particular speech falls close to the line separating the lawful and the unlawful, the possibility of mistaken factfinding—inherent in all litigation—will create the danger that the legitimate utterance will be penalized. The man who knows that he must bring forth proof and persuade another of the lawfulness of his conduct necessarily must steer far wider of the unlawful zone than if the State must bear these burdens. This is especially to be feared when the complexity of the proofs and the generality of the standards applied . . . provide but shifting sands on which the litigant must maintain his position. How can a claimant whose declaration is rejected possibly sustain the burden of proving the negative of these complex factual elements? In practical operation, therefore, this procedural device must necessarily produce a result which the State could not command directly. It can only result in a deterrence of speech which the Constitution makes free.[21]

I might note at this point that proponents of economic due process had similar concerns. The reader may recall Justice McReynolds's plea in *Nebbia v. New York:* "If necessary for appellant to show absence of the asserted conditions, the little grocer was helpless from the beginning—the practical difficulties were too great for the average man."[22]

Although *Speiser* and its progeny did not entirely eliminate balancing in speech cases, they did weigh the scale heavily in favor of freedom of expression. Instead of requiring a speaker or publisher to show that the legislature did not have sufficient cause for imposing the restraint, the Court placed the burden of justification on the state. In subsequent cases, the Court said that the state's explanation would be subject to strict scrutiny and could survive judicial review only if the state could show that a compelling public interest necessitated the law.

The major purpose of freedom of expression is to provide the electorate, the ultimate decision-makers in our society, with information about political affairs and events. Justice Jackson once observed that the Founding Fathers protected expression "because they knew of no other way by which free men could conduct representative democracy."[23] The vehicle is the marketplace of ideas, for which the Supreme Court has shown an extraordinary appreciation in recent decades, even to the extent of relying on it as a solvent for errors and possibly wrongdoing. In certain situations the Court is willing to tolerate falsehoods, exaggerations, distortions, and defamations on the theory that competition and not authority provides the remedies most in the public interest. The market itself suppresses those ideas that the public believes to be wrong or harmful, and any effort to interfere in this competition limits or denies entry to potentially acceptable ideas. In the words, already quoted, of Justice Holmes: "[T]he ultimate good desired is better reached by free trade in ideas—...the best test of truth is the power of the thought to get itself accepted in the competition of the market."[24] Those who strive to succeed will have to produce new, better, different, and more attractive ideas. In short, the High Court has applied and enforced the wisdom of Adam Smith to this one selected area of human endeavor.

To be sure, not everything that is printed or said is safeguarded. The Court has excluded from protection expression—for example, obscenity, incitement to crime, and libel—that it thinks does not further society's interests. The existence of gradations of expression was recently revealed by Justice Stevens's widely quoted remark: "[F]ew of us would march our sons and daughters off to war to preserve the citizen's right to see 'Specified Sexual Activities' exhibited in the theaters of our choice."[25] The Court has also accepted Justice Black's belief that whenever expression is manifested in conduct, it is not necessarily protected.

Three major cases involving free press are especially illustrative of the extent of the Supreme Court's commitment to competition in the marketplace of ideas. Each places a severe restraint on the state's authority to restrict expression, and together they grant a large degree of immunity from governmental oversight to one of the country's major industries. If for no other reason, this result is noteworthy because we live during an era when industry in general is increasingly subject to regulation. Brief summaries of these cases follow.

The first case is *New York Times Co. v. Sullivan* (1964).[26] The Court applied the First and Fourteenth amendments to strike down in the instance of public officials the prevailing common law rule that a defendant could escape liability for defamation only by proving the truth of the expression. The *New York Times* had printed an advertisement soliciting contributions critical of Montgomery, Alabama police conduct during the civil rights protests. It contained factual errors of which the paper was unaware. Sullivan, a Montgomery city commissioner in charge of the police department, sued the *Times* and four clergymen, whose names appeared on the ad, for personal libel. A jury verdict awarding damages of $500,000 was upheld by the Supreme Court of Alabama, but was overruled by a unanimous United States Supreme Court. Writing for the Court, Justice Brennan held that a public official could not recover damages for a defamatory falsehood relating to his official conduct unless he proved that the statement was made with "actual malice"—that is, with knowledge that it was false or with reckless disregard for the truth. Subject to this qualification, this rule enables the press to publish untruths about a public official, while leaving that person without recourse, despite damages sustained.[27] Brennan provided two explanations for the rule.

> [W]e consider this case against the background of a profound national commitment to the principle that debate on public issues should be uninhibited, robust, and wide-open, and that it may well include vehement, caustic, and sometimes unpleasantly sharp attacks on government and public officials....
> ...Allowance of the defense of truth, with the burden of proving it on the defendant, does not mean that only false speech will be deterred.... Under such a rule, would-be critics of official conduct may be deterred from voicing their criticism, even though it is believed to be true and even though it is in fact true, because of doubt whether it can be proved in court or fear of the expense of having to do so. They tend to make only statements which "steer far wider of the unlawful zone."[28]

The second case also involves the *New York Times: New York Times Co. v. United States* (1971).[29] In *Near v. Minnesota*,[30] Chief Justice Hughes had enunciated three exceptions to the rule against prior restraint, one of which concerned publications affecting military security. In this second *Times* case, the government sought to enjoin temporarily the publication of excerpts from the surreptitiously obtained "Pentagon Papers," which were a classified study of the nation's involvement in the Viet Nam War. Both parties acknowledged that *Near* meant that an injunction could not lie unless publication would injure national security. The government asked for temporary relief to permit it to study and assess the impact on national security of the release of these voluminous documents. It claimed that publication might prolong the war by providing the enemy with classified information and might also embarrass the country's diplomatic endeavors. A dissenting judge in a lower court warned that publication could result in "the death of soldiers, the destruction of alliances, the greatly increased difficulty of negotiations with our enemies, the inability of our diplomats to negotiate."[31] A majority of the Justices thought that publishing the documents might be harmful to the nation and that the publishers might be prosecuted eventually for violating various espionage statutes. However, the per curiam opinion (with six justices concurring and three dissenting) declared that prior restraint, even of material that falls within a recognized exception, requires a heavy burden of justification and the government in this instance had not met that burden. Justices Black and Douglas controverted the existence of a limited "military security" exception;[32] Justices Stewart and White believed that the exception was to be construed narrowly and utilized only when disclosure "will surely result in direct, immediate, and irreparable damage to our Nation or its people";[33] and Justice Brennan countenanced restraint only when the government alleges and proves that "publication must inevitably, directly, and immediately cause the occurrence of an event kindred to imperiling the safety of a transport already at sea [an example used in *Near*]."[34] Each of the nine Justices, including the three dissenters, expressed his view separately and accepted the concept that prior restraint is presumptively unconstitutional.

The case involved the executive and judicial branches, neither of which is covered by the First Amendment's expression guarantee that is confined by its terms to laws passed by Congress. None of the Justices raised this issue, apparently accepting application of the constitutional provision to these branches, notwithstanding its limiting terminology.

The third case, *Miami Herald Publishing Co. v. Tornillo* (1974),[35] points up the enormous inequalities that exist in the marketplace of ideas. The influence of the ordinary citizen or small periodical is virtually nonexistent when compared with that of many daily newspapers. As one technique to lessen this inequality, a number of commentators have recommended that access requirements be imposed on the printed media. These requirements would demand, among other things, that newspapers air minority tastes and viewpoints, print replies to personal attacks that appeared in the news or editorial columns, and accept all paid advertisements offered to them.

The access movement suffered a probably fatal setback as a result of the case in question, involving a Florida right-to-reply law that had been invoked against the Miami *Herald* by Pat Tornillo, a candidate for the state legislature. The statute provides that if a newspaper assails the personal character or official record of a candidate for political office, it must upon demand print his reply in the same amount of space, free of charge. The newspaper's failure to comply is a misdemeanor. On its editorial pages, the *Herald* had excoriated Tornillo, a teachers' union official, for his actions in connection with teacher strikes. Pursuant to the Florida law, Tornillo demanded the right to reply. The *Herald* refused, contending that the statute was unconstitutional, and Tornillo filed suit.

He complained that the newspaper had the power to destroy his bid for public office and that the law should be upheld because it moderated that power in the public interest. His attorney argued that the right-to-reply statute assured that the marketplace of ideas would be as open and competitive as possible in the face of great concentrations of power, and would encourage the press to exercise its power more responsibly. The Florida Supreme Court upheld the act, but the United States High Court unanimously overruled this decision, stating that "[i]t has yet to be demonstrated how governmental regulation of this crucial [editorial] process can be exercised consistent with First Amendment guarantees of a free press...."[36]

Tornillo examines the breadth of the Holmesian concept of the marketplace of ideas where the only test of truth is acceptance by the consumer. Florida's statute was a seemingly modest regulation, intended to perfect the market by reducing inequalities among producers. It did not forbid or require the publication of specific material and operated to compel publication only when a prescribed market failure occurred. Chief Justice Burger's opinion held it unconstitutional because it did mandate publication of material that an editor would not otherwise publish. Any compulsion, said Burger, to publish that which reason tells a publisher should not be published is unconstitutional. "[P]ress responsibility is not mandated by the Constitution and like many other virtues it cannot be legislated."[37]

Furthermore, the restraint would inhibit the functioning of the marketplace. Burger explained that if the law were invoked, the publisher would incur the cost of composing and printing replies and would lose income from space that otherwise could be devoted to more remunerative material. Faced with this potential, editors might conclude that the safest course is to avoid controversy. The result would be to deter rather than foster "uninhibited, robust and wide-open" discussion of public issues. Thus, alleviating the problem of access would result in limiting the scope and vitality of the market. This legislative means for achieving greater dissemination of opinion is remote to the accomplishment of that end. Under this reasoning, the statute could not stand because it did not further a compelling state interest.

Of the three preceding cases, *Tornillo* may have the widest significance for society, because it was another version of the continuing struggle between equality and freedom—except that the outcome differed from the typical result in contemporary times. Professor Jerome Barron was Tornillo's attorney and has been a leading advocate of laws requiring the communications industry to provide for the airing of minority viewpoints that might not otherwise be disseminated. He

has written that under current conditions in the communications industry, "constitutional theory is in the grip of a romantic conception of
free expression" and that as a "constitutional theory for the communication of ideas, laissez-faire is manifestly irrelevant."[38] This is the kind
of plea for equality that has frequently proven irresistible to both legislators and courts in the economic and social areas. It did not succeed in
Tornillo because the justices are more favorably disposed to the operation of the marketplace for ideas.[39] Basically the same issue continually
confronted the Old Court in the context of economic activity, and the
outcome was frequently the same as in *Tornillo*. The similarities and
differences between the marketplace for ideas and that for goods and
services are further discussed in chapter 11.

Other Fundamental Interests

The Right of Privacy

The initial decision in this series is *Griswold v. Connecticut,* discussed
in chapter 1, in which Justice Douglas raised to a fundamental right the
privacy surrounding the marriage relationship. He explained this right
as follows:

> We deal with a right of privacy older than the Bill of Rights—older
> than our political parties, older than our school system. Marriage is a
> coming together for better or for worse, hopefully enduring, and
> intimate to the degree of being sacred. It is an association that pro
> motes a way of life, not causes; a harmony in living, not political
> faiths; a bilateral loyalty, not commercial or social projects. Yet it is
> an association for as noble a purpose as any involved in our prior
> decisions.[40]

Griswold led in time to the abortion decisions, among the most important and controversial adjudications in the High Court's history. In
Roe v. Wade, the leading abortion case, the Court declared that the
fundamental right to privacy was "broad enough to encompass a woman's decision whether or not to terminate her pregnancy."[41] Therefore,
only a compelling state interest would justify governmental restraint of
that decision. In voiding the Texas abortion statute, which permitted
an abortion only on medical advice that it was necessary to save the
woman's life, Justice Blackmun, author of the majority opinion, separated pregnancy into three distinct time periods and used the concept
of compelling state interest to define the extent of regulation, if any, the
state may impose on each. For the first trimester, the abortion decision

must be left to the medical judgment of the attending physician. Between the first trimester and viability, the state may regulate the abortion procedure in ways that are reasonably related to the woman's health. After viability, the state may regulate and even proscribe abortion, except when it is necessary to the woman's life or health. Thus, the Court went much further than invalidating the law; it wrote an abortion statute for all the states.

The second abortion decision, *Doe v. Bolton,*[42] dealt largely with the provisions of a Georgia statute that regulated the performance of a lawful abortion. Employing the compelling interest standard, Blackmun held that certain statutory conditions, such as requiring the use of an accredited hospital and subjecting the doctor's medical judgment to committee approval and confirming consultations, were unduly restrictive of the patient's right to obtain an abortion. The Justice referred to the statutory requirement of overview as unduly infringing upon a licensed physician's right to administer medical care based on his own best judgment.

Subsequently, the Court, again per Justice Blackmun, nullified provisions of a Missouri statute requiring written consent to the abortion by the spouse during the first trimester of pregnancy, or written consent of one parent during that same period for an unmarried woman under the age of eighteen.[43] Blackmun asserted that the state cannot "delegate to a spouse a veto power which the state itself is absolutely and totally prohibited from exercising during the first trimester of pregnancy."[44] Thus the Court has determined that at a certain stage of pregnancy neither the state's concern to protect the fetus, nor the interests of the father and the woman's family are sufficient to subordinate the woman's right to an abortion. The right to an abortion does not, however, require that the state fund it for indigents according to *Maher v. Roe,*[45] a 1977 decision, discussed later in this chapter.

The Court has in other respects enlarged the scope of the privacy right established in *Griswold* and the abortion cases. Relying on these and other holdings, a majority of the Justices in another 1977 case held that the decision of whether or not to beget or bear a child is of fundamental status. The Court struck down provisions of a New York law banning sales of nonmedical contraceptives to minors and allowing their sale to adults only by licensed pharmacists.[46]

The Right to Travel

The right to travel, although not set forth specifically in the Constitution, has long been judicially recognized and protected as furthering one of the basic reasons for the formation of the union—namely, facilitating commercial, intellectual, cultural, and physical movement among the states.[47] We are, said Chief Justice Taney, "one people, with one common country."[48] In *Shapiro v. Thompson,* this right achieved the rank of the constitutionally exalted. As more fully explained in chapter 14, a 6–3 majority invalidated a one-year residency requirement for welfare eligibility imposed by Congress and two states largely on the basis that the restraint impeded the right of interstate travel.[49] Subsequently, in *Memorial Hospital v. Maricopa County,*[50] the Court applied the precedent to declare unconstitutional a county residency requirement of one year as a condition for an indigent person's receiving nonemergency hospitalization or medical care at county expense. The Court found that the residency requirements in both cases penalized the right of travel, asserting that denial of welfare benefits to one who has recently exercised the right of travel across state lines was sufficiently analogous to a criminal fine to justify strict judicial scrutiny. Had no fundamental right been involved, the Court would have had to evaluate the classification distinguishing those who have and have not resided for the disputed period under the minimal scrutiny test, which would have made reaching the same result much more difficult (although Justice Brennan, author of the *Shapiro* opinion, observed that application of the lesser standard would have led to the same result in that case).

In these cases the Court's opinions not only strike down the laws, but also operate to compel the state to provide welfare benefits for a certain category of indigents. In effect, the Court has written new spending legislation for the state. These cases raise the distinction between rulings that eliminate restraints on people and those that impose them on the legislature, a matter discussed in chapter 14. Two subsequent cases have limited the meaning of *Shapiro* and *Maricopa: San Antonio Independent School District v. Rodriguez,*[51] which denied that education is a fundamental right, and *Maher* referred to above. The latter, which is analytically comparable to *Shapiro,* sustained a Connecticut welfare department curb on state medicaid benefits for first-trimester abortions except for those deemed medically necessary. The state funded indigents' medical expenses for pregnancy and childbirth. Two indigent women, unable to obtain a physician's certificate of medical necessity, challenged the law, which a three-judge district court found unconstitutional on the basis of the abortion cases and *Shapiro* and *Maricopa.*[52] Justice Powell, for a 6–3 majority, disagreed:

Roe did not declare an unqualified "constitutional right to an abortion," as the District Court seemed to think. Rather, the right protects the woman from unduly burdensome interference with her freedom to decide whether to terminate her pregnancy. It implies no limitation on the authority of a State to make a value judgment favoring childbirth over abortion, and to implement that judgment by the allocation of public funds . . . .

. . . The State may have made childbirth a more attractive alternative, thereby influencing the woman's decision, but it has imposed no restriction on access to abortions that was not already there. The indigency that may make it difficult—and in some cases, perhaps, impossible—for some women to have abortions is neither created nor in any way affected by the Connecticut regulation.[53]

Accordingly, the laws of Connecticut did not prevent abortion; the indigency of the women seeking this service was responsible for their plight. Thus the issue raised in Connecticut was not one of the legal right to abortion, but rather of a law affecting people on the basis of their economic resources. Such a law would require strict scrutiny only if wealth or poverty were suspect classifications, which neither are.[54]

Criminal Appeals and Voting

Although the Court has not considered it as a suspect category, poverty—or denial of equal access to rights because of financial constraint—apparently provides the common thread running through the cases that found criminal appeals, voting, and travel (in recent years) fundamental. Like the right to travel, the rights of appeal from criminal conviction and of the franchise are not independently secured in the Constitution.

In *Griffin v. Illinois*,[55] the Court held that in a criminal appellate review an indigent defendant is entitled to a transcript of the proceedings at the state's expense when the bill of exceptions needed for such review could not be prepared without a transcript. By charging for trial transcripts, Illinois had created in effect a classification that was detrimental to those whose means were inadequate to purchase one. The Supreme Court majority of five stressed the concept of equal justice for poor and rich, weak and powerful, alike. The state was required to cure the burden its rule placed on indigent criminal appellants. Subsequently in *Douglas v. California*,[56] the Court held that a state had to provide indigent appellants with counsel for their first appeal as of right. *Griffin* and *Douglas* did not, however, require a state to fund discretionary appeals of an indigent state prisoner, according to a subsequent opinion.[57] In *Harper v. Virginia Board of Elections*, an annual poll tax of $1.50 on all residents was invalidated because the Supreme Court concluded that "a State violates [equal protection] whenever it makes the affluence of the voter or payment of any fee an electoral standard. Voter qualifications have no relation to wealth nor to paying or not paying this or any other tax."[58]

In the cases we have been considering in this section, the cavalier treatment the Justices have accorded the constitutional basis (or lack thereof) for finding interests fundamental is remarkable. In *Griffin:* "It is true that a State is not required by the Federal Constitution to provide appellate courts or a right to appellate review at all."[59] In *Harper:* "[T]he right to vote in state elections is nowhere expressly mentioned. It is argued that the right to vote in state elections is implicit...."[60] In *Shapiro:* "We have no occasion to ascribe the source of this right to travel interstate to a particular constitutional provision."[61]

The two-tier approach to equal protection intervention can be justified as limiting judicial review exclusively to matters of fundamental interest to society. The ordinary and less vital interests are thus left entirely for resolution to the legislature and executive. In this respect, the two-tier system imposes substantial restraint on the Court. But Professor Gunther's analysis of the 1971 Court term discloses a change in the Court's previous willingness to confine itself to the two tiers.[62] In seven of the fifteen basic equal protection decisions of that term outside of race and reapportionment areas, the Court upheld the claim or remanded it for consideration without invoking the strict scrutiny formula. Gunther concluded that a majority was prepared to acknowledge equal protection claims on the basis of an intermediate standard. Subsequent decisions have confirmed the existence of such policy and with it, a much greater potential for the application of judicial discretion. Among the classifications subject to intermediate review are those involving gender and illegitimacy.

Irrebuttable Presumptions

Those who believe that the contemporary Court has resurrected substantive due process to serve its own ideological designs find support in another string of cases which have been decided by the Warren-Burger Courts on the basis of the irrebuttable presumption doctrine. Under this doctrine, the Court has struck down statutes conclusively presuming the existence of a certain state of facts that might in reality be wrong in a particular situation. Although the cases are frequently argued on equal protection grounds, the Supreme Court has held these laws invalid because such an "irrebuttable presumption" violated due process. The opinions are not always clear on whether the doctrine is founded in procedural or substantive due process. It is difficult, however, to dispute the position of commentators and dissenting Justices that substantive protection is being accorded certain liberties. Consider some examples:

In *Cleveland Board of Education v. LaFleur,*[63] the Cleveland School Board required every pregnant schoolteacher to take a maternity leave without pay beginning five months before the expected birth of her child. In declaring the rule invalid, the majority, per Justice Stewart, asserted the provision amounted to a conclusive presumption that all pregnant teachers in their fifth month of pregnancy were physically unfit to teach. Concluding that this presumption was not necessarily true, Stewart construed the due process clauses as requiring the school board to employ administrative procedures to determine fitness. The Court reasoned that the regulation operated to penalize the pregnant teacher economically for deciding to bear a child and was therefore a heavy burden on the exercise of freedom of personal choice in matters of marriage and family life, which were protected under the due process clause. Justice Rehnquist in dissent charged that substantive due process was being invoked, and contended that the decision would impair the legislative process because of the widespread use of classifications that can be construed as illegal irrebutable presumptions.

Vlandis v. Kline[64] concerned a Connecticut statute under which students failing to meet certain residency requirements would be conclusively presumed to remain nonresident for tuition purposes. The complainants possessed Connecticut driver's licenses, car registrations, and voter's registrations, but because they had not met the specific criteria of the statute, they were barred from the educational benefits granted to "residents." Justice Stewart, for the majority, held that since the statute "precluded the appellees from ever rebutting the presumption . . . [it] operated to deprive them of a significant amount of their money without due process of law."[65]

Bell v. Burson[66] is cited by the Supreme Court frequently in irrebuttable presumption decisions for doctrinal support. In that case, a Georgia statute provided for suspension of the motor vehicle registration and driver's license of an uninsured motorist involved in an accident, unless security for damages claimed was posted. It conclusively presumed fault from the fact that an uninsured motorist was involved in the accident. The Court unanimously invalidated the act as violating procedural due process, since it did not provide a prior hearing for determination of evidence of fault. Subsequent decisions refer to *Burson* mainly for the irrebuttable presumption implicit in the state regulation—that uninsured motorists are conclusively presumed to be at fault whenever involved in motor vehicle accidents. This case, like the prior two, rests in large part on a desire to protect against arbitrary deprivation of economic interests. Justice Brennan stated:

> Once licenses are issued, as in petitioner's case, their continued possession may become essential in their pursuit of a livelihood. Suspension of issued licenses thus involves state action that adjudicates important interests of the licensees.[67]

Using irrebuttable presumption or equal protection rationale, the Court has invalidated certain primarily economic criteria for obtaining social security and food stamp benefits. However, a majority in other cases has gone along with Justice Rehnquist's belief that "a noncontractual claim to receive funds from the public treasury enjoys no constitutionally protected status."[68] Commentators have found it extremely difficult to reconcile the decisions in this area.[69]

The irrebuttable presumption cases raise issues associated with the old substantive due process: a high degree of scrutiny; relationship of the means to the legislative ends; the availability of less onerous means for achieving the statutory purposes. Were only procedural due process involved, the courts would not be concerned about the substantive implications of the legislation. The issue of irrebuttable presumptions surfaced during the 1920s, and was used chiefly to strike down tax statutes.[70] The lineup on the Court of that period in matters of substantive due process remained steadfast in these cases, with Holmes, Brandeis, and Stone being the principal dissenters. These opinions, while concerned to an extent with procedural rules, were reasoned along lines consistent with the then prevailing notions of substantive due process.

The irrebutable presumption doctrine protects various economic interests, but not those of the entrepreneur. A *Michigan Law Review* note describes its relevancy to that concern.

> The Kansas legislature [in *Ferguson v. Skrupa*][71] had precluded laymen from the business of debt-adjusting, although lawyers were not so precluded, on the presumption that "financially distressed debtors require 'debt adjustment' services and advice which no laymen...however honest, can possibly supply." ... [U]nder the *Vlandis* standard, this statutory presumption seems far from "universally or necessarily true in fact," since many experienced debt

adjustors surely have as much competence to engage in that business as the average lawyer. Moreover, "reasonable alternative means" are available to the state in the form of licensing and regulation of the debt-adjusting trade. Since competence to engage in debt-adjusting could be measured by objective tests, it would seem easier to determine than a college student's domiciliary intent. In terms of the individual impact, the individuals who were forced to give up their livelihood by the Kansas statute surely suffered greater hardship than the *Vlandis* appellees, who paid higher tuition rates but were able to remain in school and did receive some state subsidy....[72]

Reincarnation

From what we have seen, if the enactment places significant limits on activity designated as a fundamental interest or creates a suspect or other classification that appears arbitrary to a majority of the Justices, the Court is likely to strike it down. Frequently the majority insists its judgment is distinguishable from substantive due process, and almost inevitably the dissenters cry that it is nothing less. The Constitution does not disclose the extent to which speech should be protected, nor does it state that privacy, travel, criminal appeals, and voting should be fundamental rights, nor does it reveal that certain classifications are beyond the legislature's capacity. Our Supreme Court continues to respond in accordance with its members' own individual ideas about the meaning of the Constitution.

10   Protecting Certain Material Rights

This chapter will examine those areas in which rulings of the contemporary High Court have safeguarded economic interests of producers and sellers. We shall probe the undefinable line that separates protected and unprotected economic endeavors. As the preceding chapter demonstrates, economic and political rights are frequently interchangeable in the constitutional scheme. For example, freedom of contract could safeguard publishers and the publishing industry to no less a degree than does freedom of expression. It could also protect family and privacy liberties, and the right to travel.

Under current legal thought, freedom of contract receives judicial protection only as a result of its relationship to those endeavors that the judiciary is willing to safeguard. Freedom of contract for the publisher, writer, parent, doctor, and patient is maintained because of decisions concerning other liberties. Only those whose activities also fit within the protected categories have their economic interests afforded special judicial recognition. As a result, two constitutional levels for economic interests have been established; a high level of judicial protection is accorded one group and virtually none is given the other. Perhaps the economic interests thus favored are the more important, but even if this proposition is true, it is the result of totally fortuitous circumstances.

Conceptual and Material Rights Converge

The two-level approach allows people in the advertising business, real estate brokers, and lawyers to enjoy certain economic rights now deemed near fundamental. These rights are the ones closely allied with freedom of expression. Thus, during the last several years commercial advertising has been placed within the ambit of protected speech.

If one were to select the economic activities that should be accorded special legal recognition, advertising would probably not receive the highest priority. The removal of controls on pricing, entry, production, distribution, and property use would surely be stronger contenders for this distinction. Of course, the importance of advertising in bettering the human condition should not be denigrated. In our society a consumer's interest in the free flow of commercial information "may be as keen, if not keener by far, than his interest in the day's most urgent political debate."[1] But not long ago prevailing sentiment among economists about advertising was that at worst it created monopolistic power and at best it was a wasteful and undesirable allocation of resources.[2]

Until the recent spate of cases on the subject, serious doubt existed that commercial advertising would be considered protected expression. Unlike political speech, commercial speech has long been regulated by federal and state agencies. In 1943, the United States Supreme Court unanimously ruled in *Valentine v. Chrestensen* that the "Constitution imposes no . . . restraint on government as respects purely commercial advertising."[3] For many years the *Chrestensen* principle remained sufficiently intact to enable the Court to apply it narrowly to advertising that was largely financially motivated. However, this rule (a "casual, almost offhand" statement, according to Justice Douglas, that has not survived reflection)[4] was steadily eroded as a number of regulatory laws were struck down and was finally demolished in three cases, discussed below, that were decided during 1976 and 1977.

In a democracy speech is protected primarily in order to enlighten public decision-making. That commercial activity should be included under even the broadest umbrella is hardly a fulfillment of this objective. The line between political and commercial commentary may be difficult to draw, but had it been so disposed, the Court could have accepted Justice Rehnquist's contention that this difficulty was not cause for eliminating the distinction.[5]

In the three recent cases, the High Court reasoned in both economic and legal theory, but the explanation for the elevation of commercial speech to special protection must lie with the persuasiveness of the economic argument made in the first and elaborated and applied in the later two. The outcome was also encouraged by the unsatisfactory and confusing state of the law on the subject. Although the existing distinctions were clear in theory, they were hard to execute in practice.

For many years a two-level approach applied to commercial speech. A communication intended primarily to generate business profits enjoyed no First Amendment protection. In contrast, if the communication's primary purpose was to convey information or opinions on political matters, it was entitled to full protection. When paid political advertising carried a political message, it was within the protected area. But what if the advertising was for a commercial service that also furthered or concerned political issues or conveyed information of interest or value to an audience other than those immediately serviced? *Bigelow v. Commonwealth of Virginia,* decided in 1975, raised this question with respect to an advertisement in a Virginia paper for a New York abortion service.[6] The advertisement was violative of a Virginia statute that made encouraging or permitting the procuring of an abortion a misdemeanor. The Court reasoned that the part of the ad reading 'Abortions are now legal in New York. There are no residency requirements" involved communicating information and disseminating opinion.[7] It therefore overturned a conviction under the law and set up a balancing test to determine the validity of commercial speech. This test required a case-by-case analysis without establishing a preference for advertising. Such was the state of the law prior to the decisions in the three cases mentioned above—decisions that I shall now discuss.

1. *Virginia State Board of Pharmacy v. Virginia Citizens Consumer Council, Inc.*[8] A Virginia statute provided that a pharmacist licensed in the state was guilty of unprofessional conduct if he or she published, advertised, or promoted in any manner, any amount, price, fee, premium, discount, rebate, or credit terms for any drugs that may be dispensed only by prescription. The legal attack against the act was brought by a number of prescription drug consumers who claimed that they would greatly benefit if the prohibition were lifted and advertising freely allowed. The three plaintiffs included a Virginia resident who suffered from a disease that required her to take prescription drugs daily, a Virginia consumer organization, and the state's AFL-CIO. An

associate of Ralph Nader represented the plaintiffs before the United States Supreme Court.

The High Court ruled 7–1 that the advertising ban violated freedom of expression, stating that the First Amendment's "protection . . . is to the communication, to its source and to its recipients both."[9] Justice Blackmun, explaining why this advertising warranted First Amendment protection, wrote that Virginia's ban prevented consumers from learning about differences in the prices of prescription drugs, principally to the very serious disadvantage of older people, who are the biggest users of such drugs and who frequently subsist on modest fixed incomes. Because elderly people are less mobile than the rest of the population, they cannot shop around for bargain prices. In the absence of advertising, pharmacists can charge relatively high prices, secure in the knowledge that many of their customers will not be able to learn that the cost is less elsewhere. For example, surveys disclosed that in Richmond the price of forty achromycin tablets ranged from $2.59 to $6.00, and that in the Newport News–Hampton area, the price of tetracycline varied from $1.20 to $9.00. According to the Federal Trade Commission, such price discrepancies prevail throughout the nation, largely because thirty-four states impose significant restrictions on the dissemination of drug price information.

Such statistics evidence the importance to the elderly of knowledge about prices. As Justice Blackmun stated, "When drug prices vary as strikingly as they do, information as to who is charging what becomes more than a convenience. It could mean the alleviation of physical pain or the enjoyment of basic necessities."[10] The dissemination of this commercial information could enhance the lives of people more than the publication of political information, and therefore should not lack constitutional protection.

However, the opinion made plain that this result does not mean that commercial speech is legally the same as other forms of expression. Common sense differentiates between speech that does no more than propose a commercial transaction and speech that, for example, deals with political issues. In the latter instance only the most minimal restraint may be imposed. In the former, regulation is more broadly permissible with respect to time, place, and manner, falsehoods or deceptions, and possibly errors or omissions.

Blackmun stressed that only the regulation of commercial advertising by pharmacists was being considered and expressed no opinion on the applicability of the ruling to other professions. The case was also distinguishable on the basis of the product being advertised; that the pharmaceuticals could be obtained only with a physician's prescription practically eliminated the possibility that the advertising was advancing goods and services that might prove detrimental to health and safety.

Blackmun's opinion presented several arguments equating political and economic interests in our society.

> So long as we preserve a predominantly free enterprise economy, the allocation of our resources in large measure will be made through numerous private economic decisions. It is a matter of public interest that those decisions, in the aggregate, be intelligent and well informed. To this end, the free flow of commercial information is indispensable.... And if it is indispensable to the proper allocation of resources in a free enterprise system, it is also indispensable to the formation of intelligent opinions as to how that system ought to be regulated or altered....
>
> ...As to the particular consumer's interest in the free flow of commercial information, that interest may be as keen, if not keener by far, than his interest in the day's most urgent political debate....
>
> ...It appears to be feared that if the pharmacist who wishes to provide low cost, and assertedly low quality, services is permitted to advertise, he will be taken up on his offer by too many unwitting customers....
>
> ...There is, of course, an alternative to this highly paternalistic approach. That alternative is to assume that this information is not in itself harmful, that people will perceive their own best interests if only they are well enough informed, and that the best means to that end is to open the channels of communication rather than to close them. If they are truly open, nothing prevents the "professional" pharmacist from marketing his own assertedly superior product, and contrasting it with that of the low-cost, high-volume prescription drug retailer. But the choice among these alternative approaches is not ours to make or the Virginia General Assembly's. It is precisely this kind of choice, between the dangers of suppressing information, and the dangers of its misuse if it is freely available, that the First Amendment makes for us.[11]

Why did Virginia attempt to prohibit the advertising of prescription drug prices? Perhaps, as Justice Rehnquist said, the public interest against the promotion of drugs for every ill, real or imaginary, is extremely strong.[12] However, it may also be that small drugstore owners favored the legislation as protection against chain stores and discounters that engage in considerable advertising and frequently have cheaper prices. The legislation likely reflects the greater political strength of small drugstore owners.

2. *Linmark Associates v. Township of Willingboro.*[13] Justice Marshall's opinion in this case is another affirmation, this time supported by all eight participating justices, of the importance of commercial expression. Willingboro, New Jersey, is located in the southern part of the state near Fort Dix Army Base and McGuire Air Force Base, and as of the 1970 census had a population of about 44,000. Between 1970 and 1973 the white population declined by almost 2,000 while the non-white population expanded by more than 3,000. In the early 1970s, the local authorities of Willingboro became fearful that too many white families were selling their homes and moving from the municipality. In an effort to avoid "panic selling" and to stem "white flight," they passed an ordinance in March 1974 prohibiting the posting of "For Sale" and "Sold" signs on property.

A corporation owning realty in Willingboro and a local real estate agency filed suit to declare the ordinance unconstitutional. At the trial, several real estate agents testified that 30 to 35 percent of their clients came to them because they had seen one of their "For Sale" or "Sold" signs. In one broker's estimation, based on his experience in a neighboring community that had already banned signs, selling realty without signs takes twice as long as selling with signs.

Ordinarily this kind of hardship is not sufficient to cause a court to declare a land or property use law unconstitutional. Law books are filled with cases in which relief was denied to property owners who suffered much greater deprivations, ranging up to millions of dollars. Every zoning ordinance contains a wide variety of restrictions upon the use of property, many severely depressing values.

Willingboro's sign ordinance, by comparison, was a minor restraint. It was unlikely to cause an owner serious loss or lead to waste or misuse of property. Marshall's explanation of the adverse impact of the sign ordinance discloses that the alternatives, although not as satisfactory, were far from drastic:

> The options to which sellers realistically are relegated—primarily newspaper advertising and listing with real estate agents—involve more cost and less autonomy than "For Sale" signs;...are less likely to reach persons not deliberately seeking sales information;...and may be less effective media for communicating the message that is conveyed by a "For Sale" sign in front of the house to be sold....[14]

Nevertheless, the United States Supreme Court, which usually does not intervene in local zoning decisions, found this ordinance unconstitutional. The law had a technical defect not present in most land use restrictions: it abridged freedom of commercial speech. The eight Justices agreed that the ordinance impaired the "flow of truthful and legitimate commercial information,"[15] and was not necessary to achieve a compelling state interest. In reaching this decision, the Court relied principally on the *Board of Pharmacy* case, stating that the Willingboro council, like the Virginia legislature, had attempted to prevent its residents from obtaining certain information important to their well-being. For the Court, Justice Marshall asserted that the sign ordinance might interfere with one of the most significant choices that individuals have a right to make, the decision about where to live and raise their families. The restraint was not constitutionally justifiable.

> The Council had sought to restrict the free flow of these data because it fears that otherwise homeowners will make decisions inimicable to what the Council views as the homeowners' self-interest and the corporate interest of the township: they will choose to leave town.... If dissemination of this information can be restricted, then every locality in the country can suppress any facts that reflect poorly on the locality, so long as a plausible claim can be made that disclosure would cause the recipients of the information to act "irrationally."[16]

The Justice rejected this paternalistic approach, quoting from Blackmun's observation in the *Board of Pharmacy* case that people will perceive their own best interests if only they are well enough informed.

To bridge the gap between commercial and political speech, Marshall quoted from Brandeis's concurrence in *Whitney v. California:* "If there be time to expose through discussion the falsehood and fallacies, to avert the evil by the process of education, the remedy to be applied is more speech, not enforced silence. Only an emergency can justify repression."[17] And in comparing the interest in information about housing to the consumer interests (abortion and drugs) that the Court had vindicated in earlier decisions, Marshall stated:

> If the Willingboro law is to be treated differently from those [previously] invalidated...it cannot be because the speakers—or listeners—have a lesser First Amendment interest in the subject matter of the speech that is regulated here. Persons desiring to sell their homes are just as interested in communicating that fact as are sellers of other goods and services. Similarly, would-be purchasers of realty are no less interested in receiving information about available property than are purchasers of other commodities in receiving like information about those commodities. And the societal interest in "the free flow of commercial information"...is in no way

lessened by the fact that the subject of the commercial information here is realty rather than abortions or drugs.[18]

3. *Bates v. State Bar of Arizona.* The appellants, licensed attorneys and members of the Arizona State Bar, operated a legal clinic in Phoenix. They sought to provide legal services at modest fees to people with moderate incomes who did not qualify for governmental legal aid. They accepted only routine matters and because of their low rates had to depend on substantial volume. When, after two years of practice, their business remained insufficient to sustain them financially, the appellants began to advertise. A complaint was filed with a committee of the state bar charging them with transgressing the state supreme court's disciplinary rule prohibiting attorneys from advertising in newspapers or other media. The Arizona Supreme Court upheld the bar committee conclusion that the appellants had violated the rule, rejecting their claim that the prohibition was contrary to the Sherman Antitrust Act and the First Amendment. The United States Supreme Court held that the rule was not subject to attack on the former ground but that it was unconstitutional on the latter. The Court thus clarified one of the questions left open in the *Board of Pharmacy* ruling by applying the reasoning in that opinion to price advertising by lawyers.

Justice Blackmun, for a 5–4 majority, rested his arguments concerning the applicability of the First Amendment on the *Board of Pharmacy* ruling, emphasizing the importance of consumers having access to legal fee information and fending off attacks premised on the alleged problems inherent in deregulation. He held the advertising was protected, and found no compelling state interest justifying the state's ban of it. He quoted a dissent by one of the Arizona Supreme Court justices, who wrote that price information is indispensable to the formation of an intelligent opinion by the public on how well the legal system is working and on whether it should be altered or regulated. This observation was intended to close whatever conceptual gulf existed between lawyers' advertising and the dissemination of political information. However, the underlying basis of the decision was a pragmatic one. Elimination of the advertising ban would increase competition and make legal services less costly and more widely available to people with moderate and average incomes.

Blackmun countered the dissenters' justifications for the ban. He contended that price advertising will not adversely affect professionalism, that attorney advertising is not inherently misleading, that such advertising will not have a negative influence on the administration of justice, that it will not increase the costs of legal services, that it will not lower the quality of those services, and that regulation is not required to prevent misleading or deceptive price advertising. He chided the opponents of legal advertising:

> It is at least somewhat incongruous for the opponents of advertising to extol the virtues and altruism of the legal profession at one point, and, at another, to assert that its members will seize the opportunity to mislead and distort. We suspect that, with advertising, most lawyers will behave as they always have: They will abide by their solemn oaths to uphold the integrity and honor of their profession and of the legal system. For every attorney who overreaches through advertising, there will be thousands of others who will be candid and honest and straightforward. And, of course, it will be in the latter's interest, as in other cases of misconduct at the bar, to assist in weeding out those few who abuse their trust.[19]

Within several years after *Bates,* hundreds of legal clinics had opened that emphasized high volume and low-cost services. Advertising is essential to the operation of these clinics, which, it has been reported, frequently charge prices 30–35 percent below those of the more conventional law offices.[20] The decision has had little effect on that part of the profession engaged in servicing wealthy corporations and individuals.

As we have seen, the Supreme Court has now said that purchasers of pharmaceuticals, houses, and legal services are better able to pursue their welfare in the absence of prohibitions on advertising. Governmental controls are interfering with the market in a manner harmful to the public by causing an increase in prices, most adversely affecting those least able to bear the cost. The dissenting Justices in these cases remind us that many problems arise in an uncontrolled marketplace, and of course they are correct. However, the possibility of detriment in *Near,* both *New York Times* cases, and *Tornillo* (discussed above in chapters 7 and 9) was not sufficient to overcome the benefits of freedom in the marketplace. Presumably the Justices have compared the harm caused by authority to the harm caused by freedom and have come down heavily in favor of the latter. With respect to pharmaceutical advertising, the Federal Court has ruled no differently from the state courts that continue to observe substantive due process, except that these courts do not have to become embroiled in interpreting an expression guarantee. In challenges to statutes similar to the Virginia act, three state supreme courts found no substantial relationship be-

tween the means used by the statute and the legislative ends of furthering the public health and safety.[21] The restraint on the plaintiffs,
who were drugstore owners, was therefore unreasonable and arbitrary.
In these situations the state and federal courts have achieved the same
results. But this outcome has occurred only because of the fortuitous
circumstance of the federal interpretation of the speech guarantee.

   Carey v. Population Services International,[22] decided in 1977, advanced further the economic thrust of the preceding three decisions.
Provisions of the New York Education Law made it a crime (1) for
anyone other than a licensed pharmacist to distribute contraceptives to
people over sixteen; (2) for anyone including a licensed pharmacist to
advertise or display contraceptives; and (3) for any person to sell or
distribute any contraceptive to a minor under sixteen. The complainant
in a suit brought to decide the law's constitutionality was a corporation
engaged in the mail-order retail sale of nonmedical contraceptive devices from its offices in North Carolina. It regularly advertised its
products in periodicals published or circulated in New York, accepted
orders from New York residents, and filled orders by mailing contraceptives to New York purchasers without regard for their age. The
court gave the corporation standing to assert the interests of potential
consumers disadvantaged by the statute.

   The United States Supreme Court, with seven Justices joining or
concurring in the opinion and two dissenting, upheld a district court
opinion declaring all provisions unconstitutional. Justice Brennan's
decision interpreted *Griswold v. Connecticut* and its progeny as protecting individual choices in matters relating to conception and bearing
of children from any governmental intrusion not justified by a compelling state interest. He declared that access to contraceptives is essential to making these choices and that limiting distribution of nonprescrip-
tion contraceptives to licensed pharmacists imposed an unjustified
burden on the right of individuals to use contraceptives if they so
chose. While the burden was not as great as a complete ban, this
restriction upon distribution to a small fraction of the total number of
possible retail outlets "renders contraceptive devices considerably less
accessible to the public, reduces the opportunity for privacy of selection and purchase, and lessens the possibility of price competition."[23]

   The Justice included the purchase by minors of contraceptives as
protected under the right of privacy. Brennan further held that the
advertising ban was contrary to the *Board of Pharmacy* ruling. Because the statute suppressed completely any information about the
availability and price of contraceptives, it required strong justification

New York contended that advertising contraceptive products would be offensive and embarrassing to some and that permitting such advertisements would legitimize sexual activity among young people. Brennan rejected these reasons as not constituting a compelling state interest sufficient to sustain the statute. Employing a free speech rationale, he explained that at least when obscenity is not involved, the fact that protected speech may be offensive to some does not justify its suppression. Nor, he said, citing *Brandenburg*'s standard, could such advertising be characterized as "inciting or producing imminent lawless action and . . . likely to incite or produce such action."[24]

Carey can be distinguished, of course, from other freedom of contract cases on the ground that the statute in question applied to personal decisions on begetting children which the Court found to be within the fundamental right of privacy. While technically correct, the explanation makes little sense in a real world, for it isolates the facts of the case from their obvious similarity to legal infringements on the production and distribution of food, shelter, and clothing. The complainant in *Carey* was seeking to exercise liberty of contract, to sell a particular product that appears to be no more important to bettering the human condition than a wide variety of other commodities and services. The question arises, why contraceptives and not also groceries, houses, and wearing apparel? Regulation restricting production or sales in these other areas renders them likewise "considerably less accessible to the public, reduces the opportunity for privacy of selection and purchase, and lessens the possibility of price competition."

Because almost everyone in a private enterprise society continually enters into contractual relationships to buy or sell goods and services, it is difficult to contain the economic implications of decisions premised on nonmaterial rights. Thus, a California court of appeal (an intermediate court) postulated in a 2–1 decision that as a result of the abortion cases "[t]here exists in the doctor licensed to practice medicine a right, constitutional in nature, as yet ill defined, to treat and to treat by unorthodox modalities—as yet unapproved by the state board—an informed, consenting patient."[25] The court, partly on this basis, reversed the conviction of a physician for prescribing laetrile to a cancer victim in violation of a California statute prohibiting the prescription of non-FDA-approved drugs for the cure of cancer. Subsequently, however, the California Supreme Court affirmed the conviction.[26]

The First Amendment shield for business activity can at times be exceedingly broad. In the 1961 case, *Eastern Railroad Presidents Conference v. Noerr Motor Freight Inc.*,[27] the High Court unanimously held that understandings and agreements among competitors that could traditionally be regarded as an illegal conspiracy in violation of the Sherman Antitrust Act were beyond reach of the statute if they constituted attempts to influence government decisions. A complaint for treble damages and a restraining order was filed under the Sherman Act by forty-one Pennsylvania truck operators and their trade association against twenty-four eastern railroads, associations of the presidents of those railroads, and a public relations firm, alleging that the defendants had conspired to restrain trade in and to monopolize the long-distance freight business. The gist of the alleged conspiracy was that the railroads had engaged the public relations firm to conduct a publicity campaign against the truckers that was designed to foster the adoption of laws and law enforcement practices destructive of the trucking business, to create among the general public an atmosphere of distaste for the truckers, and to impair the relationship existing between the truckers and their customers.

Subsequently, the defendants filed a counterclaim, alleging that the truckers were guilty of essentially the same conduct. The district court held that that railroads had voilated the Sherman Act while the truckers had not. Its judgment rested first, upon findings that the railroads' publicity campaign, insofar as it was actually directed at lawmaking and law-enforcing authorities, was malicious and fraudulent—malicious because its only purpose was to destroy the truckers as competitors, and fraudulent because it was predicated upon deception of the authorities. Second, the district court found that the railroads' campaign had as an important if not overriding purpose the destruction of the truckers' reputation among both the general public and the truckers' existing customers and thus that it had injured the truckers in ways unrelated to the passage or enforcement of law.

In reversing the lower court, Justice Black held that these findings did not constitute illegal activity. The Sherman Act could not be construed to regulate the rights to petition and other politically motivated conduct "simply because those activities have a commercial impact and involve conduct that can be termed unethical."[28] Considerable litigation has centered on *Noerr*, and at present its rule seems confined to protecting concerted efforts to influence the political arena and public officials through petitioning and communicating, regardless of ultimate purpose.

The commercial advertising and *Noerr* line of decisions raise the question of whether laws barring or regulating entry into business do not infringe upon First Amendment rights. Producing, distributing, and

elling require communication of possibly otherwise unavailable in-
ormation to consumers. Sellers inform potential customers about the
oods and services that they offer, about conditions in the market, and
bout competitive products. Sometimes they discuss their products
nd services within the context of current political affairs. This avenue
·f communication is limited when businesses are excluded from the
narket. Under the rationale of the *Board of Pharmacy* case, is it too
emote to consider that regulations barring or limiting entry into a
narket shut off the communication of information important to the
·/ell-being of consumers and thus constitute an infringement of free-
lom of speech? With more producers and sellers in the market, a
onsumer is likely to be better informed with respect both to a pro-
·osed purchase and to the functioning of the marketplace. (Consumers
night even have a better understanding as to whether it should be
egulated.) *Noerr* perhaps suggests that no bars on entry or production
hould exist that would operate to deny the public and officials in-
ormation about competitors and competitive conditions.

The disturbing aspect about this line of reasoning is the fact that it
nakes free speech the guardian of the economic system. This approach
; hardly consistent with either the intention of the Founding Fathers or
easonable constitutional construction. In any case, the inter-
elationship of rights apparent in these situations makes illogical the
xisting exclusion of economic rights from judicial protection.

qual Protection

Iotions of equal protection may also remove regulations on the pur-
hase and sale of products from the minimal scrutiny standard. Such a
·sult was illustrated by the 1976 case of *Craig v. Boren*,[29] in which a
censed vendor (referred to as a saloonkeeper by Justice Burger) of 3.2
·ercent beer successfully challenged a 1972 Oklahoma statute pro-
·ibiting the sale of this product to males under twenty-one and to
·males under eighteen. The vendor was given standing to assert the
·ights of eighteen-to-twenty-year-old males to purchase this drink.
·ight of the Justices thought that the statute was not irrational with
·spect to the end of achieving greater highway safety. However, using
·he intermediate standard of review applicable to gender-based classi-
·cations, a plurality of four, per Justice Brennan, held that the act
·invidiously discriminated" against males eighteen to twenty years of
·ge. Three Justices concurred in the judgment, with two dissenting.

Justice Rehnquist's dissent rejected the position that a standard (
review more stringent than rationality be invoked for discriminatio
against the males: "There is no suggestion in the Court's opinion tha
males in this age group are in any way peculiarly disadvantaged, sul
ject to systematic discriminatory treatment, or otherwise in need (
special solicitude from the courts."[30]

This dissent raises some obvious dilemmas for judicial policy. Wh
should the statute be treated differently from countless legislativ
classifications unrelated to sex that have been upheld under th
minimum rationality standard? Is there something special about a ce
tain group of male beer drinkers that entitles them to preferentia
treatment not accorded many more who consume other goods an
services of at least equal importance to well-being?

As the preceding discussion indicates, the key to overturning eco
nomic laws lies not in how arbitrary, perverse, or senseless they are
but in whether they touch on sensitive areas. Another excellent illu
tration is provided by cases dealing with the exclusion of aliens fro
government employment. These cases bring forth memorable expre
sions on the "right to work," which would be just as pertinent an
telling in cases dealing with regulatory controls that operate to lim
employment opportunities. In *Hampton v. Mow Sun Wong*,[31] Justic
Stevens quoted approvingly Justice Hughes's statement that "the rig
to work for a living in the common occupations of the community is (
the very essence of the personal freedom and opportunity that it wa
the purpose of the [Fourteenth] Amendment to secure."[32] The 5-
majority in *Hampton* invoked a standard of scrutiny that enabled the
to strike down, as violative of the Fifth Amendment due proces
clause, regulations of the United States Civil Service Commission tha
barred aliens from employment in the federal competitive civil servic
Three years earlier, the Court, by an 8–1 margin, ruled that Ne
York's civil service laws allowing only United States citizens to ho
permanent positions in the competitive classified state civil servic
infringed the equal protection and supremacy clauses.[33] In both ir
stances the Court examined the justifications for the regulations, an
found they unnecessarily deprived aliens of their liberties.

Such an inquiry is, of course, inappropriate under the rational rel
tion rule. Yet countless regulations proliferate throughout the nation
economy that directly or indirectly deny persons the opportunity t
work in a chosen vocation. Because aliens frequently are margina
employees—that is, the last hired and first fired—almost any legal in
pediment to employment is likely to be adverse to their interests. Du

o language and educational limitations, they also are less likely to pass
tate licensing examinations.

Regulations that limit employment opportunities emanate from two
ources. First, occupational licensing laws preclude many qualified
eople from pursuing particular lines of work (as discussed in chapter
). Second, economic regulations that inhibit production and distribu-
ion curtail work opportunities. Land use laws provide an example. By
estricting construction, zoning laws limit employment for construction
vorkers. In many parts of the country, unions have joined with man-
gement to fight zoning and environmental laws that impede develop-
nent. Thus the economic and social laws ignored by the Court may be
reating more unemployment for "insular and discrete"[34] minorities
han those that it condemns.

Obligation of Contracts Clause

ustice Brennan, dissenting in two recent cases, suggested that a
najority of his colleagues were using the obligation of contracts clause
o invalidate economic legislation that otherwise would readily satisfy a
ninimal scrutiny test. The first of these cases was *United States Trust
Co. of New York v. New Jersey*,[35] in which the courts struck down, as
iolative of the contracts clause, 1974 legislation adopted by both New
'ork and New Jersey. The legislation repealed a 1962 covenant made
y these states that limited the ability of the New York and New Jersey
'ort Authority to subsidize rail passenger transportation from revenues
nd reserves pledged as security for bonds issued by the Authority.
Acknowledging that the contracts clause is not an absolute bar to a
tate's subsequent modification of its prior commitments, Justice
Blackmun for a 4–3 majority explained that an impairment may be
onstitutional only if it is reasonable and necessary to serve an im-
ortant public purpose. In applying this standard, complete deference
o a legislature's assessment of reasonableness and necessity is not
ppropriate because the state's self-interest is at stake. Brennan con-
ended that the contracts clause does not provide authority for the
Court to invalidate purely economic and social legislation of the type in
uestion.

In *Allied Structural Steel Co. v. Spannaus*,[36] Justices Stewart and
Brennan debated whether a Minnesota statute increasing an em-
loyer's pension liabilities impaired its existing pension obligation or
vas purely an economic regulation. The steel company was an Illinois
orporation that maintained an office in Minnesota employing thirty

people. It established in 1963 a pension plan entitling its employees t
receive, under certain conditions, pensions at the age of 65. In 197
Minnesota enacted a Private Pension Benefits Act, subjecting ever
private employer of 100 or more workers (at least one of whom was
Minnesota resident) to a "pension funding charge" if it terminated
pension plan or closed its Minnesota office. Shortly afterwards, in
move planned before passage of the act, Allied closed its Minnesot
office. The state thereafter notified the company that it owed approx
mately $185,000 for nine employees covered by the pension protectio
statute.

In his 5–3 opinion, Stewart held that a purpose of the constitution
provision was to protect the contractual expectations of the parties. B
increasing the amount a company owed employees for past services
wrote Stewart, the Minnesota law nullifies "express terms of the com
pany's contractual obligations and imposes a completely unexpecte
liability in potentially disabling amounts."[37] Stewart asserted that n
societal problems existed to warrant such action by the state. Brenna
replied: "There is nothing sacrosanct about expectations rooted i
contract that justify according them a constitutional immunity denie
other property rights."[38]

The reader may recall Justice William Johnson's complaint in 182
that the Court was forced frequently to "toil up hill" to apply th
contracts clause because of the erroneous interpretation it had give
the ex post facto clause.[39] As the *Allied Steel* case shows, curre
judicial policy on economic liberties similarly forces the High Court t
"toil up hill."

Property

Under *Village of Euclid v. Ambler Realty Co.*,[40] the presumption c
validity in zoning controversies rests with the municipality—a fac
that places a difficult burden on the plaintiff who must prove tha
the ordinance has no substantial relationship to the public welfare
However, in the context of fundamental rights, the burden shifts to th
municipality and it must satisfy the more severe compelling stat
interest standard. In *Moore v. City of East Cleveland*,[41] decided i
1977, Justices Powell, Blackmun, Brennan, and Marshall, resuscitatin
substantive due process, designated extended family life as a funda
mental right in order to protect the inhabitants of a household fro
zoning restrictions. Justice Stevens's concurrence on other ground
provided a majority. The latter reasoned that the ordinance constitute

a deprivation of property in violation of the Fourteenth Amendment's due process clause.

Establishing a fundamental right for the family would have accomplished no more in *Moore* than the safeguarding of a property owner's rights would have, and seems entirely superfluous given the existence of a property guarantee in the taking and due process clauses. However, zoning decisions have so crippled the meaning of the taking clause, the Constitution's principal guarantee of property rights, that it is more of a sieve than a bulwark against restrictions, even in the most dire circumstances. This statement is supported by the fact that three of the four Justices who dissented in *Moore* were unable to find that a taking of property had occurred despite the extreme situation presented by that case. Some of the majority Justices may also have thought that absent a fundamental interest approach, existing precedent did not warrant overturning the ordinance.

"Unbelievable" is an apt description of the facts of the case. An East Cleveland, Ohio, zoning ordinance made criminal a grandmother's living with her two grandchildren if the grandchildren are cousins but not if they are siblings. Inez Moore, aged sixty-three, resided in an East Cleveland home with her son Dale and her grandchildren, Dale, Jr., and John, Jr., who are cousins. John's mother died when he was one year old, and he had lived with Moore subsequently. At the time of the United States Supreme Court decision, John was ten years old. Some time after he came to live with Moore, the city served notice that John was an "illegal occupant" under the zoning ordinance and directed her to remove him from her home. When she failed to comply, the city filed a criminal charge. Moore was subsequently convicted and sentenced to five days in jail and fined $25.00. The conviction was upheld by an Ohio appellate court and reversed, 5–4, by the United States Supreme Court.

In support of his position that family life is a fundamental right, Powell wrote that the Constitution protects the sanctity of the family because it is an institution deeply rooted in this nation's history and traditions. East Cleveland's zoning law, he said, unnecessarily interfered with this basic relationship. He explained that the tradition of uncles, aunts, and especially grandparents sharing a household with parents and children has origins deserving constitutional recognition.

Powell's reasoning, however, should not obscure the fact that the case essentially involved a land use regulation. Moore wanted to use her property for certain purposes, including the housing and raising of John, that were prohibited by the city. Certainly, as Justice Powell asserted, this use is important to society. But in a private enterprise economy, the same can be said about a large number of other uses, such as apartments, stores, and factories. These uses, unlike the one in the East Cleveland case, are intended to generate business profits—a fact that makes it possible to classify them separately. However, this is a distinction without a difference, for nearly all uses of property, including the one East Cleveland prohibited, have an economic effect. Moore could have sold her home and bought or rented in another locality which would not have penalized her for roofing John. Presumably she would have sustained a hardship in so acting, but any such hardship does not differ in principle from the economic losses other owners sustain when zoning laws deny them permission to utilize their property as they wish.

The *Moore* case again reveals the close relationship between social and economic concerns. Just as John will benefit from the Supreme Court's decision, thousands of tenants, would-be homeowners, workers, and business people would gain from the elimination of countless zoning restrictions preventing construction of residential units and projects. The family life of many who are unable to afford new housing or of those who will have to pay more for it because of zoning restrictions would be enhanced—in some cases possibly preserved—if these restrictions were lifted. Justice Marshall's opinion in *Willingboro* is a strong statement on the harmful consequences of even relatively minor regulation in the housing market. However, the opinions in the *Moore* decision indicate that the Court is not about to recognize these social problems by limiting the *Euclid* decision.

Outside the regulatory context, the Court has shown considerable concern for owners of property interests. In these situations, the post–New Deal Court has increasingly protected property owners, broadening the meaning of "property"[42] and "just compensation"[43](in the Fifth Amendment's provision that private property will not be taken for public use without just compensation). However, it has also reduced the definition of "public use" to the equivalent of "public purpose" and thereby eliminated this qualification as a protection against unwanted takings.[44] The harm to unwilling property owners resulting from this change is reduced by the greater generosity afforded through the Court's augmented "just compensation" interpretation.

Traditional eminent domain theory would seem to require governmental possession or dominion over the property before compensation is awarded. Thus, among the more significant taking clause decisions of recent years are those that have expanded its coverage to include dam-

ages to property arising from governmental actions not previously considered a taking. In a 1946 opinion, *United States v. Causby*,[45] Justice
Douglas, writing for the 7–1 majority, ruled that frequent low over-
flights by United States military planes amounted to taking an ease-
ment or air corridor over the property, entitling the owner to just
compensation for loss of this portion of his property. This opinion
settled the previously uncertain state of the law with respect to losses
incurred by property owners as an incidental result of government
actions in furtherance of an authorized and valid public project. Douglas elevated the owners' claims to a constitutional level over the objections of Justice Black, who characteristically argued that no constitutional question was involved because the taking clause was not
intended to apply to this situation.[46]

In *Causby*, Douglas thus solidified the federal law on what is referred
to as inverse condemnation. Under this doctrine, compensation has
been required both when an actual, physical invasion of property has
taken place and when impairment or destruction of property interests
has occurred by reason of certain governmental actions. A large variety of conduct is covered, with the marked exception of land use regulation. Although regulation can lower property values no less than do
other governmental actions, property owners are generally denied
compensation for the losses. The difference in treatment is accentuated
by the fact that on the one hand, after an inverse condemnation has
occurred—and its definition continues to broaden—the sole question
remaining is one of the damages suffered. On the other hand, the property owners aggrieved by zoning ordinances confront the double
problem of an unfavorable presumption of validity and a remedy that
usually does not go further than invalidating the ordinance without compensation for any legal and holding costs, both of which may at times
be substantial.[47] Thus the label given the proceedings is critical to the
property owner.

> Lay people (and many lawyers) reading opinions on eminent domain
> and inverse condemnation would find unbelievable the tenor and
> results of cases involving the regulation of land use. The pattern of
> concern for property rights stops abruptly when regulation is in-
> volved. Unless a zoning ordinance removes all economic value from
> property, there is little certainty as to how it will fare in the courts. It
> is even possible that the judges may at times uphold regulations that
> eliminate virtually all commercial values.[48]

Property rights seem to assume high priority when out of the zoning
context, sometimes even when the competing interest is free expres-

sion. *Hudgens v. NLRB*[49] provides such an example. In that case, strikers picketed in front of their employer's store, which was located in a shopping center. When the center's manager threatened them with arrest for criminal trespass, they left. Subsequently their union filed an unfair labor practice charge with the NLRB against the shopping-center owner. The board entered an order in favor of the union, concluding that the First Amendment guaranteed the union's right to picket the employer's store in the center. In a 6–2 opinion, the High Court disagreed and held that the strikers did not have any such constitutional right. Five of the Justices, in two separate opinions, joined to reverse a 1968 Supreme Court decision that would have supported the union's position.[50] The majority made clear its belief that the typical shopping center has all the characteristics of private property and that the public entering it has only those privileges accorded by the owner. The Court rejected the position that the modern shopping center must allow the exercise of free speech within its confines. The Justices have demonstrated that they would not be so solicitous of property rights if zoning were involved.

This concern with preserving property interests against a First Amendment challenge was manifest again in *Zacchini v. Scripps-Howard Broadcasting Co.*,[51] the human cannonball case, decided in 1977 (a 5–4 decision with one dissent on different grounds). Hugo Zacchini is an entertainer whose act consists of being shot from a cannon onto a net approximately two hundred feet away. Each performance takes about fifteen seconds. Against Zacchini's wishes, a TV station videotaped the act at a fair and ran it on a news program. Zacchini sued the station on the ground that it had unlawfully appropriated his "professional property." He acknowledged that the media could have reported his performance but denied that the station could broadcast the entire act without his permission. Such coverage of course substantially lessened his act's value because people could see it free on television. The station rejected liability, asserting that its presentation was protected by the right of free speech, for it had only been reporting a newsworthy event.

The Supreme Court of Ohio agreed with the station, ruling against Zacchini, but was reversed by a closely divided United States Supreme Court. The Court held that the constitutional protection of speech and press does not make the media immune from property rights violations when it broadcasts a performer's entire act without consent. Three of the dissenters argued that Zacchini should be given protection only if the news broadcast was a cover for private or commercial exploitation.

Interstate Commerce

Measured by number of cases decided, the commerce clause is currently the nation's strongest weapon against economic special-interest legislation. Section 8 of Article I conferring upon Congress the power to regulate domestic commerce has been construed by the federal High Court as not only an authorization for congressional action but also as a restriction on permissible state regulation of commerce. The Court has held that a state may not (1) discriminate against interstate commerce, (2) unreasonably burden it, or (3) regulate commerce which is essentially interstate in character. The key question in these cases is whether a local measure inhibiting the flow of interstate commerce can be justified as effectuating a legitimate local purpose. The standard of review is substantially stricter than that conducted under the minimal scrutiny rule.

The burden to show discrimination rests on the party challenging the validity of the statute, but "[w]hen discrimination against commerce ... is demonstrated, the burden falls on the state to justify it both in terms of the local benefits flowing from the statute and the unavailability of nondiscriminatory alternatives adequate to preserve the local interest at stake."[52] When considering the purpose of a challenged statute, the Court is not bound by the "name, description, or characterization given it by the legislature and the courts of the State," but will determine for itself the practical impact of the law.[53] The reasoning resembles that utilized under economic due process. The court probes legitimacy of purposes, employs means-ends analysis, and considers the availability of less drastic alternatives that would accomplish the same legislative purposes. Cases decided in recent years illustrate the application of these standards in various factual situations.

In *Raymond Motor Transportation Inc. v. Rice*,[54] the High Court annulled a Wisconsin regulation prohibiting operation of trucks sixty-five feet in length because it burdened interstate commerce and did not "make more than the most speculative contribution to highway safety." *Hunt v. Washington State Apple Advertising Commission*[55] struck down a North Carolina statute prohibiting the marking of Washington State apple grades on closed containers of apples shipped into the state. Only the labeling of the applicable U.S. grade or standard was permitted. North Carolina contended that the primary purpose of the statute was to eliminate the multiplicity of state grades which might deceive and confuse buyers. The Court concluded, how-

ever, that the law was intended to advantage the local apple industry at
the expense of out-of-state producers, and that less arduous
alternatives were available to minimize deception and confusion.

Philadelphia v. New Jersey[56] concerned a New Jersey law banning
the importation of most solid or liquid waste which originated or was
collected outside the territorial limits of the state. Suit was brought by
operators of private land fills in New Jersey and several cities in other
states that had agreements with these operators for waste disposal. In
annulling the law, the Court held that New Jersey had not shown
sufficient basis for discriminating against the articles of commerce
coming from outside the state. The Court rejected the conclusions of
the New Jersey Supreme Court that local environmental and health
interests warranted the discrimination. *Hughes v. Oklahoma*[57] overturned an Oklahoma law forbidding transport or shipment for sale outside the state of minnows seined or procured within the state's waters.
The Court found the law defective because the minnows were articles
of commerce that could not be limited to the use of citizens of one state
to the exclusion of others when equally effective, nondiscriminatory
conservation measures were available to serve the same legislative
purposes.

The New Property

To be sure, the creation of the dual standard of judicial review as
described in Part III of this book did not imply that the Justices were
oblivious to material well-being. Unlike the majority of the earlier
Court, many of the new Justices believe that legislative and administrative processes are the best guardians of economic welfare. These
Justices were not unwilling to assert power when they thought economic necessities of ordinary citizens were at stake. Evidence for this
conclusion is provided by the majority's acceptance in 1970 of Professor Charles Reich's concept of the "new property" the "ownership" of which is largely in the hands of the common people. Reich,
writing in 1964, defined the new property as a product of government largess,[58] a form of property that proponents of the welfare state could defend quite comfortably. By reason of the enormous growth of government and the welfare state, large numbers
of the public have become dependent on government for employment,
income, benefits, services, franchises, licenses, contracts, subsidies,
and use of public resources. Reich contended that such claims on gov-

ernment constitute a "new property" entitled to both substantive and procedural constitutional protection. Justice Brennan, writing the majority opinion in *Goldberg v. Kelly*,[59] recognized Reich's thesis that

> [t]he law of government largess has developed with little regard for procedure. Reversal of this trend is long overdue.
> The grant, denial, revocation, and administration of all types of government largess should be subject to scrupulous observance of fair procedures. Action should be open to hearing and contest, and based upon a record subject to judicial review.[60]

Brennan held, in that case, that a state could not terminate public assistance payments to a recipient without affording the opportunity for an evidentiary hearing prior to termination. Welfare entitlements, said Brennan, are more like "property" than "gratuity."

The consequence of this decision was a due process revolution, with a flood of suits seeking review of administrative procedure that operated adversely to claimants. The Court was confronted with the need to formulate a comprehensive set of criteria to determine the validity of the administrative processes under which termination of entitlements are considered. Thus, in recent years, the Court has ruled on such disparate matters as terminating disability benefits under the social security system, the discharge of a policeman from the Marion, North Carolina police force for failure to perform his duties properly, and the reasonableness of gas service termination notices used by a municipally owned utility.[61]

The contention that the "new property" cases involve only procedural due process is not very persuasive. Thus in the *Goldberg* case, the Court required the government to continue paying welfare benefits until the termination of the prescribed hearings. The government had stopped payments upon its determination that the recipients were no longer eligible, arguing that they would not be in a financial position to return the amounts collected if the decision went against them. Moreover, the Court's imposition of procedural rules has accorded a particular group substantive rights to these procedures.

Civil Rights Jurisdiction

As we have seen, the Supreme Court in contemporary times has attempted to follow a course that distinguishes between material and nonmaterial liberties. Yet when confronted with the issue as to whether the dichotomy is realistic, the Court has replied in the negative.

Lynch v. Household Finance Corp.[62] required the Court to consider in a particular context the core issue of the dual standard of review: was there a distinction between personal liberties and proprietary rights for purposes of jurisdiction under the Civil Rights Act? It had been argued that the act was not applicable to property interests. Justice Stewart, for all seven Justices participating, observed that a compelling reason for rejecting a "personal liberties" limitation upon the act is the great difficulty of drawing a line between personal and property rights with any consistency or principled objectivity.

> [T]he dichotomy between personal liberties and property rights is a false one. Property does not have rights. People have rights. The right to enjoy property without unlawful deprivation, no less than the right to speak or the right to travel, is in truth a "personal" right, whether the "property" in question be a welfare check, a home, or a savings account. In fact, a fundamental interdependence exists between the personal right to liberty and the personal right in property. Neither could have meaning without the other. That rights in property are basic civil rights has long been recognized. J. Locke, of Civil Government...; J. Adams, A Defence of the Constitutions of Government of the United States of America...; 1.W. Blackstone, Commentaries....[63]

Lynch involved wages deposited in a savings account, which the Court held was subject to the civil rights statutes. Stewart noted that other courts have found civil rights jurisdiction in areas that involve commercial concerns, such as claims alleging discrimination in business licenses and in employment and in relation to the termination of leases in public housing projects.

Conclusion

As the preceding discussion reveals, certain entrepreneurs, property owners, and consumers enjoy more constitutional protection than do others who essentially are similarly situated. For the former, the document stands as a barrier against the actions and designs of the holders of executive, legislative, and administrative power to no less a degree, and sometimes to an even greater degree, than existed in the substantive due process period. Unfortunately from the standpoint of a rational and just society, these individuals owe their gratitude more to the vagaries of jurisprudence than to its wisdom.

IV *Safeguarding Economic Liberties*

11   The Remaining Dichotomy

Dichotomies in the law, which exist in many areas, are rarely clear-cut. The one initiated in the late 1930s between material and nonmaterial rights is, as we have seen, no exception. The differentiation between the two has become smaller and more blurred in recent years, as the Supreme Court has increasingly protected economic activities under a variety of rubrics. However, the dichotomy remains, as evidenced by the vast gulf separating judicial treatment of government regulation affecting expression and that affecting production and distribution of goods and services. In the remainder of this book, I shall discuss this and other aspects of the dichotomy. The present chapter will be devoted to exploring the basis for the high priority given expression and the applicability of this reasoning to the protection of economic interests.

Government supervision over private activity is commonly referred to as *censorship* when applied to the press and *regulation* when implemented elsewhere. However, these labels becloud the similarities. A robust, uninhibited press is far from trouble free, but it is preferable to censorship; and the same logic can be applied to economic activity.

Different Treatment for Different Marketplaces?

Felix Frankfurter tells us that Justice Holmes was convinced that progress is to a considerable extent the displacement of error, which had at one time held sway as accepted truth, by beliefs that in turn yield to other beliefs; and that therefore no rights should be considered more fundamental in an open society than speech.[1] From the perspective of Professor Hayek, Holmes touched on only one factor explaining the advancement of human society: Hayek believes that the freedom to do material things is likewise critical to progress.[2] According to Hayek, the process that brings about new development is best understood in the intellectual sphere where the results are new ideas. Most people comprehend that intellectual advances often spring from the unforeseen and undesigned and therefore agree that barriers must not be imposed curtailing the intellectual process. However, Hayek observes, this freedom is most important as the final step in a process of action—of doing things. Unfortunately, many people underestimate the necessity for liberty of action in experimenting with the established material facilities of our civilization. They do not realize that new ideas are born from the innovative use of these facilities, and that only ultimately do these ideas enter the highly regarded intellectual realm. "The importance of freedom, therefore, does not depend on the elevated character of the activities it makes possible. Freedom of action, even in humble things, is as important as freedom of thought."[3] Hayek explains:

> To extol the value of intellectual liberties at the expense of the value of the liberty of doing things would be like treating the crowning part of an edifice as the whole. We have new ideas to discuss, different views to adjust, because those ideas and views arise from the efforts of individuals in ever new circumstances, who avail themselves in their concrete tasks of the new tools and forms of action they have learned.[4]

It is this process that society looks to for new, better, different, or less costly goods and services, essential elements in the pursuit of progress and well-being. Participants in the economic marketplace, as Professor Kirzner reminds us, are engaged in an incessant race to get or keep ahead of one another—and to be ahead always means "to be offering the most attractive opportunities to other market participants."[5] It follows, therefore, that any circumstances that inhibit individual initiative and creativity impede advancement, whether it be in the marketplace of ideas or of goods and services.

Other distinguished commentators, including economists Milton Friedman, Aaron Director, and Ronald Coase and political scientist Robert McCloskey, criticize judicial policies that limit recognition of economic interests. The economists believe that freedom of producers and consumers in one industry should be no less than that in another.

McCloskey favors application of a modest standard of judicial review in economic fields.

Professor Director asserts that a remarkable similarity exists between the underlying rationale for complete laissez-faire in the market for ideas and in the market for goods and services. During the foreseeable future most members of society will have to devote a considerable part of their lives to pursuing economic opportunities, and for them freedom of choice in areas of employment, investment, and consumption is fully as important as freedom of discussion and participation in government. Moreover, it is only under a system of voluntary exchange that freedom is maximized and the widest array of voluntary associations is possible. The justification for the marketplace of ideas has been its utilitarian value. While empirical tests are not possible between markets, the economic marketplace gives stronger, or at least less ambiguous, historical evidence of utilitarian achievement. The greatest material progress has occurred in the absence of economic restraint.

Director maintains that undue importance has been attached to solving economic problems through discussion. Much of what passes for rational discussion of economic issues—for example, foreign trade, price control, and agricultural subsidies—is far beyond the voters' expertise, and is not likely to be superior to the competitive economic marketplace which automatically makes countless decisions tending to allocate resources efficiently. Efforts to bring economic processes under "rational" control will on the whole not achieve better results than similar endeavors directed at expression.[6]

Professor Coase notes the contradictions in favoring one market over another:

> In the market for goods, the government is commonly regarded as competent to regulate and properly motivated. Consumers lack the ability to make the appropriate choices. Producers often exercise monopolistic power and, in any case, without some form of government intervention, would not act in a way which promotes the public interest. In the market for ideas, the position is very different. The government, if it attempted to regulate, would be inefficient and its motives would, in general, be bad, so that, even if it were successful in achieving what it wanted to accomplish, the results would be undesirable. Consumers, on the other hand, if left free, exercise a fine discrimination in choosing between the alternative views placed before them, while producers, whether economically powerful or weak, who are found to be so unscrupulous in their behavior in other

markets, can be trusted to act in the public interest, whether they publish or work for the *New York Times,* the *Chicago Tribune* or the Columbia Broadcasting System.[7]

Professor Friedman believes freedom to be indivisible, at least to the extent that political liberty requires economic liberty and that economic liberty demands political liberty. Rights are so intertwined and inseparable that infringements on one affect the other. Dissent becomes extremely difficult when government exercises a large measure of control. For example, business people and academicians dependent for financial support on government largess cede some or all of their rights to criticize their particular benefactors and possibly other governmental entities. Campaign contributions to and services in behalf of candidates are influenced by the likelihood of obtaining economic rewards from government. Thus appreciable government involvement in the economic system has a "chilling effect" on conceptual freedom.[8] John Stuart Mill made the point this way:

[If the] great joint stock companies, the universities and all the public charities, were all of them branches of the government;...if the employés of all these different enterprises were appointed and paid by the government, and looked to the government for every rise in life; not all the freedom of the press and popular constitution of the legislature would make this or any other country free otherwise than in name.[9]

Political scientist Robert McCloskey contends that the legal distinction between economics and civil rights is tenuous because most people probably feel that an economic right is at least as important to them as the right to speak their minds. Entrepreneurial and occupational freedom is no less indispensable than are civil rights to the "openness" of society, and individuals denied economic opportunity, such as access to an occupation, require judicial protection since, like discrete minorities, they do not present a united front and thus have great difficulty influencing the legislative process. McCloskey says that the dedication to free choice in the intellectual and spiritual realms has the "smell of the lamp about it."[10]

[I]t may reflect the tastes of the judges and dons who advance it, rather than the real preferences of a commonality of mortals. Judges and professors are talkers both by profession and avocation. It is not surprising that they would view freedom of expression as primary to the free play of their personalities.[11]

Professor Director adds the following:

> Everyone tends to magnify the importance of his own occupation and to minimize that of his neighbor. Intellectuals are engaged in the pursuit of truth, while others are merely engaged in earning a livelihood. One follows a profession, usually a learned one, while the other follows a trade or business.[12]

The same view is more bluntly expressed by Professor Coase:

> The market for ideas is the market in which the intellectual conducts his trade. The explanation of the paradox is self-interest and self esteem. Self-esteem leads the intellectuals to magnify the importance of their own market. That others should be regulated seems natural, particularly as many of the intellectuals see themselves as doing the regulating. But self-interest combines with self-esteem to ensure that, while others are regulated, regulation should not apply to them. And so it is possible to live with these contradictory views about the role of government in these two markets. It is the conclusion that matters. It may not be a nice explanation, but I can think of no other for this strange situation.[13]

For those who believe that results control legal decisions, the comments of McCloskey, Director, and Coase may explain the dichotomy under discussion. The allocation of rights might be far different, for example, were economists and business people assigned the judicial task.

But the present dichotomy may be consistent with constitutional principles, and it is to that issue that we now turn. The question to be resolved is whether the Constitution either explicitly or implicitly creates or accepts the dichotomy.[14]

No one all-encompassing rationale explains the emphasis placed on free expression. Judges and commentators have justified their support by a variety of reasons. Brandeis, as previously noted, believed that free expression would, among other things, develop individual faculties, foster happiness, and provide a safety valve for society. Professors Meiklejohn, Emerson, and Kalven have eloquently described the benefits that unrestrained speech confers on the search for truth, understanding, and sensitivity and the attainment of individual self fulfillment and dignity.[15] Many other commentators have likewise expressed the importance of speech and press in bettering and elevating the human condition. Some extol the press as being virtually ordained to ferret out and expose public waste and corruption.[16]

All these ideas are supplementary, however, to those that I believe have been the three principal theories advanced over the years for according expression the special legal treatment it presently enjoys. These are, first, that the Framers of the First Amendment intended the rights of expression to be absolute or nearly so; second, that unrestricted expression is essential to the functioning of a representative society; and third, that government cannot competently or desirably regulate expression. Let us now examine more fully the three theories.

The Original Meaning of the First Amendment

Justices Brandeis, Holmes, Black, and Douglas are the Justices most associated with historical views that the Framers intended to maximize the free exercise of speech and press. As previously noted (see chapter 7), Justice Brandeis's *Whitney* opinion does not provide facts and data upon which to judge the extent of the guarantee. His footnotes refer to, among others, Harold Laski, Zachariah Chafee, Jr., and Thomas Jefferson, an invocation that does not establish a historical basis for a very broad interpretation. The technique employed in *Whitney* bears strikingly little resemblance to the "Brandeis brief," a document noted for its compilation of objective data to support a particular position. Justice Holmes, who during his years on the Court changed his position on the extent to which the Constitution protects expression (as discussed in chapter 7), was not much more informative in his final resolution of the problem.

In contrast, Justice Black's opinions in the expression cases are marked by extensive historical exposition vividly detailing the tyranny suffered by publishers and speakers under English rule. Black and Douglas postulated that the Founding Fathers were, as a result of the English experience, determined to reject all forms of censorship and that they accomplished this objective in the absolute and unqualified language of the First Amendment that "Congress shall make no law...abridging the freedom of speech, or of the press...." This absolute theory, however, has never received the approval of a majority of the Justices. Some claim that even Black departed from it because he differentiated between speech and conduct and thereby excluded many activities involving expression.

The absolute theory encounters serious technical difficulties. The initial problem is that the amendment is confined to Congress and does not affect the executive or judicial branches of the federal government, or the states in any respect. The Fourteenth Amendment absorbs the First (according to our High Court), and its protection can hardly be greater in the scope of its application to state government. Those who insist upon observing a literal interpretation of the First and Fourteenth Amendments will find difficulty in imposing an expression restraint against all segments of the federal and state governments. They should also be most hesitant in accepting the idea that the Fourteenth absorbed the expression guarantee of the First Amendment (as discussed in chapter 2). Another problem is that the absolute interpretation rejects definitive meanings for the key portions of the clause—*abridge, freedom of speech and the press,* and *law.* For example, is every utterance speech? Is every symbol press? Is every restraint a law or an abridgment? The words used in the amendment are far from absolute and precise in meaning; they are not beyond interpretation.

No one has ever shown that the Framers intended the provision on expression to be absolute. Far less concern for free speech and press existed during the nation's early years than exists now. Many of the nation's early leaders were not opposed to punishing people for making political statements that today would pass largely unnoticed.[17] Prior to the ratification of the First Amendment, the common law of seditious libel provided for criminal punishment for the maker of any statement about government that could be deemed either detrimental to it or conducive to a breach of the peace. Blackstone asserted that freedom of the press, while it bars prior restraint, does not relieve the writer from censure for improper, mischievous, and illegal publication, and he supported the common law of seditious libel.

> [T]o punish (as the law does at present) any dangerous or offensive writings, which, when published, shall on a fair and impartial trial be adjudged of a pernicious tendency, is necessary for the preservation of peace and good order, of government and religion, the only solid foundations of civil liberty.[18]

One of the continuing debates about the First Amendment is whether the Framers intended to eliminate this severe restraint on speech and press. History does not support the belief of many contemporary Justices that the First Amendment eradicated seditious libel. Consider the views of Professor Leonard Levy, a leading scholar on the subject:

> What is clear is that there exists no evidence to suggest an understanding that a constitutional guarantee of free speech or press meant the impossibility of future prosecutions of seditious utterances. The traditional libertarian interpretation of the original meaning of the First Amendment is surely subject to the Scottish verdict: no proven. Freedom of speech and press, as all the scattered evidence

suggests, was not understood to include a right to broadcast sedition by words. The security of the state against libelous advocacy or attack was always regarded as outweighing any social interest in open expression, at least through the period of the adoption of the First Amendment. The thought and experience of a lifetime, indeed the taught traditions of law and politics extending back many generations, supplied an a priori belief that freedom of political discourse, however broadly conceived, stopped short of seditious libel....[19]

Seven years after the First Amendment was ratified, Congress adopted the Sedition Act of 1798, designed, among other things, to silence what the Federalist majority regarded as subversive expression by its political opponents. Although this law was never directly tested in the United States Supreme Court, Levy reports that every member of the Court in 1798–1800 ruled while on circuit that the act was constitutional. The Federalists generally thought it was constitutional and the Republicans contended it was not. Professor Levy believes that a broad libertarian position on freedom of speech and press did not emerge in the United States until the Republicans were forced to defend themselves against the sedition law.

Professor Walter Berns contends that even at that time, and for some years thereafter, the libertarian position did not receive widespread support.[20] Jefferson himself, after his election to the presidency, wrote a letter condemning the "licentiousness" and "lying" that he perceived in the Federalist press and saying in part: "I have therefore long thought that a few prosecutions of the most eminent offenders would have a wholesome effect in restoring the integrity of the presses."[21]

Justice Story in 1833 commented that the First Amendment

imports no more, than that every man shall have a right to [express] his opinions..., without any prior restraint, so always, that he does not injure any other person... and so always, that he does not thereby disturb the public peace, or attempt to subvert the government. It is neither more nor less, than an expansion of the great doctrine, recently brought into operation in the law of libel, that every man shall be at liberty to publish what is true, with good motives and for justifiable ends.[22]

The Relationship of Free Expression to Representative Government

Regardless of constitutional meaning, clearly the existence of a representative society in which the voters are the ultimate and final authority necessitates the broad dissemination of information to the public. Voters cannot intelligently make their decisions unless they can acquire the needed knowledge and understanding. It does not necessarily follow, however, that the complete absence of government intervention is required for the marketplace of ideas to function at the optimal level. The contemporary Court's belief in a free market for ideas was not widely shared in earlier periods of our history and is far from universally accepted today.

Had the Framers of the Constitution or of the First Amendment conceived that the American political process requires near unlimited expression, they surely would have applied a speech guarantee to the states. In the absence of this requirement, the states were at liberty to control expression. Nor does the evidence indicate that compelling free expression in the states was a leading concern for the framers of the Fourteenth Amendment. The Supreme Court did not impose a speech guarantee on the states for fifty-seven years after ratification of that amendment. Although the rhetoric of Holmes and Brandeis implied a demand for unlimited expression, their clear and present danger test allowed for considerable judicial discretion to restrain expression. Federal and state governments would have greater power over expression under this test than they now do.

The belief that a free market in ideas is superior to a moderately controlled one is not based on empirical evidence. No studies have been undertaken to prove the point; obtaining or evaluating meaningful comparisons would be very difficult. If, as is widely proclaimed, regulation softens the excesses and overcomes the limitations of a private market, it can hardly be assumed that these results are not possible in the instance of expression.

Some observers contend that government could not fairly administer press regulations because it is a partisan in the political arena. While not to be minimized, this problem is no more insurmountable than the one that occurs when boards and commissions are created to regulate and administer election practices. Such appointees can also greatly influence public policies and the course of events. To overcome these defects, terms of newspaper commissioners could be fixed and staggered, covering more than one administration; appointments from different parties and legislative confirmation could be required. Such controls are in effect for many agencies and commissions. A nation frequently has to sacrifice absolute neutrality on the part of its officials in order to achieve particular societal benefits. Federal and state supreme court justices are indebted to incumbent officials for their jobs, but this fact does not disqualify them from making decisions affecting the administration, policies, and practices of presidents and governors who appoint them. The FBI, the IRS, and many other agencies usually are more partisan to government than to citizens. Federal, state, and city attorneys are given wide discretion to use the criminal process against citizens, a power highly susceptible to partisan abuse in an area of the gravest concern to freedom. Accordingly, while I would find the very thought of an official press commission abhorrent, I question whether its results would be more outrageous than those of some other governmental bodies.

The Basis of Press Freedom: Fear of the Censor

A near unlimited freedom for the press is maintained in this country not because the Constitution mandates it or because our system of government requires it. The explanation lies with the disapproval and fear our society expresses against censorship. (I continue to use the word *censorship* in a broad sense to cover governmental limitations on expression, including both prior and post publication restraints.)

To be sure, a representative society demands an informed electorate; but regulation eliminating media distortion, inaccuracy, unfairness, and misrepresentation would fulfill that objective. The problem, of course, is that removal of undesirable expression requires censorship—and that is highly objectionable. Better to suffer the evils and abuses of liberty than of authority. Our commitment to freedom of expression rests on the general repudiation of censorship.

Free expression is desirable because the alternative is likely to be much worse. This kind of reasoning explains why relatively few advocate significant curbs on the press regardless of how serious its defects and derelictions. Press freedom is maintained and augmented notwithstanding a record that is replete with imperfections.[23] In a day when almost any real or imagined failure of the economic marketplace is an excuse for imposing regulation, the continued exemption of the press is remarkable. The legislatures and the courts accept, in the instance of publishing, a conclusion that they reject for most other industries: freedom brings with it a certain amount of excesses and abuses that over-all are usually less harmful to the public interest than are the consequences of state intervention and coercion. In the words of Professor Director: "The absolute doctrine of [expression] is defended even though it necessitates the protection of speech which no reasonable man wants or should want to see protected."[24]

The chronology of free expression in the English-speaking countries begins in 1694 when the Licensing of the Press Act expired and was not renewed, thereby eliminating censorship in advance of publication. According to Macaulay, the English Parliament did not reenact the law chiefly because it was so troublesome. "The Licensing Act is condemned, not as a thing essentially evil, but on account of the petty grievances, the exactions, the jobs, the commerical restrictions, the domiciliary visits, which were incidental to it . . . . Such were the arguments which did what Milton's *Areopagitica* had failed to do."[25]

In the United States, the federal Supreme Court, using common-law technique, broadened over the years the scope of protected expression on a case-by-case basis. At each step, it weighed and evaluated a particular restraint, often against a background of argument reminiscent of the controversy in England before censorship was lifted. Curbs on expression are invariably attacked as censorship—a cry that has a profound and disturbing meaning in our society. Western culture repudiates the notion that the censor can act selflessly and altruistically; it portrays the censor as an arbitrary, clumsy, and even sinister figure, dedicated to the execution of his or her own designs. Consequently, regulation of the press would be carried out tyrannically and incompetently. *Near*, the two *New York Times* decisions, and *Tornillo* (discussed in chapters 7 and 9) are among the most important expression cases, and all stand for the proposition that government does not know how to temper press freedom without destroying that freedom's functions and purposes.

Near and the first *Times* decision provide particularly persuasive support for the thesis that fear and antipathy for the censor chiefly account for the contemporary judicial priority accorded speech. As the reader may recall from prior discussion of these cases, both involve the validity of laws that operated to restrain printed attacks on public officials. *Near* enlarged the forbidden area of prior restraint and limited the power of judges to act as censors. *Times* had a comparable impact on postpublication restraint and restricted the censorial authority of juries.

The statute struck down in *Near* authorized public authorities to seek injunctions against an owner or publisher printing scandalous and defamatory material. Unless the defendant produced evidence satisfying a judge that the accusations were true and were published with good motives and for justifiable ends, the newspaper or periodical would be suppressed and any further such publications would be punishable as a contempt of court. "This is the essence of censorship," concluded Chief Justice Hughes.[26]

The published material in *Near* charged local office-holders with official derelictions. Under authority of the statute, judges could halt publication and thereby possibly stifle political expression intended to expose malfeasance and encourage more faithful performance of official duties. The fact that this authority could also be employed to prevent abuse by "miscreant purveyors of scandal" did not lessen the need for giving the press broad opportunity to find and report on official misconduct. Censorship even when imposed by a judge after a fair hearing was still viewed by the Supreme Court as a threat to political processes.

The logic of *Near* also applies to postpublication restraints. In the words of Justice Cooley, "the liberty of the press might be rendered a mockery and a delusion, and the phrase itself a byword if, while every man was at liberty to publish what he pleased, the public authorities might nevertheless punish him for harmless publications."[27] The *Times* situation showed that under the then-existing libel laws, juries in determining damage awards could effectively exercise censorship by deterring future publications. In that case, the defendants could not plead truth in their defense because the advertisement in question contained misstatements of facts. The jury was instructed to determine compensatory and punitive damages, which it did in the total amount of $500,000 without specifying the amount of each. Given the emotion-laden conditions of that period, the size of the award raised considerable concern. Many perceived it not as compensation for the harm sustained, but as a blow struck by the jury in favor of one side of the civil rights struggle in which the country was then engaged. Thus it was questionable just how much the plaintiff's reputation was harmed. Of *The New York Times* issue containing the advertisement, only 394 copies were distributed in Alabama, and 35 in Montgomery County, the community in which the plaintiff claimed injury to his reputation. The misstatements did not name or directly refer to the plaintiff. Also, in view of the climate of opinion in the county, charges that excessive and illegal force was used against black students and civil rights workers might not be very harmful to one's local reputation. The large sum awarded by the jury for damages demonstrated that juries could operate, in certain situations, as very potent censors of the press. It followed that for the press to remain "uninhibited, robust and wide open," the jury's power would have to be limited. Rather than allow censorship, the Court was willing to subject society to the harm that results from the dissemination of untruthful and inaccurate information.

Near and *Times* reveal a fear of censorial power even when exercised by the most respected legal institutions. The American legal system is predicated on the integrity and competency of judges and juries and it accords them great power over life and property. These are the official bodies considered least vulnerable to corruption and expediency. If official discretion has to be exercised, the prevailing wisdom would consider them most capable of implementing it responsibly and reasonably. Nevertheless, the High Court found these fundamental institutions incapable of properly and desirably censoring the press. If judges and juries are unsuited to this responsibility, who in society can possibly perform it?

Comparing Censorship and Regulation

Once we resolve that neither the text of the Constitution nor the governmental system it establishes mandates absolute or nearly unlimited expression, the technical distinctions separating the conceptual and economic marketplaces have been removed. We are then left to compare pragmatically censorship—the fear of which I believe keeps the conceptual marketplace free—with regulation. Society condemns censorship for two reasons: first, because it would operate tyranically and oppressively, and second, because the censors would perform their task incompetently, and even counterproductively. In the balance of this chapter I shall compare these explanations for the rejection of censorship with the operation and impact of regulation. Our inquiry is to determine whether the kind of controls the society believes are unwise and destructive for one market can be appropriate and desirable for another.

Professor Thomas I. Emerson has set out in great detail the inherent unworkability and inequity of press censorship.[28] The crux of the problem, he says, is that regulation must be applied by one group of human beings to other groups of human beings—the eternal question of who will control the controllers. He presents five reasons why government restraints will not produce a more effective system of free expression.

1. Most people have strong inclinations to suppress opposing opinions, even when differences in viewpoint are comparatively slight.

Those in power cling to their economic, political, and social positions and frequently reject dissent. Attacks on cherished notions threaten most the "authoritarian personality" and others who seek to control the society. Unless the rules are precise and readily enforceable, those desiring increased restriction will break through the openings; freedom of expression will thus become the exception, and suppression the rule.

2. It is exceedingly difficult to frame limitations on expression that will cover only the problem areas. As a result, the restraints are almost necessarily constructed and administered so as to restrict a much broader area of expression than is required.

3. Those assigned the job of censor already have, or soon develop, a tendency to pursue their task zealously. Their livelihood may depend on their accomplishments in enforcing censorship, for success in this field is often measured by how much is banned.

4. Although well intended, the restrictions usually are readily subject to distortion and to use for ulterior purposes. Censors may prevent publication because they oppose ideas or because such action will obtain for them personal or partisan advantage.

5. Limitations are seldom applied except in an atmosphere of public fear and hysteria. Most administrators and publishers will find accommodating these pressures easier than opposing them.[29]

Emerson writes that experience under expression controls imposed by the Sedition Act and during World War I supports his conclusions and shows that *(a)* a tendency existed to constantly overestimate the need for restriction; *(b)* the restrictions were applied to the extreme; *(c)* the language used in the restriction was vague while the safeguards designed to mitigate their effect operated poorly, almost to the point of ineffectiveness; *(d)* administration of the restrictions resulted in the creation of an enforcement apparatus that employed obnoxious practices, including the use of informers, professional witnesses, excessive search and seizure, and government surveillance; *(e)* the restrictions were applied to achieve objectives quite different from the theoretical purpose of the laws they were constructed to support; *(f)* in neither period was the country's security or welfare appreciably enhanced; *(g)* the impact of the restrictions was felt not only by those convicted but also by many more who were merely prosecuted and by countless others who could not accurately determine the boundaries of legal expression; *(h)* the restrictions resulted in corruption and decline in the credibility of government.[30] Emerson presents an excellent exposition of the operation of the administrative process engaged in censorship.

His article persuasively asserts that censorship must inevitably function contrary to elementary notions about the inviolability of the rule of law and the meaning of due and fair process in a free society.

For me, most of Emerson's observations are not merely matters of theory. In more than two decades as a practicing attorney, I appeared many times before zoning authorities and other regulatory bodies. During these years I constantly encountered acts and conduct comparable to those he describes. Reprehensible practices are not exclusive to the regulators of expression. Neither are the unfortunate consequences of decisions. Government is no more wise, compassionate, or understanding when it regulates the economic marketplace than when it censors expression. In zoning matters rules are often adopted to satisfy demands, sometimes bordering on the irrational, made by homeowners, environmentalists, and other pressure groups. Considerations fundamental to the purpose of land-use regulation are swept away as the authorities succumb to their own desires and fears as well as of those who exert most pressure on them.[31]

In appearing before regulatory authorities, one soon learns the enormity of the power that they exercise; plausible explanation can always be found to excuse even the most corrupt acts. A large number of subjective factors are invariably involved, allowing the decision-makers almost unlimited opportunity to rule virtually as they wish. Officials with zoning power frequently have to consider a very diverse array of elements, including compatibility, economic feasibility, market conditions, existing competition, consumer demand and need, property values, existing use, adjoining and nearby uses, traffic, schools, utilities, topography, future growth, and environmental impact. Illustrating the enormity of discretion given many agencies is Professor Kenneth Culp Davis's description of the policies that must be considered by Civil Aeronautics Board members in performing their duties: he lists twenty-nine major questions that Congress left open to the board's judgment.[32] As the discussion in the next chapter will show, it is doubtful that regulatory agencies can function effectively without having great discretion.

A major reason for imposing regulation is to prevent or minimize externalities; government intervention is continually demanded to avoid harm to third parties. Over a period of two decades, I have heard in forums, public hearings, and courtrooms arguments about the perils of certain proposed uses of land that homeowners feared would endanger their environment and lower property values. Such apprehensions are not uncommon. Much regulation is founded on fears of the marketplace.

Even assuming that hazards are of the magnitude alleged in the calls for regulation, they cannot pose so great a risk to the public welfare as misleading, distorted, or false information. Expression may be the most dangerous of all freedoms. It can lead to war, depression, tyranny, terrorism, revolution, and insurrection, since the final decision on these and numerous other critical issues rests with a public dependent on news media for accurate information.

The dissemination of ideas and information is exceedingly influential in electing the officials who will make vital decisions. An inaccurate or partisan story close to voting time or one or more misleading reports in a particular newspaper may provide a margin of victory in a close election.[33] In many instances, the marketplace of ideas does not overcome lies and distortions. Very few voters have the time and inclination to read, study, and evaluate carefully all the available data on the candidates and issues. Many citizens subscribe to or read the political editorials and news in only one publication. Newspapers, radio, and television can give only limited coverage to political matters. Sometimes gross errors are never corrected or the corrections are never assimilated in the public mind. In my experience as a resident of two major cities, I found the press frequently attacked for being partisan about candidates and issues. By today's prevailing criteria, few industries are as appropriate for regulation as is the press. And yet in spite of the temptations and provocations, the nation wisely continues to abide by the reasoning of James Madison:

> Some degree of abuse is inseparable from the proper use of everything, and in no instance is this more true than in that of the press. It has accordingly been decided by the practice of the States, that it is better to leave a few of its noxious branches to their luxuriant growth, than, by pruning them away, to injure the vigour of those yielding the proper fruits.[34]

Some Concluding Observations

I shall close this chapter with some observations on what has already been discussed and what is yet to come.

1. Eight Supreme Court Justices have agreed that the public's interest in the free flow of commercial information may be as keen as, if not

keener by far than, its interest in the day's most urgent political debate[35]—that is, for many people economic concerns tend to outweigh political ones. This proposition is more likely to be true as incomes descend and comfort and convenience become more closely related to the expenses of living.

2. Is government supervision over business and industry required to enhance economic well-being? The prevailing answer to a comparable question concerning expression is a resounding "No!"—an answer, as I have said, based largely on faith and not on surveys and studies. Faith also frequently accounts for the belief that government economic controls are beneficial and should be maintained as the legislature wills. I am inclined to conclude that the difference between the legal treatment of conceptual freedoms and that of material freedoms is grounded in large measure on the belief that the public welfare requires state intervention in one area and not in the other.

3. A great many studies show that government regulation *actually* is as harmful in the economic sphere as it is *thought* to be in the conceptual realm. These studies are discussed in chapter 13.

4. The United States Supreme Court has concluded that advertising is generally in the consumer's interest because it provides price and other economic information. The studies discussed in chapter 13 show that free entry, competition, and unrestrained production benefit the consumer to no less an extent.

5. As the *Tornillo* case reveals, even the most benign regulation of the press impedes the production of ideas. Similarly, governmental economic restraints hinder material production. In both instances, the major victims are those at the lower end of the economic scale. An increased production of ideas means that the uninterested, uninformed, disadvantaged, and even illiterate are more likely to be reached. Maximum material production likewise augments the welfare of the less fortunate; they are able to acquire more food, clothing, and shelter, and to enjoy a better living standard. For example, the production of more cars, refrigerators, or homes will enable more people of average income or less to acquire one, whether new or used.

Judicial review of economic restraints will not cure all the problems of regulation. But at least review might curb its excesses and abuses. Regardless of their merit, changes beneficial to both freedom and material welfare are not as likely to be realized if the legislature remains the final arbiter of economic liberties. In the chapter that follows, I shall proceed to examine the legislative processes.

12 The Limitations and Infirmities of the Legislative Processes

In the absence of judicial review, neither the principle of checks and balances nor the principle of the separation of powers is applicable to social and economic legislation. The popularly elected branches assume the burden and responsibility for implementing and protecting the often conflicting interests of the state and of the person. The prevailing judicial wisdom maintains that, regardless of any historical basis for judicial oversight, society functions better when final determinations in the socioeconomic area rest with the legislature and the executive. We examine this assumption in this and the next chapter.

The Irrational Rational Relation Test

The minimal scrutiny level of judicial review is referred to as the "rational relation test." Under this rule a court will uphold socioeconomic legislation not infringing on specially protected rights if it can find that the measure is or might be rationally related to a public purpose. Because every economic regulation serves some purpose, the rational relation standard essentially presupposes judicial withdrawal. This withdrawal occurs even if a statute imposes severe and unnecessary restraints on a large number of people and was passed as the result of the most reprehensible legislative conduct. Despite all the political shenanigans to which the country has been subjected after 1936, the

Supreme Court has not invalidated any economic regulations since tha year on due process grounds.[1]

Judges respond to these criticisms by insisting that our system doe provide relief for legislative derelictions: vote the offending legislator out of office.[2] This response has little basis in fact. It is simply un realistic to believe that very many individuals and corporations arbi trarily aggrieved by the legislature can persuade a majority of the vot ers or of the legislature to repeal the offensive legislation. The peopl harmed are frequently those with the least influence in the electio process. If these people had more power, they would never have foun themselves in their predicaments. In addition, elections are hel periodically, and by the time new legislators have been selected anc new laws adopted the damage may have become irreparable. The maxim "justice delayed is justice denied" applies no less in thes circumstances. Neither is the possibility of an executive veto a feasibl alternative for most losers in legislative procedures. With this branc too, political reality overrules the impact of the powerless.

While heralded for its rulings on minority rights, the Warren Cour was also much dedicated to the concept of majoritarianism in th political process. In the historic *Reapportionment Cases,*[3] it con centrated on protecting the interests of numerical majorities in the stat legislatures. In order to achieve the goal of "one person–one vote, on vote–one value," it reduced the legislative representation of rural so cial and economic interests. Rejecting the dissenters' position that th interests of groups other than those who compose numerical majoritie should be represented in the state legislatures, Chief Justice Warre and most of his colleagues insisted on majoritarianism as an essentia principle of state government.

Warren believed that reapportionment was his most important ac complishment as Chief Justice of the Supreme Court, presumably be cause it reinforced the most important of all democratic rights. Justic Black had similar convictions on the power of free expression t further intelligent use of the franchise. Both Justices had a suprem faith in the democratic processes and used the judicial power to remov barriers to majoritarian rule. In a system striving to make everyone' vote equal, with a free press spreading maximum political knowledg and understanding, the people would be able to govern wisely an justly—to support the correct issues and to elect as leaders those bes suited to provide for the over-all good.

Unfortunately the reality does not bear out the vision. As the ensuin discussion will explain, the legislative process is seriously flawed i important respects. First, the relationship between the will of the majority and the passage of laws is often highly tenuous. Second, many laws that are adopted are not very efficient or effective, and therefore needlessly deprive some people of their liberties. Third, small special interest groups continually succeed in obtaining the passage of laws beneficial to them and harmful to much larger numbers. Fourth, even in the absence of these infirmities, legislatures still pass laws that are arbitrary and oppressive to some. Fifth, administrative agencies exercise much rule-making authority in the society, and their relationship to the popular will is remote. To explain these conclusions requires consideration of the country's lawmaking processes.

Voting and Elections

Although few societies have encouraged voting and free speech more than ours, participation in the election process wanes, both because a great many people do not vote and because a large number of potential candidates do not enter politics.

Results of state and city elections held in November 1978 show a continuation of the substantial drop in the percentage of people voting that has occurred nationwide for nearly two decades. In the most important election—that for President—eligible voter turnout was 63 percent in 1960, 62 percent in 1964, 60 percent in 1968, 55.4 percent in 1972 (after enfranchisement of 18-to-20-year-olds), and 56.5 percent in 1976. Percentages of eligible voter participation in the midterm elections of 1958, 1962, 1966, 1970, 1974, and 1978 were 43, 46, 45, 44, 36, and 36 respectively. The November 1977 statistics show that a large portion of the population is not interested in participating in the electoral process, regardless of how effortless such participation is made. The Committee for the Study of the American Electorate reports that in the November elections that year, the decline in voter participation ironically was sharpest in the states permitting postcard registration; the rate of voting increased slightly in the cities but changed little over-all in the states adopting election-day registration. (Postcard registration eliminates the need to register in person, and election-day registration obviates any effort other than going to the polls.) New York, New Jersey, and Pennsylvania allowed postcard registration prior to the 1977 elections, but voting still declined by 15 to 30 percent from the 1967 figure. This study also disclosed that the sharpest decrease in voting occurred in New Jersey, where for the first time since World War II, the turnout fell below 40 percent in a gubernatorial election, and in New York City, where less than 30 percent voted, the lowest percentage in thirty years.[4]

One simple statistic suggests how politically apathetic the population is. When polled by Gallup in March and September 1970 on the question "Do you happen to know the name of the present Representative in Congress from your district?" 53 percent replied "yes" and 47 percent "no." Among college graduates, 35 to 36 percent replied "No."[5]

These data call into question the legitimacy of government and its powers. Usually the presence of a majority of the members of an official body or organization is required to constitute a quorum for transacting business. When only 36 to 46 percent of the eligible citizens vote, proving that our laws represent the people's will is difficult. Legislators cannot point to the majority as the source of their power.

Moreover, the party and ideological preferences of those who do vote are not always reflected in the makeup of the legislature. According to the Gallup organization, in the 1978 elections for the U.S. House of Representatives, 55 percent of the voters cast ballots for Democrats and 45 percent for Republicans. Yet they chose 275 Democrats and 158 Republicans (with two races still undecided at that time), or a House 63.5 percent Democratic and 36.5 percent Republican. Gallup reports that in 1970 the national popular vote for House candidates was 54 percent Democratic and 46 percent Republican. The voters in that year elected a House consisting of 254 Democrats, 180 Republicans (one contest undecided), or 58.6 percent Democratic and 41.4 percent Republican.[6] If, as is commonly believed, Republicans tend to be more conservative than Democrats, the House in these years at least did not adequately mirror the nation's conservative voters.

Nor does the other side of the election equation seem to function well. In spite of the glamor and glory accompanying political office, a very limited number of people are attracted to such public service. Primaries in congressional districts containing hundreds of thousands of voters rarely attract as many as a half dozen candidates. Running for office is a highly speculative venture, and apparently many qualified and gifted people prefer to take other types of risk.

Many people who do vote do not act deliberately and dispassionately, considering only the merits of the candidates and the issues. Arnold Steinberg, an election consultant who has written two books explaining the art and practice of politics for those who professionally manage political campaigns, believes that the most significant problem common to campaign managers, coordinators, and news directors is a failure to perceive that most voters are not very interested in politics in general, let alone in a specific campaign. Steinberg tells us that every campaign is a public relations effort to sell the candidate to the voters.[7]

He does not deny that some candidates or political parties are so appealing and certain issues so important to voters that almost no amount of public relations will affect the outcome. In these situations the interest of a majority of voters is likely to be represented. That is the way the system is supposed to function. However, in many situations numerically small but well-organized special-interest groups are able to obtain preferential treatment from government because of legislatures' innate tendency to cater to such groups. Professor Milton Friedman observes: "The most potent group in a democracy such as ours is a small minority that has a special interest which it values very highly, for which it is willing to give its vote, regardless of what happens elsewhere, and about which the rest of the community does not care very strongly."[8] He explains that by combining enough small groups into a coalition advocating special interests, a candidate for public office can achieve a majority vote. If one group wants a tariff on chemicals—an issue about which most people are unconcerned—hardly anyone will vote against a candidate who voices this commitment so long as the candidate remains in favor of something the voters want. By making a number of such pledges, the office-seeker will be on the way to receiving a majority of the vote.

Legislatures consider thousands of measures, and few voters can amass information about how prospective candidates will view them all. Ideological leanings may be indicative, but they are far from conclusive on any one question, and in any case most legislators embrace the middle course and not the extremes. Moreover, many voters are not well versed in the liberal or conservative positions on particular questions, and many are unconcerned about various matters. It is frequently difficult to contend that election results provide a mandate on any one issue. Although 80 percent of the people may dislike red neckties, they might nevertheless have voted for the candidate who stood for red ties if he or she had also advocated what to them was the more critical issue of blue suits.[9] Single issue voting—abortion, gun control, civil rights, the economy, concern for ancestral lands—is a prominent characteristic of recent elections.

Nor does the public always vote solely on the issues. A study by the Historical Research Foundation sought to discover why voters in six districts had voted, apparently inexplicably, to elect individuals whose voting record was contrary to the majority's philosophical bent (a conservative district choosing liberals and liberal districts voting for conservatives). The successful candidates appeared to overcome philosophical differences by being friendly, accessible, energetic, and providing services.[10]

Voters frequently are not knowledgeable about critical political facts. Polls show that in the early 1970s, many voters found deciding between potential presidential candidates Edward Kennedy and George Wallace difficult; yet the two support diametrically opposed policies. A poll taken before the New Hampshire presidential primary of 1968 revealed that a majority of the voters questioned were unaware that Eugene McCarthy was a "dove" candidate. It would seem that everyone in California would remember that in 1978 Governor Jerry Brown strongly opposed Proposition 13 (which sharply cut property taxes). Yet a poll taken after the initiative had been approved showed that 41 percent of the sample thought Brown had supported it, with only 31 percent correctly recalling his opposition. Brown's strong efforts to implement the proposition may have accounted for the confusion, but it is nevertheless a dramatic illustration of voter ignorance.

It is said that political scientists believe that government is perfectible even if humanity is not, a belief reflected especially among liberally oriented private groups organized to achieve better government. Typically their officers and publications suggest solving our political problems by educating and informing the public so that the most competent and honest people are elected. This laudable goal is widely accepted and should be encouraged; that these endeavors will eliminate the problems of representative government is most doubtful. The educational level of the American people has increased at a substantial pace with what appears to be little corresponding improvement in the quality of our politics. Consider the number of women and men obtaining college degrees. Between 1870 and 1970, while population increased 500 percent, the number of college degrees conferred rose about 9,000 percent—roughly seventeen to eighteen times more than the population. A great many people would question whether American government has improved at a similar pace.

Consider in this regard what should be an elementary tenet of popular government, that the people will hold elected officials accountable for their actions, removing when possible the rascals and incompetents. The experience of judicial retention elections illustrates that this assumption is unrealistic. Under this plan the judge runs only on his or her own record, not against an opponent, and is required to obtain a certain percentage of the vote (50 or 60) in order to remain in office. Sixteen states in 1976 employed merit-retention elections for some or all of their judges. In the thirteen states that conducted such elections in that year, the voters apparently rejected only 3 out of 353 trial and appellate judges standing for retention. Either the judiciary is performing incredibly well or the retention system is not operating as intended.

Citing these and other figures, Professor William Jenkins, Jr., contends that the process has become a rubber stamp and thus does not assure judicial accountability.[11] By contrast, when judges run for re-election against opponents, as occurs in other political contexts, they are more likely to be defeated—possibly for reasons that have nothing to do with merit. Missouri originated the retention plan more than twenty years ago and has removed exactly one judge since then. Even in the states that require 60 percent of the vote in order to retain office, removing a judge from office is very difficult. Jenkins writes that in 1976 five judges up for retention in Cook County, Illinois, encountered the combined opposition of the Chicago Bar Association, the Chicago Council of Lawyers, and all three of the city's newspapers. Yet only one judge was defeated under the Illinois 60 percent approval requirement, and he received 58.85 percent of the vote, sufficient for retention in some states and qualifying as a victory of almost landslide proportions in an ordinary contest. The other four judges garnered 60.8, 61.8, 61.9, and 63.0 percent of the votes. The rejected judge was only the second to be ousted in the state's twelve-year history of retention balloting.

Clearly voter performance belies the theoretician's beliefs. Voters may, of course, be expressing values of overriding importance to them, having to do with judicial experience and judicial independence. Proponents of the retention plan thought that because many voters would not have contact with judges or understand their records, they would rely in part on lawyers' informed recommendations. Prior to the 1976 Arizona election, a local bar association polled its members to rate the judges on a variety of characteristics connected with the judicial function. The three judges with the lowest bar ratings were retained by safe margins. Each ranked low in legal knowledge—an aptitude that lawyers should be able to recognize. The lowest ranking judge in the bar survey received a rating of only 33 percent but obtained 69 percent of the votes, an acceptance rate not much different from the 78 percent attained by the judge who received a score of 99 percent from the bar.

Jenkins asserts that these results are not inconsistent with those nationwide. He says that even the lowest bar ratings seldom reduce the margin of victory by more than 10 to 15 percent, usually not enough to result in defeat. One Arizona political writer quoted by Jenkins concluded that short of committing incest at high noon at the city's busiest intersection, "it would appear our honorable judges now have lifetime sinecures."[12]

The irrational and erratic nature of the popular franchise should caution us about relying on it as an ultimate solution to contemporary problems.

Majoritarianism

Even at its theoretical best, when enlightened and dedicated voters cast ballots in large numbers, majoritarianism—that is, rule by 50 percent plus one—should not be the final arbiter of human affairs. Even the most dedicated majoritarians, among whom are Justices appointed during the Warren Court era, would be outraged at the slightest suggestion that the concept be applied to political and civil liberties. Alexis de Tocqueville's book, *Democracy in America,* devotes two chapters to the problems of majoritarianism in our nation. He wrote that in France the prevailing attitude was that the king could do no wrong, while for Americans, it was the majority who possessed this perfection. He continued: "When I see that the right and the means of absolute command are conferred on a people or upon a king, upon an aristocracy or a democracy, a monarchy or a republic, I recognize the germ of tyranny, and I journey onwards to a land of more hopeful institutions."[13] De Tocqueville saw majoritarianism as a threat to the goals of the American state:

> A majority taken collectively may be regarded as a being whose opinions, and most frequently whose interests, are opposed to those of another being, which is styled a minority. If it be admitted that a man, possessing absolute power, may misuse that power by wronging his adversaries, why should a majority not be liable to the same reproach? Men are not apt to change their characters by agglomeration; nor does their patience in the presence of obstacles increase with the consciousness of their strength. And for these reasons I can never willingly invest any number of my fellow-creatures with that unlimited authority which I should refuse to any one of them.[14]

As we have seen, the Constitutional generation sought protection for minority interests. Hamilton said that one objective of government was to protect the weak as well as the strong: "In a society under the forms of which the stronger faction can readily unite and oppress the weaker, anarchy may as truly be said to reign as in a state of nature, where the weaker individual is not secured against the violence of the stronger...."[15]

Tyranny is not the only problem. Majorities do not necessarily have enough knowledge, insight, or expertise to assure wisest action. Domestic issues such as inflation, unemployment, and economic controls require expertise and understanding far beyond that which is possessed by the majority. Even the most knowledgeable people differ on the answers to these problems, and someone must therefore be wrong. The collective wisdom is not likely to be less fallible. Hayek rejects the dedication to majority superiority as being inconsistent with human experience: "It is only because the majority opinion will always be opposed by some that our knowledge and understanding progress."[16]

Moreover, majorities shift before and after elections, and the laws that fleeting alliances produce may long outlast the forces that created them. Election polls indicate that popular opinion does not remain steady but rather can be quite fickle, and at times may swing sharply. Were laws able to constantly reflect the majority's opinion, the legislators might spend much of their time undoing what they had only recently decreed. An election operates like a speed camera recording a segment of ongoing movement. We are told that had the 1968 election been held a week or two later, Hubert Humphrey would have been president instead of Richard Nixon. Jerry Brown, it is also said, owes his accession to the California governorship to the fact that the election was held the first and not the second or third week in November. In both cases public sentiment was moving away from the eventual victor. According to the polls, Jimmy Carter had a more than 25-point lead over President Ford early in the 1976 campaign, but only a few percentage points separated them on election day. In fact some polls showed that Ford was favored toward the end of the campaign.

Elections of course must be held at intervals greater than weeks or months. And although the verdicts do not remain constant, elections do provide an authority generally acceptable to most people. The popular election as a means for resolving public differences has proven superior to all other techniques. However, these obvious benefits should not blind us to the fallibility of majoritarianism. The majority should not be consecrated with the authority to trample the rights of those not fortunate enough to belong to it.

Legislating

Legislation in this nation emanates from federal, state, and local levels of government. While the process differs in certain respects at each tier, all legislators confront common burdens and responsibilities. Under our system, a legislature is charged with implementing the public's political will. To fulfill this obligation, a lawmaker must be able to comprehend well both the social problems and the legal means for coping with them so that the popular will prevails through efficient and effective legislation. For a number of reasons, these responsibilities are frequently beyond most legislators' ability and capacity. To vote intelligently on proposed statutes demands reasonably expert knowledge of the subject matter, which few legislators possess about a great portion of measures they consider. Because the number of measures proposed is so great, and because politicians must fulfill many social, personal, and constituent obligations to remain in office, legislators lack the time, and probably also the will and inclination, to become very knowledgeable. Moreover, in many matters implementing constituents' opinions is not possible because those opinions are based on individual values and are not sufficiently clear to provide mandates on issues. Nor are legislators always free agents to implement the public's will; on many measures they are subject to strong pressures exerted by lobbyists, contributors, and organized groups of constituents. And finally, efficiency and effectiveness are limited by the constant need for compromise and expediency that are political realities. I shall consider these problems in the succeeding pages.

The business of legislating covers the spectrum of human activity. Although in most instances legislators are generalists and not specialists, they have enormous powers to decide matters that require great expertise. In Washington, legislators decide issues concerning war and peace, economic well-being and recession, authority and liberty, and the complexities of taxation. In cites and towns all over the country, legislators regulate the use of private property and the taxing and spending of people's money. On every level legislators pass laws affecting enterprise and restraining individuals and corporations. Yet rarely are these politicians expert or even very knowledgeable about these matters. On the contrary, they usually are primarily expert only in that specialized part of political science involved in getting elected to, and remaining in, office. Few who seek public office have an impressive background in any of the matters he or she will vote on if elected.

To some extent the situation is ameliorated by officials employing staff members who become knowledgeable on particular issues. My conversations with legislators at federal and state levels of government suggest, however, that most staff time is devoted to dealing with constituents and their problems. Except possibly for chairmen of committees employing technically trained help, legislators are limited in the amount of information and advice they can obtain from their staffs.

Many people are elected to office because of accomplishments or backgrounds that provide little help in carrying out their responsibilities in office. Tom Dewey was elected governor of New York because he put a number of crooks in jail; Edward Kennedy, Barry Goldwater, Jr., and Adlai Stevenson III had the advantage of widely recognized family names (when he was running for an Illinois office, Stevenson's billboards carried only the words "Adlai III"). Jerry Brown would probably never have been elected to the governorship of California at the age of thirty-six had he not been the son of a two-time governor of that state, and Ronald Reagan might never have held that position had he not achieved fame as an actor. U.S. Senator Bill Bradley owes his membership in the World's Greatest Deliberative Body to his excellence as a basketball player. Good looks, family background, money, speaking ability, an abundance of energy, and a positive public relations image are attributes essential to winning elections, but they provide scant help in analyzing and deciding critical policy issues.

Some believe that representative government demands only that the elected legislators carry out the will of their constituency and that therefore their own knowledge is not important. Such a portrayal of the legislative function is not accurate. Constituents may have several views, none of which attracts a majority. Such situations raise the well-discussed paradox of voting: a majority position results from a chance combination of first and second choices.[17] In many matters the ordinary voter has only a vague idea about which actions will accomplish his or her preferred goals. Today, much legislation is so complex that simply favoring the concept involved is meaningless; the terms and provisions of legislation are more important than is its actual passage.

Consider, for example, the national land use measures before Congress during the 1970s that I had occasion to study and about which I testified before both Senate and House committees. Many people favored in principle the passage of such legislation. However, enormous differences can separate bills directed toward this general purpose. One bill may emphasize environmental and open-space objectives over employment and business, another vice versa. The bill may establish a large or small bureaucracy or a strong or minor federal role.

The complexity of legislation is evident merely from perusing the legislative bills. Land use measures presented at local and federal levels some years ago provide illustrations. S.268, reported by the Senate Committee on Interior and Insular Affairs in June 1973, contained more than seventy-five pages. The House version, H.R.10294, as originally introduced in September 1973, consisted of fifty-five pages. In California, Assembly Bill No. 15, introduced 2 December 1974, relating to the preservation of prime agricultural land, was composed of twenty-nine pages. I studied each for several hours, and although I am a lawyer with considerable knowledge in the area, serious questions as to meaning and intent were raised by a great many provisions. To vote intelligently on these measures requires considerable study, possibly weeks for persons not well-informed in the field. Committee meetings, hearings, and summaries alleviate to some extent the informational problem, but even then, newcomers to the field would be far from expert. Judging from my personal experience, I do not believe many congressmen understood well the problems and the proposed or alternative solutions. Yet each of these bills would have affected considerably the lives and fortunes of a great many. (None of these measures was enacted.)

Even if the legislator envisions his or her role as purely representative of the voters, translating the latters' desires into laws that will operate effectively still requires considerable study, information, and often expertise. Because the demand for laws and regulations is great, legislators confront an immense responsibility. The California legislature reportedly considered more than 7,000 proposals during the 1975–76 session. Congress was expected to process as many as 6,000 items in the session beginning in 1977. All these measures require at least committee study, and every legislator will have to review a large variety of proposals, either in committee or on the floor. Unfortunately, most legislators do not have the time, will, or inclination to give these matters the attention they warrant.

Being a federal, state, or local lawmaker is a full-time job, and much of this time is occupied with activities that will assure retention in office. These activities include meeting, communicating with, entertaining, and addressing constituents, and traveling to and from and participating in political meetings. Even if the inclination is there, little time is left in which to study and understand the hundreds of highly complex bills that are constantly introduced.

Because of the subjectivity involved in political issues, unanimity rarely prevails. But politics is said to be the art of the possible, and here the possible means continual compromise. This ingredient also severely retards the effectiveness of the political process. Assuming the Perfect Plan is introduced in the legislature, it is likely to be quite imperfect by the time it clears public hearings, committee, and floor votes. Sometimes the situation can be compared to surgery conducted by a team composed of Christian scientists, exorcists, and surgeons.

Moreover, it is becoming increasingly evident that there can be little certainty about the importance of any legislation until after it has become law. Remember that modest congressional resolution that eventually sent hundreds of thousands of Americans to fight in Viet Nam? The Tonkin Gulf Resolution was not a declaration of war and contained only six paragraphs; few legislators who voted for it imagined that it would be used by two presidents as authority to wage a major war in Southeast Asia. Similar problems arise, as we shall see, when regulatory commissions are created to implement legislation.

The preceding discussion may be inadequate in describing "legislating" because it does not account for the actions of legislators who consciously strive to improve the human condition. Clearly, many people in public office have avid supporters who believe in the dedication, objectivity, and integrity of their representatives. Terms such as "over-all good," "public interest," and "general welfare" are part of the jargon of the political world, and surely even cynics would agree that some legislators at some times are motivated by such goals. The problem is that these terms have no precise meaning. In every controversy politicians have the task of choosing among competing interests and values. Policies that will benefit some will harm others. The struggle is not necessarily between good and bad, but often involves degrees of good and bad with perhaps the choice turning on the means and not the ends. Contemplate Professor Bruce Johnson's thoughts on the subject:

> The *public interest* (or the common good) is an empty phrase unless it is interpreted literally to mean an unambiguous improvement in the situation of each and every member of society or, on a weaker criterion, to leave no one any worse off. Since it is difficult to even imagine an activity that does not hurt someone, let alone uniformly increase the lot of everyone, the concept is empty—a piece of rhetoric used to persuade others through the political process. In fact, public interest arguments usually mean that the good of some men takes precedence over the good of others. In certain cases the common good appears to mean the good of the majority versus the good of the minority or of the individual.[18]

In the absence of any objective guide, and a determination to be bound by it, subjective concerns tend to enter and influence or dominate the decision. Issues become personal in the sense that although a vote for either side may not be critical to society as a whole, it may substantially affect an individual's future. The rhetoric notwithstanding, what reasons exist to believe that unlike those of every other ambitious person, politicians' day-to-day judgments will not be made to further their own goals? Can legislators with even the noblest of intentions ignore their personal welfare in the determinations that they make?

A law that is poorly conceived or drafted or results from significant compromises tends to be inefficient and ineffective. Such legislation poses threats to personal liberties by being far more restrictive than necessary to achieve the legislative purpose.

Special Interests

Posner suggests that the lawmaking process creates a market for legislation in which politicians "sell" legislative protection to those who can help their electoral prospects with money and/or votes.[19] Professor Michael Granfield likens the legislature to a general store whose inventory includes monopolies, preferences, and concessions. He writes that the politician sells the goods, as any astute storeowner will, to that group offering the highest price. The process does not necessarily include bribery or any other illegal activity; it may simply involve a legal contribution or a promise of votes.[20] Chapters 8 and 13 contain many illustrations of economically preferential enactments, and in reality the list is much longer. One wonders, for example, what prompted the enactment of automobile franchise laws, presently operative in at least eighteen states, that control the location of new auto dealerships? In California such a law enables existing dealers to prevent or delay the location of new dealerships in their territory. Naturally, the California law states that it was intended, among other things, to ensure that dealers provide adequate and sufficient services to consumers. But it is hard to conceive of consumers arising en masse to demand limitations on their shopping opportunities.[21]

The process that leads to legislation benefiting comparatively few people is not difficult to understand. Those who would be helped substantially by laws have the incentive to wage a strong lobbying effort, whereas those who would bear the costs without sharing the benefits frequently do not have a sufficient personal stake. This is a major defect of a democratic society whose laws are in theory supposed to tilt toward the majority. The concentration of benefits provides an incentive for creating a narrow political lobby, whose small size makes organizing relatively easy. On the other side, a larger number of citizens are involved, they are often widely dispersed, and the costs of the legislation are spread so that no one person suffers very much—a reality that limits organizational incentive. As a result the cost of spending measures, subsidies, and special economic preferences are passed along, often to an unknowing and uncomplaining public.[22] The description fits the activities not only of financial groups but also of many social activists.

In this environment, the well-being of politically powerless entrepreneurs can be precarious. Reform groups who distrust market mechanisms and business interests who seek to eliminate competition have considerable opportunity to achieve their goals, particularly when they have common aims, as has often occurred.

Professor Hayek believes that never in the whole of history were governments so much under the necessity of satisfying the particular wishes of numerous special interests as they are today. He believes that an omnipotent democratic government, such as exists in England, simply cannot exercise restraint against these pressures.

> If its powers are not limited, it simply cannot confine itself to serving the agreed views of the majority of the electorate. It will be forced to bring together and keep together a majority by satisfying the demands of a multitude of special interests, each of which will consent to the special benefits granted to other groups only at the price of their own special interests being equally considered. Such a bargaining democracy has nothing to do with the conceptions which were used to justify the principle of democracy.[23]

The Agencies

Carrying out the will of Congress frequently requires the creation of administrative positions and agencies. Since the 1887 passage of the Interstate Commerce Act establishing the commission of the same name, federal and state legislatures have created hundreds of commissions and boards to implement and administer regulatory legislation. By such actions lawmakers achieve various goals. First, the existence of agencies is often essential to the fulfillment of the legislative design, for lawmaking bodies are not in a position to implement and enforce regulatory measures. Second, difficult decisions and conflicts can be

avoided by creating commissions and delegating to them broad authority to administer generalized programs. Third, commissions are
established in response to public demands.

The question of delegation of power in these situations raises serious
legal and political issues. In some instances, the delegation has been
relatively specific. However, the more usual tendency has been to
make the delegation of power general, broad, and inclusive. Professor
Kenneth Culp Davis has stated that Congress often tells the agency:
"Here is the problem; deal with it." Davis explains that the lack of
meaningful standards almost always results from one or more of three
factors (and usually from a mixture of all three):

> (1) Each legislator and each assistant to a legislator concerned with a
> bill has limited confidence in his own capacity in the time available to
> dig very far into the specialized subject matter, and such a state of
> mind produces general and vague formulations of objectives, not
> specific and precise ones. (2) Developing policies with respect to
> difficult subject matter often can best be accomplished by consider-
> ing one concrete problem at a time, as an agency may do; generaliz-
> ing in advance is often beyond the capacity of the best of minds. (3)
> Subject matter calling for delegation is often highly controversial; the
> more specific the statement of legislative objectives the more difficult
> the achievement of a consensus that can be supported by a majority
> of each house and win the signature of the executive; the more vague
> and general the statement of legislative objectives the more likely is
> the achievement of such a consensus; if bills are to be enacted, the
> legislative process must be allowed to make its own determination of
> what degree of specificity or generality is attainable.[24]

Although the delegation of power solves one portion of the legislative dilemma, it creates another of at least comparable dimension: it
removes from the representative process a large area of decision-
making. No matter how determined the public is to be in charge, it has
little control over extremely important decisions made daily by administrative agencies that affect a large percentage of the population.
With the advent of these agencies, the theory that a knowledgeable and
understanding electorate would rule wisely and well, elect the ablest,
and throw the rascals out became inoperative in a vast portion of
political life. Agency officials with far-reaching powers do not have to
submit themselves to public approval, and even though their executive
and legislative superiors do, the gap between the public will and the
exercise of authority has been widened substantially. When the delegation is not precise, the agencies are not bound by any rule of law
that the representative process has established.

Moreover, although administrative agencies are supposed to be depositories of knowledge and expertise, many of the matters with which they deal are not susceptible to scientific or certain resolution. Much of their time is spent adjusting the claims of the various competing groups and interests vying for their favor—essentially a legislative and not an administrative undertaking. In exercising their discretion, these agencies are not bound by a basic maxim of a free society, that the ultimate test of truth is acceptance in the marketplace of ideas. The administrative agencies, isolated and insulated from the representative process, are too far removed from the public to make Holmes's belief in the wisdom of the political process meaningful for vast portions of the population.

The people appointed to these commissions exercise enormous economic powers. Consider some of the issues that the commissions decide. Prior to the deregulatory legislation of 1978, the Civil Aeronautics Board determined what companies could enter the industry, how much airfare should be charged, and where each airline could fly. The Federal Communications Commission chooses which of four qualified contenders should be licensed to own and operate a television or radio station. The Interstate Commerce Commission creates rates and rules for railroads and truckers. Local zoning authorities decide what may be built where—and sometimes even how it is to be built.

Different people, regardless of how wise and expert they are, can decide these matters differently. Absent precise and detailed standards by which rulings can be measured, decisions arrived at for the worst reasons—graft, favoritism, or political ambition—can just as readily be rationalized as those decided for the noblest ones. Commissioners with a certain ideological bent can be as rigid and unshakable as those influenced by corruption. Important rules, affecting great numbers of people, can be created purely by chance, depending on the voting mixture of the day. The rule of law, the individual's most important defense against arbitrary power, can exist only in very attenuated form in such circumstances.

Conclusions

In dissolving an injunction issued by a three-judge district court preventing implementation of California's Automobile Franchise Act, Justice Rehnquist (in his capacity as circuit justice) wrote that at any time a state is enjoined by a court from effectuating statutes enacted by representatives of its people, it suffers a form of irreparable injury.[25] I think that, with all due respect, the Justice would have considerable difficulty in proving this assertion with empirical evidence. Interestingly, the statute in question, as I have previously indicated, appears to be an excellent illustration of special-interest legislation that is not responsive to general public concern.[26] Clearly, most of his colleagues would not agree with the Justice's conclusion if the laws related to the intellectual liberties. Moreover, many distinguished Americans of earlier generations would be disinclined to accept Rehnquist's generalization, for our country was born with a distaste for the finality of parliamentary judgments.

> When in 1767 this modernised British Parliament, committed by now to the principle of parliamentary sovereignty unlimited and unlimitable, issued a declaration that a parliamentary majority could pass any law it saw fit, it was greeted with an outcry of horror in the colonies. James Otis and Sam Adams in Massachusetts, Patrick Henry in Virginia and other colonial leaders along the seaboard screamed "Treason!" and "Magna Carta!" Such a doctrine, they insisted, demolished the essence of all their British ancestors had fought for, took the very savour out of that fine Anglo-Saxon liberty for which the sages and patriots of England had died.[27]

These concerns are no less valid and appropriate in our times. The infirmities of the political and administrative processes are many and widespread; judicial abdication in the rational relation rule ignores and rejects the realities of government. In the good society, some measure of protection is always appropriate for those who for good and bad reasons lose in the political or administrative struggles. We should find entrusting the legislatures and the agencies with final discretion over economic liberties as absurd as we find entrusting them with such discretion over the political liberties. Commands of the state should never be inviolate, lest its very purpose be eroded.

13   The Failure of Regulation

The experience of American jurisprudence re-
veals that pragmatism is an important element in judicial decision-
making. No matter how principled and objective judges seek to be,
they cannot always dissociate themselves from a concern for the
extralegal consequences of their decisions. Justice Holmes's famous
description of the common-law process is applicable also to constitutional interpretation:

> The life of the law has not been logic: it has been experience. The felt
> necessities of the time, the prevalent moral and political theories,
> intuitions of public policy, avowed or unconscious, even the preju-
> dices which judges share with their fellow-men, have had a good deal
> more to do than the syllogism in determining the rules by which men
> should be governed.[1]

Our concern in this book is with the Justices and their positions on
economic liberties. As we have seen, a strong correlation existed on
the Taft and Warren Courts between the philosophical inclinations of
Justices and their views on constitutional liberties. Holmes's oft-
quoted statement about the influence of economic theory on the majority's decision in *Lochner* (suggesting the majority was implementing
laissez-faire economics) was no less applicable to many other Justices
with whom he served, including in particular his colleague in dissent,
Justice Brandeis. For Justices and others concerned with the social and

economic consequences of government intervention in the economy, this chapter presents summaries of fifty-three studies of regulation.

The New Attitude toward Regulation

Judges who are convinced that governmental economic restraints are on the whole essential to the well-being of the public may find overturning regulatory and welfare legislation difficult, sometimes despite their judicial responsibilities. They may acknowledge the limitations and infirmities of the legislative and administrative processes and nevertheless conclude that the nation is best situated when the judiciary does little to impede them. The low esteem in which economic due process is held suggests to many that judicial review of economic matters is undesirable and harmful and that the judiciary should accept without reservation almost all legislative and administrative solutions to social and economic problems. Society was worse off, the proponents of this approach contend, as a result of the interventions of the "laissez-faire" Court.

At the time of Brandeis's dissent in *New State Ice Co. v. Liebmann* (1932),[2] this position was more persuasive than it is today. In that opinion the Justice cited the writings of contemporary liberal reformers who were critical of unregulated free enterprise, and the Depression, which the country was then suffering, provided poignant support for their views. However, these critics arrived at their conclusions on the basis of theory, not experience, for at that time little was known or understood about governmental regulation and its consequences. Thus Brandeis felt the need to explain extensively the meaning of a certificate of convenience and necessity, which in 1932 was a relatively new and not widely recognized device that governmental agencies used to control entry into regulated industries. Today such an extensive explanation would not be required.

While the results of the regulatory process went untabulated and unevaluated, the attitude toward regulation expressed in Brandeis's dissent increasingly attracted allies. One indicator of this growing approval was the crescendo of fury and invective that arose in 1944 when Friedrich Hayek's *Road to Serfdom* was published in this country.[3] This perceptive work explains the inefficiency of regulation and the serious threat it poses to individual freedom. The reaction to Hayek's conclusions was in large measure prompted by a lack of knowledge, for in this country, regulation was still in its infancy, and his reasoning was incomprehensible to those who, on the basis of hope and not experience, had been fervently preaching greater government involvement in economic matters. Today a similar response would be much more difficult to justify. We now have hundreds of federal and state agencies regulating some aspect of private activity, and we no longer have to evaluate them on the basis of theory and hope.

Consider the case of the Civil Aeronautics Board (CAB), the federal agency responsible for the economic regulation of the airlines. We now know that until the CAB's abrupt change in policy in 1976, rates for airline travel controlled by the CAB were far higher than those on routes it did not regulate. Studies have been made of federal airline regulation disclosing that its most significant accomplishment is the raising of airline fares.

CAB is not an isolated illustration. People all along the ideological spectrum who have studied the agencies are now aware that they are far from being guardians of the public interest, and that they have often been created for reasons having little to do with the general welfare. Thus, very persuasive evidence exists that railroad regulation in the late nineteenth century, the nation's first major regulatory effort, did not come about simply because of public outrage at the robber barons, as is commonly supposed. It turns out that most railroads supported regulation in 1887 when Congress created the Interstate Commerce Commission. They believed the ICC would help them impose an industry-wide cartel, something they had not been able to accomplish by themselves. And they were not wrong.[4]

The realities of over forty years of welfarism and regulation have eroded the enthusiasm that once existed for governmental activism, and few today, even among those most dedicated to the welfare state, would be likely to launch an attack on its opponents comparable to that which met the *Road to Serfdom*. For example, Senator Edward Kennedy, whom many observers would probably have expected to be in Brandeis's camp on this issue, has become one of the leading and most effective proponents of economic deregulation. Hardly a free-market zealot, still he believes that "[t]he problems of our economy have occurred, not as an outgrowth of laissez-faire unbridled competition. They have occurred under the guidance of federal agencies, under the umbrella of federal regulations."[5] He asserts that the loss to our economy from unnecessary and anticompetitive regulation is staggering. According to the senator, the failure of regulation has led perversely to even greater government intervention, further aggravating economic difficulties.[6]

Kennedy was a leader in the successful fight for passage of the 1978 airline deregulation bill, and had the support of many liberal reformers, such as Ralph Nader and prominent members of the Carter administration. The principal opponents of deregulation—and in this respect the cast has not changed since *New State Ice*—were most of the major airlines. Among their supporters were their lenders, the AFL-CIO, and the labor unions connected with the airline industry. If, as the proregulators have been telling us for years, regulation is intended to curb industrial giants in order to protect consumers, why, one wonders were so many of the "predators" eager to retain the system?

In March of 1978, Kennedy introduced a bill entitled "The Competition Improvements Act of 1978," an earlier version of which one writer described as "so sweeping in its potential effect, as to strike fear in the hearts of every federal agency as well as the businessmen and unions hovering under their protection."[7] The bill applies to the Interstate Commerce Commission, the Federal Communications Commission the Securities and Exchange Commission, the Civil Aeronautics Board, the Federal Maritime Commission, and the Nuclear Regulatory Commission. It requires that before an agency takes an action that may lessen competition, it must, among other things, find that: (1) the anticompetitive effects are clearly outweighed by demonstrable public benefits; and (2) the same result could not be substantially accomplished by alternative measures having a lesser anticompetitive impact. If its action is challenged in court, the agency would have the burden of establishing by substantial evidence that it has met these standards.

The bill declares the country is committed to a private enterprise system in the belief that competition protects consumers, promotes efficiency, and spurs innovation. It further declares that regulation has created unnecessary losses for consumers, fostered inefficiency, and stifled innovation.

I have already mentioned Ralph Nader's condemnation of economic regulatory agencies, which he delivers with an intensity that even Milton Friedman, Friedrich Hayek, and their ideological colleagues do not surpass. Nader leads the consumer movement in supporting the establishment of a federal consumer protection agency that would represent consumer interests before the regulatory commissions. The push for the agency is predicated on two beliefs: first, that the consumer has received abysmal treatment from the federal bureaucracy and second, that the consumer desperately needs protection from the agencies. However, opponents appropriately charge that Nader's proposal would produce yet another bureaucracy, with no assurance that it would not revert to the customary, criticized practices of the other agencies.

In at least twenty-four states, measures that are dubbed "sunset laws" have been introduced requiring state regulatory agencies to justify their existence at specified intervals; absent such justification, they would be abolished. This type of law originated in Colorado and required all of that state's forty-one regulatory agencies to prove, every six years, the need for their continuance. In 1977, Senator Edmund S. Muskie, along with forty-two cosponsors, introduced in the United States Senate the Sunset Act of 1977, which in substance received unanimous committee approval under the title "The Program Evaluation Act of 1977." The popularity of such laws along the entire ideological spectrum is strong evidence of the skepticism with which regulation is viewed.

Legislative termination of regulation is not in sight, however. Kennedy, Nader, and many other liberal-reformers favor regulation whenever health or safety is involved—for example, in such areas as the environment, drugs, and working conditions. Kennedy advocates wage-price ceilings. Many conservatives are strong proponents of zoning, environmental, and obscenity controls. Every regulatory agency has a constituency battling efforts to terminate it. New forms of government restraint continue to evolve. Clearly, however, the perspective evident in Brandeis's dissent has given way to a new realism about regulation.

Economic regulation is no longer a nebulous phenomenon about which people can theorize at will; its effects are now well known and understood. While every regulation serves or accomplishes a purpose desired by many, such results may come at the expense of other objectives of the good society. Numerous studies have measured or evaluated the benefits and costs of the regulatory agencies. The following pages present short resumes of those available in scholarly books and professional publications.

Studies of Regulation

Included in this chapter are studies coming to my attention that I regard as scholarly and able investigations or analyses of regulatory programs. It was not feasible for purposes of this book to consider and summarize every significant study in this field. Consequently the compilation presented may not necessarily be representative of existing learned opinion on government regulation. However, the number of both the areas covered and the researchers involved is sufficiently large and varied to warrant serious consideration of the conclusions presented. I believe a representative sampling of the scholarly literature would not yield an appreciable difference in opinion about the results of regulation.

The studies reported herein are classified by the industry or other subject matter with which they deal. When appropriate, there is comparison of those studies covering the same or similar regulation. The original studies contain many pages of important information necessarily omitted in these short summaries. The reader is therefore urged to refer to the original writings for a better comprehension of the subject matter. Excluded from this chapter are studies of minimum wage laws on which I have reported in preceding pages (see above, chapter 6) and studies of natural gas regulation prepared following the energy crisis of 1974, which are so numerous and varied as to be beyond the scope of this book.

The Transportation Industry

Studies made of airline regulation include Keeler (1972), the Report of the Subcommittee of the United States Senate Judiciary Committee (1975), and the Report of the CAB Special Staff (1975).* The basis of airline regulation is price, entry, and output control. All three studies assert that regulation substantially elevates prices and distorts competition and efficiency by causing airlines to compete on the basis of service rather than price.

In a related study, Levine (1975) discusses airmail transportation, the rates and routes of which are regulated by the CAB. Levine finds that as a result of these regulations, the postal service must pay higher prices than it otherwise would for identical or even inferior service, and consequently carrier utilization is less than optimal. The main purpose of the regulation was to benefit carriers, and in this aspect it has succeeded. However, Levine concludes that the regulations have caused misallocation of resources and a net loss to society.

Eckert and Hilton (1972) and Kitch, Isaacson, and Kasper (1971) have researched taxicab regulation. The former discuss the effect on jitneys of regulations imposed by state and local governments during the period 1914 to 1920. Despite their regional or local origin, these provisions were frequently so similar as to almost suggest a common or national source. Their stated purpose was to make jitneys license common carriers and therefore more responsible and responsive to public needs; however, the major agitation for the regulation came

---

*References for this chapter will be found on pp. 366–68.

from jitney competitors—the street railways and regular taxicabs. As a result of regulation, jitney business in the nation collapsed. From an estimated fleet of 62,000 in 1915, only 35,000 continued to operate in January 1916, while reportedly less than 6,000 remained by October 1918. By the early 1920s they had virtually disappeared, although subsequent sporadic revivals have occurred. The demise of the jitneys eliminated an alternative form of transportation that Eckert and Hilton believe served the community well. They conclude that only a very limited form of regulation was actually required to protect the public.

The Kitch study of Chicago taxicabs also concludes that taxicab regulation has not been beneficial. In that city regulations resulted in the establishment of a protected taxicab monopoly. Its elimination would increase service by from 42 to 54 percent and decrease fares by 14 percent. The study notes that a major purpose of the regulations was to benefit the taxi industry, and that this objective has been achieved only partially. Owners have fared better than drivers, the latter obtaining relatively small benefits. Kitch found that the most pernicious consequence of the regulation has been to limit the use of the auto as a public transportation alternative.

Spann and Erickson (1970) studied the need for and effect on railroads of regulation at the time of its inception in 1887 through the creation by Congress of the Interstate Commerce Commission (ICC). A main feature of the original regulation, according to the authors, was its attempt to link two dissimilar markets by imposing anticompetitive controls on the competitive long-haul market in order to limit monopoly power in the noncompetitive short-haul market. The regulations required similar charges for long and short hauls. Prior to the regulations, the railroads had sought, with little success, to establish cartels; regulation tended to stabilize the cartel and kept long-haul rates from falling. Although the authors state that their conclusions are not necessarily inevitable, they do believe that regulations linking competitive and noncompetitive sectors are seldom likely to result in an increase in net welfare. They found that in 1890, the losses suffered by long-haul customers from increased rates were twice the gains accruing to short-haul customers from decreased rates.

Breen (1977) studied interstate moving companies, an industry subject to ICC regulation. Certificates required for operation have substantial value, but would not exist in the absence of regulation. He estimates that the capitalized value of monopoly rents accruing to the owners of all outstanding certificates was in 1971 in the neighborhood of $60.8 million, with total industry revenue in that year about $910 million. This and other evidence indicate that regulated interstate rates are above competitive levels. Breen does not believe that without regulation these carriers would engage in destructive competition resulting in a single monopoly.

Peltzman (1975) discusses automobile safety regulations imposed by the National Highway and Traffic Safety Administration. These regulations require automobile design modifications, including seatbelts for all occupants, energy absorbing steering columns, penetration resistant windshields, dual braking systems, and padded instrument panels. The purpose of the regulations is to decrease highway injuries and deaths. Peltzman found, however, that the regulations have been ineffective and therefore unnecessary.

Moore (1978) reports on the price impact of trucking regulations. In 1950, some products that had been transported only by regulated carriers were declared by the courts to be commodities exempt from ICC regulation. As a result of these decisions, prices declined substantially, by from 12 to 59 percent in particular markets, with an unweighted average of 33 percent for fresh poultry and 36 percent for frozen, and a weighted average decline for frozen fruit and vegetables of 19 percent. Member firms of the National Broiler Council ship fresh poultry by exempt carriers and cooked poultry by regulated carriers. In surveying rates for the same routes between the same points, the council found that the average unregulated rates were 33 percent less than the regulated ones. Comparisons of trucking rates between countries show that rates in those with little or no regulation were 43 percent lower than rates in West Germany (with strict controls) and the United States. Moore concludes that three-quarters of the cost to shippers, and ultimately to consumers, of trucking regulations takes the form of income transfers to labor and capital engaged in that industry.

Sloss (1970) discusses the effect of regulation on trucking rates, using as an example the Canadian experience. There, differences in regulation exist among the provinces, and higher trucking prices accompany regulation. Sloss extends and modifies this analysis to fit the United States, where trucking regulation is comprehensive. Acknowledging that his figures are far from precise, the author nevertheless suggests that rates for trucking services would be substantially reduced if they were not regulated.

Brown and Fitzmaurice (1972) studied entry controls imposed by the ICC on the surface-freight forwarders. Members of this industry (which does not include air or ocean freight forwarders) arrange freight transport from shipper via surface carrier. The authors found that the assumption upon which regulation is based—namely, that the industry is a natural monopoly—is incorrect. Competition has been severely restricted because of limitations on new entry and on entry by pro-ducers into new service areas, and the result is higher prices for re-duced service.

Bonsor (1977) studied the impact of transportation costs on regional economic development with special reference to northern Ontario in Canada. That province tightly controls entry into the trucking industry. Such a policy causes truck freight rates to rise to artificially high levels, causing rail freight rates, which can be adjusted under Canadian law to meet those set for truckers, to rise correspondingly. The rate structure hinders the development of secondary (that is, support) manufacturing in the region.

The Electric Utility Industry

The articles on the electric utility industry fall into two subgroups. One deals with the general effectiveness of electric utility regulation; the other with a particular effect of such regulation. The former is dis-cussed by MacAvoy (1970), Stigler and Friedland (1962), Pike (1967), Moore (1970), and Goddard (1971), who comments on Moore's article. MacAvoy does a cost-benefit analysis of the Federal Power Commis-sion's (FPC) electric power regulation, which sets rates and fosters increases in service. For a typical year during the 1960s, he estimates that the cost of the regulations, one-half of which were required expen-ditures by the companies, was $3 million, while the increase in output resulting from the regulation amounted to only $1 million dollars. Thus the costs of the regulation are much higher than the benefits.

Comparing statistics before and after regulation, Stigler and Fried-land found that state regulation of electric utilities is ineffectual and without impact either on the average level of rates charged or on the amounts sold to domestic as compared to commercial users. They also found that unregulated utilities were not more profitable than regulated ones. Moore discovered that regulation has caused a slight, barely significant decrease in rates—no more than 5 percent. Goddard, in his comment on Moore's article, indicates that Moore's estimate of price reduction may be understated. However, both agree that the regulators have imposed distorted pricing programs that lead to resource mis-allocations and inefficiencies. Pike tested whether different methods of utility rate determination might alter the effectiveness of regulation, and concluded that no one kind appreciably affects residential consumer rates.

The next group of articles tests the Averch-Johnson hypothesis[8] that utility regulation causes firms to engage in inefficient production by overutilizing capital. Regulations usually specify an allowable rate of return on capital investment, so presumably firms can increase profits by increasing their capital base. Moore asserts that electric utility companies do not operate in this manner. However, Spann (1974), Courville (1974), and Petersen (1975) believe that firms do overutilize capital. Courville estimates the amount of inefficiency in 1962 at $436.5 million, or 11.95 percent of total production costs. Goddard also believes that severe inefficiency may exist. Baron and Taggart (1977) agree that inefficiency is present, but think that firms under- rather than overutilize capital, for the firms operate according to the premise that the amount of capital they invest is negatively related to the prices set by the regulatory authorities. A utility has an incentive to produce inefficiently if such action will lead to a higher regulated price, and if the firms have the ability to alter their capital and labor stock between rate reviews. Baron and Taggart's study of forty-eight utilities in 1970 suggests that undercapitalization may be present, and that regulators therefore set price below that which unregulated firms would set given their chosen capital stock. (However, the authors caution that their results are based on one year's statistics and therefore urge further study.)

The Natural Gas Industry

Regulation of the natural gas industry is discussed by Wellisz (1963), Gerwig (1962), and MacAvoy (1970 and 1971). Wellisz discusses regulation of natural gas pipeline companies, which purchase field gas and transport it to consumers. In particular, he looks at the Federal Power Commission's method of ascribing costs to the regulated sales, and of determining peak and offpeak prices. This researcher determined that prices are established contrary to economic efficiency: when opportunity costs are low, prices are set high and vice versa. He also found that regulation discourages the building of storage facilities (even though they would be an efficient use of resources) and encourages an overuse of capital. Wellisz states that regulations are contrary to the interests of consumers and that the allocation pattern imposed by the formula may even be worse than no regulation at all.

MacAvoy's (1970) conclusion provides a contrast to Wellisz's. The former believes that FPC pipeline regulation has brought about positive results. In a cost-benefit analysis, regulation added $6 million to FPC and company expenditures, but saved the consumer $9 million in lower rates.

Gerwig and MacAvoy discuss the effect of regulations that governed the rates charged by natural gas companies in years prior to the current energy shortage. Gerwig confines his study to 1956–58 and to the Gulf Coast area (south and east Texas and Louisiana). He discovered that regulations imposed costs on producers amounting to 7 percent of the product's value. In addition, he found that producers pass these costs on to consumers, with the result that prices in regulated markets are higher than those in relatively unregulated markets.

MacAvoy (1970) evaluated, on a cost-benefit basis, FPC gas field price regulations during the 1960s and found residential rates lower than they would have been in the absence of controls. However, such regulation is extremely costly to both the FPC and producers. The only clear benefits are those of income redistribution. Additionally, consumers experience losses caused by possible output restriction.

MacAvoy (1971) deals with regulation of prices at the gas wellhead. Although the FPC strictly controls residential gas resale, regulation of industrial resale is loose or nonexistent. The FPC efforts have resulted in lower consumer prices; however, not all consumers have benefited from them. The artificial price has caused a severe restriction of output. Evidence indicates that the burden of this restricted output has fallen on domestic consumers, as output has been reallocated from domestic to industrial users. Thus, the group which the regulation was designed to help—domestic consumers—has actually suffered detriment.

The Banking Industry

Four articles discuss various aspects of banking industry regulations. Peltzman (1965) and Edwards and Edwards (1974) deal with bank entry regulation. Peltzman found that this regulation has achieved its goal of reducing bank entry, for the entry rate would have been twice as great had the regulation not been imposed. Thus entry into banking has become more attractive, and economic factors have been subordinated to the discretion of the government officials. "Free banking," which proponents of regulation argued could result in the collapse of many banks or even of the system itself, has been ended, and as a consequence competition in the industry has been seriously reduced.

Edwards and Edwards revised downward some of Peltzman's figures, but also concluded that bank entry regulations have reduced entry. They found that bank entry policies are not applied to maximize the income of those regulated—that the regulators have not been "captured." Instead, they believe that the regulators are acting in a manner consistent with the view that they are furthering the public interest. However, the regulation has resulted in higher profits.

Cohen and Reid (1967) discuss the effects of new banking laws in the State of Virginia allowing more mergers and branching. The Virginia law prohibits *de novo* branching outside the immediate area of a given bank—so that any bank could gain entry at a certain locale only by absorbing a bank already in business there. Bank managers and small bank owners were found to benefit from this prohibition, while other investors, stockholders, and consumers do not. The authors do not compare quantitatively the gains and losses of various groups.

Peltzman (1970) deals with regulations governing bank capital investments. The intent here is to prevent bank failures, and regulators therefore have sought to compel greater solvency and liquidity in banks. However, the author found that regulation now has virtually no effect on banking investment behavior, and that it probably never did. Peltzman's study casts great doubt on the effectiveness of banking investment regulation.

The Securities Industry

Five articles treat regulation in the securities industry. Jaffe (1974) tested the effectiveness of regulations designed to prevent corporate insiders from speculating on and benefiting from inside information. These regulations were largely unenforced until 1961. He discovered that the regulations as since enforced by the Securities and Exchange Commission (SEC) have had little effect on either the profitability or the volume of insider trading.

Horwitz and Kolodny (1977) discuss the SEC disclosure rule promulgated in 1971, requiring corporations to disclose, in their annual reports, profits by line of business. The authors analyzed the behavior of two sets of fifty firms during a period of nine years, one set operating with and the other without such a disclosure rule, and found that the rule affected neither the risk nor the return of securities. Thus the evidence indicates that the information, which is costly to provide, is of little value to investors, and that the new rule has not been effective.

Schwert (1977) uses data from the securities market to test the hypothesis that producers (in this study, members of the New York and American Stock Exchanges) benefit from government regulation. He concludes that the profitability of membership in the exchanges fell when the SEC was first established and that it has never recovered from this fall.

The Report of the Special Study of the Securities Market of the Securities and Exchange Committee (1963) concerned the adequacy of the SEC regulation of the securities market. It did not find "the prevalence of gross abuses" that were characteristic of the era which preceded the enactment of the securities law and concluded that the regulation was responsible for this improvement. Nevertheless, because the evidence showed that existing regulation had proved deficient in important respects, the report urged the imposition of much more stringent controls.

Stigler (1975) criticized the report for poor use of either empirical evidence or economic theory to support its proposals. In his article, Stigler evaluated the overall effectiveness of SEC policy. Because the general purpose of the regulation is to protect the investor, he sought to determine empirically whether investors have in fact benefited from it. He concludes that the SEC has no important effect on quality of new securities; in fact, he has grave doubts whether, if the costs of regulation are considered, the SEC has saved the purchasers of new issues any money.

The Broadcasting Industry

Regulations in the broadcasting industry are discussed by Crandall (1972 and 1978) and Levin (1964). Crandall's study (1972) deals with the Federal Communications Commission (FCC) rules forbidding suppliers of programs to network companies from selling syndication rights and shares of profits to the network, and forbidding such purchases by the networks. He identifies the main purpose of the regulation as protection of independent producers from the networks. However, he concludes that these producers are not in need of such special protection, and that the rules have limited the market for them with the consequence that they have had either to assume more risks, and/or to sell syndication interests to a more limited number of buyers.

Crandall's 1978 study, which is based on data from 1972 and 1973, concludes that the FCC's regulation of commercial television has restrained competition, fostered monopoly profits in broadcasting, and provided the means for subsidizing whatever the FCC deems "merit" programing—actually local and national news and public affairs, along with almost anything else that is locally produced. Merit programing is the *quid pro quo* demanded from broadcasters in return for those benefits received from the FCC policy restricting entry. Estimating the cost of merit programing as the difference between a potential 70 percent net return on investment compared to the 29 percent actual broadcaster earnings, Crandall concludes that although the FCC policy is extremely expensive, it nevertheless allows monopoly profits. He suggests another societal detriment of these policies, namely, that viewers are given an FCC-prescribed diet and deprived of a variety of alternative programs that could be offered if the FCC increased the number of television channels or other outlets to allow greater competition.

Levin measured the effects of FCC licensing policies on the value of broadcasting licenses. He found that the benefits conferred on radio and television networks by licensing provisions have been capitalized by the market and are reflected in the selling price of stations. However, these benefits are not uniform, but rather depend on the conditions of the market and the terms of the license. Thus license holders who operate in markets where competition is limited and few restrictions are placed on their economic activity benefit the most, and the difference in market value of stations can be substantial. Levin shows that regulation has decreased competition in the television broadcast industry and thereby increased the value of stations.

The Food and Beverage Industry

Studies in this group cover three areas: the liquor, meat, and milk industries. The liquor industry was studied by Urban and Mancke (1972) and Luksetich (1975). The former discuss the Federal Alcohol Administration labeling regulations. They found that prior to 1972 the regulations requiring that the label disclose the product's age discriminated against a particular kind of whisky (American light), with the result that this whisky was eventually driven out of the market. *Age* was defined as the amount of time the whisky was kept in new barrels before bottling. Because only heavy-bodied whiskies are aged in new barrels, light-bodied American whiskies could not, under the regulation, claim to be aged, even though they had been aged in used barrels—a practice that was standard for such whiskies. Foreign producers were exempt from the regulation. The FAA required the light whisky manufacturers to print "less than one month old" on the label.

As a result, competition in the whisky industry was lessened, and consumer choices were reduced. Only a select group of producers benefited from the regulation. In addition, the regulations acted counter to their purposes of protecting consumers from deception and of increasing competition.

Luksetich deals with a different aspect of liquor regulation: the effect of Minnesota resale price maintenance regulation from 1951 to 1969, and the results of its suspension thereafter. The regulation's stated purpose was to promote temperance and eliminate retail price wars. Both goals were accomplished at the cost of higher prices for those consumers who did not wish to be temperate. After the regulation was suspended, Luksetich says that wholesale and distiller prices did not fall but that retail prices did. He suggests that because retailers benefited most, they probably were instigators of the regulation, and he minimizes the influence of temperance and consumer groups in its adoption.

Knutson (1969) and Kessel (1967) cover regulation in the milk market. Knutson deals with the Minnesota Diary Industry Unfair Trade Practices Act of 1957 prescribing a host of rules limiting competition and "unfair trade practices." The act purportedly was intended to aid milk consumers and producers, and resulted from a period of intense competition and price wars in the industry. Knutson found that after passage of the act, consumers had to pay higher retail milk prices and that no observable benefits occurred for producers. However, milk processors did benefit. Therefore, the regulations did not fulfill their major purpose. The act also stifled competition and encouraged inefficiencies.

Kessel discusses the federal regulation of milk prices in 1967, under which about 60 percent of all milk shipped from farms passed through bottlers or dairies whose prices and other marketing practices were regulated. The regulations in effect permitted milk producers to exercise control over the dairies. He found that regulated producers benefited but that unregulated producers did not. The legislation favors the suppliers of fluid milk products and injures suppliers of milk for manufacturing. It raises the price of a necessity—milk—and lowers the price of luxuries—for example, ice cream. By raising its price, the regulation encourages too much production of milk so that resources over-all are not being used most efficiently. The regulation also decreases competition and efficiency in the industry. Kessel concludes that the gains to some classes are outweighed by the losses to others and that therefore the regulation results in a net loss.

Weiss (1964) studied federal meat inspection, and his conclusions are mixed. He found that in some areas federal inspection regulations are necessary and that they increase consumer welfare. However, in other areas, regulations simply codify into law actions that producers had previously taken as a matter of course. Additionally, some labeling and product standards reduce consumer choices. Moreover, although he found that, on balance, total eradication of the regulations would not increase social welfare, he also concludes that the unnecessary regulations are those that involve inadequacies detectable by consumers and that over-all welfare would increase if these regulations were removed.

Zoning

Four studies discuss the consequences of zoning. Siegan (1972) studied Houston's system of nonzoning and concludes that the system had made land use more responsive to consumer demand than it generally is with zoning. He compared prices of single-family houses and rent for multi-family dwellings in Houston and zoned areas, principally Dallas. His research indicates that for the period studied, the absence of zoning did not appreciably affect single-family prices, but did result in lower rents than would have been the case under zoning. Siegan believes that the pattern of land use in Houston is probably not appreciably different from what it would have been under zoning.

Sagalyn and Sternlieb (1973) studied certain zoning and building requirements in New Jersey. They conclude that reducing three major zoning requirements (lot size, lot frontage, and living area) would reduce prices considerably and enlarge the effective housing market provided of course that builders made a concomitant reduction in design of the housing offered—an action that they probably would take. Changing two building code specifications (thickness of exterior wall sheeting and size of foundation cinder block) would also lower selling prices, but not to the same degree as would altering zoning policies.

Maser, Riker, and Rosett (1977) analyzed some of the effects of zoning in the urbanized area of Rochester, New York, in order to determine whether zoning significantly modifies outcomes in the urban land market, or whether market forces negate the forces of regulation. They conclude that the amount of control embodied in the zoning they studied appeared to be small and episodic, and that zoning is largely ineffective. From their limited comparisons, they found no significant land price effects attributable to zoning.

As a result of their zoning study in Pittsburgh, Crecine, Davis, and Jackson (1967) conclude that the urban property market is in large measure immune to the externality and neighborhood effect that zoning is supposed to reduce or eliminate. They suggest that the entire practice of zoning and land planning should be reconsidered, for it may be predicated on false or inadequate assumptions. Rueter (1973) studied zoning in Pittsburgh to determine if the expected undesirable external effects of land use upon which the zoning concept is based actually arise in urban property markets. He concludes that many of the restrictions specified in zoning ordinances could be eliminated without any adverse influence on property values.

Pharmaceuticals

Peltzman (1973) evaluated the 1962 Kefauver-Harris amendments to the food and drug laws that required the Food and Drug Administration (FDA) to regulate efficacy of pharmaceuticals (for many years before then, only safety was controlled). Peltzman found that the regulations result in a net loss to society. He estimates the benefit from decreased spending on ineffective drugs to be approximately $100–150 million annually, and the costs from a reduced flow of both drugs and information to consumers (doctors) to be $300 to $400 million, with price increases adding about $50 million. Peltzman claims that the 1962 amendments have increased the cost of entering the drug market, prolonged testing, and resulted in less output and higher prices. He writes that the post-1962 flow of new drugs was less than one-half of the pre-1962 flow, without corresponding benefit in the efficacy of the drugs produced.

Wardell (1974), a clinical pharmacologist, compared the availability and therapeutic quality of new chemical entities introduced by the pharmaceutical companies in the United States and Great Britain between 1962 and 1971. Prior to 1962, regulation was similar in both countries, but after that year, American regulation became much more stringent as a result of the Kefauver-Harris legislation. He found that during the nine-year period that he studied, many more drugs were introduced in Great Britain and that the greater supply was on the whole more beneficial to society. Wardell concludes that it appears the United States has, on balance, lost more than it gained from adopting a more restrictive regulatory approach during the period studied.

Federal regulation has probably doubled the cost of introducing a new pharmaceutical, according to Grabowski, Vernon, and Thomas (1978). They found that regulation stemming from the 1962 amendments was the leading (but not the sole) cause of a sharp decline of new drug introductions into the United States during contemporary years. Their conclusions also are based on comparing output of pharmaceuticals in the United States with that in Great Britain between 1962 and 1971.

Miscellaneous

Other articles do not logically fit into any of the other categories. Joskow (1973) examined state rate-making and risk-classification regulations in the property liability insurance industry, finding that regulations restrict competition and increase prices. In addition, they cause an expansion of capacity beyond the efficient level. Joskow further concludes that the basis for the regulation is faulty. Using as an example California, which since 1947 has employed minimal regulation over the industry, he shows that relatively open competition can be allowed with excellent results. California premiums are lower, and no mass bankruptcies or price wars have occurred. Although supply shortages exist, they are less severe than in other states. The study recommends movement away from rate regulation and cartel pricing to open competition as a means of eliminating prevailing performance problems in the industry.

Cochran (1951) surveyed agricultural price support regulations—those intended to raise the incomes of rural people. He concludes that the regulations have not fulfilled their purpose. Rather, the incomes of only the largest producers have increased significantly, while smaller producers have hardly benefited. The emphasis on price supports to raise rural incomes originated from pressure from commercial agriculture and public confusion over purposes and possible results. Cochran proposes a different program of price supports and advocates more extensive regulation to improve the lot of rural dwellers.

Benham (1972) examined restrictions on advertising in the eyeglass industry. In 1963, the year during which Benham collected his data, approximately three-quarters of the states had some regulation against advertising. Some states prohibited price advertising, while others allowed virtually no information on eye examinations or eyeglasses to be disseminated for commercial purposes. These laws are intended to protect consumers from fraudulent advertising affecting their health and to maintain professional standards among sellers and practitioners.

Benham, who found eyeglass prices to be substantially lower in states that allowed advertising, estimates the restrictions were reflected in prices ranging from 25 to more than 100 percent higher for what seemed to be the same quality product. The author concludes that established optometrists and other professionals within a state benefit most from such restrictions.

Some Conclusions about Regulation

These studies do not, of course, cover all the regulatory agencies, nor do they include all surveys of regulation; accordingly, they are not conclusive on the subject. They do, however, explain why so many economists along every portion of the political spectrum voice criticism of government regulation. Many of the preceding studies were originally published in the *Journal of Law and Economics,* whose editor, economics professor Ronald H. Coase, summarized in 1974 existing research on regulation in this manner:

> [T]here have been more serious studies made of government regulation of industry in the last fifteen years or so, particularly in the United States, than in the whole preceeding period. These studies have been both quantitative and nonquantitative.... The main lesson to be drawn from these studies is clear: they all tend to suggest that the regulation is either ineffective or that when it has a noticeable impact, on balance the effect is bad, so that consumers obtain a worse product or a higher-priced product or both as a result of the regulation. Indeed, this result is found so uniformly as to create a puzzle: one would expect to find, in all these studies, at least some government programs that do more good than harm.[9]

The preceding pages indicate that, as measured by the tools of the economist, regulations very often operate negatively—the disadvantages outweigh the advantages. To be sure, the conclusions arrived at through such analysis can be quite different from the perspective of those who laud regulations for achieving objectives that these people regard as of special value not translatable into numbers. Some environmentalists, for example, reject the economic analysis. They contend that the preservation of natural resources should not be based on numbers and dollars which reflect only a fraction of the values that people hold dear.

Similar approaches can justify regulation of almost any industry or any area, because regulation will achieve certain purposes that are of great importance to some people. Thus, under strict CAB regulation in effect prior to 1976, the commercial airlines were far from disintegrating; air travel in the United States was dependable, comfortable, and convenient, particularly for the affluent who could afford first class or day rates. Some localities were served in spite of low traffic yields. Airline investors and managers did not lie awake at night in fear of competitive invasion—a fact that leads to a certain amount of personal security and tranquillity.

However, regulation cannot be judged by only one variable. Censorship of speech and press likewise accomplishes some good, but it would indeed be folly to evaluate a regulated press by an isolated standard of achievement. Although Mussolini made the trains run on time, he subjected his country to tyranny. Thousands of lives could be saved annually by eliminating automobiles, but not even the most dedicated humanitarians advocate this course. Most of the preceding studies come as close to comprehensive and systematic evaluation as can be expected, given the wide range of values and interests inherent in the analysis.

The existence of a large number of negative studies should be of great concern to those who have to evaluate regulation. While almost every regulation accomplishes some good, a very sustantial portion fails an analysis that weighs the disadvantages against the advantages. The foregoing studies, along with those discussed earlier in this book, reveal that much regulation has resulted in a reduction of economic efficiency, misallocation of resources, and the redistribution of income from consumers to the regulated group. A common finding is that regulation raises prices: first, by restricting the market from competition, and second, by imposing a variety of requirements on producers and sellers that increase costs. Those of average and lesser incomes, those least likely to afford higher prices, are the most adversely affected. This wide consensus should dispel any doubt that the problem lies with regulation itself and not with those who administer it.

The studies effectively disclose the error in the approval by constitutional scholars and historians of the New Deal emphasis on government intervention to solve existing economic problems. The studies demonstrate that the very people who these commentators believe require the regulators' assistance—those at the lower end of the economic spectrum—actually suffer greatly from regulation. Those well-intended government controls struck down by the old, unreconstructed Court would, for the most part, have had a detrimental effect on that portion of the population with whose welfare the commentators say they are most concerned. The scholars are proving the wisdom of the Old Court's guiding principle, that freedom of contract is the rule and restraint the exception. Though the maxim is founded on constitutional interpretation, it applies to economic welfare as well. Once again, the conclusion is warranted that the Old Court's policy of review is, on the basis of the very standards used by its most vehement critics, preferable to the contemporary Supreme Court's abdication.

14　Negative and Affirmative Jurisprudence

The preceding two chapters disclose the difficulties inherent in legislative and administrative endeavors to solve social problems. In contemporary times, judges and others have sought, by expanding the judiciary's role, to fill the gap between what is being done and what they believe should be done by government to enhance the public welfare. People who, in the earlier part of the century, would have condemned the judicial power as undemocratic and autocratic began to view it, in Warren Court years, as a way to maximize social benefits. As we saw in chapter 4, this approach raises questions of legitimacy and authority, for it requires the United States Supreme Court to assume powers not constitutionally granted and to enter areas that properly belong to other branches. Although it is couched in utilitarian terms, this type of judicial activity also presents pragmatic questions about the ability of judges and judicial remedies to solve social and economic problems.

Because this affirmative form of jurisprudence frequently conflicts with the traditional, negative kind, acceptance of the former may diminish the latter and the social benefits accompanying it. Those concerned with preserving economic and property rights have a vital stake in this controversy, for the two approaches treat these interests differently. Judicial utilitarians often subordinate individual interests to notions of the collective good, while under the original conception of the judicial role, the protection of individual liberty is the major goal.

The traditional approach can also be defended as more likely to achieve greater social benefits. We consider these issues in this chapter.

Separating Judicial and Legislative Concerns

When people discussed rights and liberties during the nation's early days, they were concerned with governmental action that might abridge these rights and liberties. In contrast, during contemporary times the word *right* has been used in a far different sense. For example, the Universal Declaration of Human Rights, adopted by the General Assembly of the United Nations in 1948, speaks of the rights to work, to equal pay for equal work, to an adequate standard of living, to rest and leisure, and to education.[1] Lawyers have sought constitutional sanction for rights to housing, education, medical service, clean environment, and "just wants." Rights in this more recent context demand affirmative governmental action to provide goods and services for certain sections of the population, action that traditionally has been considered a function of political decision-making, entirely different from the judicial function of interpretation implemented by veto—of naysaying. In fact, the two views of rights may be in direct conflict, for achieving an affirmative right frequently requires eliminating or diminishing an existing or vested interest.

According to Chief Justice Marshall, "The province of the Court is, solely, to decide on the rights of individuals, not to inquire how the executive, or executive officers, perform duties in which they have a discretion. Questions in their nature political, or which are, by the constitution and laws, submitted to the executive, can never be made in this court."[2] Marshall's observations on executive responsibilities are also applicable to the responsibilities of the legislature, and, for the purposes of this discussion, especially to its fiscal responsibilities.

Regardless of constitutional theory, however, the judicial process enables judges to impose affirmative solutions to social problems. I have already discussed judicially supervised programs, which I have referred to as affirmative jurisprudence. Judges can also impose their social theories on the legislature by striking down existing spending policies, thereby forcing the lawmakers to adopt judicially inspired alternatives. The fact that courts employ the veto in this process does not disguise the affirmative purpose and outcome. Judicial endeavors to direct legislative and administrative spending are another manifestation of affirmative jurisprudence.

It has been said that rights are not static and that "part of our current problem is to address the idea of right to our current needs." The author of this statement continues:

> The unrestrained exploitation of our resources and the debasement of the environment require a recognition that all citizens together have a natural right to enjoy their common resources and environment, a right more compelling than the freedom once claimed in the name of laissez-faire to plunder resources, pollute the air, and impair the amenities of living.[3]

Throughout our nation's history, comparable pleas have been made for government prohibition and regulation. Prior to the ratification of the Constitution, state governments passed statutes retroactively limiting creditors' collection of obligations that they had contracted for under previously existing law. Proponents of such laws claimed that they were reprieving debtors for humanitarian reasons and to protect the social order; the state, it was explained, would be undermined if people lost their possessions because of economic conditions over which they had no control. Repugnance toward and fear of such retroactive laws encouraged the formation of the federal union and a constitutional system intended in part to secure the interests of creditors and contracting parties and thereby to maintain social stability. In more recent times, government found that interning people of Japanese ancestry was necessary in the belief that the national security in wartime is more important than are the civil rights of a certain group. The decision upholding this action as constitutionally justifiable[4] has been subject to great criticism.

Perhaps, in our time, environmental issues do raise uniquely important questions. However, the theory of our constitutional system is that no public need or desire is important enough to derogate concern for those who claim to be aggrieved by the state's action. The majority's will may not be final lest it destroy the liberties of those who oppose it.

The Federal Constitution was created not to supervise relations between private individuals, but rather to embody a social compact that prevents government from invading the area of personal autonomy. Nearly all of the constitutional provisions guaranteeing liberties secure the individual and corporation only from the federal or state government. The High Court has accordingly created the doctrine of state action which requires that persons asserting that their rights have been violated show that the harm complained of is the result of government action, except in those instances when private conduct is officially delegated or mandated or is otherwise tantamount to government action. The doctrine operates as a restraint on judicial review, confining it to state-related controversies and precluding the judiciary from imposing constitutional requirements on the vast array of private relationships. It is a bar to judicial intrusion on the powers of other branches, and therefore to the exercise of affirmative jurisprudence.

A Comparison of the Warren and Burger Courts

Although clearly not immune to legislative proclivities, the Burger Court has avoided certain of the Warren Court's failings in this area.[5] The different perspectives are epitomized by two opinions already discussed briefly: *Shapiro v. Thompson,*[6] decided by the Warren Court, and *San Antonio Independent School District v. Rodriguez,*[7] decided by the Burger Court. Plaintiffs in both cases contended that fundamental rights were at issue, requiring the Court to apply a strict scrutiny standard to determine whether existing classifications complied with the equal protection clause. The objective was to achieve a ruling on economic equality by way of asserting a denial of a fundamental right. *Shapiro* concerned Connecticut, Pennsylvania, and District of Columbia statutes that denied welfare assistance to new arrivals in the jurisdiction who had resided there for less than one year prior to their initial application for assistance. In holding the law unconstitutional, Justice Brennan reasoned in this manner: first, the law inhibited those who receive welfare assistance in one state from moving to any state having such a residency requirement. Second, the requirement consequently curtailed the right to travel of the person so affected. Third, the right to travel is a fundamental right, and therefore classifications impacting it must meet the strict scrutiny–compelling interest standard. Fourth, under this standard, the differentiation for welfare purposes between residents and nonresidents fails as a violation of equal protection. Brennan explained that a state may reduce or even eliminate expenditures for welfare but that once it provides such benefits, it may not discriminate between residents and nonresidents unless such a course is necessary to achieve a compelling state interest.

This approach enabled the Supreme Court to enter the decision-making process relating to the administration of welfare programs, which are supported by tax revenues. The result was that the Court required a state to fund the right to travel. The benefits to the disadvantaged are dubious; because the extent to which the public is prepared to finance welfare is limited, the monies for new residents may be taken from those otherwise designated for established residents. Thus people previously entitled to welfare assistance may be subsidizing this right to travel. Income redistribution between richer and poorer persons would occur only if new taxes were imposed to pay for assisting new residents, in which event the Court would be entering further into local taxing and spending decisions.

Subsequently, in *Dandridge v. Williams*,[8] the Supreme Court recognized the perils of such affirmative jurisprudence when it sustained a Maryland regulation mandating a monthly welfare limit of $250.00 for each family, regardless of the family's size or need. Justice Stewart explained for the majority:

> [T]he intractable economic, social, and even philosophical problems presented by public welfare assistance programs are not the business of this Court. . . . [T]he Constitution does not empower this Court to second-guess state officials charged with the difficult responsibility of allocating limited public welfare funds among the myriad of potential recipients.[9]

Shapiro marks the culmination of an affirmative approach intended to reduce economic disadvantage. Clearly the Burger Court has receded from such use of judicial review. There has been, writers say, a "retreat from activism." *Dandridge* signaled a departure from the promised land of *Shapiro* that had held out hope against any classification denying needed access to "food, shelter and other necessities of life."[10] According to one commentator, "[j]ust as *Nebbia v. New York* ended the stewardship of substantive due process in the reign of laissez-faire economics, *Dandridge* halted equal protection's expanding role as the rationalizing legal premise of Roosevelt liberalism."[11]

Rodriguez contains the Burger Court's most exhaustive statement on affirmative jurisprudence. This suit attacked as violative of equal protection the Texas system of financing public education under which a considerable disparity exists in the amount of money collected for public education in various areas of the state. Districts with high assessed property valuations had more funds available for schooling than those having low assessed valuations. In Texas for the period involved in the litigation, 50 percent of school funding came from the state, 40 percent from local revenues, and 10 percent from federal sources. For the year in question, the district in which the plaintiffs resided had $356.00 to spend on educating each student, while the most affluent district in their city had $594.00. Finding that education is a fundamental interest and wealth a suspect classification, the lower federal court held that the Texas system would be sustained only if the state could show that it was premised on some compelling state interest. The lower court could find neither a compelling nor even a reasonable ground for the disparity.[12]

In reversing, the Supreme Court (5–4), per Justice Powell, said that no deprivation had occurred that would cause it to intrude into the field of state taxation, in which the Court has traditionally deferred to state legislatures. It rejected both bases of the lower court decision.

Powell wrote that the Court had never previously held that wealth discrimination was a suspect classification. Nor did the case concern the infringement of a right since government had not denied or interfered with the plaintiffs' opportunity to acquire an education. Instead, the suit involved the plaintiffs' desire for additional funding for a service already offered by the state. Failure on the part of the state to extend it as the plaintiff demanded did not deny nor dilute it. "[W]e have never presumed to possess either the ability or the authority to guarantee to the citizenry the most *effective* speech or the most *informed* electoral choice.... [These] are not values to be implemented by judicial intrusion into otherwise legitimate state activities."[13]

According to the majority, the facts presented matters suitable for decision by the local political process instead of by the judiciary. Powell stated that the Court lacks both the expertise and the familiarity with local problems so necessary to the raising and disposing of public revenue. In addition it has limited knowledge about the relationship between public financing and the proper goals of education—goals about which even experts dispute. Further, the federal-state relationship demands the Court exercise utmost caution before abrogating education financing systems used in almost every state.

Powell observed that no proof was offered at the trial discrediting or refuting the state's assertion that it was providing an adequate education for the children of all its residents. However, he did not close the door completely on judicial involvement in this area. He suggested that a far more compelling set of circumstances for judicial intervention would be presented by a public system that charged tuition, thereby foreclosing the opportunities for children of indigents to obtain an education. Presumably this deprivation would be sufficiently arbitrary to enable the law to be invalidated without the need for considering education as a fundamental liberty or poverty as a suspect classification.

Rodriguez denies *Shapiro*'s implication that the United States Supreme Court has certain affirmative responsibilities for increasing the material welfare of the poor. In *Maher v. Roe*,[14] discussed in chapter 9, the Court affirmed the rationale of *Rodriguez* by holding that the Constitution does not require public funding for abortions. A decision requiring the funding of nontherapeutic abortions would also inject the Supreme Court into the policy question of how public welfare monies should be spent. Many considerations apply in the situation that require its resolution by the bodies with taxing and spending responsibilities. If the state pays for such surgery, less will be available from the funds the public is willing to allocate for welfare needs—which means that some recipients will be contributing to the welfare of others. Some argue that in the long run, the birth of unwanted children will be more costly to the state; also that unwanted children will not have the chance to develop their talents and may be the butt of child abuse. Others contend that private charities may help the mother, that the adoption market may alleviate the problem of unwanted children, and that abortions may preclude the birth of very gifted individuals (an "Einstein") capable of enhancing the lives and well-being of others. Of course, the public in its wisdom may be willing to accept additional costs stemming from certain policies (especially when moral issues are involved). Efficient allocation of monies is hardly a responsibility of the judiciary. Adding to the complexity of the problem is the fact that the economic discrimination argument raised in *Maher* cuts both ways. Opponents of funding point out that the state's policy favors the unborn children of the poor. The situation presented by *Maher* is another example of welfare spending allocations that the court in *Dandridge* referred to as judicially intractable.

Had *Rodriguez* and *Maher* been decided differently, any societal structure with serious wealth inequalities would have been threatened. At some point the Court would have had to decide that a person does not have a fundamental right to food, clothing, medicine, housing, legal assistance, or other "just wants."[15] If it did not in time so hold, the Court would have imposed a guaranteed annual income that would have been supplied from the pockets of people not represented in the making of these decisions.

"No taxation without representation" is an old and honored American adage. Our Constitution observes the principle so literally that it requires all bills for raising revenue to originate in the House of Representatives. This principle was applicable to the reign of King George III and is similarly relevant to rule by small groups appointed to lifetime positions, the monetary consequences of whose decisions can be quite high. "[I]t is estimated that federal court decisions striking down various state restrictions on welfare payments, like residency requirements, made an additional 100,000 people eligible for assistance."[16]

When the federal judiciary requires the national government to spend money, it acts contrary to the constitutional provision that "No Money shall be drawn from the Treasury, but in Consequence of Appropriations made by Law" (Art. I, Sec. 9, cl. 7). Only the Congress can make appropriations, and a judiciary which required spending by the federal government would be usurping this power. While no such provision exists with respect to the states, the implication of the provision is clear. The judiciary does not have the appropriation power and should not use the veto as a means to exercise it.

In a society that considers private incentives a primary means to economic progress, affirmative jurisprudence creates serious pragmatic problems. Despite the fact that he is a proponent of an affirmative "just wants" role for the courts, Professor Michelman is nevertheless willing to accept economic inequalities when their elimination would prove counterproductive to the interests of the disadvantaged and "insofar as they were necessary to incentives and market allocations thought to make the economy more efficient and productive than it could otherwise be."[17] Although such a caveat should be unnecessary, its repetition should make proponents of affirmative jurisprudence exceedingly wary of abandoning the traditional judicial function in pursuit of complex and ambiguous social objectives. The experience of recent decades provides ample evidence of the frequency with which welfare laws are counterproductive. Courts operating on a case-by-case basis are not in a position to overcome the enormous difficulties inherent in this kind of economic determination.

Moreover, judges do not have the same options as legislators, who may choose among a great number of competing interests and values. Judges do not have the option of deciding, for example, how much taxes should be collected and how much should be spent; they cannot determine the amount of funds that should be designated for welfare or any other purpose, and how funds within the welfare or other budgets should be allocated among competing interests. Nor can it be maintained that the courts are better situated to solve social problems than politically dominated legislatures, since solutions in these areas usually involve ideology and personal predilections.

Pragmatic Benefits of Negative Jurisprudence

The courts' traditional role in protecting individual rights remains the most promising judicial means of reducing the burdens of economic

312 Safeguarding Economic Liberties

inequality. The recent record of the New Jersey Supreme Court in zoning litigation provides strong support for this position. Since 1970, the courts of that state have been undoing the results of a prior judicial policy, long in effect, that allowed municipalities mostly free rein in zoning matters.

In 1975 the New Jersey Supreme Court issued a widely noted decision in a case filed by the NAACP and others against the Township of Mount Laurel.[18] This opinion requires that each developing community with sizable vacant areas zone enough land for moderate- and low-income housing so as to accommodate its fair share of the number of such units needed within a region. This was affirmative jurisprudence, intended to integrate the affluent suburbs, both economically and racially. The Court was in effect finding a right to housing under the state constitution's due process and equal protection clauses.

The *Mount Laurel* decision met considerable hostility from the suburban populace and rejoicing from most of those who wrote about it. A large number of commentaries on the case appeared in professional journals, and the vast majority appeared to favor the decision. The suburbs would no longer be enclaves of the rich; instead they would have to accept all people, regardless of their wealth or race. A new day had dawned.

Despite all the hullabaloo, the *Mount Laurel* decision was a failure. Its direct mandate resulted in very little new housing for its intended beneficiaries. The explanation is that low- and moderate-income housing requires government subsidies and that relatively meager federal and state funds are available for this purpose. Although the court could compel land to be zoned for lower income housing, it had neither the power nor the funds to cause the housing to be built.

The New Jersey court recognized the problem, and in 1977, a 4–3 majority in *Oakwood at Madison, Inc. v. Township of Madison*[19] substantially modified the *Mount Laurel* ruling. The court again deplored zoning practices that excluded poorer people from the suburbs, but this time it followed largely the negative route of striking down zoning restrictions through which exclusion of lower cost housing was accomplished. Without mentioning property or economic rights of owners or developers, the court, again interpreting the state constitution, overturned a variety of zoning regulations that impeded the production of lower cost housing. The court's concern was directed at governmental practices excluding lower income buyers and renters from the suburban housing market. The decision was consumer and not producer in orientation, but in major respects the result would have differed little had its basis been the substantive due process rights of owners and developers.

In both *Mount Laurel* and *Oakwood at Madison,* the New Jersey court dealt with the entire zoning ordinances of the municipalities involved, and its ruling in each instance determined the provisions required for such ordinances to be sustained. It ruled in the later case that developing municipalities may not utilize zoning to prevent the construction of significant amounts of "least-cost housing"—that is, the lowest cost conventional housing that could be erected consistent with reasonable standards of health and safety. The decision leaves intact zoning powers relating to commercial, industrial, and luxury residential development, except as these are used to obstruct the construction of least-cost housing. The court acknowledged the inadequacy of the *Mount Laurel* fair-share formula. Rejecting such a quota approach, the majority declared:

> [A]ttention . . . to the *substance* of a zoning ordinance under challenge and to *bona fide* efforts toward the elimination or minimization of undue cost-generating requirements . . . represents the best promise for adequate productiveness without resort to formulaic estimates of specific unit "fair shares" of lower cost housing by any of the complex and controversial allocation "models" now coming into vogue.[20]

To the objection that even in areas classified for least-cost housing, industry cannot build inexpensively enough for low- and moderate-income families, the court replied that these families would benefit indirectly through the filtering process (frequently but not fairly referred to as "trickle down") started by the new conventional construction that the decision would encourage. The opinion cites a study showing that when a thousand new units are constructed, a succession of about thirty-five hundred moves occurs as existing units are vacated because of the availability of the new housing. Over one-third of these moves are made by people in low- and moderate-income brackets who will probably move to improved housing. Occupants of slums and deteriorating housing will have greater opportunity to move to more desirable areas.[21] The court thus recognized the benefits to the less affluent resulting from removal of legal restraints on housing production.

The *Mount Laurel* decision removes the presumption of validity for zoning ordinances not meeting the standards required by the court and places the burden of proving the ordinance's constitutionality in these instances on the locality. *Oakwood at Madison* retains this procedure.

Other portions of the majority opinion in the latter case veto unreasonable restraints upon the exercise of economic liberties (as phrased in terminology appropriate to "exclusionary" zoning):

1. The majority stated that the exactions municipalities required from developers may be unreasonable when they "exert an exclusionary influence." They found that Madison Township had zoned certain tracts in such a manner that the developers would have to spend large sums to install sewer and water facilities and build and improve roads. The municipality could render such exactions nondiscriminatory either by requiring proportional donation from other property owners or by relocating the less restrictive zoning to tracts nearer to utility hookups.

2. The court said that another cost-generating requirement is the length of the subdivision approval process. Delays can result in high carrying charges and have the potential for reducing the project's feasibility. Madison had added to its approval process a third "informal, preliminary application stage," which required an additional forty days for completion. Finding that this stage generated undue delay and that it was not required under New Jersey statutes, the court ordered its elimination.

3. The township advanced ecological and environmental considerations to justify large-lot zoning. The court replied that despite these considerations the locality had sufficient vacant land to provide for adequate amounts of least-cost housing. The court reiterated that while such factors and problems were always to be given consideration in zoning, "the danger and impact must be substantial and very real (the construction of every building or the improvement of every plot has some environmental impact)—not simply a makeweight to support exclusionary housing measures or preclude growth."[22]

Judged by a literal standard of negative jurisprudence, *Oakwood at Madison* is not an entirely satisfactory decision. Although the court refused to mandate that developing municipalities affirmatively provide zoning for additional low-income housing, it did impose supervision over Madison by ordering it to submit a revised zoning ordinance to the trial court within ninety days that complied with the requirements set forth in the opinion. The court also ordered the rezoning of plaintiff's 200 acres for a 2400-unit multi-family project. Otherwise, said the opinion, the plaintiff, who had spent six years in the litigation and prevailed in two trials and the appeal, might win only a pyrrhic victory. The township, as has occurred elsewhere, might rezone the property to an unacceptable classification, entailing still more litigation.

But these affirmative aspects do not disturb the basically negative thrust of the New Jersey decision. The *Oakwood at Madison* decision presents a realistic hope that many more people of moderate means will have better housing. Instead of establishing affirmative quotas, it removes regulatory inhibitions on production and supply of shelter. The opinion supports the methods through which the private market traditionally has provided material betterment for the masses. Ironically, *Oakwood at Madison* applies the principles of economic due process which the Old Court, in *Village of Euclid v. Ambler Realty Co.*,[23] did not.

Some Conclusions about the Judiciary's Responsibility

In *Shapiro,* the Court achieved income redistribution, but we cannot be certain about the source of the money; it may have come from other welfare recipients, other state programs, increased taxes, or perhaps some combination of these. The conventional assumption that income redistribution involves a transfer from those who have too much to those who have too little probably was not realized. Existing welfare recipients, with little, if anything to spare, may be the major contributors. Consequently what may be the leading case of judicially sponsored income redistribution may well have been a failure in this respect. While this experience does not condemn all such efforts, the lesson of the judiciary's limitations in pursuing this policy is apparent.

The province of the judiciary is not to undertake wealth redistribution or to make some people wealthier than others; its role is limited to ensuring that when the legislature engages in such tasks, it does not do so oppressively at the expense of individual liberties. The Framers did not desire, and the Constitution does not warrant, that the Supreme Court legislate. The Court has a role in progress, equality, and redistribution, but it is one that is tied to individual achievement, initiative, and creativity. As the protector of individual liberties, the Court assures society that private people, as the major source of progress, will continue, individually or in concert with others, to apply themselves to undertakings of their own choice. The greatest threat to progress and well-being comes when legislators eliminate the opportunity for individual advancement.

Negative and positive constitutional interpretations cannot coexist; when the courts attempt affirmative jurisprudence, they necessarily have to abandon their obligation to defend existing material rights. Beginning with some of the earliest decisions in the land, judges have acknowledged their responsibility to prevent the legislature from taking from *A* to give to *B*.[24] They have predicated this authority on the natural law, the contracts clause, due process, and of course the Fifth Amendment's taking clause. Using such authority, the courts must assume a protective role for owners and entrepreneurs in order to ensure that their rights are not violated. Affirmative jurisprudence, on the other hand, requires the judiciary to assume a reverse role at the expense of ownership. The fact that the transfer relates to personal and not real property is unimportant. Whether the property is represented by a house or by funds in the bank after it is sold, the burden on the owner is the same.

Commentators who urge the courts to provide more monetary benefits to the poor should recognize that these funds have to be obtained from somewhere and that the consequences of the transfer cannot be ignored. Taxpayers already pay substantial portions of their earnings to government, at great risk to the incentive policies of our society. Even when they are the result of extensive legislative deliberations, programs for economic redistribution and reform have been far from universally successful. The American system is replete with social programs that do not work, that harm productive members of society, and that limit the productivity and efficiency of the economy upon which the solution to social problems ultimately depends. Income redistribution is utter folly if the outcome is that fewer poor people are better off.

In the first chapter of this book, I explained that the meanings given popular or technical concepts change over time. The ensuing chapters have presented numerous illustrations of this assertion, and constitutional law texts provide many more. This book is concerned with liberties that have undergone great change in meaning over the years. The Constitution neither defines the word *liberty* nor makes plain which and to what extent liberties are protected by various provisions that I have discussed (the due process, ex post facto, and obligation of contracts clauses). Over the years judges have supplied definitions. Courts of different periods have employed disparate meanings, and commentators have been able to chart American constitutional law on the basis of a given era's perspectives, tendencies, approaches, and attitudes.[25] Each Supreme Court is said to reflect the enlightenment of its day.

But what makes nine lawyers the best interpreters of the current wisdom? If this be the criterion, why not let the legislature be the final authority on the fundamental law, as it is in some other countries with constitutions? An excellent argument can be made that with all its faults, the legislature better reflects contemporary thoughts, feelings, and beliefs. Some might reply that people appointed to the High Court have more training, background, and ability to comprehend and apply the law than does the average legislator. Such an argument implies that people having these abilities make wiser or better interpreters of the human situation. However, it does not take into account the enormous difference in perspective that exists among highly talented people. The presence or absence of wisdom and understanding does not explain the difference in outlook separating Frankfurter and Harlan on the one side from Black and Douglas on the other. The explanation may lie more in the irrational processes of the human mind that have much to do with personal likes, choices, and preferences. If decision-making draws on the irrational portions of the human personality, the reputed advantages of judges over legislators erodes. I am not aware that smart people possess better or stronger psyches.

Separation of power between judicial and legislative branches is not intended to result in a contest over which one better reflects the conceptual approaches of the day. The difference between the two branches is fundamental; it lies in function. The legislature is the protector of the governor and the judiciary of the governee. The legislature equates the public interest with the creation of laws; the judiciary, with the preservation of liberty. Each must look to its constituency in the exercise of its responsibility. However, finality under our system must be with the branch of government charged with safeguarding liberty. Thus, as Francis Lieber perceived the constitutional perspective of his day, everything in favor of the authority of government is to be closely construed, while everything that pertains to the security of the individual is to be interpreted broadly. This practice is essential because by its nature public power increases while the individual eternally requires protection.[26]

15   Conclusion: Reinterpreting the Due Process Clauses

    The most persuasive argument favoring the current Supreme Court policy that rejects judicial review of governmental restraints on economic activity is simply that it exists and is long established and therefore should not be abandoned without strong, compelling reasons. As Robert McCloskey has observed, "The American Constitution is not merely the document of 1789; it also comprises the judgments attached to it by subsequent generations."[1] The material presented in this book that advocates a revised policy meets this rigorous standard for changing judicial course. This concluding chapter will summarize the preceding information and arguments, and will provide additional support for the change in judicial position that is proposed here.

    Reversing current policy is justified for five reasons.

    1. *Judicial review of social and economic legislation is firmly rooted in the Constitution.* A major objective of the Constitution's Framers was protecting and preserving the right of property. The Framers expected the federal judiciary to exercise judicial review insofar as civil liberties were concerned, primarily to secure property and other economic interests. They believed that the natural law was the highest legal authority, except as modified in the Constitution, and that it safeguarded the prerogatives of ownership. Consistent with this perspective, the Marshall Court protected property rights even without explicit

constitutional authority, holding invalid as contrary to natural principles abridgements of vested property interests.

To be sure, we find no mention of the property right in the text of the original Constitution; but the reason seems to be that the Framers expected that the ex post facto clauses would secure this right. The evidence is persuasive that *Calder v. Bull* was incorrect in restricting the applicability of these clauses to retroactive criminal laws. Had these provisions not been so confined, they would have applied to retroactive restraints on the use, enjoyment, and disposition of property. The national and state governments would have been curtailed in their powers to adopt measures regulating business and industry. The states' power over economic activity would have been even more circumscribed if Chief Justice Marshall's broad interpretation of the obligation of contracts clause had prevailed in *Ogden v. Saunders*. Similar concerns may also have motivated the Framers of the Fourteenth Amendment as the four dissenting Justices in the *Slaughter-House Cases* maintained. The decisions in *Calder, Ogden,* and the *Slaughter-House Cases* were subsequently *sub silentio* reversed through interpretation of the Fourteenth Amendment's due process clause.

Accordingly, the Framers' intentions, the rulings of the Marshall Court implementing them, the strong probability of error in one or more of the three mentioned decisions, the construction to that effect given for a lengthy period to the due process clauses, all provide powerful constitutional support for judicial review of economic and social regulation. Whatever doubts remain about this issue should give way before the judicial purpose of providing a forum for persons aggrieved by government and of serving as a check on the other branches.

2. *The judiciary has no authority to eliminate constitutional protection for economic liberties.* Individual liberties can be evaluated from the perspective both of the individual and of the society. Because liberties are personal matters, no one can or should determine what is vital or important to another. However, organized society cannot accept the pursuit of all interests at all times; therefore, it must establish priorities and rules governing them. The test of a just society is the ability to resolve this issue in the most logical, reasonable, and comfortable manner possible. Because of the subjectivity involved, the solution can be neither too precise nor always consistent, but at least it should be the product of our most profound wisdom, arrived at through those state systems authorized for and suited to this purpose.

Establishing the priority of liberties is a political judgment. Not being provided for in the Constitution, it is beyond the authority of the High Court. Those who framed and those who ratified the Constitution never intended to grant political authority to this branch of government. Reflecting the predominant sentiments of his day, Hamilton considered the judicial review power to be limited to the negative veto for the judiciary would "have neither FORCE nor WILL but merely judgment."[2] The judicial branch would have no influence over either the sword or the purse, and no direction either of the strength or of the wealth of the society.[3] The courts of justice, declared Hamilton, were to be no more than the bulwarks of a limited Constitution against legislative encroachments.[4] The judicial purpose was to temper, not create, laws.

Judicial withdrawal from the protection of economic activity violates Article III, which provides that the "judicial power shall extend to all cases in law and equity, arising under this Constitution." Although Justices cannot be expected to treat every interest and concern the same, excising from constitutional protection liberties that affect substantial numbers of people is a judgment exceeding the bounds of discretion inherent in judicial decision-making. The judiciary lacks legitimacy to discriminate against certain liberties.

3. *Because much welfare and regulatory legislation has proved economically harmful, judicial review of such legislation serves the pragmatic interests of society.* During the substantive due process years opposition to judicial review came largely from the left side of the political spectrum. These critics demanded social reforms and income redistributions, which could be effected only by Congress and the state legislatures. They viewed the judiciary as a serious impediment to such ends. What the reformers apparently did not comprehend was that while judicial review would annul some liberal measures, it would also dispose of legislation favorable to the rich and special-interest groups. Although legislatures pass statutes intended to help the disadvantaged, they also impose regulations that serve the wealthy and small special interest groups at the expense of the poor.

Modern understanding of the regulatory processes reveals that many of the most controversial opinions of the Supreme Court during the substantive due process period were well founded in economic theory. A substantial number of economists would now accept the majority opinions in *Lochner, Adkins,* and *New State Ice,* and the dissenting opinion in *Nebbia,* as beneficial to the more disadvantaged members of society.

In recent years, studies of economic and social regulation show that very frequently the detriments outweigh the benefits. Both federal and state regulation have often resulted in a reduction of economic efficiency, a misallocation of resources, and the distribution of income from consumers to the regulated group. Ironically, the people repeatedly harmed by regulation are those at the lower end of the economic spectrum, the ones whose interests the regulatory policies were supposedly designed to safeguard. Therefore, there is little pragmatic basis for denying the Framers' intentions to secure property and economic liberties by restraining governmental authority.

4. *Because of its limitations and infirmities, the legislature should not be the final authority in socioeconomic matters.* A strong case can be made that on many issues Congress and state legislatures do not reflect the views of their constituents. The evidence is similarly persuasive that numerous critical provisions of statutes do not represent or are contrary to majoritarian will. These problems of legitimacy are compounded by problems of competency. Many legislators do not have the knowledge, understanding, incentive, or time to create efficient and effective statutes that will not unnecessarily deprive people of their liberties. Even when legislators do have the requisite qualifications, their effectiveness is limited by the need for compromise and for placating politically important constituents.

Of particular concern is the influence that special-interest groups have on the legislative process. Small groups seeking material or ideological favors have proved to be extremely convincing in the legislative councils. Although large numbers of citizens may oppose such legislation, individually they lack the incentive and dedication to organize and lobby. This political imbalance results in the passage of laws that are disadvantageous to the general public and that may be particularly harmful to some individuals.

These limitations and infirmities compromise the credibility of the legislature as the representative of the political majority and therefore its entitlement to final authority over legislation. The legitimacy of imposing restraints on the public diminishes as the legislative role and purpose become less credible. Therefore, the need for the judiciary to safeguard liberties of those affected by legislation increases.

5. *The policy of judicial withdrawal from review of socioeconomic legislation is not coherent or principled.* Despite the Justices' insistence that the Court will not intervene in economic and social matters, such intervention frequently occurs. However, form reigns over substance. Thus, advertising by pharmacists, lawyers, and real estate brokers, and the sale of contraceptives to minors are secured, but the production and distribution of most goods and services are not.

Municipalities are prohibited from banning "For Sale" and "Sold" signs, but may impose much more stringent zoning controls on real estate development. Economic competition is extolled in decisions protecting advertising under the First Amendment, but ignored when challenges are made to laws severely restraining competition. Similarly, the right to work is judicially relevant when equal protection claims are asserted, but not in the context of regulation which denies it.

The economic or social importance of an activity is not decisive; what counts is whether a majority of our high court is willing to fit it within a protected constitutional category. Economic legislation is not overturned according to how arbitrary, perverse, or senseless it is. Adding to the confusion is the Court's willingness to engage in extensive review to provide procedural and some substantive safeguards for the "new property" created by government largess. As these illustrations indicate, the area of judicial abdication in economic matters has grown smaller over the years and now stands out as an aberrant (although very important) exception to the Court's role in safeguarding liberties.

Expanding the Scope of Review in Social and Economic Matters

In matters affecting the people's freedoms, the scope of judicial review should be defined by its general goal of protecting and preserving liberty. A foremost principle for a society which has limited its government in order to maximize freedom is that no one should be needlessly deprived of liberty. Thus, a law that has no benefit for society yet restrains human action has no legitimate purpose or utility. The same holds true for a law that impedes individual choice much more than necessary to achieve the legislative objective. Nor should one be restrained to accomplish an illegitimate goal.

The principle under discussion is fundamental to English and American jurisprudence. For Locke and Blackstone, laws imposing excessive restraint were arbitrary and oppressive. Referring to civil liberty, the latter wrote:

> [Civil liberty] is no other than natural liberty so far restrained by human laws (and no farther) as is necessary and expedient for the general advantage of the public. Hence we may collect that the law, which restrains a man from doing mischief to his fellow citizens, though it diminishes the natural, increases the civil liberty of mankind: but every wanton and causeless restraint of the will of the subject, whether practised by a monarch, a nobility, or a popular

assembly, is a degree of tyranny. Nay, that even laws themselves, whether made with or without our consent, if they regulate and constrain our conduct in matters of mere indifference, without any good end in view, are laws destructive of liberty.... [T]hat constitution or frame of government, that system of laws, is alone calculated to maintain civil liberty, which leaves the subject entire master of his own conduct, except in those points wherein the public good requires some direction or restraint.[5]

In constitutional adjudication, Blackstone's exposition takes the form of tests to determine whether the legislative means substantially achieves the legislative ends; whether the means and ends are legitimate; and whether when restraint is necessary, the one utilized is the least onerous to liberty. Thus, Chief Justice Marshall declared that for legislation to be constitutional, the end has to be legitimate, and the means appropriate and plainly adopted to that end.[6] Both substantive due process and the clear and present danger test required inquiry along these lines. Similarly, as we saw in chapter 9, the contemporary Court will not countenance measures limiting the exercise of fundamental liberties that cannot be vindicated under a rigorous application of these standards.

The foregoing tests are appropriate and suitable for determining the constitutionality of social and economic legislation. In a 1972 article, Professor Gerald Gunther proposed to raise the level of minimum review under equal protection adjudication by requiring a determination that the legislative means substantially further the legislative ends.[7] He would have the Court assess the means in terms of legislative purposes that have a substantial basis in actuality, not merely in conjecture. Such review would occupy a position subordinate to strict review, which would continue to be reserved for suspect classifications and fundamental rights. It would be applicable to social and economic regulatory legislation, except for the "intractable" variety that involves fiscal policies of government.

Gunther prefers to apply the equal protection rather than the due process clause, in part because he believes economic due process remains unacceptable to the legal community. This position, however, raises some conceptual difficulties. Due process has a much firmer constitutional basis for these purposes than does equal protection, whose scope was not intended to go beyond race relations. Gunther's approach in this respect might inject into the required analysis notions of a vague and undefined equality that hover around equal protection and that are inconsistent with emphasizing the preservation of individual and corporate liberty. Application of the same standard under due process would more clearly differentiate between the interest of the state and that of the person.

Subsequently in *Craig v. Boren* (1976),[8] Justice Brennan in a plurality opinion held that to withstand an equal protection challenge "classifications by gender must serve important governmental objectives and must be substantially related to the achievement of those objectives."[9] Brennan's standard requires scrutiny of the ends as well as the means, whereas Gunther is concerned only with the means. To be fully effective, a means-ends test must be accompanied by a restraint on impermissible ends as well, since almost every statute does accomplish some goal. The model I advocate would add an additional component to Brennan's test: a less-drastic-alternative analysis. It would apply with this modification under the due process clauses to the broad area of legislation as contemplated by Gunther.

The due process review herein proposed would be less exacting than strict scrutiny. Always to subject the legislature's will to an extreme standard of justification might eliminate it as a viable branch of government. Nor is it likely, in the absence of constitutional direction to this effect, that the American people would accept virtual legislative abandonment of social and economic remedies. As envisioned here, due process scrutiny would apply generally to legislation and regulation except for the intractable variety, and would borrow heavily from economic due process and fundamental liberties jurisprudence. In suits challenging the validity of restraints, the government would have the burden of persuading a court utilizing an intermediate standard of scrutiny, first, that the legislation serves important governmental objectives; second, that the restraint imposed by government is substantially related to achievement of these objectives, that is, as Brennan explained, the fit between means and ends must be close; and third, that a similar result cannot be achieved by a less drastic means.

The important governmental objectives requirement incorporates the principle that laws must serve legitimate purposes. Thus, a law prohibiting the exercise of a fundamental liberty is illegal unless it is necessary to achieve a compelling state interest. For the reasons previously advanced in this book, I propose that a statute or ordinance should not be deemed valid if, in the absence of justification by the government under an intermediate standard of judicial scrutiny, it *(a)* denies an owner of the use and disposition of property without just compensation,[10] or *(b)* denies an individual or corporation freedom to engage in an occupation, trade, profession, or business of one's or its choosing, or *(c)* denies an individual or corporation freedom of contract to produce and distribute goods and services.

In its review, the Court should strive for a realistic evaluation of the challenged enactment to determine the legislative purpose.[11] This requires delving beyond the stated purposes and post hoc rationalizations into the history of and political circumstances attending the enactment to ascertain what the lawmakers sought to achieve. Determining legislators' motivations may sometimes present very difficult problems, but it constitutes considerable improvement over the judiciary concocting explanations (as perhaps in *Dukes*).

The burden of proof in these cases should be borne by the government. At present, in suits concerning "taking" and other economic regulatory controversies, this burden rests with the private party. Our constitutional system presumes substantial freedom to engage in the material pursuits, and this presumption is entitled to no less recognition in the courtroom. When government proscribes these liberties, it has an obligation and responsibility to prove justification for the restraint. The presumption that the state is correct in curtailing people's activities can only be accepted in societies where restraint is normal—those which, unlike ours, equate government direction and control with the public interest.

The preceding observations are taken for granted in our criminal as well as fundamental liberties jurisprudence. It is also accepted that in interstate commerce cases, the state bear the burden of proof. Demanding that the aggrieved party assume this obligation operates, as Justice Brennan explained in *Speiser*, to limit freedom. Such a rule, Justice McReynolds pointed out in *Nebbia*, makes it, as a practical matter, quite difficult and at times impossible for the individual to obtain judicial vindication.[12]

The standards herein proposed for determining validity of economic restraints require the exercise of considerable judicial discretion. This raises obvious questions. As Justice Rehnquist asked in his *Boren* dissent, how is this Court to determine what legislative objectives are important and whether a law is or is not substantially related to the achievement of such objectives? Much of this book is devoted to explaining the importance of securing economic liberties—so that further discussion is not required here. With respect to the second query, Rehnquist and other commentators have described the complex and knotty problems involved in means-ends tests.[13] However, the Justice himself is not prepared to dispense with them. In a concurring opinion in a 1979 freedom of press case, Rehnquist stated that a means-ends analysis is appropriate when expression is involved. The challenged law in that case prohibited newspapers but not the electronic media from disclosing the names of juvenile offenders. He concluded that the law "largely fails to achieve its purposes" to provide anonymity for juveniles since radio and TV were not barred from disclosure.[14]

Thus, for the Justice, the test itself is not objectionable. Like many constitutional concepts, means-ends analysis can be a complex and not very precise or always satisfying undertaking. Nevertheless, Rehnquist and likely most judges and lawyers are willing to employ it to protect certain liberties.

Nor is it used solely for high and intermediate rights. Often applying economic analysis, the High Court subjects challenged local restraints on interstate commerce to means-ends and less-restrictive-alternative inquiries: to evaluate whether the legislation serves its purported objectives, or arbitrarily interferes with national commerce. A means-ends test would also seem relevant under the more recent interpretation of the contract clause. (Both the interstate commerce and contract clause decisions are discussed in chapter 10.) State courts that enforce economic due process necessarily utilize means-ends analysis.

The legal tests previously discussed require the application of judgment, which is after all the essence of the judicial process. Determining reasonableness is at the crux of constitutional construction. If the difficulty of resolving issues were cause for limiting the judicial role, judges might be left with little to do. In the words of Professor McCloskey, "while doubts about judicial expertise and power warrant withdrawal from some economic questions, they cannot justify withdrawal from all such questions, unless the doubter is willing to go the full distance . . . and give up most of the residue of modern judicial review."[15]

The possibility of judicial dereliction is not to be dismissed, but then neither are the benefits of the proposed policy. So much regulation is adverse that the likelihood of harm from an overzealous court is not very great. "The injury which may possibly be done by defeating a few good laws will be amply compensated by the advantage of preventing a number of bad ones."[16] The history of economic due process does not suggest a contrary result. The Old Court accepted a considerable amount of welfare and regulatory legislation. However, its jurisprudence led to fewer laws, more individual liberties, less government, less regulation that raises costs and prices, and greater production.

Policy Questions

Four policy arguments can be advanced in opposition to applying economic due process to statutes barring or regulating economic activities. First, such application would limit social and economic experimentation by Congress and the states; second, it would violate the basic tenets of federalism by giving the federal courts discretion over state and local interests; third, the federal courts would be subjected to a greatly increased case load; and fourth, the economic power of corporations would be augmented.

The first two objections involve the same issue: namely, whether political and material rights should be judged differently. Experimentation and federalism are involved when the federal courts strike down limitations on speech, press, religion, privacy, and travel. Thus, the question is really about equal treatment for liberties; questions of experimentation and federalism are entirely subordinate to that issue and are resolved by its resolution. My position is that there is no constitutional basis for the federal courts discriminating against economic liberties.

On its face, the prevailing theory of legislative experimentation in social and economic matters appears plausible: the politicians should be able to pass laws that they deem necessary, and if the laws do not work, they can be repealed. There are two problems with this position. First, laws affect lives. Some people might have to sacrifice precious liberties while the "experiment" is in progress. Second, legislation creates vested interests that are not readily terminable.

In his *New State Ice* dissent, Justice Brandeis urged that the Oklahoma law be given a chance to prove whether it worked. He presented an analogy to the approach taken in the sciences: "The discoveries in physical science, the triumphs in invention, attest the value of the process of trial and error."[17] Brandeis evidently believed that the public process functions like a laboratory in which experiments can be ended at will. The current effort to deregulate industry demonstrates his error; it is not easy to stop a political experiment. Regulation creates vested interests in both public and private sectors which will strongly oppose efforts to eliminate it.

Had the Oklahoma ice law been held valid, those companies insulated from competition would not have taken kindly to efforts to end the "experiment" and to force them to compete in the unrestricted marketplace. Obviously they would have vigorously protested legislation eliminating their special privileges. Likewise, airlines and trucking companies today have geared their investments and operations to the will of the government regulators, and many fear the results of changing to meet competition under deregulation. These companies, which understandably fight deregulation, complain they will suffer serious financial losses if it occurs.

Frequently when an ordinance restricts entry into a service, value attaches to the licenses issued under these controls. Taxi licenses, for example, are often bought and sold, with their sales price dependent upon the actual number of cabs allowed. In 1978 taxicab licenses reportedly were for sale in New York for $50,000 and in San Francisco for $28,000. A comparable situation prevails currently in the trucking industry as a result of regulation. ICC records on forty-three transactions for truck route operating rights occurring from 1967 through 1971 disclose that these rights were purchased originally for a total of $776,800 and were later sold for a total of $3,844,100.[18] In an unregulated market, no trucker would enjoy exclusive rights to any route.

Those who purchase licenses or operating rights from others will lose this investment if the regulation is eliminated and entry is no longer curbed. They will strenuously oppose deregulation as not being in their best interests. And many will sympathize with their plight. Because of such opposition, many "experiments," despite their failure, will never end.[19]

Federal economic due process would not significantly alter the federal-state balance. Although this doctrine would prevent state authorities from imposing a certain amount of regulation, it would have the same effect on the national government, thereby limiting the federal presence in the states. In those states whose courts already observe economic due process, the impact might be minimal. Moreover, the problems usually associated with federal authority—distant government and arbitrary power—have little relation to the exercise of a veto intended to preserve individual liberties by removing government restraints. Unlike the usual federal presence that increases authority, judicial review is intended to emphasize liberty.

Expanding due process coverage will probably add to the existing federal case load, but that consideration should not be decisive if the values embodied are important to the nation. In our system, it is difficult to regard the protection of liberty as burdensome. Moreover, the increases in cost that economic due process causes the judicial branch might be more than offset by the resultant decrease in the total cost of government. As applied in its original sense, judicial review is a device for reducing the authority and size of government. It has the potential to eliminate costly economic and social programs that increase both the size of governmental budgets and the cost of goods and services. Professor Gunther has suggested that litigation in this area, even when the statute is upheld, would encourage the airing and criticizing of programs with desirable fallout for the political process.[20]

Concern for the burden on the judicial docket should lead to the retrenchment of affirmative jurisprudence that, unlike negative review, increases the size and cost of government. Judges that do not legislate will have more time to devote to their judicial responsibilities.

The fourth argument related to the power of corporations. Both individuals and corporations are persons under the due process clauses, and both would benefit from judicial expansion of those provisions. In favoring a revitalization of economic due process, Professor McCloskey implies a reservation about extending this relief to large corporations.[21] Professor Tribe observes that McCloskey's concern can be met by utilizing the Fourteenth Amendment's privileges and immunities clause as the vehicle of change, for this clause does not apply to corporations.[22] Their theory is that big corporations are not in need of additional judicial relief because they possess the political and economic resources to overcome any disadvantages in the courts.

However, treating corporations differently for purposes of economic due process would go far to defeat the reason for change. Corporations are owned and operated by individuals. Frequently corporations or substantial owners of corporate stock have fewer resources than some people. When relief for property or economic deprivations is denied corporations, the owners of small corporations who utilize this legal form for business purposes also sustain injury. As of 1972, only 11 percent of the nation's corporations had receipts of $1 million or more; 93.4 percent of all corporations had assets under $1 million.[23] Because we cannot be certain how much power the big corporations actually possess, the risk of their failure to overcome judicial policy is borne in part by their moderate-income stockholders and the pension funds of labor unions and other organizations that invest substantially in these companies.[24] Moreover, to suggest that large corporations are not fully entitled to defend their economic interests is just as objectionable as suggesting that the big corporate owners of news publications should not be able to protect their rights to a free press.

Recent judicial experience rejects the notion that the interests of large corporations and consumers are necessarily antagonistic. Big corporations have opposed, in both the legislatures and the courts measures that increase consumer prices. Two instances have been previously reported: Exxon corporation fought the Maryland law that prohibited oil company ownership of service stations,[25] and General Motors contested the California statute regulating the location of new car dealers.[26] Economic due process would further the interests only of corporations seeking greater competition.

To emphasize the legal entity is to ignore the major issues: protecting private property and economic liberty and maximizing economic competition. In the words of Walter Lippmann: "[T]he issue between the giant corporation and the public should not be allowed to obscure the truth that the only dependable foundation of personal liberty is the economic security of private property."[27]

Finally in this connection, it should be noted that existing policy is favorable to those corporations that are able to obtain preferential treatment from the legislatures and the regulators. If McCloskey and Tribe are correct in their assumptions about corporate powers, we should worry about the special-interest legislation that they are capable of obtaining and should seek the widest application of judicial review to abrogate such legislation. The inability of those using the corporate form to obtain relief would limit their opportunity to contest such special legislation.

Rehabilitating Constitutional Principles

When the Constitution was framed, separation of powers, checks and balances, and judicial review were political and economic ideas. They would safeguard the individual in his personal, business, or professional life from governmental oppression. Society would benefit because liberty was regarded as the greatest encouragement to wisdom, productivity, creativity, and contentment. The same reasoning remains applicable today. We still rely on freedom to advance understanding and culture as well as to supply food, clothing, and shelter. But those constitutional concepts now operate to augment liberty in one area and not in the other.

Prior to the ratification of the Constitution, the state legislatures were the final arbiters in economic affairs—much as now. We have it on the authority of Madison, Hamilton, and Marshall that the legislatures used this power in a manner that seriously harmed individuals and the economy. These practices may have been a leading factor prompting the framing and adoption of the Constitution.

The situation is little improved today. In earlier times in our history, the success of a business was dependent upon its acceptability in the marketplace. Entrepreneurs who best satisfied consumers prospered, while those less competent or efficient fared poorly or were forced out of business. Today this economic competition is increasingly replaced by political competition. Losers in the economic arena seek relief from legislators who have the power to make them winners. One law can offset a score of inefficiencies. The scenario is no different when it comes to occupations, trades, and professions, for here again political power enjoys supremacy over ability, talent, and competence.

The application of judicial review to economic matters will not restore laissez-faire to our economy, but at least we should expect reduction of legislative and administrative excesses and abuses. This is an outcome not to be minimized. The rewards of liberty are vast and unpredictable.

Notes

Chapter One

1. City of New Orleans v. Dukes, 427 U.S. 297 (1976).
2. Dukes v. City of New Orleans. The United States District Court for the Eastern District of Louisiana at New Orleans, Jack M. Gordon, J. rendered summary judgment for the city and the mayor on 9 October 1973. Civil Action No. 72–2042, sec. I.
3. Dukes v. City of New Orleans, 501 F.2d 706 (5th Cir. 1974).
4. 427 U.S. at 303–04.
5. Calder v. Bull, 3 U.S. (3 Dall.) 386 (1798).
6. Ogden v. Saunders, 25 U.S. (12 Wheat.) 213 (1827).
7. Slaughter-House Cases, 83 U.S. (16 Wall.) 36 (1873).
8. Munn v. Illinois, 94 U.S. 113, 125 (1877).
9. *Cf.* Mugler v. Kansas, 123 U.S. 623 (1887); Yick Wo v. Hopkins, 118 U.S. 356 (1886).
10. Allgeyer v. Louisiana, 165 U.S. 578 (1897).
11. West Coast Hotel Co. v. Parrish, 300 U.S. 379 (1937).
12. Olsen v. Nebraska, 313 U.S. 236 (1941); *cf.* Lincoln Federal Labor Union v. Northwestern Iron & Metal Co., 335 U.S. 525 (1949).
13. 354 U.S. 457 (1957). As a result of the reversal of this decision, the outcome in federal litigation is the same whether economic legislation is challenged as violating equal protection or due process.
14. Ogden v. Saunders, 25 U.S. (12 Wheat.) 213, 356 (1827) (Marshall, C.J., dissenting).
15. Herbert Wechsler, *Toward Neutral Principles of Constitutional Law,* 73 HARV. L. REV. 1, 20 (1959).
16. 83 U.S. (16 Wall.) 36 (1872).
17. *Id.* at 81.
18. Harper v. Virginia Bd. of Elections, 383 U.S. 663, 669 (1966).

19. Home Bldg. & Loan Ass'n v. Blaisdell, 290 U.S. 398, 443 (1934).

20. LEONARD W. LEVY, LEGACY OF SUPPRESSION: FREEDOM OF SPEECH IN EARLY AMERICAN HISTORY (New York: Harper Torchbooks, 1963).

21. *Id.* at 4.

22. William Ray Forrester, *Are We Ready for Truth in Judging?*, 63 A.B.A. J. 1212 (1977).

23. While its members differed in various respects on the issue, the Constitutional Convention did accept the existence of slavery in certain states. U.S. CONST. art. 1, §§ 2, 9. The Union could not otherwise have been formed. In this regard, there has been an enormous change in sentiment, since it is inconceivable that compromise on this issue could have been effected in contemporary times.

24. *See* Richard A. Posner, *Blackstone and Bentham*, 19 J. L. & ECON. 569 (1976).

25. *Compare* CHARLES A. BEARD, AN ECONOMIC INTERPRETATION OF THE CON- STITUTION OF THE UNITED STATES (New York: Macmillan, 1913), *and* Martin Diamond, *Democracy and the Federalist: A Reconsideration of the Framers' Intents*, 53 AMERI- CAN POL. SCI. REV. 52 (1959).

26. *E.g.* Korematsu v. United States, 323 U.S. 214 (1944); Home Bldg. & Loan Ass'n v. Blaisdell, 290 U.S. 398, 426 (1934); Pennsylvania Coal Co. v. Mahon, 260 U.S. 393, 415 (1922); Schenck v. United States, 249 U.S. 47, 52 (1919).

27. *See* Richardson v. Mellish, 2 Bing. 229, 130 Eng. Rep. 294 (1824); Richard A. Epstein, *Unconscionability: A Critical Reappraisal*, 18 J. L. & ECON. 293 (1975).

28. Hirabayashi v. United States, 320 U.S. 81 (1943); Korematsu v. United States, 323 U.S. 214 (1944).

29. *See* RAOUL BERGER, GOVERNMENT BY JUDICIARY 412–13 (Cambridge, Mass. Harvard University Press, 1977).

30. 1 W. BLACKSTONE, COMMENTARIES *61.

31. WILLIAM B. LOCKHART, YALE KAMISAR & JESSE H. CHOPER, CONSTITUTIONAL RIGHTS AND LIBERTIES: CASES AND MATERIALS 124 (St. Paul: West Publishing Co., 4th ed. 1975).

32. *See* Mary Cornelia Porter, *That Commerce Shall Be Free: A New Look at the Old Laissez-Faire Court*, 1976 SUP. CT. REV. 135, 136 n.4, citing Ralph K. Winter, Jr. *Poverty, Economic Equality, and the Equal Protection Clause*, 1972 SUP. CT. REV. 41, 100.

33. Kahn v. Shevin, 416 U.S. 351, 356 n.10 (1974) (Douglas, J.).

34. 381 U.S. 479, 482 (1965).

35. *Id.* at 484.

36. However, there is doubt as to the kind of restraint that would be acceptable. *See* Eisenstadt v. Baird, 405 U.S. 438 (1972).

37. Meyer v. Nebraska, 262 U.S. 390 (1923); Pierce v. Society of Sisters, 268 U.S. 510 (1925).

38. 381 U.S. at 486 (Goldberg, J., concurring).

39. 381 U.S. at 507 (Black, J., dissenting).

40. *Id.* at 501 (Harlan, J., concurring).

41. Wesberry v. Sanders, 376 U.S. 1 (1964); Reynolds v. Sims, 377 U.S. 533 (1964).

42. U.S. CONST. art. I, § 10, cl. 1.

43. City of El Paso v. Simmons, 379 U.S. 497, 517 (1965) (Black, J., dissenting).

44. Harper v. Virginia Bd. of Elections, 383 U.S. 663, 670 (1966) (Black, J., dissent- ing).

45. 381 U.S. at 517–18 (Black, J., dissenting).

46. Moore v. City of East Cleveland, 431 U.S. 494, 502 (1977).

47. *Quoted by* JAMES BRADLEY THAYER, OLIVER WENDELL HOLMES AND FELIX FRANKFURTER ON JOHN MARSHALL 85 (Chicago: University of Chicago Press, Phoenix ed., 1967).

48. Meyer v. Nebraska, 262 U.S. 390 (1923); Pierce v. Society of Sisters, 268 U.S. 510 (1925).

49. Palko v. Connecticut, 302 U.S. 319, 325 (1937).

50. Roe v. Wade, 410 U.S. 113 (1973); Doe v. Bolton, 410 U.S. 179 (1973).

51. Moore v. City of East Cleveland, 431 U.S. 494 (1977).

52. Shapiro v. Thompson, 394 U.S. 618 (1969).

53. Memorial Hosp. v. Maricopa County, 415 U.S. 250 (1974).

54. 394 U.S. at 677 (Harlan, J., dissenting).

55. Thus President Jefferson denounced the opinion in Marbury v. Madison. In more contemporary times, the Warren Court has been subject to much criticism. See *Hearings before the Subcomm. on Separation of Powers of the Comm. on the Judiciary*, U.S. Senate, 90th Cong., 2d Sess. (1968).

56. Nebbia v. New York, 291 U.S. 502 (1934). (See discussion in chapter 6 *infra*).

57. New State Ice Co. v. Liebmann, 285 U.S. 262 (1932). (See discussion in chapter 6 *infra*).

58. Adkins v. Children's Hospital, 261 U.S. 525 (1923). (See discussion in chapter 6 *infra*).

59. FORTUNE MAGAZINE's list of the 500 largest United States corporations for 1977 shows Time, Inc. as number 198 with sales of $1,249,816,000; Times-Mirror (Los Angeles) as 219 with sales of $1,129, 630,000; Knight-Ridder Newspapers, 293 and sales of $751,712,000; New York Times, 385, $509,520,000; Washington Post, 435, sales of $436,102,000. THE FORTUNE DOUBLE 500 DIRECTORY (1978). It is hard to conceive of any owners of major daily newspapers as not being well off financially.

60. New York Times Co. v. Sullivan, 376 U.S. 254 (1964); Gertz v. Robert Welch, Inc., 418 U.S. 323 (1974).

61. Nebraska Press Ass'n v. Stuart, 427 U.S. 559 (1976).

62. New York Times Co. v. United States, 403 U.S. 713 (1971).

63. Miami Herald Publishing Co. v. Tornillo, 418 U.S. 241 (1974).

64. *Id.*

65. 198 U.S. 45 (1905).

66. *E.g.*, John Hart Ely, *The Wages of Crying Wolf: A Comment on Roe v. Wade*, 82 YALE L.J. 920 (1973); Richard Epstein, *Substantive Due Process by Any Other Name: The Abortion Cases*, 1973 SUP. CT. REV. 159. *See* Laurence H. Tribe, *The Supreme Court 1972 Term, Foreword: Toward a Model of Roles in the Due Process of Life and Law*, 87 HARV. L. REV. 1, 5–50 (1973).

67. Pennsylvania State Bd. of Pharmacy v. Pastor, 441 Pa. 186, 272 A.2d 487 (1971); Maryland Bd. of Pharmacy v. Sav-A-Lot, Inc., 270 Md. 103, 311 A.2d 242 (1973). *See* Guy Miller Struve, *The Less-Restrictive-Alternative Principle and Economic Due Process*, 80 HARV. L. REV. 1463 (1967); Note, *State Economic Substantive Due Process: A Substantive Approach*, 88 YALE L.J. 1487 (1979).

68. Virginia State Bd. of Pharmacy v. Virginia Citizens Consumer Council, Inc., 425 U.S. 748 (1976); Linmark Associates v. Township of Willingboro, 431 U.S. 85 (1977); Bates v. State Bar of Arizona, 433 U.S. 350 (1977).

69. Allied Structural Steel Co. v. Spannaus, 438 U.S. 234 (1978); United States Trust Co. of New York v. New Jersey, 431 U.S. 1 (1977).

70. *See, e.g.,* Lynch v. Household Finance Corp., 405 U.S. 538, 552 (1972); Hudgens v. NLRB, 424 U.S. 507 (1976); Hughes v. Oklahoma, 441 U.S. 322 (1979).

Chapter Two

1. 2 EDWARD COKE, INSTITUTES OF THE LAWS OF ENGLAND 46, 47, 63 (London: W. Clarke and Sons, 1817). Kent and Story cite pages 50 and 51. 2 JAMES KENT, COMMENTARIES ON AMERICAN LAW 10 (New York: Da Capo Press, 1971); 3 JOSEPH STORY, COMMENTARIES ON THE CONSTITUTION OF THE UNITED STATES 661 (New York: Da Capo Press, 1970). Both Kent and Story applied natural justice to invalidate confiscatory legislation, as discussed later in this chapter and in chapter 4. Coke's discussion referred to above concerns chapter 29 of a subsequent issue of the charter which was broader in scope than the original chapter 39. Coke's interpretation of the common law on monopolies is not generally accepted. See William L. Letwin, *The English Common Law concerning Monopolies,* 21 U. CHI. L. REV. 355 (1954).

2. 1 W. BLACKSTONE, COMMENTARIES *135; *see* also 117–41.

3. Bank of Columbia v. Okely, 17 U.S. (4 Wheat.) 235, 244 (1819).

4. Bowman v. Middleton, 1 S.C.L. (1 Bay) 252 (1792).

5. Trustees of the University of North Carolina v. Foy, 5 N.C. (1 Mur.) 58 (1805).

6. Trustees of Dartmouth College v. Woodward, 17 U.S. (4 Wheat.) 518, 581 (1819). Justice Thomas Cooley apparently regarded this statement as the best definition of due process of law. THOMAS M. COOLEY, A TREATISE ON THE CONSTITUTIONAL LIMITATIONS 353–54 (New York: Da Capo Press, 1972).

7. *Quoted* in BENJAMIN FLETCHER WRIGHT, THE CONTRACT CLAUSE OF THE CONSTITUTION 22 (Cambridge, Mass.: Harvard University Press, 1938). This action was subsequently litigated before the Supreme Court in Fletcher v. Peck, 10 U.S. (6 Cranch) 87 (1810). For Hamilton's views on natural law, see GERALD STOURZH, ALEXANDER HAMILTON AND THE IDEA OF REPUBLICAN GOVERNMENT (Stanford, Cal.: Stanford University Press, 1970). Hamilton's thoughts on due process are in 4 THE WORKS OF ALEXANDER HAMILTON 321–32 (New York: Knickerbocker Press, 1904).

8. Dash v. Van Kleeck, 7 Johns. (N.Y.) 477, 506 (1811).

9. *E.g.,* CHARLES GROVE HAINES, THE AMERICAN DOCTRINE OF JUDICIAL SUPREMACY (New York: Russell & Russell, 1959); Edward S. Corwin, *The Doctrine of Due Process of Law before the Civil War* (pt. 1), 24 HARV. L. REV. 366 (1911); Edward S. Corwin, *The Basic Doctrine of American Constitutional Law,* 12 MICH. L. REV. 247 (1914); J. A. C. Grant, *The Natural Law Background of Due Process,* 31 COLUM. L. REV. 56 (1931); Thomas Grey, *Do We Have an Unwritten Constitution?,* 27 STAN. L. REV. 703 (1975); 3 *id.* 1 (1924); Lowell J. Howe, *The Meaning of "Due Process of Law" Prior to the Adoption of the Fourteenth Amendment,* 18 CALIF. L. REV. 583 (1930); Roscoe Pound, *Liberty of Contract,* 18 YALE L.J. 454 (1909).

10. Corwin, *Basic Doctrine, supra* note 9, at 253.

11. *See, e.g.,* Pound, *supra* note 9; BERNARD BAILYN, THE IDEOLOGICAL ORIGINS OF THE AMERICAN REVOLUTION (Cambridge, Mass.: Belknap Press, 1967); EDWARD S. CORWIN, LIBERTY AGAINST GOVERNMENT (Baton Rouge, La.: Louisiana State University Press, 1948); BERNHARD KNOLLENBERG, ORIGIN OF THE AMERICAN REVOLUTION 1759–1766 (New York: Free Press, 1965) and GROWTH OF THE AMERICAN REVOLUTION 1766–1775 (New York: Free Press, 1975); 3 MURRAY N. ROTHBARD, CONCEIVED IN LIBERTY: ADVANCE TO REVOLUTION, 1760–75 (New Rochelle, N.Y.: Arlington House Publishers, 1976); GORDON S. WOOD, THE CREATION OF THE AMERICAN REPUBLIC 1776–1787 (Chapel Hill, N.C.: University of North Carolina Press, 1969).

12. ARCHIBALD COX, THE ROLE OF THE SUPREME COURT IN AMERICAN GOVERN-MENT 31 (New York: Oxford University Press, 1967).

13. *See* texts cited in *supra* note 11.

14. BAILYN, *supra* note 11, at 27.

15. *See* THE FEDERALIST PAPERS; Cecilia M. Kenyon, *Men of Little Faith: The Anti-Federalists on the Nature of Representative Government*, 12 WILLIAM AND MARY QUARTERLY 3 (1955); JOHN TURNER MAIN, THE ANTIFEDERALISTS (Chapel Hill, N.C.: University of North Carolina Press, 1961); Wood, *supra* note 11, at 519–64, 607–15.

16. Wood, *supra* note 11, at 376.

17. 2 MAX FARRAND, THE RECORDS OF THE FEDERAL CONVENTION OF 1787, at 582, 587–88 (rev. ed. 1937) (New Haven, Conn., and London: Yale University Press, 1966).

18. THE FEDERALIST PAPERS No. 84 (A. Hamilton) at 513 (New York and Scarborough, Ont.: A Mentor Book, 1961).

19. *Id.*

20. 3 STORY, *supra* note 1, at 715–16.

21. 3 DEBATES ON THE ADOPTION OF THE FEDERAL CONSTITUTION 620 (Jonathan Elliot, ed.) (New York: Burt Franklin, 1888).

22. 2 FARRAND, *supra* note 17, at 611, 617, 618, 620. Madison states the vote was 7–4, *id.*, at 618.

23. *Id.* at 618.

24. *Id.* at 376.

25. *Id.*

26. *Id.*

27. Calder v. Bull, 3 U.S. (3 Dall.) 386 (1798).

28. 1 W. BLACKSTONE, COMMENTARIES *134, 135, 140.

29. 1 THE JAMES MADISON LETTERS 350 (Philadelphia: J. B. Lippincott, 1865).

30. 1 FARRAND, *supra* note 17, at 134; THE FEDERALIST PAPERS, *supra* note 18, No. 44 (J. Madison), at 282–83. Chief Justice Marshall voiced similar thoughts in Ogden v. Saunders, discussed in chapter 3. According to Hamilton, writing in 1801, "creditors had been ruined or in a very extensive degree, much injured, confidence in pecuniary transactions had been destroyed, and the springs of industry had been proportionately relaxed," due to the failure in the states to enforce property rights. 25 THE PAPERS OF ALEXANDER HAMILTON 479 (Harold C. Syrett, ed.) (New York: Columbia University Press, 1977). Albert Beveridge, Marshall's biographer, relates that Marshall and Madison were most distressed at the antics in the mid-1780s of the Virginia House of Delegates, of which they were members. The delegates refused to pass legislation allowing enforcement of debts owed by Virginians to the British, payment of which had been suspended during the war. 1 ALBERT BEVERIDGE, THE LIFE OF JOHN MARSHALL 223–32 (Boston and New York: Houghton Mifflin, 1916). Marshall said in Virginia's ratification convention that economy and industry were essential to happiness, but the Confederation took away "the incitements to industry by rendering property insecure and unprotected." The Constitution, on the contrary, "will promote and encourage industry." *Id.* at 416–17. Beveridge concludes that the "determination of commercial and financial interests to get some plan adopted under which business could be transacted, was the most effective force that brought about [the Philadelphia Convention]." *Id.* at 242.

31. 1 FARRAND, *supra* note 17, at 422–33.

32. THE FEDERALIST PAPERS, *supra* note 18, No. 60 (A. Hamilton) at 369; 25 THE PAPERS OF ALEXANDER HAMILTON, *supra* note 30, at 478.

33. *See* discussion in chapter 4.

34. Vanhorne's Lessee v. Dorrance, 2 U.S. (2 Dall.) 304, 310 (1795).

35. Wilkinson v. Leland, 27 U.S. (2 Pet.) 627, 657 (1829).
36. 3 U.S. (3 Dall.) 386 (1798).
37. *Id.* at 387–88.
38. *Id.* at 399 (Iredell, J., concurring).
39. *Id.*
40. Thus, Justice Black charged his colleagues with applying natural law. *See* Griswold v. Connecticut, 381 U.S. 479, 511 (1965) (Black, J., dissenting).
41. JOHN LOCKE, OF CIVIL GOVERNMENT, Second Treatise, ch. IX, sec. 124 (Chicago, Ill.: Henry Regnery, 1955).
42. *Id.* at ch. XI, sec. 137.
43. *Id.* at ch. XI, sec. 138.
44. 77 Eng. Rep. 646 (K.B. 1610).
45. *Id.* at 652.
46. 1 W. BLACKSTONE, COMMENTARIES *156.
47. *Id.* at *125, 130, 134. For an example of how Blackstone's views were used as a basis for decision-making, *see* Ritchie v. People, 155 Ill. 101, 104, 40 N.E. 454, 456 (1895).
48. 10 U.S. (6 Cranch) 87 (1810).
49. U.S. CONST. art. I, § 10, cl. 1.
50. 10 U.S. at 135.
51. *Id.* at 139.
52. *Id.* at 143 (Johnson, J., concurring).
53. 17 U.S. (4 Wheat.) 235 (1819).
54. *Id.* at 244.
55. 13 U.S. (9 Cranch) 43 (1815).
56. *Id.* at 50–51.
57. 25 U.S. (12 Wheat.) 212 (1827).
58. *Id.* at 346–47 (Marshall, C.J., dissenting).
59. *Id.* at 354 (Marshall, C.J., dissenting).
60. 27 U.S. (2 Pet.) 627 (1829).
61. *Id.* at 657.
62. 6 F. Cas. 546 (C.C.E.D. Pa. 1823) (No. 3,230).
63. *Id.* at 551.
64. *See* LAURENCE H. TRIBE, AMERICAN CONSTITUTIONAL LAW, at 405–08 (Mineola, N.Y.: The Foundation Press, 1978).
65. Barron v. Mayor of Baltimore, 32 U.S. (7 Pet.) 243 (1833).
66. *See* BERNARD SCHWARTZ, FROM CONFEDERATION TO NATION, at 14–15 (Baltimore and London: The Johns Hopkins University Press, 1973).
67. 68 U.S. (1 Wall.) 175 (1864).
68. *Id.* at 206–07.
69. Loan Association v. Topeka, 87 U.S. (20 Wall.) 655 (1875).
70. *Id.* at 669 (Clifford, J., dissenting).
71. 2 ALEXIS DE TOCQUEVILLE, DEMOCRACY IN AMERICA 272 (New Rochelle, N.Y.: Arlington House, 1965).
72. Murray's Lessee v. Hoboken Land and Improvement Co., 59 U.S. (18 How.) 272 (1855).
73. Dred Scott v. Sandford, 60 U.S. (19 How.) 393 (1857).
74. *Id.* at 450.
75. *Id.* at 450–51.

76. *Id.* at 453.

77. 55 U.S. (14 How.) 539 (1853).

78. *Id.* at 553.

79. Nor, of course, did Taney's definition obtain majority approval.

80. For an argument that the adoption of the taking clause in the Fifth Amendment reflected the sense of the country on the issue of just compensation and was therefore relevant to the law of New York, which had no such provision, see Chancellor Kent's decision in Gardner v. Newburgh, 2 Johns. Ch. (N.Y.) 162 (1816), discussed at greater length later in this chapter.

81. J.A.C. Grant, *The "Higher Law" Background of the Law of Eminent Domain*, 6 WISC. L. REV. 67, 70 (1931).

82. MORTON J. HORWITZ, THE TRANSFORMATION OF AMERICAN LAW 1780–1860, at 64 (Cambridge, Mass.: Harvard University Press, 1977).

83. William B. Stoebuck, *A General Theory of Eminent Domain*, 47 WASH. L. REV. 553, 583 (1972).

84. Corwin, *Basic Doctrine, supra* note 9, at 247, 256.

85. CORWIN, *supra* note 11, at 75–81.

86. Wilkinson v. Leland, 27 U.S. (2 Pet.) 627, 658 (1829).

87. Grant, *supra* note 81.

88. *See* Cooley, *supra* note 6, at 523–71.

89. Hairston v. Danville & West. Ry., 208 U.S. 598, 606 (1907).

90. Allen v. Peden, 4 N.C. (Term) 442 (1816).

91. Hoke v. Henderson, 15 N.C. (4 Dev.) 1 (1833).

92. *Id.* at 16.

93. *In re* Dorsey, 7 Port. 293 (1838).

94. *See* Lowell J. Howe, *The Meaning of "Due Process of Law" Prior to the Adoption of the Fourteenth Amendment*, 18 CAL. L. REV. 583, 592 (1930).

95. CORWIN, *supra* note 11, at 96, and *Doctrine of Due Process, supra* note 9, at 460.

96. 1–4 Kent, *supra* note 1.

97. 2 Johns. Ch. (N.Y.) 162 (1816).

98. People v. Platt, 17 Johns. (N.Y.) 195 (1819); Bradshaw v. Rodgers, 20 Johns. (N.Y.) 103 (1822); Sinnickson v. Johnson, 17 N.J.L. 129 (1839).

99. Cooley, *supra* note 6, at 541–57. Pumpelly v. Green Bay Co., 80 U.S. 166 (1871), brought Gardner within federal law, but the principle of "inverse condemnation" remained unsettled under the United States Constitution until United States v. Causby, 328 U.S. 256 (1946), discussed in chapter 10.

100. CORWIN, *supra* note 11, at 98.

101. 4 Hill (N.Y.) 140 (1843).

102. Westervelt v. Gregg, 12 N.Y. 202, 209 (1854).

103. 13 N.Y. 378 (1856).

104. *Id.* at 393.

105. CORWIN, *supra* note 11, at 107.

106. Beebe v. State, 6 Ind. 501 (1855).

107. Jackson v. State, 19 Ind. 312 (1862).

108. CORWIN, *supra* note 11, at 114–15.

109. COOLEY, *supra* note 6, at 356.

110. *Id.*

111. *Id.* at 357–58.

112. Cooley was critical of laws banning liquor sales, stating that they make the

merchant of yesterday the criminal of today. He did not criticize these laws as being violative of due process. *Id.* at 583–84.

113. 83 U.S. (16 Wall.) 36 (1872).

114. *Id.* at 53.

115. 6 F. Cas. 546 (C.C.E.D. Pa. 1823) (No. 3,230).

116. *Id.* at 551–52.

117. 83 U.S. at 78.

118. *Id.* at 80–81.

119. *Id.* at 81.

120. *See* Alexander M. Bickel, The Morality of Consent 44 (New Haven, Conn.: Yale University Press, 1975).

121. Act of 9 April 1866, ch. 31, 14 Stat. 27.

122. Raoul Berger, Government by Judiciary, 391, 22–36 (Cambridge, Mass.: Harvard University Press, 1977). *See* Charles Fairman, *Does the Fourteenth Amendment Incorporate the Bill of Rights? The Original Understanding,* 2 Stanford L. Rev. 5, 15–18, 37–40 (1949); Lynch v. Household Finance Corp., 405 U.S. 538, 543–51 (1972). Nor is there sufficient basis for concluding that the Fourteenth Amendment's first section was intended to apply the Bill of Rights to the states. Fairman *supra.*

123. Bartemeyer v. Iowa, 85 U.S. (18 Wall.) 129 (1873).

124. *Id.* at 135.

125. Davidson v. New Orleans, 96 U.S. 97, 102 (1877).

126. 25 Feb. 1862, ch. 33, 12 Stat. 345.

127. Hepburn v. Griswold, 75 U.S. (8 Wall.) 603, 624 (1870).

128. Knox v. Lee (Legal Tender Cases), 79 U.S. (12 Wall.) 457, 553 (1871).

129. 83 U.S. at 101 (Field, J., dissenting).

130. *Id.* at 122 (Bradley, J., dissenting).

131. *Id.* at 128 (Swayne, J., dissenting).

132. *Id.* at 90–91 (Field, J., dissenting).

133. *Id.* at 116, 122 (Bradley, J., dissenting).

134. *Id.* at 127 (Swayne, J., dissenting).

135. William E. Nelson, *The Impact of the Antislavery Movement upon Styles of Judicial Reasoning in Nineteenth Century America,* 87 Harv. L. Rev. 513, 552 (1974).

136. *Id.* at 555–57.

137. *See id.* at 547–66.

138. *See, e.g.,* Plessy v. Ferguson, 163 U.S. 537 (1896), upholding "separate but equal" transportation; Blyew v. United States, 80 U.S. (13 Wall.) 581 (1871); United States v. Cruikshank, 92 U.S. 542 (1876). *See generally* Leonard W. Levy, *Judicial Review, History and Democracy* in Judicial Review and the Supreme Court 34–35 (Leonard W. Levy, ed.) (New York, Evanston, and London: Harper Torchbooks, 1967).

139. Butchers' Union Co. v. Crescent City Co., 111 U.S. 746 (1884).

140. 165 U.S. 578 (1897).

141. Pound, *supra* note 9, at 470.

142. 94 U.S. 113, 136 (1876) (Field, J., dissenting).

143. *Id.* at 143.

144. 113 U.S. 27 (1885).

145. 127 U.S. 678 (1888).

146. 118 U.S. 356 (1886).

147. *Id.* at 366.

148. *Id.* at 370.

149. Railroad Comm'n Cases, 116 U.S. 307 (1886).

150. *Id.* at 331.

151. Smyth v. Ames, 169 U.S. 466 (1898). *See* Mary Cornelia Porter, *That Commerce Shall Be Free: A New Look at the Old Laissez-Faire Court,* 1976 SUP. CT. REV. 135.

152. Chicago, Milwaukee & St. Paul Ry. Co. v. Minnesota, 134 U.S. 418 (1890).

153. Smyth v. Ames, 169 U.S. 466 (1898).

154. Powers v. Shepard, 45 Barb. (N.Y.) 524 (1865).

155. People v. Marx, 99 N.Y. 377, 2 N.E. 29 (1885).

156. *In re* Jacobs, 98 N.Y. 98 (1885).

157. *Id.* at 110.

158. Godcharles & Co. v. Wigeman, 113 Pa. 431, 437, 6 A. 354, 356 (1886).

159. Leep v. St. Louis, I. M. & S. Ry. Co., 58 Ark. 407, 415, 422, 25 S.W. 75, 77, 79 (1894).

160. Eden v. People, 161 Ill. 296, 43 N.E. 1108 (1896). *Contra,* People v. Havnor, 37 N.Y.S. 314 (1896), *aff'd* 149 N.Y. 195.

161. Ritchie v. People, 155 Ill. 101, 40 N.E. 454 (1895). *Contra,* Commonwealth v. Hamilton Mfg. Co., 120 Mass. 383 (1876); Bergman v. Cleveland, 39 Ohio St. 651 (1884); State v. Buchanan, 29 Wash. 602, 70 P. 52 (1902); Wenham v. State, 65 Neb. 394, 91 N.W. 421 (1902); State v. Muller, 48 Or. 252, 85 P. 855 (1906); Starnes v. Albion Mfg. Co., 147 N.C. 556, 61 S.E. 525 (1908).

162. State v. Fire Creek Coal and Coke Co., 33 W. Va. 188, 10 S.E. 288 (1889).

163. State v. Julow, 129 Mo. 163, 31 S.W. 781 (1895); Gillespie v. People, 188 Ill. 176, 58 N.E. 1007 (1900); State *ex rel.* Zillmer v. Kreutzberg, 114 Wis. 530, 90 N.W. 1098 (1902); Coffeyville Vitrified Brick & Tile Co. v. Perry, 69 Kan. 297, 76 P. 848 (1904); People v. Marcus, 185 N.Y. 257, 77 N.E. 1073 (1906); State *ex rel.* Smith v. Daniels, 118 Minn. 155, 136 N.W. 584 (1912).

164. State v. Loomis, 115 Mo. 307, 22 S.W. 350 (1893); State v. Haun, 61 Kan. 146, 59 P. 340 (1899); Godcharles & Co. v. Wigeman, 113 Pa. 431, 6 A. 354 (1886); State v. Goodwill, 33 W. Va. 179, 10 S.E. 285 (1889); *but see* Peel Splint Coal Co. v. State, 36 W. Va. 802, 15 S.E. 1000 (1892). *Contra,* Hancock v. Yaden, 121 Ind. 366, 23 N.E. 253 (1890); Opinion of the Justices, 163 Mass. 589, 40 N.E. 713 (1895); Harbison v. Knoxville Iron Co., 103 Tenn. 421, 53 S.W. 955 (1899); International Text Book Co. v. Weissinger, 160 Ind. 349, 65 N.E. 521 (1902).

165. *In re* Aubry, 36 Wash. 308, 78 P. 900 (1904); Bessette v. People, 193 Ill. 334, 62 N.E. 215 (1901); People v. Beattie, 96 App. Div. 383, 89 N.Y.S. 193 (1904). In passing on legislation restricting entry into occupations, the courts considered relationships to public health. The exercise of the police powers was upheld in licensing of doctors, State v. Carey, 4 Wash. 424, 30 P. 729 (1892); of dentists, State *ex rel.* Smith v. Board of Dental Examiners, 31 Wash. 492, 72 P. 110 (1903); and of plumbers, People *ex rel.* Nechamcus v. Warden of City Prison, 144 N.Y. 529, 39 N.E. 686 (1895); but not for horseshoeing.

166. *In re* Morgan, 26 Col. 415, 58 P. 1071 (1899).

167. Low v. Rees Printing Co., 41 Neb. 127, 59 N.W. 362 (1894).

168. *Ex parte* Kuback, 85 Cal. 274, 24 P. 737 (1890); People v. Coler, 166 N.Y. 1, 59 N.E. 716 (1901); Street v. Varney Electrical Supply Co., 160 Ind. 338, 66 N.E. 895 (1903); *contra,* State v. Atkin, 64 Kan. 174, 67 P. 519 (1901); *In re* Broad, 36 Wash. 449, 78 P. 1004 (1904). Citing cases from 1835 to 1861, Warren observes that laws were upheld regulating sale of anthracite coal by weight; regulating the weight and price of bread; prohibiting open restaurants after 10:00 P.M; prohibiting the playing of music and the

entry of females in saloons after midnight; forbidding storekeeping on Sunday; licensing lawyers; and licensing bowling alleys. Charles Warren, *The New "Liberty" under the Fourteenth Amendment,* 39 HARV. L. REV. 431, 442–43 (1925). *See* general discussion of state judicial review of economic regulation in Pound, *supra* note 9, at 466–70.

169. *Quoted in* Slaughter-House Cases, 83 U.S. at 110.

170. LOCKE, *supra* note 41, ch. V, sec. 27.

171. 4 THE JAMES MADISON LETTERS 478 (March 27, 1792) (New York: Townsend Mac Coun., 1884).

Chapter Three

1. Slaughter-House Cases, 83 U.S. (16 Wall.) 36, 78 (1873).

2. As to the common law powers of the federal government, see United States v. Hudson & Goodwin, 11 U.S. (7 Cranch) 32 (1812), and United States v. Coolidge, 14 U.S. (1 Wheat.) 415 (1816). *See also* Swift v. Tyson, 41 U.S. (16 Pet.) 1 (1842); Erie R.R. v. Tompkins, 304 U.S. 64 (1938).

3. 2 U.S. (2 Dall.) 304 (1795).

4. 3 U.S. (3 Dall.) 386 (1798).

5. 10 U.S. (6 Cranch) 87 (1810).

6. 13 U.S. (9 Cranch) 43 (1815).

7. 10 U.S. (6 Cranch) at 138.

8. See United States v. Brown, 381 U.S. 437 (1965).

9. 10 U.S. (6 Cranch) at 138.

10. *See* pp. 69–70, 73–76 *infra.*

11. 25 U.S. (12 Wheat.) 213, 332 (1827) (Marshall, C.J., dissenting).

12. McMillan v. McNeill, 17 U.S. (4 Wheat.) 209, 212–13 (1819). However, all the majority opinions in *Ogden* confined *McMillan* to a bankruptcy discharge under the laws of a state other than the one in which the contract had been executed. In *Ogden* a dissenting Justice Marshall agreed with this interpretation. 25 U.S. (12 Wheat.) at 333 (Marshall, C.J., dissenting).

13. 25 U.S. (12 Wheat.) at 256.

14. Sturges v. Crowninshield, 17 U.S. (4 Wheat.) 122 (1819).

15. 25 U.S. (12 Wheat.) at 276.

16. *E.g.,* 1 WILLIAM WINSLOW CROSSKEY, POLITICS AND THE CONSTITUTION 359 (Chicago: University of Chicago Press, 1953); 4 ALBERT J. BEVERIDGE, THE LIFE OF JOHN MARSHALL 480–81 (Boston and New York: Houghton Mifflin, 1919).

17. 2 CROSSKEY, *supra* note 16, at 1324 n.7.

18. 1 *id.* at 359.

19. 25 U.S. (12 Wheat.) at 322.

20. LAURENCE H. TRIBE, AMERICAN CONSTITUTIONAL LAW at 467 (Mineola, N.Y.: Foundation Press, 1978); BENJAMIN FLETCHER WRIGHT, JR., THE CONTRACT CLAUSE OF THE CONSTITUTION 50 (Cambridge, Mass.: Harvard University Press, 1938); BEVERIDGE, *supra* note 16, at 481.

21. 25 U.S. (12 Wheat.) at 334 (Marshall, C.J., dissenting).

22. *Id.* at 335.

23. *Id.* at 356. Thus, it is pertinent that the important Northwest Ordinance adopted by Congress in 1787 protected only "private contracts . . . previously formed."

24. Given the "master rule" that all existing rules are subject to change, no contractual obligation can be considered very secure. TRIBE, *supra* note 20, § 9–6, at 468.

25. Home Bldg. & Loan Ass'n v. Blaisdell (The Minnesota Mortgage Moratorium Case), 290 U.S. 398 (1934). "Not only are existing laws read into contracts in order to fix obligations as between the parties, but the reservation of essential attributes of sovereign power is also read into contracts as a postulate of the legal order." *Id.* at 435. The Legal Tender Cases, 79 U.S. (12 Wall.) 457, 550–51 (1871), had fashioned the result with a dictum that contracts between private individuals are subject to the police power. Although that case dealt with the power of the federal government, the language is applicable to the contracts clause.

26. 25 U.S. (12 Wheat.) at 346 (Marshall, C.J., dissenting).

27. *Id.* at 346–47.

28. *Id.* at 355.

29. CHARLES A. BEARD, AN ECONOMIC INTERPRETATION OF THE CONSTITUTION OF THE UNITED STATES 181–82 (New York: Macmillan, 1913). Beard views Marshall as closely reflecting the Framers' perspectives—hardly a compliment given the source. *See generally* WRIGHT, *supra* note 20, at 27–61.

30. BEARD, *supra* note 29, at 182.

31. CHARLES A. MILLER, THE SUPREME COURT AND THE USES OF HISTORY 26 n.54 (New York: Clarion Books, Simon & Schuster, 1972).

32. 25 U.S. (12 Wheat.) 354–55 (Marshall, C.J., dissenting).

33. *See* discussion in chapter 2, note 30 and accompanying text. However, Wright believed that the Framers were concerned primarily about state laws affecting the money supply and that they thought that the solution to this problem lay in prohibiting state powers over money. Only secondarily were they concerned about the contract clause. WRIGHT, *supra* note 20, at 5–6.

34. See pp. 72–73 *infra*.

35. WRIGHT, *supra* note 20, at 51.

36. 1 CROSSKEY, *supra* note 16, at 355.

37. Allied Structural Steel v. Spannaus, 438 U.S. 234 (1978); United States Trust Co. of New York v. New Jersey, 431 U.S. 1 (1977). Both cases are discussed in chapter 10.

38. 2 MAX FARRAND, THE RECORDS OF THE FEDERAL CONVENTION OF 1787, at 596–97 (rev. ed. 1937) (New Haven, Conn. and London: Yale University Press, 1966).

39. *Id.* at 636; 4 *id.* at 59.

40. *See* 1 CROSSKEY, *supra* note 16, at 357–58; WRIGHT, *supra* note 20, at 9 n.20. Crosskey believed that the Framers intended to grant Congress supremacy over all the nation's commerce. He supports this position in part by reasoning that Congress was given power over the entire field of contracts so that the states could not interfere with the federal authority. CROSSKEY at 358.

41. 2 FARRAND, *supra* note 38, at 619.

42. Society for the Propagation of the Gospel v. Wheeler, 22 F. Cas. 756, 767 (C.C.D.N.H. 1814) (No. 13,156).

43. 3 U.S. (3 Dall.) 386, 391, 393, 394 (1798).

44. 1 CROSSKEY, *supra* note 16, at 346, *citing* 3 FARRAND, *supra* note 38, at 73, 589; 4 *id.* at 72, 73.

45. 3 U.S. (3 Dall.) at 397.

46. *Id.* at 399–400.

47. 10 U.S. (6 Cranch) 87, 138–39 (1810).

48. 25 U.S. (12 Wheat.) at 286 (emphasis added).

49. Satterlee v. Matthewson, 27 U.S. (2 Pet.) 380, 681 app. (1829).

50. *Id.* at 683–84, *citing* Wilkinson v. Meyer, 2 Lord Raym. 1350–52 (1724).

51. 27 U.S. (2 Pet.) at 686.

52. *Id.* at 685–86.

53. *Id.* at 687.

54. Trustees of Dartmouth College v. Woodward, 17 U.S. (4 Wheat.) 518 (1819).

55. JAMES MADISON, JOURNAL OF THE FEDERAL CONVENTION (E.H. Scott, ed.) (Freeport, N.Y.: Books for Libraries Press, 1970 [n.p. 1840]). The official journal provides little information on the subject.

56. *Id.* at 586–87 (footnote omitted).

57. *Id.* at 620–21.

58. *Id.* at 625–26.

59. *Id.* at 727–28.

60. 2 FARRAND, *supra* note 38, at 440 n.19.

61. *See* pp. 73–76 *infra.*

62. *See* pp. 69–70 *supra.*

63. William Winslow Crosskey, *The True Meaning of the Constitutional Prohibition of Ex-Post-Facto Laws,* 14 U. CHI. L. REV. 539 (1947); *The Ex-Post-Facto and the Contracts Clauses in the Federal Convention: A Note on the Editorial Ingenuity of James Madison,* 35 U. CHI. L. REV. 248 (1968).

64. 1 CROSSKEY, *supra* note 16, chs. XI & XII at 324–60.

65. *Quoted in id.* at 325–26.

66. 1 W. BLACKSTONE, COMMENTARIES 132–33 (W.G. Hammond ed., 1890).

67. 2 U.S. (2 Dall.) 304, 319 (1795).

68. Turner v. Turner's Executrix, 9 Va. (4 Call) 234, 237 (1792); Elliot's Executor v. Lyell, 8 Va. (3 Call) 268, 286 (1802); Den v. Goldtrap, 1 N.J.L. 315, 319 (1795); State v. Parkhurst, 9 N.J.L. 427, 444 app. (1802), *citing* Taylor v. Reading, unrep.

69. Turner v. Turner's Executrix, 9 Va. (4 Call) 234, 237 (1792).

70. 2 FARRAND, *supra* note 38, at 617.

71. Oliver P. Field, *Ex Post Facto in the Constitution,* 20 MICH. L. REV. 315 (1922).

72. 3 FARRAND, *supra* note 38, at 100, *quoted in* Field, *supra* note 71, at 331.

73. EDWARD S. CORWIN, LIBERTY AGAINST GOVERNMENT, 70–72 (Baton Rouge, La.: Louisiana University State Press, 1948).

74. 3 JOSEPH STORY, COMMENTARIES ON THE CONSTITUTION OF THE UNITED STATES 212–13 (New York: Da Capo Press, 1970).

75. THOMAS M. COOLEY, A TREATISE ON THE CONSTITUTIONAL LIMITATIONS 264 (New York: Da Capo Press, 1972).

76. CHARLES GROVE HAINES, THE ROLE OF THE SUPREME COURT IN AMERICAN GOVERNMENT AND POLITICS 1789–1835, at 157 (Berkeley and Los Angeles: University of California Press, 1944).

77. Dash v. Van Kleeck, 7 Johns. (N.Y.) 477, 505 (1811).

78. 14 Annals of Congress, 8th Cong., 2d Sess., 1083 (1805).

79. *Id.* at 1096.

80. MORTON J. HORWITZ, THE TRANSFORMATION OF AMERICAN LAW 1780–1860, at 7 (Cambridge, Mass.: Harvard University Press, 1977).

81. 1 FARRAND, *supra* note 38, at 422–23.

82. 3 *id.* at 450. These observations are contained in a note written by Madison, apparently in 1821, explaining views he set forth during the convention.

83. THE FEDERALIST PAPERS No. 10, at 78 (J. Madison) (New York: Mentor Books, 1961).

84. 1 FARRAND, *supra* note 38, at 533–34 and 541–42.

85. *Id.* at 428, 469–70, 542; 2 *id.* at 202; 3 *id.* at 110.

86. Stanley N. Katz, *Thomas Jefferson and the Right to Property in Revolutionary America,* 19 J.L. & ECON. 467, 469–70 (1976).

87. *Id.* at 468.

88. U.S. CONST. amend. 5: "nor shall private property be taken for public use, without just compensation."

89. Francis S. Philbrick, *Changing Conceptions of Property in Law,* 86 U. PA. L. REV. 691, 712–13 n.68 (1938).

90. THE FEDERALIST PAPERS, *supra* note 83, No. 7, at 65.

91. *See* pp. 30, 71 *supra.*

92. However, the Bill of Rights did not apply to the states, the source of most such problems. Barron v. Mayor of Baltimore, 32 U.S. (7 Pet.) 243 (1833).

93. 2 Annals of Congress (1790) at 1206, 1214, 1216–24, 1227, 1249; 1 CROSSKEY, *supra* note 16, at 338–39. Madison, as previously noted, expressed the limited view of ex post facto in this debate.

94. LEONARD W. LEVY, LEGACY OF SUPPRESSION: FREEDOM OF SPEECH IN EARLY AMERICAN HISTORY, vii–viii (New York: Harper Torchbooks, 1963).

95. 3 U.S. (3 Dall.) at 400.

96. Kohl v. United States, 91 U.S. 367, 371–72 (1876). *See generally* William B. Stoebuck, *A General Theory of Eminent Domain,* 47 WASH. L. REV. 553, 557–69 (1972).

97. 2 U.S. (2 Dall.) at 311.

98. C. VAN BYNKERSHOEK, QUAESTIONUM JURIS PUBLICI 218 (T. Frank transl. 1930), quoted in Stoebuck, *supra* note 96, at 560.

99. New York Times Co. v. Sullivan, 376 U.S. 254, 276 (1964).

Chapter Four

1. 1 MAX FARRAND, THE RECORDS OF THE FEDERAL CONVENTION OF 1787, at 533–34, 541–42 (rev. ed. 1937) (New Haven, Conn. and London: Yale University Press, 1966) (hereinafter cited as FARRAND). THE FEDERALIST PAPERS No. 10 (J. Madison) (New York: Mentor Books, 1961) (hereinafter cited as THE FEDERALIST).

2. THE FEDERALIST No. 79 (A. Hamilton) at 472.

3. 3 JOSEPH STORY, COMMENTARIES ON THE CONSTITUTION 661 (New York: Da Capo Press, 1970).

4. *See generally* CHARLES A. BEARD, THE SUPREME COURT AND THE CONSTITUTION (Englewood Cliffs, N.J.: Prentice-Hall, 1962); EDWARD S. CORWIN, THE DOCTRINE OF JUDICIAL REVIEW (Princeton, N.J.: Princeton University Press, 1914) and COURT OVER CONSTITUTION (Gloucester, Mass.: P. Smith, 1957); HORACE A. DAVIS, THE JUDICIAL VETO (Boston and New York: Houghton Mifflin, 1914); LOUIS B. BOUDIN, GOVERNMENT BY JUDICIARY (New York: Russell & Russell, 1968); Frank E. Melvin, *The Judicial Bulwark of the Constitution,* 8 AM. POL. SCI. REV. 167 (1914); 2 WILLIAM W. CROSSKEY, POLITICS AND THE CONSTITUTION 976–1007 (Chicago, Ill.: University of Chicago Press, 1953) (hereinafter cited as CROSSKEY).

5. 1 FARRAND at 21.

6. 1 FARRAND at 131, 140 (6 June); 2 FARRAND at 71, 80 (21 July); 2 FARRAND at 295, 298 (15 Aug.).

7. 5 U.S. (1 Cranch) 137 (1803).

8. *See* CHARLES GROVE HAINES, THE AMERICAN DOCTRINE OF JUDICIAL SUPREMACY 148–70 (New York: Russell & Russell, 2d ed. 1959).

9. 1 ALBERT J. BEVERIDGE, THE LIFE OF JOHN MARSHALL 452 (Boston and New York: Houghton Mifflin, 1916).

10. CORWIN, *supra* note 4, at 2.

11. BENJAMIN FLETCHER WRIGHT, THE GROWTH OF AMERICAN CONSTITUTIONAL LAW 15–16 (New York: Holt, 1942).

12. 1 FARRAND at 97, 98, 109; 2 FARRAND at 73, 76, 78, 298, 299, 376, 391, 430.

13. Bayard v. Singleton, 1 Martin (N.C.) 42 (1787); the New Hampshire cases are unreported and arose under the so-called "Ten Pound Act." See 2 CROSSKEY 968–74; Leonard W. Levy, *Judicial Review, History and Democracy: An Introduction in* JUDICIAL REVIEW AND THE SUPREME COURT 10 (Leonard W. Levy, ed.) (New York, Evanston, and London: Harper Torchbooks, 1967); HAINES, *supra* note 8, at 112–20.

14. HAINES, *supra* note 8, at 89–112.

15. *See* discussion in 2 CROSSKEY at 938–75.

16. 2 FARRAND 28.

17. Thomas C. Grey, *Origins of the Unwritten Constitution: Fundamental Law in American Revolutionary Thought*, 30 STANFORD L. REV. 843, 868 n.111 (1978), citing VINER'S ABRIDGEMENTS which first appeared in 1742–53, apparently regarded as the leading law encyclopedia of the time; HAINES, *supra* note 8, at 223–27; EDWARD S. CORWIN, LIBERTY AGAINST GOVERNMENT 39–40 (Baton Rouge: Louisiana State University Press, 1948).

18. *See* 2 CROSSKEY 976–1046.

19. Chief Justice Marshall in Marbury v. Madison, 5 U.S. (1 Cranch) at 179.

20. Charles A. Beard, *Supreme Court: Usurper or Grantee?* in ESSAYS IN CONSTITUTIONAL LAW 45 (Robert G. McCloskey, ed.) (New York: Alfred A. Knopf, 1962).

21. HAINES, *supra* note 8, at 204–31.

22. *Id.* at 209–10.

23. *Id.* at 215–16.

24. ANDREW C. MCLAUGHLIN, THE COURTS, THE CONSTITUTION AND PARTIES 105–06 (Chicago, Ill.: University of Chicago Press, 1912).

25. EDWARD S. CORWIN, THE DOCTRINE OF JUDICIAL REVIEW 27 (Princeton, N.J.: Princeton University Press, 1914). Prof. C. H. MCILWAIN has developed this perspective in great depth in CONSTITUTIONALISM: ANCIENT AND MODERN (Ithaca, N.Y.: Great Seal Books, rev. ed. 1947) and CONSTITUTIONALISM AND THE CHANGING WORLD (Cambridge, Mass.: Cambridge University Press, 1939). Corwin vacillated during his life regarding the question of whether the Framers intended review over congressional legislation. *See* Levy, *supra* note 13, at 3–4.

26. *See generally* THE FEDERALIST PAPERS.

27. THE FEDERALIST No. 78 (A. Hamilton) at 466–67; *see also* No. 81 (A. Hamilton) at 481–91.

28. Marbury v. Madison, 5 U.S. (1 Cranch) at 163.

29. MCILWAIN, CONSTITUTIONALISM AND THE CHANGING WORLD, *supra* note 25, at 64.

30. THE FEDERALIST No. 73 (A. Hamilton) at 443.

31. 2 U.S. (2 Dall.) 304 (1795).

32. 3 U.S. (3 Dall.) 386 (1798).

33. 27 U.S. (2 Pet.) 627 (1829).

34. 10 U.S. (6 Cranch) 87 (1810).

35. 13 U.S. (9 Cranch) 43 (1815).

36. Trustees of Dartmouth College v. Woodward, 17 U.S. (4 Wheat.) 518 (1819).

37. 4 BEVERIDGE, *supra* note 9, at 251–52, 256–57; J. A. C. Grant, *The Natural Law Background of Due Process*, 31 COL. L. REV. 56, 61–63 (1931).

38. Slaughter-House Cases, 83 U.S. (16 Wall.) 36, 115 (1873) (Bradley, J., dissenting). "In internal matters, in England itself, there are many fundamental rights of the subject that parliament in modern times has never dreamt of infringing and could only infringe at the cost of revolution." McILWAIN, CONSTITUTIONALISM AND THE CHANGING WORLD, *supra* note 25, at 279–80.

39. 83 U.S. at 114 (Bradley, J., dissenting).

40. People v. Croswell, 3 Johns. Cas. (N.Y.) 337, 344 app. (1804) (argument presented in behalf of defendant).

41. THOMAS M. COOLEY, A TREATISE ON THE CONSTITUTIONAL LIMITATIONS 175–76 (New York: Da Capo Press, 1972).

42. *See* p. 71 *supra*.

43. THE FEDERALIST No. 44 (J. Madison) at 282.

44. 3 U.S. (3 Dall.) 386 (1798).

45. Wilkinson v. Leland, 27 U.S. (2 Pet.) 627, 657 (1829).

46. Dash v. Van Kleeck, 7 Johns. (N.Y.) 477, 505 (1811).

47. People v. Croswell, 3 Johns. Cas. (N.Y.) 337, 358 app. (1804) (argument presented in behalf of the defendant).

48. Declaration and Resolves of the First Continental Congress, 14 Oct. 1774.

49. However, according to an early Supreme Court decision, the Constitution did not incorporate all the common law. Originally, some observers assumed that the provision in Article III, sec. 2, cl. 1, extending the judicial power to "the Laws of the United States," provided common-law jurisdiction to the federal judiciary on the basis that the common law was a law of the United States. United States v. Hudson & Goodwin, 11 U.S. (7 Cranch) 32 (1812), presented the question of whether federal circuit courts could exercise jurisdiction in common-law criminal cases. Justice Johnson stated that lower federal courts are tribunals of limited jurisdiction and do not have the power to enforce the criminal common law in the absence of congressional legislation conferring it. *Cf.* United States v. Coolidge, 14 U.S. (1 Wheat.) 415 (1816). *See* Swift v. Tyson, 41 U.S. (16 Pet.) 1 (1842) and Erie R.R. v. Tompkins, 304 U.S. 64 (1938).

50. 1 JAMES KENT, COMMENTARIES ON AMERICAN LAW 315–16 (New York: Da Capo Press, 1971).

51. *See id.* at 321–22, 465–79; J. A. C. Grant, *Our Common Law Constitution*, 40 BOSTON L. REV. 1 (1960); GORDON S. WOOD, THE CREATION OF THE AMERICAN REPUBLIC 1776–1787 at 9–13 (Chapel Hill, N.C.: University of North Carolina Press, 1969).

52. WOOD, *supra* note 51, at 10.

53. Grant, *supra* note 51, at 1–2.

54. COOLEY, *supra* note 41, at 429.

55. Grant, *supra* note 51, at 19.

56. HAINES, *supra* note 8, at 217. See Vanhorne's Lessee v. Dorrance, 2 U.S. (2 Dall.) 304 (1795); Beard, *supra* note 20, at 51–54; Corwin, *supra* note 17, at 58–76; ROBERT KENNETH FAULKNER, THE JURISPRUDENCE OF JOHN MARSHALL 65–79 (Princeton, N.J.: Princeton University Press, 1968). Hamilton wrote that one of the

purposes of federal judicial review was to protect property rights in the states. 25 THE PAPERS OF ALEXANDER HAMILTON 478 (Harold C. Syrett, ed.) (New York: Columbia University Press, 1977).

57. Marshall in Fletcher v. Peck, 10 U.S. (6 Cranch.) 87, 132 (1810). KENT, *supra* note 50, at 273; STORY, *supra* note 3, at 426, citing Kent.

58. 1 MOORE'S FEDERAL PRACTICE at 701.22–23, and authorities cited (New York: Matthew Bender, 2d ed. 1964). U.S. CONST., art.III, §2.

59. THE FEDERALIST No. 33 (A. Hamilton) at 201–05 and No. 44 (J. Madison) at 283–87.

60. THE FEDERALIST No. 41 (J. Madison) at 261–64.

61. THE FEDERALIST Nos. 30 & 34 (A. Hamilton).

62. 4 THE WORKS OF ALEXANDER HAMILTON 152 (Henry Cabot Lodge, ed.) (New York and London: G. P. Putnam's Sons, 1904).

63. 2 FARRAND 303–04, 308–11, 321–26, 344, 351, 611, 615–16, 620.

64. *See* 3 FARRAND 375–76.

65. *See* ROBERT HESSEN, IN DEFENSE OF THE CORPORATION 65–66, 28 (Stanford, Cal.: Hoover Institution Press, 1979); 1 WILLIAM D. GRAMPP, ECONOMIC LIBERALISM 106–08 (New York: Random House, 1965). The corporation in the Constitutional period was a different institution than it is today. Chartering of corporations then usually accompanied a grant of exclusive economic privileges.

66. 2 FARRAND 615–16 (Madison's notes). The official journal shows the vote was taken "To grant letters of incorporation for Canals & ca." *Id.* at 611. The notes of James McHenry, delegate from Maryland, generally corroborate Madison. *Id.* at 620.

67. 2 FARRAND 611, 616, 620.

68. 3 FARRAND 362. Views on this matter were also expressed by Gerry, *id.*, Jefferson and Hamilton, *id.* at 363, and Baldwin, *id.* at 375–76.

69. 3 FARRAND 463, 494–95. *See* Hamilton and Jefferson's explanation for the action, 3 FARRAND 363–64. *See* also remarks of Senator T. W. Cobb arguing that the Constitution does not authorize Congress to construct canals. 3 FARRAND 464–66.

70. THE FEDERALIST No. 45 (J. Madison) at 293.

71. THE FEDERALIST No. 42 (J. Madison) at 267–68.

72. 3 FARRAND 478.

73. THE FEDERALIST No. 10 (J. Madison) at 84. See chapter 2, note 30 and accompanying text.

74. H. Howard Mann, *The Marshall Court: Nationalization of Private Rights and Personal Liberty from the Authority of the Commercial Clause,* 38 IND. L. REV. 117 (1963).

75. 1 GRAMPP, *supra* note 65, at 109.

76. *Id.*

77. ADAM SMITH, THE WEALTH OF NATIONS 712 (Edwin Cannan, ed.) (New York: Modern Library, 1937).

78. MILTON FRIEDMAN, CAPITALISM AND FREEDOM 127–28 (Chicago and London: University of Chicago Press, 1962).

79. Martin Diamond, *Democracy and the Federalist: A Reconsideration of the Framers' Intents,* 53 AMERICAN POL. SCI. REV. 52 (1959).

80. THE FEDERALIST No. 10 (J. Madison) at 78.

81. Ralph Lerner, *Commerce and Character: The Anglo-American as New-Model Man,* 36 WILLIAM AND MARY QUARTERLY 3 (1979).

82. See discussion of affirmative jurisprudence in chapter 14 *infra.*

83. Robert F. Nagel, *Separation of Powers and the Scope of Federal Equitable Remedies*, 30 STAN. L. REV. 661, 661–62 (1978).

84. United States v. Hudson & Goodwin, 11 U.S. (7 Cranch) 32, 34 (1812).

85. Kilbourn v. Thompson, 103 U.S. 168, 191 (1881).

86. Meriwether v. Garrett, 102 U.S. 472, 521 (1880) (Field, Miller, and Bradley, J. J., concurring).

87. *See* HAINES, *supra* note 8, at 88–121.

88. BENJAMIN N. CARDOZO, THE NATURE OF THE JUDICIAL PROCESS 124–25 (New Haven, Conn.: Yale University Press, 1921). *See* Zechariah Chafee, Jr., *Do Judges Make or Discover Law?*, 91 PROCEEDINGS OF THE AMERICAN PHILOSOPHICAL SOCIETY 405 (1947).

89. Osborn v. Bank of the United States, 22 U.S. (9 Wheat.) 738, 866 (1824).

90. THE FEDERALIST No. 78 (A. Hamilton) at 465.

91. 1 BLACKSTONE, COMMENTARIES at *69. *Cf.* 2 BLACKSTONE at *117.

92. *Quoted* in MORTON J. HORWITZ, THE TRANSFORMATION OF AMERICAN LAW 1780–1860, at 9 (Cambridge, Mass.: Harvard University Press, 1977) *citing* 2 LEGAL PAPERS OF JOHN ADAMS 127 (L. Wroth and H. Zobel, eds., 1965).

93. Marbury v. Madison, 5 U.S. (1 Cranch) 137, 170 (1803).

94. THE FEDERALIST No. 78 (A. Hamilton) at 466.

95. THE FEDERALIST No. 47 (J. Madison) at 303.

Chapter Five

1. Lincoln Federal Labor Union v. Northwestern Iron & Metal Co., 335 U.S. 525, 535 (1949).

2. 165 U.S. 578 (1897).

3. *Id.* at 589.

4. *Id.* at 589–90 *citing* Butchers' Union Co. v. Crescent City Co., 111 U.S. 746, 762 (1883) (Bradley, J., concurrring).

5. *Id.* at 590 *citing* Powell v. Pennsylvania, 127 U.S. 678, 684 (1888).

6. 198 U.S. 45 (1905).

7. People v. Lochner, 76 N.Y.S. 396 (1902).

8. People v. Lochner, 177 N.Y. 145, 69 N.E. 373 (1904).

9. 198 U.S. at 76 (Holmes, J., dissenting).

10. *Id.* at 57–58.

11. *Id.* at 59.

12. *Id.* at 54. The reference is to Holden v. Hardy, 169 U.S. 366 (1898).

13. People v. Beattie, 96 App. Div. 383, 89 N.Y.S. 193 (1904); *In re* Aubry, 36 Wash. 308, 78 P. 900 (1904); Bessette v. People, 193 Ill. 334, 62 N.E. 215 (1901).

14. People v. Beattie *supra*.

15. Low v. Rees Printing Co., 41 Neb. 127, 59 N.W. 362 (1894); Godcharles & Co. v. Wigeman, 113 Pa. 431, 6 A. 354 (1886).

16. Muller v. Oregon, 208 U.S. 412 (1908).

17. Bunting v. Oregon, 243 U.S. 426 (1917).

18. 198 U.S. at 59.

19. See p. 117 *infra*.

20. In the small bakeries with the long working time, the employees were not engaged in physical activity throughout their working hours, but were idle and even slept while

awaiting completion of a phase in the baking process. New York Times, 27 Dec. 1896, at
1, cols. 5–6. The index of output per man hour for workers in manufacturing increased
from 36.6 in 1909 to 114.3 in 1950 (1947 = 100), which is an average annual com
pound rate of increase of approximately 2.8 percent. The corresponding figure for
bakery workers is 59.6 in 1947 and 105.5 in 1970 (1967 = 100), which constitutes an
average annual compound rate of increase of about 2.5 percent. THE STATISTICAL
HISTORY OF THE UNITED STATES FROM COLONIAL TIMES TO THE PRESENT at 950 (New
York: Basic Books, 1976). These figures suggest the parameters of annual productivity
gains. Unlike the Lochner situation where only working hours would be limited, these
gains also encompass advances caused by new or improved technology, better manage
ment methods, and educational training of labor. See discussion in CARROLL R
DAUGHTERTY, LABOR PROBLEMS IN AMERICAN INDUSTRY 82–83, 186–208 (Boston,
Mass.: Houghton Mifflin, 1938); PAUL SAMUELSON, ECONOMICS 741–42 (New York:
McGraw-Hill, 10th ed. 1976).

21. 1 WILLIAM G. PANSCHAR, BAKING IN AMERICA 45–84 (Evanston, Ill.: Northwestern University Press, 1956).

22. HAZEL KYRK AND JOSEPH STANCLIFFE DAVIS, THE AMERICAN BAKING INDUSTRY
1849–1923 AS SHOWN IN THE CENSUS REPORTS 35–37, 96 (Stanford, Cal.: Stanford
University, 1925).

23. BUREAU OF THE CENSUS, DEPT. OF COMMERCE AND LABOR, MANUFACTURES
1905, Part II States and Territories tables 24, 25, at 726, 729 (Washington: Government
Printing Office, 1907).

24. New York Times, 16 May 1896, at 9, cols. 1–2.

25. New York Times, 8 Apr. 1896, at 6, col. 5.

26. New York Times, 16 May 1896, at 9, col. 2.

27. "The length of time which is considered a day's labor in bakeries varies greatly—
those conducted on a modern plan, with improved appliances and proper workrooms,
rarely work their men more than ten hours a day; while in those which were found in
noisome cellars and unfit surroundings the men were compelled to work twelve to
twenty-two hours." TENTH ANNUAL REPORT OF THE FACTORY INSPECTORS OF STATE
OF NEW YORK 42 (Albany and New York: Wynkoop Hallenbeck Crawford, 1896).

28. The Statistics of the Journeyman Bakers of the State of New York, BAKERS'
JOURNAL (Brooklyn, N.Y.), 3 June 1896, at 1, cols. 1, 2.

29. The manager of an Albany (New York) biscuit company commented favorably on
the law, but criticized enforcement practices. BAKERS' JOURNAL, 22 Jan. 1896, at 1, col.
2. Nine "employing bakers," both individuals and companies in New York and
Minnesota (which adopted a similar statute), wrote letters to the editor supporting
the regulation in whole or in part. BAKERS' JOURNAL, 20 Nov. 1895, at 1, cols. 3–4.

30. See New York Times, 3 Jan. 1907, at 6, col. 3; and 8 Aug. 1896, at 5, col. 2.

31. KYRK AND DAVIS, supra note 22, at 60–61.

32. PAUL H. DOUGLAS, REAL WAGES IN THE UNITED STATES 1890–1926, at 112
(New York: Augustus M. Kelley, 1966). Working hours were also declining in other
industries. See infra notes 54 and 55 and accompanying text.

33. Wall Street Journal, 31 May 1978, at 1, col. 1.

34. 198 U.S. at 59–60.

35. 348 U.S. 483 (1955).

36. Id. at 487.

37. City of New Orleans v. Dukes, 427 U.S. 297, 303–04 (1976).

38. Walter Guzzardi, Jr., What the Supreme Court Is Really Telling Business, FOR-
TUNE, 147, 149 (Jan. 1977).

39. RICHARD A. POSNER, ECONOMIC ANALYSIS OF LAW 271 (Boston and Toronto: Little, Brown, 1972).

40. 198 U.S. at 64.

41. 208 U.S. 161 (1908).

42. 236 U.S. 1 (1915).

43. 208 U.S. at 174–75.

44. 236 U.S. at 17.

45. *Id.*

46. CHESTER WHITNEY WRIGHT, ECONOMIC HISTORY OF THE UNITED STATES 618–19 New York: McGraw-Hill, 2d ed. 1949). Union membership grew to a peak of 17.5 percent in 1920 following the war, but declined to 9.3 percent in 1930. *Id.*

47. William E. Nelson, *The Impact of the Antislavery Movement upon Styles of Judicial Reasoning in Nineteenth Century America,* 87 HARV. L. REV. 513, 557 (1974) citing *n re* Higgins, 27 F. 443, 445 (C.C. N.D. Tex., 1886).

48. *Quoted* in HENRY HAZLITT, THE CONQUEST OF POVERTY 139 (New Rochelle, N.Y.: Arlington House, 1973).

49. CHARLES O. GREGORY & HAROLD A. KATZ, LABOR LAW: CASES, MATERIALS AND COMMENTS 122 (Charlottesville, Va.: Michie Casebook Corp., 1948).

50. U.S. Bureau of Labor Statistics, News Release for Labor Day Weekend, 1977, No. 77-771, table 2.

51. WRIGHT, *supra* note 46, at 429, 889.

52. THE STATISTICAL HISTORY, *supra* note 20, at 224.

53. GEORGE F. WARREN & FRANK A. PEARSON, GOLD AND PRICES 316–17 (New York: ohn Wiley & Sons, 1935) (wages and wholesale prices); BUREAU OF LABOR STATISTICS, HISTORY OF WAGES IN THE UNITED STATES FROM COLONIAL TIMES TO 1928 at 521 Washington, D.C.: Government Printing Office, 1934) and THE STATISTICAL HISTORY upra note 20, at 211 (wages and consumer prices). According to these sources, wholesale and consumer prices were virtually the same in 1914–15 as in 1840 while wage ates per hour for all industries other than agriculture for which data are available rose hreefold for this period. On this basis, the purchasing power of nonagricultural wages increased between 1840 and 1914–15 at an average annual compound rate slightly in excess of 1.5 percent.

54. DAUGHERTY, *supra* note 20, at 192.

55. DOUGLAS, *supra* note 32, at 116.

Chapter Six

1. Chapters 2 and 5 *supra.*

2. Lawton v. Steele, 152 U.S. 133, 137 (1894).

3. Mary Cornelia Porter, *That Commerce Shall Be Free: A New Look at the Old Laissez-Faire Court,* 1976 SUP. CT. REV. 135, 140–45.

4. Nebbia v. New York, 291 U.S. 502 (1934) and West Coast Hotel v. Parrish, 300 U.S. 379 (1937).

5. 243 U.S. 426 (1917).

6. 261 U.S. 525 (1923).

7. *Id.* at 564 (Taft, C.J., dissenting).

8. EDWARD S. CORWIN, THE TWILIGHT OF THE SUPREME COURT 86 (New Haven, Conn.: Yale University Press, 1934).

9. 272 U.S. 365 (1926).

10. Ray A. Brown, *Due Process of Law, Police Power, and the Supreme Court*, 40 Harv. L. Rev. 943, 945 n.11 (1927).

11. Wallace Mendelson, *Separation, Politics and Judicial Activism*, 52 Ind. L.J. 313, 322 (1977).

12. 260 U.S. 393 (1922).

13. *Id.* at 416 (Brandeis, J., dissenting).

14. *Id.* at 415–16 (citations omitted).

15. *Id.* at 414–16 (citations omitted).

16. 260 U.S. at 418 (dissenting opinion).

17. 272 U.S. at 395.

18. Tyson & Brother v. Banton, 273 U.S. 418, 446 (1927) (Holmes, J., dissenting).

19. Adkins v. Children's Hospital, 261 U.S. 525, 568 (1923) (dissenting opinion).

20. Ferguson v. Skrupa, 372 U.S. 726 (1963).

21. 285 U.S. 262 (1932).

22. *Id.* at 272, *citing* 1925 Okla. Sess. Laws C.147.

23. *Id.* at 310–11 (Brandeis, J., dissenting).

24. *Id.* at 277.

25. *Id.* at 279.

26. *Id.* at 280.

27. *Id.* at 304 (Brandeis, J., dissenting).

28. *See* p. 138 *infra*.

29. 285 U.S. at 292.

30. Adam Smith, The Wealth of Nations 141 (Edwin Cannan, ed.) (New York: Modern Library, 1937).

31. Richard Posner, Economic Analysis of Law 269 (Boston and Toronto: Little, Brown, 1972). Posner notes that Brandeis was evaluating possible justifications for the law and accordingly his expressions may not necessarily represent his own views. However, the Justice rarely found justification for upholding laws limiting the exercise of speech and press. *See* chapter 7 *infra*.

32. Michael Levine, *The Economics and Politics of Airline Deregulation* in The Interaction of Economics and the Law 70 (Bernard H. Siegan, ed.) (Lexington, Mass.: D.C. Heath, 1977).

33. Milton Friedman, There Is No Such Thing as a Free Lunch 11–14 (LaSalle, Ill.: Open Court, 1975). *Cf.* Milton Friedman, Capitalism and Freedom 125–26 (Chicago and London: University of Chicago Press, 1962).

34. Ralph Nader, *Regulatory Reform*, Statement Submitted to the Consumer and Environmental Subcommittees, Committee on Commerce, U.S. Senate, 23 June 1975, pg. 2.

35. 285 U.S. at 273.

36. Posner, *supra* note 31, at 269.

37. Nashville, C. & St. Louis Ry. v. Walters, 294 U.S. 405 (1935); Thompson v. Consolidated Gas Utilities Corp., 300 U.S. 55 (1937).

38. 285 U.S. at 301–02.

39. Nebbia v. New York, 291 U.S. 502 (1934).

40. West Coast Hotel Co. v. Parrish, 300 U.S. 379 (1937).

41. 291 U.S. at 548 (McReynolds, J., dissenting).

42. *Id.* at 548–49, 551 (McReynolds, J., dissenting).

43. *Id.* at 557–58 (McReynolds, J., dissenting).

44. *Id.* at 558–59 (McReynolds, J., dissenting).

45. *Id.* at 556 (McReynolds, J., dissenting).

46. New York Times, 1 Apr. 1933, at 1, col. 5; and Editorial, 6 Apr. 1933, at 16, col. 4.

47. Editorial, New York Times, 12 May 1933, at 16, col. 2.

48. New York Times, 21 Apr. 1934, at 17, col. 8.

49. New York Times, 26 Apr. 1934, at 18, cols. 3–4.

50. A friend whose parents owned a small grocery store on Chicago's West Side during the 1930s advised me that his father worked six days a week, from 8 A.M. to 8 P.M. and four hours on the seventh day. His mother worked 30 to 35 hours per week. Their annual income in 1937 and 1938 was about $2,200 plus food for the family exclusive of meat and fish, which was purchased elsewhere.

51. 291 U.S. at 558 (McReynolds, J., dissenting).

52. Act of 19 Sept. 1918, 40 Stat. 960, c.174.

53. 261 U.S. 525 (1923).

54. *Id.* at 553.

55. *Id.* at 561.

56. *Id.* at 563 (Taft, C.J., dissenting).

57. *Id.* at 570 (Holmes, J., dissenting).

58. 300 U.S. 379 (1937).

59. *Id.* at 391.

60. Califano v. Webster, 430 U.S. 313, 316–17 (1977); Craig v. Boren, 429 U.S. 190, 197 (1976).

61. *Cf.* Orr v. Orr, 99 S. Ct. 1102 (1979); Califano v. Webster, 430 U.S. 313 (1977).

62. In recent times, some Justices have sought to subject sex classifications to the most rigorous standard of review. Justice Brennan for himself and three other Justices declared in Frontiero v. Richardson, 411 U.S. 677 (1973), that classifications based upon sex, like those based upon race, are inherently suspect and require strict scrutiny. Because four other Justices refused to accept his reasoning, and one Justice dissented, Brennan's position does not have the force of law.

63. Jude Wanniski, *A Conversation with Munoz Marin,* WALL STREET JOURNAL, 24 Aug. 1977, at 14, col. 3–4.

64. Finis Welch, *The Rising Impact of Minimum Wages,* REGULATION (Nov./Dec. 1978) 28, 30.

65. *Cited id.* at 34. Welch lists these studies (at 37):

Gramlich, Edward M. *Impact of Minimum Wages on Other Wages, Employment, and Family Incomes,* in 2 BROOKINGS PAPERS ON ECONOMIC ACTIVITY 409–51 (1976).

Hashimoto, Masanori, and Mincer, Jacob. Employment and Unemployment Effects of Minimum Wages (Washington, D.C.: National Bureau of Economic Research, 1970), mimeo.

Kaitz, Hyman. *Experience of the Past: The National Minimum,* in BUREAU OF LABOR STATISTICS, YOUTH UNEMPLOYMENT AND MINIMUM WAGES, Bulletin no. 1657 (Washington, D.C.: BLS, 1970).

Kosters, Marvin, and Welch, Finis. *The Effects of Minimum Wages on the Distribution of Changes in Aggregate Employment,* 62 AM. ECON. REV. 323–32 (June 1972).

Mincer, Jacob. *Unemployment Effects of Minimum Wages,* 84 J. POL. ECON. S87-S104 (August 1976).

Ragan, James. *Minimum Wages and the Youth Labor Market,* 59 REV. ECON. & STAT. 129–36 (May 1977).

Welch, Finis. *Minimum Wage Legislation in the United States,* 12 ECON. INQUIRY 285–318 (September 1974) and "Reply" in 15 *id.* at 139–42 (January 1977).

Welch, Finis, and Cunningham, James. *Effects of Minimum Wages on the Level and Age Composition of Youth Employment*, 60 REV. ECON. & STAT. 140–45 (February 1978).

66. Welch, *supra* note 64, at 36.

67. Richard Posner, *Economic Justice and the Economist*, THE PUBLIC INTEREST, 109, 110 (Fall 1973).

68. Morehead v. New York *ex rel.* Tipaldo, 298 U.S. 587, 617 (1936).

69. ELEANOR FLEXNER, CENTURY OF STRUGGLE 201 (New York: Atheneum, 1970).

70. B. BABCOCK, A. FREEDMAN, E. NORTON, & S. ROSS, SEX DISCRIMINATION AND THE LAW 24 (Boston and Toronto: Little, Brown, 1975).

71. Elizabeth Brandeis, *Hour Laws for Men* in 3 HISTORY OF LABOR IN THE UNITED STATES 1896–1932, at 540, 557–58 (John R. Commons, ed.) (New York: Macmillan, 1935).

72. FLORENCE KELLEY, SOME ETHICAL GAINS THROUGH LEGISLATION 133 (New York: Macmillan, 1905).

73. WILLIAM HENRY CHAFE, THE AMERICAN WOMAN 127 (New York: Oxford University Press, 1972).

74. 208 U.S. 412 (1908).

75. Mengelkoch v. Industrial Welfare Comm'n, 442 F.2d 1119 (9th Cir. 1971).

76. Rosenfeld v. Southern Pacific Co., 293 F. Supp. (C.D. Cal.) 1219 (1968); *aff'd.* 444 F.2d 1219 (9th Cir. 1971).

77. Adkins v. Children's Hospital, 261 U.S. 525, 561 (1923).

78. 94 U.S. 113 (1877).

79. 262 U.S. 522 (1923).

80. *Id.* at 538.

81. Tyson & Brother v. Banton, 273 U.S. 418 (1927); Ribnik v. McBride, 277 U.S. 350 (1928); Williams v. Standard Oil Co., 278 U.S. 235 (1929).

82. *See* Frank R. Strong, *The Economic Philosophy of Lochner: Emergence, Embrasure and Emasculation*, 15 ARIZ. L. REV. 419, 436–49 (1973).

83. Chickasha Cotton Oil Co. v. Cotton County Gin Co., 40 F.2d 846 (10th Cir. 1930).

84. 285 U.S. at 276.

85. Tyson & Brother v. Banton, 273 U.S. 418, 451–52 (1927) (Stone, J., dissenting).

86. Holden v. Hardy, 169 U.S. 366 (1898).

87. Muller v. Oregon, 208 U.S. 412 (1908).

88. Bunting v. Oregon, 243 U.S. 426 (1917).

89. New York Central R.R. v. White, 243 U.S. 188 (1917); Hawkins v. Bleakly, 243 U.S. 210 (1917); Mountain Timber Co. v. Washington, 243 U.S. 219 (1917).

90. Wilson v. New, 243 U.S. 332 (1917).

91. Block v. Hirsh, 256 U.S. 135 (1921); Marcus Brown Holding Co. v. Feldman, 256 U.S. 170 (1921); Edgar A. Levy Leasing Co. v. Siegel, 258 U.S. 242 (1922).

92. Schmidinger v. City of Chicago, 226 U.S. 578 (1913); P.F. Petersen Baking Co. v. Bryan, 290 U.S. 570 (1934).

93. German Alliance Ins. Co. v. Lewis, 233 U.S. 389 (1914).

94. Armour & Co. v. North Dakota, 240 U.S. 510 (1916).

95. Dent v. West Virginia, 129 U.S. 114 (1889).

96. Jacobson v. Massachusetts, 197 U.S. 11 (1905); Crossman v. Lurman, 192 U.S. 189 (1904).

97. Jones v. Brim, 165 U.S. 180 (1897); St. Louis & S.F. Ry. v. Mathews, 165 U.S. 1 (1897).

98. Miller v. Schoene, 276 U.S. 272 (1928); Hadacheck v. Sebastian, 239 U.S. 394 (1915); Reinman v. City of Little Rock, 237 U.S. 171 (1915); Murphy v. California, 225

U.S. 623 (1912); Powell v. Pennsylvania, 127 U.S. 678 (1888); Mugler v. Kansas, 123 U.S. 623 (1887).

99. Strong, *supra* note 82, at 425–27, 433.

100. Aaron Director, *The Parity of the Economic Market Place,* 7 J. L. & ECON. 1, 2 (1964).

Chapter Seven

1. 262 U.S. 390 (1923).
2. 268 U.S. 510 (1925).
3. 262 U.S. at 399–400.
4. *Id.* at 401.
5. *Id.* at 412 (Holmes, J., dissenting), citing three cases.
6. *Cf.* New State Ice Co. v. Liebmann, 285 U.S. 262, 311 (1932) (Brandeis, J., dissenting).
7. 268 U.S. at 534–35.
8. 431 U.S. 494 (1977).
9. 273 U.S. 284 (1927).
10. *Id.* at 298.
11. 197 U.S. 11 (1905).
12. 274 U.S. 200, 207 (1927).
13. 287 U.S. 45 (1932).
14. 239 U.S. 33 (1915).
15. Crane v. New York, 239 U.S. 195 (1915); Frick v. Webb, 263 U.S. 326 (1923); Ohio *ex rel.* Clarke v. Deckebach, 274 U.S. 392 (1927).
16. Plessy v. Ferguson, 163 U.S. 537 (1896); Berea College v. Kentucky 211 U.S. 45 (1908).
17. Buchanan v. Warley, 245 U.S. 60 (1917).
18. Norris v. Alabama, 294 U.S. 587 (1935). In Strauder v. West Virginia, 100 U.S. 303 (1880), the Court established that the systematic exclusion of blacks from grand or petit juries violated the equal protection clause.
19. Grovey v. Townsend, 295 U.S. 45 (1935).
20. Semler v. Oregon State Bd. of Dental Examiners, 294 U.S. 608 (1935); Packer Corp. v. Utah, 285 U.S. 105 (1932).
21. 165 U.S. 275, 281 (1897).
22. *Quoted* in Davis v. Massachusetts, 167 U.S. 43, 47 (1897).
23. 205 U.S. 454, 462 (1907). On Blackstone's definition of free expression, see chapter 11.
24. *Id.* at 465 (Harlan, J., dissenting).
25. 236 U.S. 273, 277 (1915).
26. 249 U.S. 47 (1919).
27. *Id.* at 52.
28. *Id.*
29. 249 U.S. 211 (1919).
30. 249 U.S. 204, 206 (1919).
31. *Id.* at 209. Compare Justice Sanford's remark in Gitlow in text accompanying note 49 *infra.*
32. 250 U.S. 616 (1919).
33. 268 U.S. 652 (1925), discussed pp. 170–71 *infra.*

34. Pennekamp v. Florida, 328 U.S. 331, 353 (1946) (Frankfurter, J., concurring).

35. Dennis v. United States, 341 U.S. 494, 505 (1951).

36. Harry Kalven, Jr., *"Uninhibited, Robust, and Wide-Open": A Note on Free Speech and the Warren Court,* 67 MICH. L. REV. 289, 291 n.18 (1968); Frank R. Strong, *Fifty Years of "Clear and Present Danger": From Schenck to Brandenburg–and Beyond,* 1969 SUP. CT. REV. 41, 44.

37. 260 U.S. 393 (1922).

38. Prof. Epstein observes that Holmes maintained his position that taking was a matter of degree over a forty-year period. Richard A. Epstein, *The Next Generation of Legal Scholarship?,* 30 STAN. L. REV. 635, 654–55 n.53 (1978), *citing* Rideout v. Knox, 148 Mass. 368, 19 N.E. 390 (1889).

39. 250 U.S. 616 (1919).

40. *Id.* at 628 (Holmes, J., dissenting).

41. *Id.* at 630 (Holmes, J., dissenting).

42. *Id.* at 621.

43. Wilson v. New, 243 U.S. 332 (1917).

44. Block v. Hirsh, 256 U.S. 135, 157 (1921).

45. 268 U.S. 652 (1925); 274 U.S. 357 (1927).

46. 268 U.S. at 666.

47. *Id.* at 654 *citing* New York Penal Law §161(1).

48. 274 U.S. at 360.

49. 268 U.S. at 669.

50. 268 U.S. at 673 (Holmes, J., dissenting).

51. 274 U.S. at 379 (Brandeis, J., concurring).

52. *Id.* at 375–77 (Brandeis, J., concurring).

53. Pericles, *Funeral Oration,* in 2 THUCYDIDES, THE PELOPONNESIAN WAR, chap. 40 *cited* in CHARLES A. MILLER, THE SUPREME COURT AND THE USES OF HISTORY 98 n.82 (New York: Clarion Books, Simon and Schuster, 1972).

54. Alpheus Thomas Mason, BRANDEIS: LAWYER AND JUDGE IN THE MODERN STATE 160 (Princeton, N.J.: Princeton University Press, 1933).

55. Olmstead v. United States, 277 U.S. 438, 479 (1928). For a different perspective on Brandeis *see* Melvin I. Urofsky, *The Conservatism of Mr. Justice Brandeis,* 23 MODERN AGE 39 (Winter 1979). For other Brandeis views on economic policies, *see* his dissents in Liggett v. Lee, 288 U.S. 517, 541 (1932) (Florida chain store tax), and Adams v. Tanner, 244 U.S. 590, 597 (1916) (Washington law barring employment fees from workers).

56. Lochner v. New York, 198 U.S. 45, 75 (1905) (Holmes, J., dissenting).

57. *Hearings before the Subcomm. on Separation of Powers of the Comm. on the Judiciary,* U.S. Senate, 90th Congress, 2d Sess. (1968) at 21.

58. LEONARD LEVY, LEGACY OF SUPPRESSION: FREEDOM OF SPEECH AND PRESS IN EARLY AMERICAN HISTORY 248 n.146 (New York: Harper Torchbooks, 1963).

59. 274 U.S. at 373 (Brandeis, J., concurring).

60. 2 JAMES KENT, COMMENTARIES ON AMERICAN LAW 14–22 (New York: Da Capo Press, 1971); 3 JOSEPH STORY, COMMENTARIES ON THE CONSTITUTION OF THE UNITED STATES 732–33 (New York: Da Capo Press, 1970). However, Whitney would have benefited from an 1812 High Court opinion that lower federal courts do not have jurisdiction to enforce the criminal common law in the absence of Congressional authority. United States v. Hudson & Goodwin, 11 U.S. (7 Cranch) 32 (1812).

61. 274 U.S. 380 (1927).

62. 299 U.S. 353 (1937).

63. *Id.* at 365.

64. *Id.*

65. 301 U.S. 242 (1937).

66. 283 U.S. 359 (1931).

67. 283 U.S. 697 (1931).

68. *Id.* at 713.

69. *See* MILLER, *supra* note 53, at 72–75.

70. *See* further discussion of this case in chapter 11 *infra.*

71. Village of Euclid v. Ambler Realty Co., 272 U.S. 365 (1926).

72. 239 U.S. 394 (1915).

73. 297 U.S. 233 (1936).

74. *Id.* at 250.

75. Miller, *supra* note 53, at 77.

76. 301 U.S. 103 (1937).

77. *Id.* at 139–40 (Sutherland, J., dissenting). A recent case suggests that the present Court might uphold Sutherland's view. In NLRB v. Catholic Bishop of Chicago, 440 U.S. 490 (1979), involving NLRB's authority to exercise jurisdiction over lay faculty members of church-operated schools, Chief Justice Burger writing for the majority stated that if the act asserted such authority, there would be a significant risk of infringement of the religion clauses of the First Amendment.

78. 301 U.S. at 137 (Sutherland, J., dissenting).

79. Robert H. Bork, *Neutral Principles and Some First Amendment Problems,* 47 IND. L. J. 1, 24 (1971).

80. *See id.* at 23–35.

81. United States v. Dennis, 183 F.2d 201 (2d Cir. 1950).

82. Dennis v. United States, 341 U.S. 494 (1951).

83. Robert G. McCloskey, *Economic Due Process and the Supreme Court: An Exhumation and Reburial,* 1962 SUP. CT. REV. 34, 46.

Chapter Eight

1. Morehead v. New York *ex rel.* Tipaldo, 298 U.S. 587 (1936).

2. West Coast Hotel Co. v. Parrish, 300 U.S. 379, 399 (1937).

3. Virginian Ry. v. System Federation No. 40, 300 U.S. 515 (1937); National Labor Relations Board v. Jones & Laughlin Steel Corp., 301 U.S. 1 (1937).

4. 304 U.S. 144 (1938).

5. Filled Milk Act of 4 Mar. 1923 (c.262, 42 Stat. 1486, 21 U.S.C. § 62).

6. *Id.* at 152, 154.

7. *Id.* at 152–53 n.4.

8. 313 U.S. 236 (1941).

9. 277 U.S. 350 (1928).

10. 313 U.S. at 246–47.

11. Robert G. McCloskey, *Economic Due Process and the Supreme Court: An Exhumation and Reburial,* 1962 SUP. CT. REV. 34, 38–39.

12. 335 U.S. 525 (1949).

13. *Id.* at 536–37.

14. McCloskey, *supra* note 11, at 36.

15. *See* chapters 9 and 11 *infra* on the expansion of the expression guarantees.

16. *See* New York Times, 2 March 1923, at 3, col. 6, and 14 March 1923, at 18, col. 8.

17. Martin Shapiro, *The Constitution and Economic Rights* in ESSAYS ON THE CONSTITUTION OF THE UNITED STATES at 85 (M. Judd Harmon, ed.) (Port Washington, N.Y., and London: Kennikat Press, 1978).

18. 270 U.S. 402 (1926).

19. *See e.g.,* Guy Miller Struve, *The Less-Restrictive-Alternative Principle and Economic Due Process,* 80 HARV. L. REV. 1463, 1464 (1967); Note, *State Economic Due Process: A Proposed Approach,* 88 YALE L.J. 1487 (1979).

20. Struve, *supra* note 19, at 1464.

21. 381 U.S. 479, 485 (1965), quoting NAACP v. Alabama, 377 U.S. 288, 307 (1964).

22. Kotch v. Board of River Pilot Commissioners, 330 U.S. 552 (1947).

23. *Id.* at 565 (Rutledge, J., dissenting).

24. Goesaert v. Cleary, 335 U.S. 464 (1948).

25. Daniel v. Family Security Life Ins. Co., 336 U.S. 220, 224 (1949).

26. Williamson v. Lee Optical Co., 348 U.S. 483 (1955).

27. *Id.* at 488.

28. 435 U.S. 967 (1979).

29. 342 U.S. 421 (1952).

30. *Id.* at 427 (Jackson, J., dissenting).

31. 372 U.S. 726 (1963).

32. *See* discussion of this case in chapter 9.

33. 244 U.S. 590 (1917).

34. *Id.* at 594–95.

35. 372 U.S. at 731–32.

36. Martin v. Walton, 368 U.S. 25 (1961).

37. *See In re* Anastaplo, 366 U.S. 82 (1961); Law Students Civil Rights Research Council Inc. v. Wadmond, 401 U.S. 154 (1971).

38. North Dakota State Bd. of Pharmacy v. Snyder's Drug Stores, Inc., 414 U.S. 156 (1973).

39. 278 U.S. 105 (1928).

40. *Id.* at 113.

41. *Id.* at 113–14.

42. 437 U.S. 117 (1978).

43. Governor of Maryland v. Exxon Corp., 279 Md. 410, 370 A.2d 1102 (1977).

44. 437 U.S. at 124–25.

45. 1973 Cal. Stats. ch. 996, §1.

46. Orrin W. Fox Co. v. New Motor Vehicle Bd., 440 F. Supp. 436 (C.D. Ca. 1977).

47. New Motor Vehicle Bd. v. Orrin W. Fox Co., 439 U.S. 96 (1978).

48. *Id.* at 115 (Stevens, J., dissenting).

49. Usery v. Turner Elkhorn Mining Co., 428 U.S. 1, 18–19 (1976).

50. *Id.* at 18–19.

51. Village of Belle Terre v. Boraas, 416 U.S. 1 (1974).

52. Young v. American Mini Theatres, Inc., 427 U.S. 50 (1976).

53. Penn Central Transportation Co. v. City of New York, 98 S. Ct. 2646 (1978).

54. Walter Gellhorn, *The Abuse of Occupational Licensing,* 44 U. CHI. L. REV. 6 n.2 (1976). Gellhorn does not propose judicial relief for these abuses, but proposes to rely on the legislative process.

55. *Id.* at 11–12.

56. *Id.* at 16–18.

57. Gibson v. Berryhill, 411 U.S. 564 (1973).

Chapter Nine

1. 427 U.S. 297 (1976).
2. For an early criticism of this approach, see Justice Harlan's dissent in Shapiro v. Thompson, 394 U.S. 618, 655 (1969).
3. Craig v. Boren, 429 U.S. 190 (1976); Frontiero v. Richardson, 411 U.S. 677 (1973). See comments by Justices Powell and Stevens in Craig and Justice Marshall's in San Antonio Independent School District v. Rodriguez, 411 U.S. 1, 98–110 (1973) (Marshall, J., dissenting).
4. Palko v. Connecticut, 302 U.S. 319, 325 (1937).
5. Hebert v. Louisiana, 272 U.S. 312, 316 (1926).
6. Snyder v. Massachusetts, 291 U.S. 97, 105 (1934).
7. Lisenba v. California, 314 U.S. 219, 236 (1941).
8. LEARNED HAND, THE BILL OF RIGHTS 70 (Cambridge, Mass.: Harvard University Press, 1958).
9. Konigsberg v. State Bar of California, 366 U.S. 36, 61 (1961) (Black, J., dissenting).
10. 283 U.S. 697, 708 (1931).
11. 341 U.S. 494 (1951).
12. *Id.* at 544 (Frankfurter, J., concurring).
13. 395 U.S. 444 (1969).
14. *Id.* at 447.
15. 357 U.S. 513 (1958).
16. *Id.* at 518 *citing* First Unitarian Church of Los Angeles v. County of Los Angeles, 48 Cal. 2d 419, 440, 311 P.2d 508, 521 (1957).
17. Justices Black (357 U.S. at 529) and Douglas (*id.* at 532) wrote concurring opinions. Justice Clark dissented (*id.* at 538). Chief Justice Warren took no part in consideration of the case.
18. *Id.* at 525.
19. *Id.* at 526.
20. *Id.* at 525.
21. *Id.* at 526 (citations omitted).
22. 291 U.S. 502, 548 (1934) (McReynolds, J., dissenting).
23. Thomas v. Collins, 323 U.S. 516, 545–46 (1945) (Jackson, J., concurring).
24. Abrams v. United States, 250 U.S. 616, 630 (1919) (Holmes, J., dissenting).
25. Young v. American Mini Theatres, Inc., 427 U.S. 50, 70 (1976).
26. 376 U.S. 254 (1964).
27. *Id.* at 270.
28. *Id.* at 270, 279. The *Sullivan* ruling was extended to public figures in Curtis Publishing Co. v. Butts, 388 U.S. 130 (1967). In Herbert v. Lando, 441 U.S. 153 (1979), the Court held that the First Amendment does not bar a plaintiff alleging publication of damaging falsehoods from inquiring into the editorial processes of the publishers to determine the existence of actual malice.
29. 403 U.S. 713 (1971).
30. 283 U.S. 697 (1931).
31. United States v. Washington Post Co., 446 F.2d 1327, 1330 (D.C. Cir. 1971) (Wilkey, Cir. J., dissenting).
32. 403 U.S. at 714 (Black, J., concurring); *id.* at 720 (Douglas, J., concurring).
33. *Id.* at 730 (Stewart J., concurring).
34. *Id.* at 426–27 (Brennan, J., concurring).

35. 418 U.S. 241 (1974).

36. *Id.* at 258.

37. *Id.* at 256.

38. Jerome A. Barron, *Access to the Press: A New First Amendment Right,* 80 HARV. L. REV. 1641, 1656 (1967).

39. *See* discussion chapter 11, *infra.* Within recent years editorial writers have complained about Federal Supreme Court decisions that they insist unreasonably restrict the media. See Zurcher v. Stanford Daily, 436 U.S. 547 (1978); Branzburg v. Hayes, 408 U.S. 665 (1972); Gannett Co. v. DePasquale, 99 S. Ct. 2898 (1979); Herbert V. Lando, 441 U.S. 153 (1979). Without expressing any opinion on these decisions, I would observe that the press continues to receive by far the most favored judicial treatment of any industry in the nation. This is evident from the 1978 case of Landmark Communications Inc. v. Virginia, 435 U.S. 829 (1978). Reversing a Virginia Supreme Court decision, the Federal Court ruled (7–0) that the First Amendment forbids punishment of a newspaper for divulging confidential proceedings of the state's judicial inquiry commission, conduct made illegal by the state legislature to safeguard the courts and their processes.

40. Griswold v. Connecticut, 381 U.S. 479, 486 (1965).

41. 410 U.S. 113, 153 (1973).

42. 410 U.S. 179 (1973).

43. Planned Parenthood v. Danforth, 428 U.S. 52 (1976).

44. *Id.* at 69 *citing* Planned Parenthood v. Danforth, 392 F.Supp. 1362, 1375 (E.D. Mo., 1975).

45. 432 U.S. 464 (1977).

46. Carey v. Population Services Int'l, 431 U.S. 678 (1977).

47. See Edwards v. California, 314 U.S. 160 (1941).

48. The Passenger Cases, 48 U.S. (7 How.) 283, 492 (1849) (Taney, C.J., dissenting).

49. 394 U.S. 618 (1969) (see discussion in chapter 14 *infra*).

50. 415 U.S. 250 (1974).

51. 411 U.S. 1 (1973) (see discussion in chapter 14 *infra*).

52. Roe v. Norton, 408 F.Supp. 660, 663, 664 (D. Conn. 1975).

53. 432 U.S. at 473–74.

54. *Id.* at 470–71.

55. 351 U.S. 12 (1956).

56. 372 U.S. 353 (1963).

57. Ross v. Moffitt, 417 U.S. 600 (1974).

58. 383 U.S. 663, 666 (1966).

59. 351 U.S. at 18.

60. 383 U.S. at 665.

61. 394 U.S. at 630.

62. Gerald Gunther, *The Supreme Court, 1971 Term: Foreword: In Search of Evolving Doctrine on a Changing Court: A Model for a Newer Equal Protection,* 86 HARV. L. REV. 1 (1972).

63. 414 U.S. 632 (1974).

64. 412 U.S. 441 (1973).

65. *Id.* at 452.

66. 402 U.S. 535 (1971).

67. *Id.* at 539.

68. Weinberger v. Salfi, 422 U.S. 749, 772 (1975) (per Rehnquist, J.).

69. Note, *The Irrebuttable Presumption Doctrine in the Supreme Court,* 87 HARV. L.

REV. 1534 (1974); Note, *Irrebuttable Presumptions: An Illusory Analysis,* 27 STAN. L. REV. 449 (1975).

70. Sandra Segal Polin, Substantive Due Process: A Doctrine Restored, unpublished manuscript prepared for the Institute for Humane Studies, Menlo Park, Cal. (Nov. 1976) *citing* Schlesinger v. Wisconsin, 270 U.S. 230 (1926); Hoeper v. Tax Comm'n. 284 U.S. 206 (1931); Heiner v. Donnan, 285 U.S. 312 (1932).

71. 372 U.S. 726 (1963). This case is also discussed in chapter 8.

72. Note, *The Conclusive Presumption Doctrine: Equal Process or Due Protection?* 72 MICH. L. REV. 800, 831 (1974). Footnotes omitted.

Chapter Ten

1. Virginia State Bd. of Pharmacy v. Virginia Citizens Consumer Council, Inc., 425 U.S. 748, 763 (1976).

2. ADVERTISING AND FREE SPEECH xi (Allen Hyman and M. Bruce Johnson, eds.) (Lexington, Mass.: D.C. Heath, Lexington Books, 1977).

3. 316 U.S. 52, 54 (1942).

4. Cammarano v. United States, 358 U.S. 498, 514 (1959) (Douglas, J., concurring).

5. *See* Virginia State Bd. of Pharmacy v. Virginia Citizens Consumer Council, Inc., 425 U.S. at 787 (Rehnquist, J., dissenting).

6. 421 U.S. 809 (1975).

7. *Id.* at 822.

8. 425 U.S. 748 (1976).

9. *Id.* at 756.

10. *Id.* at 763–64.

11. *Id.* at 765, 763, 769, 770.

12. *Id.* at 788–89 (Rehnquist, J., dissenting).

13. 431 U.S. 85 (1977).

14. *Id.* at 93 (citations omitted).

15. *Id.* at 98.

16. *Id.* at 96.

17. *Id.* at 97 *citing* 274 U.S. 357, 377 (1927) (Brandeis, J., concurring).

18. 431 U.S. at 92.

19. Bates v. State Bar of Arizona, 433 U.S. 350, 379 (1977).

20. Wall Street Journal, 1 May 1980, at 1, col. 5.

21. Stadnik v. Shell's City, Inc., 140 So.2d 871 (Fla. 1962); Maryland Bd. of Pharmacy v. Sav-A-Lot, Inc., 270 Md. 103, 311 A.2d 242 (1973); Pennsylvania State Bd. of Pharmacy v. Pastor, 441 Pa. 186, 272 A.2d 487 (1971).

22. 431 U.S. 678 (1977).

23. *Id.* at 689.

24. *Id.* at 701 *citing* Brandenburg v. Ohio, 395 U.S. 444, 447 (1969).

25. People v. Privitera, 55 Cal. App. 3d Supp. 39, 128 Cal. Reptr. 151 (1976).

26. 23 Cal. 3d 697, 153 Cal. Reptr. 431, 591 P.2d 919 (1979).

27. 365 U.S. 127 (1961).

28. *Id.* at 141.

29. 429 U.S. 190 (1976).

30. *Id.* at 219 (Rehnquist, J., dissenting).

31. 426 U.S. 88 (1976).

32. *Id.* at 102 n.23 *citing* Truax v. Raich, 239 U.S. 33, 41 (1915).

33. Sugarman v. Dougall, 413 U.S. 634 (1973). Aliens are not, however, protected in all lines of work. In Ambach v. Norwick, 99 S. Ct. 1589 (1979), the majority opinion explained that while states have frequently been denied the authority to exclude aliens from engaging in various activities, the courts have maintained an exception to this rule: those state functions intimately related to the operation of the state as a governmental entity. The Court upheld a statute barring aliens from certification as public school teachers. It distinguished this activity from the practice of law, having previously invalidated a statute preventing aliens from becoming lawyers. *In re* Griffiths, 413 U.S. 717 (1973). In 1978, the Court held that New York City could exclude aliens from the ranks of its police force. Foley v. Connelie, 435 U.S. 291 (1978).

34. *See* United States v. Carolene Products Co., 304 U.S. 144, 152–53 n.4 (1938), discussed in chapter 8, *supra*.

35. 431 U.S. 1 (1977).

36. 438 U.S. 234 (1978).

37. *Id.* at 247.

38. *Id.* at 261 (Brennan, J., dissenting).

39. Satterlee v. Matthewson, 27 U.S. (2 Pet.) 380, 681 app. (1829).

40. 272 U.S. 365 (1926).

41. 431 U.S. 494 (1977).

42. Armstrong v. United States, 364 U.S. 40 (1960).

43. Almota Farmers Elevator & Warehouse Co. v. United States, 409 U.S. 470 (1973).

44. Berman v. Parker, 348 U.S. 26 (1954).

45. 328 U.S. 256 (1946).

46. At 268.

47. Damage suits for violation of civil rights are possible, however. Gordon v. City of Warren, 579 F.2d 386 (6th Cir. 1978).

48. Bernard H. Siegan, Editor's Introduction: *The Anomaly of Regulation under the Taking Clause* in PLANNING WITHOUT PRICES 16 (B.H. Siegan, ed.) (Lexington, Mass.: D.C. Heath, Lexington Books, 1977).

49. 424 U.S. 507 (1976).

50. Amalgamated Food Employees Union Local 590 v. Logan Valley Plaza, Inc., 391 U.S. 308 (1968).

51. 433 U.S. 562 (1977).

52. Hunt v. Washington Apple Advertising Commission, 432 U.S. 333, 353 (1977).

53. Hughes v. Oklahoma, 99 S. Ct. 1727, 1736–37 (1979).

54. 434 U.S. 429 (1978).

55. 432 U.S. 333 (1977).

56. 437 U.S. 617 (1978).

57. 99 S. Ct. 1727 (1979).

58. Charles A. Reich, *The New Property*, 73 YALE L.J. 733 (1964).

59. 397 U.S. 254 (1970).

60. Reich, *supra* note 58, at 783.

61. Mathews v. Eldridge, 424 U.S. 319 (1976); Bishop v. Wood, 426 U.S. 341 (1976); Memphis Light, Gas & Water Div. v. Craft, 436 U.S. 1 (1978).

62. 405 U.S. 538 (1972).

63. *Id.* at 552.

Chapter Eleven

1. Kovacs v. Cooper, 336 U.S. 77, 95 (1949) (Frankfurter, J., concurring).

2. FRIEDRICH A. HAYEK, THE CONSTITUTION OF LIBERTY 32–35 (Chicago, Ill.: Henry

Regnery, 1972).

3. *Id.* at 35.

4. *Id.* at 33–34.

5. Israel M. Kirzner, Competition and Entrepreneurship 20 (Chicago and London: University of Chicago Press, 1973).

6. Aaron Director, *The Parity of the Economic Market Place,* 7 J. Law & Econ. 1 (1964).

7. Ronald H. Coase, *The Market for Goods and the Market for Ideas,* 64 Amer. Econ. Rev. 384, 384–85 (1974).

8. Milton Friedman, *The Economics of Free Speech* in Regulation, Economics and the Law (Bernard H. Siegan, ed.) (Lexington, Mass.: D.C. Heath, Lexington Books, 1979).

9. John Stuart Mill, *On Liberty* in Utilitarianism, Liberty and Representative Government 223 (New York: E.P. Dutton, 1951).

10. Robert G. McCloskey, *Economic Due Process and the Supreme Court: An Exhumation and Reburial,* 1962 Sup. Ct. Rev. 34, 46.

11. *Id.*

12. Director, *supra* note 6, at 6.

13. Coase, *supra* note 7, at 386.

14. One should not, however, disregard the idea that "To exault one Amendment is to depreciate others." Paul A. Freund, *The Supreme Court and Fundamental Freedoms* in Judicial Review and the Supreme Court 124, 129 (Leonard W. Levy, ed.) (New York, Evanston, and London: Harper Torchbooks, 1967).

15. Alexander Meiklejohn, Political Freedom (New York: Harper & Bros., 1960) and *The First Amendment Is an Absolute,* 1961 Sup. Ct. Rev. 245; Harry Kalven, The Negro and the First Amendment (Columbus, Ohio: Ohio State University Press, 1965) and *The Metaphysics of the Law of Obscenity,* 1960 Sup. Ct. Rev. 1; Thomas I. Emerson, The System of Freedom of Expression (New York: Random House, 1970) and *Toward a General Theory of the First Amendment,* 72 Yale L.J. 877 (1963).

16. *Cf.* Near v. Minnesota, 283 U.S. 697 (1931).

17. See People v. Croswell, 3 Johns. (N.Y.) 336 (1804); Walter Berns, *Freedom of the Press and the Alien and Sedition Laws: A Reappraisal,* 1970 Sup. Ct. Rev. 109.

18. 4 W. Blackstone, Commentaries *152.

19. Leonard W. Levy, Legacy of Suppression: Freedom of Speech in Early American History 236–37 (New York: Harper Torchbooks, 1963).

20. Berns, *supra* note 17.

21. *Quoted* in Levy, *supra* note 19, at 300.

22. 3 Joseph Story, Commentaries on the Constitution of the United States 732–33 (New York: Da Capo Press, 1970).

23. The brief items that follow suggest how poorly the press performs at times in covering matters of vital importance to a society based on public sovereignty.

Perhaps the most derelict press coverage of recent times occurred in the reporting of the 1968 Tet offensive during the Vietnam War. According to the former chief of the *Washington Post*'s news bureau in Saigon, the press generally failed to report that Tet was an enormous failure for the North Vietnamese and instead portrayed it as a disaster for the U.S. The press coverage led to severe changes in American policy. Peter Braestrup, Big Story: How the American Press and Television Reported and Interpreted the Crisis of Tet 1968 in Vietnam and Washington (Boulder, Col.: Westview Press, 1977).

Candidates for office frequently criticize press reporting as unfair or biased. In 1977, the *San Diego Union*'s reader's representative acknowledged that his paper's reports on a school board election were careless and had an effect on the outcome. Alfred JaCoby, *School Vote Coverage: Careless*, San Diego Union, 14 Nov. 1977, at B–6, col. 4, editorial page.

A polling firm that made pre-election surveys for the *Minneapolis Tribune* in the three major statewide races in the November 1978 elections charged that its data were "significantly altered" when the polls were published. Furious with the *Tribune*'s treatment of its findings, which were quite close to the actual outcomes, the polling firm resigned the account. San Diego Union, 18 Nov. 1978, at A–12, col. 1. Polls are important to candidates because they may affect contributions of funds and volunteer services.

24. Director, *supra* note 6, at 3.
25. 4 MACAULAY'S HISTORY OF ENGLAND 123 (London: J.M. Dent & Sons, 1906).
26. 283 U.S. at 713.
27. THOMAS M. COOLEY, A TREATISE ON THE CONSTITUTIONAL LIMITATIONS 421 (New York: Da Capo Press, 1972).
28. Emerson, *Toward a General Theory, supra* note 15.
29. *Id.* at 887–91.
30. *Id.* at 891–92.
31. *See* Note, *Zoning Variances and Exceptions: The Philadelphia Experience*, 103 U. PA. L. REV. 516 (1955); Jesse Dukeminier, Jr., and Clyde L. Stapleton, *The Zoning Board of Adjustment: A Case Study in Misrule*, 50 KY. L.J. 273 (1962).
32. KENNETH CULP DAVIS, DISCRETIONARY JUSTICE 39–40 (Baton Rouge, La.: Louisiana State University Press, 1969).
33. On the weekend before the 1977 municipal elections in San Diego, *The Church News* was distributed at churches throughout the city, praising certain candidates and issues and condemning others. One of the contests was decided by 600 votes and the losing candidate attributed her defeat in part to a *Church News* article that painted her as a choice of homosexuals. Another losing candidate denounced the publication as a political effort disguised in the cloth of religion. San Diego Union, 18 Nov. 1978, at B–2, col. 1.
34. Near v. Minnesota, 283 U.S. 697, 718 (1931) *citing Report on the Virginia Resolutions*, 4 MADISON'S WORKS 544.
35. Virginia State Bd. of Pharmacy v. Virginia Citizens Consumer Council, Inc., 425 U.S. 748, 763 (1976).

Chapter Twelve

1. As discussed in chapter 10, the Court did invalidate many economic laws that infringed on "protected" rights.
2. *See* Munn v. Illinois, 94 U.S. 113 (1877).
3. Baker v. Carr, 369 U.S. 186 (1962); Gray v. Sanders, 372 U.S. 368 (1963); Wesberry v. Sanders, 376 U.S. 1 (1964); Reynolds v. Sims, 377 U.S. 533 (1964).
4. San Diego Union, 25 Dec. 1978, at A–43, col. 1.
5. FRANK E. ARMBRUSTER, THE FORGOTTEN AMERICANS 144 (New Rochelle, N.Y.: Arlington House, 1972).
6. San Diego Union, 17 Dec. 1978, at AA–5, col. 5. Gallup reported only these years.
7. ARNOLD STEINBERG, POLITICAL CAMPAIGN MANAGEMENT: A SYSTEMS APPROACH and THE POLITICAL CAMPAIGN HANDBOOK (Lexington, Mass.: D.C. Heath, Lexington Books, 1976).

8. Milton Friedman, *Special Interest and His Law,* 51 CHICAGO BAR RECORD 434 (June 1970).

9. *Cf.* Milton Friedman, *The Line We Dare Not Cross,* 47 ENCOUNTER 8, 12 (Nov. 1976).

10. HISTORICAL RESEARCH FOUNDATION, A STUDY OF VOTERS' INCONSISTENCIES IN SELECTED CONGRESSIONAL DISTRICTS 10, 104–05 (Washington, D.C.: Historical Research Foundation, 1978).

11. William Jenkins, Jr., *Retention Elections: Who Wins When No One Loses?* 61 JUDICATURE 79 (1977). See also Kenyon N. Griffin and Michael J. Horan, *Merit Retention Elections: What Influences the Voters?* 63 JUDICATURE 78 (1979).

12. Jenkins, *supra* note 11, at 84.

13. 1 ALEXIS DE TOCQUEVILLE, DEMOCRACY IN AMERICA 250 (New Rochelle, N.Y.: Arlington House, 1965).

14. *Id.* at 249.

15. THE FEDERALIST PAPERS No. 51, at 324 (A. Hamilton) (New York and Scarborough, Ontario: Mentor Books, 1961).

16. FRIEDRICH A. HAYEK, THE CONSTITUTION OF LIBERTY 109 (Chicago: Henry Regnery Company, 1960).

17. *See* KENNETH J. ARROW, SOCIAL CHOICE AND INDIVIDUAL VALUES (New York: John Wiley and Sons, 1966); DUNCAN BLACK, THE THEORY OF COMMITTEES AND ELECTIONS (Cambridge, Mass.: Cambridge University Press, 1958); WILLIAM H. RIKER AND PETER J. ORDESHOOK, AN INTRODUCTION TO POSITIVE POLITICAL THEORY (Englewood Cliffs, N.J.: Prentice-Hall, 1973).

18. M. Bruce Johnson, *Planning without Prices: A Discussion of Land Use Regulation without Compensation* in PLANNING WITHOUT Prices 86 (Bernard H. Siegan, ed.) (Lexington, Mass.: D.C. Heath, Lexington Books, 1977).

19. RICHARD POSNER, ECONOMIC ANALYSIS OF LAW 405 (Boston and Toronto: Little, Brown, 2d ed. 1977).

20. Michael Granfield, *Concentrated Industries and Economic Performance* in LARGE CORPORATIONS IN A CHANGING SOCIETY 164 (J. Weston, ed.) (New York: New York University Press, 1975).

21. 1973 Cal. Stats. ch. 996, §1. *See* discussion in chapter 8 *supra* of New Motor Vehicle Bd. v. Orrin W. Fox Co., 99 S. Ct. 403 (1978).

22. *See* Otto A. Davis, *A Political Economist Views the Taking Issue* in PLANNING WITHOUT PRICES, *supra* note 18, at 141.

23. Friedrich Hayek, *The Miscarriage of the Democratic Ideal,* ENCOUNTER 14 (March 1978).

24. KENNETH CULP DAVIS, DISCRETIONARY JUSTICE 46 (Baton Rouge, La.: Louisiana State University Press, 1969).

25. New Motor Vehicle Bd. v. Orrin W. Fox Co., 434 U.S. 1345, 1351 (1977).

26. *See* p. 278 *supra* and discussion in chapter 8 *supra*.

27. E. MIMS, JR., THE MAJORITY OF THE PEOPLE 71 (New York: Modern Age Books, 1941).

Chapter Thirteen

1. OLIVER WENDELL HOLMES, JR., THE COMMON LAW 1 (Boston: Little, Brown, 1881).

366   Notes to Pages 284–303

2. 285 U.S. 262, 280 (1932).

3. FRIEDRICH A. HAYEK, THE ROAD TO SERFDOM (Chicago, Ill.: University of Chicago Press, 1944).

4. GABRIEL KOLKO, RAILROADS AND REGULATION 1877–1916, at 45–63 (Princeton, N.J.: Princeton University Press, 1965).

5. *Quoted* in Michael McMenamin, *The Curious Politics of Deregulation*, REASON (Jan. 1978) at 24.

6. 124 CONG. REC. S.2663–64 (daily ed. March 1, 1978) (remarks of Sen. Edward Kennedy).

7. McMenamin, *supra* note 5, at 27.

8. Harvey Averch & Leland Johnson, *Behavior of the Firm Under Regulatory Restraint*, 52 AMERICAN ECON. REV. 1053 (1962).

9. Ronald H. Coase, *Economists and Public Policy* in LARGE CORPORATIONS IN A CHANGING SOCIETY 183–84 (J. Weston, ed.) (New York: New York University Press, 1975).

References

Baron, David P. & Taggart, Robert A., Jr. *A Model of Regulation under Uncertainty and a Test of Regulatory Bias*, 8 BELL J. ECON. 151 (1977).

Benham, Lee. *The Effect of Advertising on the Price of Eyeglasses*, 15 J. L. & ECON. 337 (1972).

Bonsor, N.C. *Transportation Rates and Economic Development in Northern Ontario*, University of Toronto Press for the Ontario Economic Council, OEC Research Studies No. 7 (1977).

Breen, Denis A. *The Monopoly Value of Household-Goods Carrier Operating Certificates*, 20 J. L. & ECON. 153 (1977).

Brown, Terence A. & Fitzmaurice, J. Michael. *Entry Control in the Surface Freight Forwarder Industry*, 12 Q. REV. ECON. & BUS. 91 (1972).

Cochran, Clay L. *Price Supports and the Distribution of Agricultural Income*, 17 S. ECON. J. 330 (1951).

Cohen, Kalman J., & Reid, Samuel Richardson. *Effects of Regulation, Branching, and Mergers on Banking Structure and Performance*, 34 S. ECON. J. 231 (1967).

Courville, Leon. *Regulation and Efficiency in the Electric Utility Industry*, 5 BELL J. ECON. & MANAGEMENT SCIENCE 53 (1974).

Crandall, Robert. *FCC Regulation, Monopsony, and Network Television Program Costs*, 3 BELL J. ECON. & MANAGEMENT SCIENCE 483 (1972).

Crandall, Robert W. *Regulation of Television Broadcasting*, REGULATION 31 (Jan.–Feb. 1978).

Crecine, John P., Davis, Otto A., & Jackson, John E. *Urban Property Markets: Some Empirical Results and Their Implications for Municipal Zoning*, 10 J. L. & ECON. 79 (1967).

Eckert, Ross D., & Hilton, George W. *The Jitneys*, 15 J. L. & ECON. 293 (1972).

Edwards, Linda N., & Edwards, Franklin R. *Measuring the Effectiveness of Regulation: The Case of Bank Entry Regulation*, 17 J. L. & ECON. 445 (1974).

Gerwig, Robert W. *Natural Gas Production: A Study of Costs of Regulation*, 5 J. L. & ECON. 69 (1962).

Goddard, Frederick O. *On The Effectiveness of Regulation of Electric Utility Prices: Comment*, 38 S. ECON. J. 125 (1971).

Grabowski, Henry G., Vernon, John M., & Thomas, Lacy Glenn. *Estimating the Effects of Regulation on Innovation: An International Comparative Analysis of the Pharmaceutical Industry*, 21 J. L. & ECON. 133 (1978).

Horwitz, Bertrand & Kolodny, Richard. *Line of Business Reporting and Security Prices: An Analysis of an SEC Disclosure Rule*, 8 BELL J. ECON. 234 (1977).

Jaffe, Jeffrey F. *The Effect of Regulation Changes on Insider Trading*, 5 BELL J. ECON. & MANAGEMENT SCIENCE 93 (1974).

Joskow, Paul L. *Cartels, Competition and Regulation in the Property-Liability Insurance Industry*, 4 BELL J. ECON. & MANAGEMENT SCIENCE 375 (1973).

Keeler, Theodore E. *Airline Regulation and Market Performance*, 3 BELL J. ECON. & MANAGEMENT SCIENCE 399 (1972).

Kessel, Reuben A. *Economic Effects of Federal Regulation of Milk Markets*, 10 J. L. & ECON. 51 (1967).

Kitch, Edmund W., Isaacson, Marc, & Kasper, Daniel. *The Regulation of Taxicabs in Chicago*, 14 J. L. & ECON. 285 (1971).

Knutson, Ronald D. *The Economic Consequences of the Minnesota Dairy Industry Unfair Trade Practices Act*, 12 J. L. & ECON. 377 (1969).

Levin, Harvey J. *Economic Effects of Broadcast Licensing*, 72 J. POL. ECON. 151 (1964).

Levine, Michael E. *Regulating Airmail Transportation*, 18 J. L. & ECON. 317 (1975).

Luksetich, William A. *A Study of Regulation: The Minnesota Liquor Case*, 41 S. ECON. J. 457 (1975).

MacAvoy, Paul W. *The Effectiveness of the Federal Power Commission*, 1 BELL J. ECON. & MANAGEMENT SCIENCE 271 (1970).

MacAvoy, Paul W. *The Regulation Induced Shortage of Natural Gas*, 14 J. L. & ECON. 167 (1971).

Maser, Steven M., Riker, William H., & Rosett, Richard N. *The Effects of Zoning and Externalities on the Price of Land: An Empirical Analysis of Monroe County, New York*, 20 J. L. & ECON. 111 (1977).

Moore, Thomas Gale. *The Beneficiaries of Trucking Regulation*, 21 J. L. & ECON. 327 (1978).

Moore, Thomas Gale. *The Effectiveness of Regulation of Electric Utility Prices*, 36 S. ECON. J. 365 (1970).

Peltzman, Sam. *Capital Investment in Commercial Banking and Its Relationship to Portfolio Regulation*, 78 J. POL. ECON. 1 (1970).

Peltzman, Sam. *The Effects of Automobile Safety Regulation*, 83 J. POL. ECON. 677 (1975).

Peltzman, Sam. *Entry in Commercial Banking*, 8 J. L. & ECON. 11 (1965).

Peltzman, Sam. *An Evaluation of Consumer Protection Legislation: The 1962 Drug Amendments*, 81 J. POL. ECON. 1049 (1973).

Petersen, H. Craig. *An Empirical Test of Regulatory Effects*, 6 BELL J. ECON. 111 (1975).

Pike, John. *Residential Electric Rates and Regulation*, 7 Q. REV. ECON. & BUS. 45 (1967).

Report of the CAB Special Staff on Regulatory Reform. Washington, D.C.: Government Printing Office, July, 1975.

Report of the Special Study of the Securities Market of the Securities and Exchange Commission (Washington, D.C.: Government Printing Office, 1963) (Eighty-eight Cong. 1st Sess.).

Rueter, Frederick H. *Externalities in Urban Property Markets: An Empirical Test of the Zoning Ordinance of Pittsburgh*, 16 J. L. & ECON. 313 (1973).

Sagalyn, Lynne B., & Sternlieb, George. *Zoning and Housing Costs*. Rutgers University: Center for Urban Policy Research, 1973.

Schwert, G. William. *Public Regulation of National Securities Exchanges: A Test of the Capture Hypothesis*, 8 BELL J. ECON. 128 (1977).

Siegan, Bernard H. *Land Use without Zoning*, chs. 2, 3, & 4. Lexington, Mass.: D.C. Heath, 1972.

Sloss, James. *Regulation of Motor Freight Transportation: A Quantitative Evaluation of Policy*, 1 BELL J. ECON. & MANAGEMENT SCIENCE 327 (1970).

Spann, Robert M., & Erickson, Edward W. *The Economics of Railroading: The Beginning of Cartelization and Regulation*, 1 BELL J. ECON. & MANAGEMENT SCIENCE 227 (1970).

Spann, Robert M. *Rate of Return Regulation and Efficiency in Production: An Empirical Test of the Averch-Johnson Thesis*, 5 BELL J. ECON. & MANAGEMENT SCIENCE 38 (1974).

Stigler, George. *Public Regulation of the Securities Market*, 78–100 in THE CITIZEN AND THE STATE. Chicago: University of Chicago Press, 1975.

Stigler, George W., & Friedland, Claire. *What Can Regulators Regulate? The Case of Electricity*, 5 J. L. & ECON. 1 (1962).

Urban, Raymond, & Mancke, Richard. *Federal Regulation of Whiskey Labelling: From the Repeal of Prohibition to the Present*, 15 J. L. & ECON. 411 (1972).

U.S. Senate, Committee on the Judiciary, Subcommittee on Administrative Practice and Procedure. *Civil Aeronautics Board Practices and Procedures*. Committee Report, 94th Cong. 1st. Sess. (1975).

Wardell, William M. *Therapeutic Implications of the Drug Lag*, CLINICAL PHARMACOLOGY AND THERAPEUTICS 73 (Jan. 1974).

Weiss, Roger W. *The Case for Federal Meat Inspection Examined*, 7 J. L. & ECON. 107 (1964).

Wellisz, Stanislaw H. *Regulation of Natural Gas Pipeline Companies: An Economic Analysis*, 71 J. POLITICAL ECON. 30 (1963).

Chapter Fourteen

1. Universal Declaration of Human Rights, adopted in December 1948 by the General Assembly of the United Nations.

2. Marbury v. Madison, 5 U.S. (1 Cranch) 137, 170 (1803).

3. PAUL G. KAUPER, THE HIGHER LAW AND THE RIGHTS OF MAN IN A REVOLUTIONARY SOCIETY 21 (Washington, D.C.: American Enterprise Institute for Public Policy Research, 1974). Prof. Kauper's article otherwise contains an excellent summation of natural law concepts.

4. Korematsu v. United States, 323 U.S. 214 (1943).

5. *But see* the abortion cases: Roe v. Wade, 410 U.S. 113 (1973) and Doe v. Bolton, 410 U.S. 179 (1973). These Burger Court cases represent judicial activism at least on par with what occurred in the Warren years.

6. 394 U.S. 618 (1969).

7. 411 U.S. 1 (1973).

8. 397 U.S. 471 (1970).

9. *Id.* at 487.

10. 394 U.S. at 627.

11. Note, *The Decline and Fall of the New Equal Protection: A Polemical Approach*, 58 VA. L. REV. 1489, 1500 (1972).

12. 337 F. Supp. 280 (W.D. Tex. 1971).

13. 411 U.S. at 36.

14. 432 U.S. 464 (1977).

15. *See* Frank Michelman, *The Supreme Court 1968 Term: Foreword: On Protecting the Poor through the Fourteenth Amendment*, 83 HARV. L. REV. 7 (1969).

16. STUART SCHEINGOLD, THE POLITICS OF RIGHTS: LAWYERS, PUBLIC POLICY, AND POLITICAL CHANGE 126 (New Haven, Conn.: Yale University Press, 1974).

17. Michelman, *supra* note 15, at 15.

18. Southern Burlington County NAACP v. Township of Mt. Laurel, 67 N.J. 151, 336 A.2d 713 (1975).

19. 72 N.J. 481, 371 A.2d 1192 (1977).

20. 72 N.J. at 499, 371 A.2d at 1200.

21. JOHN B. LANSING, CHARLES W. CLIFTON & JAMES N. MORGAN, NEW HOMES AND POOR PEOPLE (Ann Arbor, Mich.: University of Michigan Institute for Social Research, 1969).

22. 72 N.J. at 544–45, 371 A.2d at 1224 *citing* Southern Burlington County NAACP v. Township of Mt. Laurel, 67 N.J. at 187, 336 A.2d at 731.

23. 272 U.S. 365 (1926). *See* chapter 6 *supra*. *Madison Township* illustrates the relationship of substantive due process to economic well-being. Thus Prof. Karlin contends that the judicial abandonment of economic due process, by encouraging the growth of regulation, has most adversely affected the poor. By raising prices for a wide variety of goods and services, regulation acts as a tax, paid by both rich and poor in the same amount, but weighing more heavily upon the latter, for whom each dollar is more precious. Norman Karlin, *Some Economic Consequences of Substantive Due Process* in FREEDOM OF CONTRACT: AN EXPLORATORY CONFERENCE 98–99 (presented by the Liberty Fund, Inc. in cooperation with the University of San Diego School of Law and Institute for Humane Studies, 12–14 Oct. 1978). For information on the substantial costs of government regulation, see Paul W. MacAvoy, *The Existing Condition of Regulation and Regulatory Reform* in REGULATING BUSINESS: THE SEARCH FOR AN OPTIMUM 3–13 (San Francisco, Cal.: Institute for Contemporary Studies, 1978); Murray L. Weidenbaum, *On Estimating Regulatory Costs*, REGULATION 14–17 (May/June 1978).

24. Calder v. Bull, 3 U.S. (3 Dall.) 386, 388 (1798).

25. *See e.g.*, LAURENCE H. TRIBE, AMERICAN CONSTITUTIONAL LAW (Mineola, N.Y.: Foundation Press, 1978).

26. FRANCIS LIEBER, ON CIVIL LIBERTY AND SELF GOVERNMENT 37–43, 143–71 (New York: Da Capo Press, 1972), *cited* in CHARLES GROVES HAINES, THE AMERICAN DOCTRINE OF JUDICIAL SUPREMACY 494 (New York: Russell & Russell, 2d ed., 1959).

Chapter Fifteen

1. Robert G. McCloskey, *Judicial Review and "The Intent of the Framers"* in ESSAYS IN CONSTITUTIONAL LAW 23 (Robert G. McCloskey, ed.) (New York: Alfred A. Knopf, 1962).

2. THE FEDERALIST PAPERS No. 78, at 465 (A. Hamilton) (New York and Scarborough, Ontario: Mentor Books, 1961).

3. *Id.*

4. *Id.* at 469.

5. 1 W. BLACKSTONE COMMENTARIES *121–22.

6. McCulloch v. Maryland, 17 U.S. (4 Wheat.) 316, 421 (1819).

7. Gerald Gunther, *The Supreme Court 1971 Term, Foreword: In Search of Evolving Doctrine on a Changing Court: A Model for a Newer Equal Protection*, 86 HARV. L. REV. 1 (1972).

8. 429 U.S. 190 (1976).

9. *Id.* at 197. This test was subsequently accepted by a majority of the Court. Califano v. Webster, 430 U.S. 313, 316–17 (1977); Orr v. Orr, 99 S. Ct. 1102 (1979).

10. Courts in at least two states place the burden of proof in exclusionary zoning cases on the municipality under what appears to be a strict review standard. The Appeal of Kit-Mar Builders, 439 Pa. 446, 268 A.2d 765 (1970); Southern Burlington County N.A.A.C.P. v. Township of Mt. Laurel, 67 N.J. 151, 336 A.2d 713 (1975). Laws severely limiting the use of property may amount to confiscation under the doctrine of inverse condemnation. Courts in such circumstances may require the payment of just compensation. My proposals for changes in existing law are not intended to preempt the operation of inverse condemnation.

11. *See* colloquium on legislative and administrative motivation in 15 SAN DIEGO L. REV. 925 (1978).

12. According to Wigmore, the allocation of the burden of proof is merely a question of policy and fairness based on experience in different situations. An important factor is that it should be borne by the party best able to know the truth and falsity of the facts. 9 J. WIGMORE ON EVIDENCE § 2486 at 275 (3d ed. 1940). Such considerations warrant that governmental authorities bear the burden of explaining and justifying why they have curbed property and economic liberties. Because an intermediate standard of review is proposed, the state would confront a less arduous undertaking than in the fundamental liberties area. *See* Justice Brennan's discussion on the allocation of the burden of proof in school desegregation cases in Keyes v. School District No. 1, 413 U.S. 189 (1973).

13. Trimble v. Gordon, 430 U.S. 762, 777 (1977) (Rehnquist, J., dissenting). Hans Linde, *Due Process of Lawmaking*, 55 NEBR. L. REV. 197 (1976); Note, *Legislative Purpose, Rationality, and Equal Protection*, 82 YALE L.J. 123 (1972); Note, *State Economic Substantive Due Process: A Proposed Approach*, 88 YALE L.J. 1487 (1979).

14. Smith v. Daily Mail Pub. Co., 99 S. Ct. 2667, 2672, 2674, n.3 (1979) (Rehnquist, J., concurring).

15. Robert McCloskey, *Economic Due Process and the Supreme Court: An Exhumation and Reburial*, 1962 SUP. CT. REV. 34, 53.

16. THE FEDERALIST, *supra* note 2, No. 73, at 444 (A. Hamilton) (referring to executive veto).

17. New State Ice Co. v. Liebmann, 285 U.S. 262, 310 (1932) (Brandeis, J., dissenting).

18. Milton Kafoglis, *A Paradox of Regulated Trucking*, REGULATION 27, 29–30 (Sept./Oct. 1977).

19. *See* discussion by Edwin Vieira, Jr., *Rights and the American Constitution* in MODERN RIGHTS THEORY 89–94 (Conference presented by the Liberty Fund, Inc. in cooperation with the Institute for Humane Studies, San Diego, Cal., 8–10 March 1979).

20. Gunther, *supra* note 7, at 47.

21. McCloskey, *supra* note 15, at 50.

22. LAURENCE H. TRIBE, AMERICAN CONSTITUTIONAL LAW 952 n.25 (Mineola, N.Y.: Foundation Press, 1978).

23. Harry J. Haynsworth, *The Need for a Unified Small Business Legal Structure*, 33 BUSINESS LAWYER 849, 852 n.7 (1978).

Notes to Pages 329–330

24. There are approximately 50,000 pension plans, almost all of which are investment funds. Approximately 70 percent of the assets of these plans are invested in shares of listed publicly owned American companies, amounting to a total pension fund portfolio of at least $140–150 billion at the end of 1974. The list price of all companies traded on the stock market at that time was about $500 billion. Those pension funds held roughly 30 percent of the total stock value of these companies. Keogh plans and individual retirement accounts held, together, about 5 percent. PETER F. DRUCKER, THE UNSEEN REVOLUTION 12 (New York, Hagerstown, San Francisco, and London: Harper & Row, 1976).

25. Exxon Corp. v. Governor of Maryland, 437 U.S. 117 (1978).

26. New Motor Vehicle Bd. v. Orrin W. Fox Co., 434 U.S. 1345 (1978).

27. WALTER LIPPMANN, THE METHOD OF FREEDOM 101 (New York: Macmillan, 1934).

General Index

Civil War, 40–41, at state level prior to Fourteenth Amendment, 41–46, after Fourteenth Amendment, 46–55, at state level after Civil War, 55–58; and rational relation test, 265–67; regulation of, compared to censorship, 260–63; as safeguarded by natural rights and social compact doctrines, 30–33, 34–37, 41–42; and substantive due process, 113–25, under Old Court, 126–55; and taking clause, 79, 80, 92, 129–30, 131, 165, 206–7, 239, 240–41, 325; threat to, of legislative process, 265–82; two-level approach to, 223–46. *See also* Due process clauses; Judicial review; Regulation; Substantive due process

Ellsworth, Oliver, 30
Emerson, Thomas, 252, 260–62
Eminent domain power, 42, 44, 79–80, 240–41
Endres, Frederick, 116
Equal protection clause (Fourteenth Amendment), 54–55, 111, 114, 120, 139, 146, 161, 191, 205, 219, 221, 235–37, 307, 323–24
Ex post facto clauses (Art. I, secs. 9 and 10), 30, 59, 60–62, 66, 67–82, 99, 238, 319

Federal Alcohol Administration, 296–97
Federal Communications Commission, 281, 286, 295–96
Federal Espionage Acts of 1917 and 1918, 163
Federalist Papers, 12, 29, 31, 85, 94, 99–100, 101, 102, 103
Federal Maritime Commission, 286
Federal Power Commission, 291, 292–93
Federal Trade Commission, 226
Field, Oliver, 51–52, 53, 54, 58, 75–76, 106
Fifth Amendment, 3, 16, 24, 78, 79, 122, 129, 130, 146, 154, 199, 205, 206–7, 240, 236. *See also* Due process clauses; Economic rights; Judicial review; Substantive due process; Taking clause
First Amendment, 9, 159, 161, 163, 164, 168, 172, 176, 179, 180, 200, 208, 209, 211–14, 225, 226, 229, 230, 233, 234–35, 242, 253–57, 322. *See also* Fundamental rights; Personal liberties; Prior restraint

clause
Food and Drug Administration, 299
Ford, Gerald, 273
Fourteenth Amendment, 3, 4, 5–6, 16, 17, 18, 20, 24, 46–55, 47, 48–51, 81–82, 97, 111, 112, 121, 122, 129–31, 139, 140, 154, 157, 161–62, 168, 179, 195, 198, 211, 236, 239, 253–54, 256, 319, 329. *See also* Due process clauses; Economic rights; Judicial review; Privileges and immunities clause; Substantive due process
Frankfurter, Felix, 165, 208, 248–49, 317
Franklin, Benjamin, 100–101, 104
Freedom of expression. *See* Fundamental rights; Personal liberties; Substantive due process
Friedman, Milton, 103, 137, 249, 251, 269, 286
Fundamental rights, 4, 15, 17, 20–21, 307, 323; as derived from fear of censor, 257–60; and freedom of expression as conceived by Framers, 253–57; and Fourteenth Amendment, 52; as interpreted by Marshall Court, 318–19; and property rights cases, 223–46; and relationship of free press to representative government, 255–57; as safeguarded by irrebuttable presumption doctrine, 219–22, by substantive due process, 204–22; and *Slaughter-House Cases*, 53; threat to, of legislative process, 265–82. *See also* Economic rights; Judicial review; Personal liberties; Substantive due process

Gellhorn, Walter, 200–202
Gerry, Elbridge, 85
Godolphin, Sidney, 69
Goldberg, Arthur Joseph, 17–19
Goldwater, Barry, Jr., 275
Government intervention. *See* Regulation
Grampp, William D., 102
Granfield, Michael, 278
Grant, J. A. C., 42, 96
Grotius, Hugo, 28, 44
Gunther, Gerald, 219, 323–24

Haines, Charles Grove, 76, 86, 87–88
Hamilton, Alexander, 15, 26, 29, 31–32,

Mendelson, Wallace, 129
Mercer, John Francis, 85
Michelman, Frank, 311
Mill, John Stuart, 124, 251
Miller, Charles, 65
Miller, Samuel, 40, 49–50, 51, 60, 106
Milton, John, 258
Moll, Conrad, 117
Montesquieu, Charles, 28, 104
Moody, William Henry, 42
Morris, Gouverneur, 30, 83, 85
Motor Carrier Act (1935), 67
Muskie, Edmund S., 287

Nader, Ralph, 137, 286, 287
Nagel, Robert F., 105
National Consumer's League, 148
National Highway and Traffic Administration, 290
National Labor Relations Act, 178
Natural law and rights doctrine, 37–40; as contractual basis of government, 28; and due process, 24, 26–33, 34; early justices' perspective on, 91–93; and judicial review, 5, 87, 91, 96; philosophical defense of, 34–37; and privileges and immunities clause, 39; as safeguard of property rights, 30–31, 34–37, 41–42; and state constitutions, 41–42
Necessary and proper clause (Art. I, sec. 8), 99–100
Negative jurisprudence. See Economic rights; Judicial review
New Deal, the, 127, 189, 302, 308
Ninth Amendment, 15, 18, 19, 29
Nixon, Richard, 273
Nuclear Regulatory Commission, 286

Obligation of contracts clause (Art. I, sec. 10), 37, 38, 92, 102, 145, 150; and public-interest businesses, 150–54; as safeguard for economic rights, 39, 60–66, 81–82, 110–13, 119, 122, 223–46, 237–38, 319
Old Court: and family rights, 156–60; and freedom of expression, 161–79; and review of economic rights, 126–55
Otis, James, 282

Panama Canal treaties, 9–10
Panschar, William, 116
Patents and copyrights, 103
Patterson, William, 32, 67, 68, 74, 80, 81
Peckham, Rufus W., 111, 112, 113–15
Personal liberties: and clear and present danger test, 163–66, 168, 169–70, 172–73, 180; and economic liberties, 157, 171, 179–81, 188, 205–6, 219, 248–64; and family rights, 156–60; and freedom of expression, 22, 156, 161–71, 207–15, 224–35; during Revolutionary and Constitutional periods, 27–33. See also Fundamental rights
Pinckney, Charles, 78, 101
Pitney, Mahlon, 122–23, 124, 129
Political liberties. See Fundamental rights; Personal liberties
Posner, Richard A., 121, 137, 278, 279
Powell, Lewis Franklin, 19, 159, 199, 217–18, 238, 239–40, 309
Prior-restraint clause (First Amendment), 176–79
Privileges and immunities clause (Fourteenth Amendment), 39, 48–50, 52, 329
Property rights. See Economic rights
Pufendorf, Samuel von, 28, 44
Pure Food and Drug Act, 189

Randolph, Edmund, 75, 84, 100
Rational relation test, 192–93, 265–67, 282
Raymond, Lord, 69
Reagan, Ronald, 275
Reasonable alternative test, 221–22
Regulation: of advertising in eyeglass industry, 300–301; and agricultural price support, 300; and airlines, 137, 285, 286, 301–2; and Averch-Johnson hypothesis, 292; and banking industry, 293–94; and broadcasting industry, 295–96; and commercial advertising, 224–31; as compared with censorship, 260–63; counterproductivity of, 118, 315–17, 320–21; and difficulty of deregulation, 327–28; of domestic commerce, 243–44; of electric utility industry, 291–92; of employer-employee relations, 56–57; of entry into business, 132–38; of expression (censorship), 248–64; of food and

Index of Cases